Turn Your Eyes Upon Jesus

Other books by George R. Knight (selected):
A. T. Jones: Point Man on Adventism's Charismatic Frontier
Angry Saints (Pacific Press)
The Apocalyptic Vision and the Neutering of Adventism
The Cross of Christ
I Used to Be Perfect (Andrews University Press)
If I Were the Devil
Joseph Bates: The Real Founder of Seventh-day Adventism
Lest We Forget
Myths in Adventism
Sin and Salvation
The Truth, the Whole Truth, and Nothing but the Truth (Inter-American Publishing Association)
A User-friendly Guide to the 1888 Message
William Miller and the Rise of Adventism (Pacific Press)

Books in the Adventist Heritage Series
A Brief History of Seventh-day Adventists
A Search for Identity: The Development of Seventh-day Adventist Beliefs
Organizing for Mission and Growth: The Development of Adventist Church Structure

Books in the Ellen White Series
Ellen White's World
Meeting Ellen White
Reading Ellen White
Walking With Ellen White

Books in the Exploring Commentary Series
Exploring Ecclesiastes & Song of Solomon
Exploring Galatians & Ephesians
Exploring Hebrews
Exploring the Letters of John & Jude
Exploring Mark
Exploring Romans
Exploring Thessalonians

A study guide for each of the books in this series is available on www.adventistbookcenter.com.

To order, call **1-800-765-6955**, or visit us at **www.reviewandherald.com** for information on other Review and Herald® products.

GEORGE R. KNIGHT

Turn Your Eyes Upon Jesus

REVIEW AND HERALD® PUBLISHING ASSOCIATION
Since 1861 | www.reviewandherald.com

Published by Review and Herald® Publishing Association, Hagerstown, MD 21741-1119

Review and Herald® titles may be purchased in bulk for educational, business, fund-raising, or sales promotional use. For information, e-mail SpecialMarkets@reviewandherald.com.

The Review and Herald® Publishing Association publishes biblically based materials for spiritual, physical, and mental growth and Christian discipleship.

The author assumes full responsibility for the accuracy of all facts and quotations as cited in this book.

This book was
Edited by Gerald Wheeler
Copyedited by Delma Miller
Designed by Review and Herald® Design Center
Cover Design by Michelle C. Petz
Typeset: Minion Pro 11/13

PRINTED IN U.S.A.

17 16 15 14 13   5 4 3 2 1

Library of Congress Cataloging-in-Publication Data

Knight, George R.
    Turn your eyes upon Jesus / George R. Knight.
      p. cm.
    1. Jesus Christ—Person and offices—Meditations. 2. Devotional calendars—Seventh-day Adventists. I. Title.
    BT203.K55 2013
    232—dc23
        2012032283

ISBN 978-0-8280-2699-4

Contents

A Word to Fellow Gazers

Turn your eyes upon Jesus. That is exactly what we will be doing for the next 365 days. And there is no better place to look. He is not only "the way, the truth, and the life" (John 14:6), but also the answer to our greatest hopes and fears. In Jesus we find meaning for both the present life and the one to come. As a result, His person and ministry are the best place to fix our gaze.

How to approach the topic was the major difficulty. At first I thought I should trace His life by focusing on one Gospel. But that would leave so much out. So I then contemplated telling the story through the eyes of all four Gospel writers. But that also was problematic, since the earthly life of Jesus is only an infinitely small fraction of who He is. As a result, I finally decided to use the evidence supplied in both biblical Testaments to trace His life from eternity in the past through eternity in the future.

Of course, not all the data could fit into one book. As a result, my treatment centers on nine focal points in Jesus' life and ministry. I have arranged the readings in a generally chronological fashion, but not slavishly so. Needless to say, some of the sections are more selective in their content than others. That is especially true for His years of ministry. A year of 365 days is just not enough to do justice to such a life. But I suppose that is good. My hope for each of us is that these 365 days will be a mere beginning of a life dedicated to daily turning our eyes upon Jesus.

Meanwhile, my prayer is that you will receive as great a blessing from this year's readings as I did in writing them.

In closing, I would like to express appreciation to my wife for typing my handwritten manuscript and to Jeannette Johnson and Gerald Wheeler for shepherding it through the publication process.

—George R. Knight
Rogue River, Oregon

DEDICATED TO BONNIE—
my best friend and wife (in that order)—
a most wonderful combination.

"I decided to know nothing among you
except Jesus Christ and him crucified."
—Paul, 1 Corinthians 2:2, RSV

"Turn your eyes upon Jesus,
Look full in His wonderful face;
And the things of earth will grow strangely dim
In the light of His glory and grace."
—Helen H. Lemmel, in *The Seventh-day Adventist Hymnal*, no. 290

"It would be well for us to spend a thoughtful hour
each day in contemplation of the life of Christ.
We should take it point by point, and let the imagination
grasp each scene, especially the closing ones."
—Ellen G. White, *The Desire of Ages*, p. 83

Part 1

Turn Your Eyes Upon Jesus as Eternal God

January 1

Where to Begin?

The angel said to them, "Be not afraid; for behold, I bring you good news of a great joy which will come to all the people; for to you is born this day in the city of David a Savior, who is Christ the Lord." Luke 2:10, 11, RSV.

Where to begin the story of Jesus? That's the problem. Of course, we could start with His birth in Bethlehem. But that would miss most of the story. After all, the Bible's portrayal of His 33 years on earth is hardly even the tip of the iceberg of an existence that runs from eternity in the past to eternity in the future. As a result, this devotional on the life of Christ will commence with His story before the Incarnation and close with His ministry after the Ascension, which extends into infinity.

The theme song for our journey through this year of beholding our Lord is Helen Lemmel's "Turn Your Eyes Upon Jesus." As part of your daily devotional experience I would suggest that you sing the chorus each day:

"Turn your eyes upon Jesus,
Look full in His wonderful face;
And the things of earth will grow strangely dim
In the light of His glory and grace."

After 365 renditions I guarantee that you will have the words memorized and that they will come to your mind repeatedly throughout the rest of your life.

Meanwhile, we need to turn our eyes upon the Jesus set forth in the angel's announcement to the shepherds in Luke 2:10, 11. Perhaps the most remarkable aspect of the passage is that it refers to the newborn baby as "Christ the Lord."

That description would have jumped right off the page to the Bible's first readers. After all, "Lord" is the word used in Greek for "Yahweh," the very name of God in the Old Testament. Thus the angel's announcement declared the child as divine. Later, Gentile readers would have picked up the same message, since the pagan world often employed the term to refer to their deities.

The term *Christ* is also an expression of Jesus' divinity, being the Greek translation of "Messiah," which means "anointed one." While one could see a king or priest as anointed, the Jews expected that in due course God would send *the* anointed one, someone who would do His will in a special way.

And what a way! The "good news" of the angel is that Jesus would become the "Savior" of "all" people. Let us rejoice with the angels (verses 13, 14).

Jesus' Real Beginning

In the beginning was the Word, and the Word was with God,
and the Word was God. John 1:1.

Here is the real beginning of the Jesus story. Whereas Matthew and Luke commence their Gospels with Jesus' miraculous birth and Mark with the inauguration of His ministry, John takes his readers back to the beginning of beginnings.

And what was that? A first thought is to go to Genesis 1:1: "In the beginning God created the heavens and the earth." But that is not where John 1:1 starts. After all, according to verse 3 Jesus already existed before the Genesis creation, being an active agent in it (cf. Col. 1:16; Heb. 1:2).

As a result, with a stroke of his pen John draws our minds not back to the Creation story of Genesis 1, but to the vast eternity before Creation and the place of Christ the Word within that boundless infinity of time. Ellen White captures the depths of that eternity when she writes that Christ "was equal with God, infinite and omnipotent. . . . He is the eternal, self-existent Son" (*Evangelism*, p. 615). When John says "beginning," he means the *real* beginning before the creation of anything.

The apostle goes on to make two other statements about the Word. The first is that He was "with God." The flow of the fourth Gospel helps us understand that "withness." It pictures Jesus as being at the Father's side (John 1:18), the Father placing everything in His hands (John 3:35), He and the Father being one (John 10:30), and so forth throughout the gospel story. Thus John's second declaration about the Word, when combined with the first, presents Christ as the Word who from all eternity has enjoyed a profound intimacy with the Father.

The last declaration about the Word equates Him with God. Here it is important to note that John is not saying that Jesus is the Father. After all, his Gospel presents the two as distinct individuals capable of talking to and about each other. Thus both the Father and the Son are identified in Scripture as "God" (cf. Heb. 1:8). We might say that They share the same family name (God) but with different functions.

Father, as we bow before You in prayer our minds are profoundly affected by the fact that the Baby born as Jesus of Nazareth is none less than eternal God. Thank You for the Gift of all gifts. As we continue our study, help us to begin to grasp the meaning of that gift for our world and our lives.

Jesus and the Other Beginning

All things were made through him, and without him was not any thing made that was made. In him was life. John 1:3, 4, ESV.

The first beginning in John's Gospel is one without a beginning, reflecting on the eternal preexistence of the divine Christ.

But John portrays a second beginning in verses 3 and 4—the beginning of Creation. Paul comments upon that one when he writes "in him all things were created, in heaven and on earth, visible and invisible, . . . all things were created through him and for him" (Col. 1:16, RSV). And the book of Hebrews states that it was through Christ that God "created the world" (Heb. 1:2, RSV).

Thus it is that the Babe of Bethlehem was much more than just one more person in the tired history of this world. The Bible sets Him forth as the Creator God, who has "life" in Himself in the same way that "the Father has life in himself" (John 5:26, RSV). *The Desire of Ages* captures that truth when it claims that "in Christ is life, original, unborrowed, underived" (p. 530).

It is that life in Himself that positioned the Word to act in Creation. And it is no accident that John describes the creative Christ as the Word. After all, it is the act of speaking that ushers in each day of Creation Week. "And God said" reflects on the meaning of the creative Word in John 1:1-5 (see Gen. 1:3, 6, 9, 14, 20, 24).

As a result, it was also that eternal Word who kept the Sabbath at the end of Creation week. "Thus," we read, "the heavens and the earth were finished, and all the host of them. And on the seventh day God finished his work which he had done, and he rested on the seventh day from all his work which he had done. So God blessed the seventh day and hallowed it, because on it God rested from all his work which he had done in creation" (Gen. 2:1-3, RSV). With that in mind, there is little wonder that Jesus noted that "the Son of man is Lord also of the sabbath" (Mark 2:28).

John's Gospel doesn't fool around when it comes to introducing Jesus. He is not merely that child born in Bethlehem.

No! He is eternal God. He is the Creator of all that is. He has life in Himself.

As we turn our eyes upon this Jesus our minds are challenged and astounded regarding the true identity of our Savior.

Jesus the Eternal "I AM"

*Jesus said to [the Jews], "Truly, truly, I say to you, before Abraham was, I am." So
they took up stones to throw at him. John 8:58, 59, RSV.*

W*hat a strange passage*, I thought to myself when first reading John's
Gospel. Why did the Jewish leaders want to stone Jesus to death because He had claimed to be "I am"? And what is the significance of that claim?

Those questions take us back to Exodus 3:13, in which Moses wanted to
know God's name in case his fellow Hebrews in Egypt asked him to identify the
Deity that he claimed had sent him to them. In reply, "God said to Moses, '*I AM
WHO I AM*'; and He said, 'Thus you shall say to the sons of Israel, "I AM has
sent me to you."' God, furthermore, said to Moses, 'Thus you shall say to the
sons of Israel, "The Lord [*Yahweh* in Hebrew], the God of your fathers, the God
of Abraham, the God of Isaac, and the God of Jacob, has sent me to you." This is
My name forever'" (verses 14, 15, NASB).

With those verses in mind it is easy to see why the Jews sought to kill Jesus
when He identified Himself as the "I AM." He was identifying Himself as no
less than the God of the covenant with the Jewish people. He was pronouncing
Himself to be Yahweh ("Jehovah" in the King James Version), the eternal I AM,
the God of the Old Testament. The word "Yahweh" means "to be," reflecting
the constant being or existence of God not only for eternity in the past and
future but also the present God who leads His people and supplies their needs
throughout Jewish history.

Thus it was the "I AM" who met with Moses on Sinai, saying, "I am the
Lord [Yahweh] your God, who brought you out of the land of Egypt, out of
the house of bondage" (Ex. 20:2, RSV). That act of divine grace called for a
response in verses 3-17—the Ten Commandments. Thus even in the Old Testament, law keeping is a response to God's redemptive grace through Christ.

How important it is to realize that the Babe of Bethlehem was not just another child. He was and is the "I AM," the God who gave the law, the God who
led His people in past ages of earthly history.

But more than that, the eternal "I AM" is still guiding His people today
and will do so throughout the ceaseless ages of eternity in the future. We serve
a magnificent Lord who not only had power to create but has the ability to save
each of us to the uttermost (Heb. 7:25).

January 5

The Prophetic Child

> *For to us a child is born,*
> > *to us a son is given;*
> *And the government will be upon his shoulder,*
> > *and his name will be called*
> *"Wonderful Counselor, Mighty God,*
> > *Everlasting Father, Prince of Peace."*
> *Of the increase of his government and of peace*
> > *there will be no end.* Isa. 9:6, 7, RSV.

The "I AM" is not only the eternal "out there" but one who would enter human history in the person of Jesus of Nazareth, the central focus of the New Testament and the subject of prophecy in the Old.

Harking back to Isaiah 7:14 and the young woman who would bear a son called "Immanuel" or "God with us," Isaiah 9:6 picks up on the word "son" and begins to fill out the profile of the person of the Godhead who would become flesh and dwell among us. The Jewish Targum (a paraphrase of the biblical Hebrew into the commonly used Aramaic of Jesus' day) helps bring out the meaning of the passage: "And there was called His name from of old, Wonderful Counsellor, Mighty God, He who lives for ever, the Messiah, in whose days peace shall increase upon us." That Messianic interpretation by the ancient Jews reflects the description of the individual being spoken of in verses 6 and 7 and cannot belong to any mere earthly ruler.

He is the "Wonderful Counselor," one who is Himself a wonder in His wisdom and kindness. The root of the word "wonder" is used in Psalm 78:12 of God who did "marvellous things . . . in the land of Egypt." The same verbal root describes the miracles God performed in Egypt, including the dividing of the sea, the leading by pillar of cloud and fire, and the cleaving of the desert rocks to provide water. The wonder of prophetic wonders is the fact that such an individual would be born a child to become the source of wisdom for God's people.

The coming Messiah would not be merely another child, but the "Mighty God." Here we have foreshadowed the miracle of incarnation and the dual nature of the coming Christ—a unique individual who would be fully human yet fully divine.

His third name is "Everlasting Father." Here we need to realize that the prophet is not confounding the divine Father with the divine Son, but rather the fact that one role of Christ was to provide the loving care of a father to His children. Finally, "Prince of Peace" of whose "government . . . of peace there will be no end" reflects upon both the nature of the eternal kingdom of God and the great prophecy of Daniel 2:44, which will bring an end to all earthly kingdoms. That kingdom "shall stand for ever" (cf. Luke 1:33).

Jesus the Divine One

*And now, Father, glorify me in your presence with the glory
I had with you before the world began. John 17:5, NIV.*

The earthly Jesus was acutely aware of the fact of His eternal deity. No one knew more than He what had to be given up when He became human. Here we find Him praying to God the Father that He might be restored to His former glory. Paul later describes the fulfillment of this prayer, noting that after Christ's life and death on the cross God "highly exalted him and bestowed on him the name which is above every name, that at the name of Jesus every knee should bow, in heaven and on earth and under the earth, and every tongue confess that Jesus Christ is Lord" (Phil. 2:9-11, RSV).

But meanwhile in John 17 Jesus is still facing the cross, still confronted with His final excruciating act as a human being. He recognizes His weakness and inability as one of us. Yet at the same time He is consciously aware of His divine nature and past glory in the courts of heaven.

Such a mental tension is beyond the experience of the rest of us mortals. We know that we possess one short life that began at birth and will end with the decay of our minds and bodies. But only the deluded have thoughts of personal divinity. The earthly Jesus faced issues and had thoughts about realities that are totally beyond our comprehension.

Yet those very thoughts reveal His earthly understanding of His part in the divine Trinity. The reality of His place in the Trinity was revealed to Him at His baptism when "the heavens were opened unto him, and he saw the Spirit of God descending like a dove, and lighting upon him" and heard a voice from heaven, saying, "This is my beloved Son, in whom I am well pleased" (Matt. 3:16, 17).

The fact that He was "the Son" as "the fullness of the Godhead manifested" in human flesh (*Evangelism*, p. 614) was a conscious part of His life. He knew without doubt that "there are three living persons of the heavenly trio . . .—the Father, the Son, and the Holy Spirit" (*ibid.*, p. 615). And Jesus reflected that trinitarian understanding in Matthew's portrayal of His last command to the disciples: "All power is given unto me in heaven and in earth. Go ye therefore, and teach all nations, baptizing them in the name of the Father, and of the Son, and of the Holy Ghost" (Matt. 28:18, 19).

What a Jesus we serve. We can understand Him—yet we can't. He became one of us, yet He was divine (and knew it). Such is the mystery of godliness.

January 7

One Sent From Heaven

No one has ascended into heaven but he who descended from heaven, the Son of man. John 3:13, RSV.

For I have come down from heaven, not to do my own will, but the will of him who sent me. John 6:38, RSV.

What kind of man is this? What kind of person would boldly state that He came down from heaven? No wonder the Jews had a difficult time with Him.

And we should, too. The hard fact of the situation is that Jesus was either who He claimed to be or some kind of delusional nut of the most dangerous kind.

C. S. Lewis caught that point when he rejected those who claimed "'I'm ready to accept Jesus as a great moral leader, but I don't accept His claim to be God.'"

"That," Lewis retorted, "is the one thing we must not say. A man who was merely a man and said the sort of things Jesus said would not be a great moral teacher. He would either be a lunatic—on a level with the man who says he is a poached egg—or else he would be the Devil of Hell. You must make the choice. Either this man was, and is, the Son of God: or else a madman or something worse. You can shut Him up for a fool, you can spit on Him and kill Him as a demon; or you can fall at His feet and call Him Lord or God. But let us not come with any patronizing nonsense about His being a great human teacher. He has not left that open to us. He did not intend to" (*Mere Christianity*, p. 56).

Such is the Jesus of the Bible. His claim demands a hearing and a decision from you and me today and every day.

And what claims He made! He came down from heaven as the Son of man. Here He picks up a title from Daniel 7:13 of a heavenly being who receives from God the Father dominion of His eternal kingdom (verse 14). "Son of man" became Jesus' favorite title for Himself. One of the last uses of it in the Bible is Revelation 14:14, in which the Son of man comes a second time out of heaven to rescue His people and set up His heavenly kingdom.

In the meantime, John tells us that Jesus not only left heaven for His earthly sojourn, but that He did so with a mission—to do God's will (John 6:38). And the central feature of that will was for Him to be lifted up on the cross so that "whoever believes in him may have eternal life" (John 3:15, RSV).

What kind of man is this? Our answer to that question is the most important decision of our lives. And it is one we need to face this very moment.

Christ's Ministry No Afterthought

You were set free by Christ's precious blood, blood like that of a lamb without mark or blemish. He was predestined before the foundation of the world, but in this last period of time he has been revealed for your sake. 1 Peter 1:19, 20, REB.

God the Son's earthly ministry was not an afterthought—something that caught God the Father off guard and forced Him into a last-minute decision to send Christ to head off our unexpected disaster. To the contrary, "He was predestined before the foundation of the world" to become the Lamb of God.

The Message paraphrase puts the issue graphically in context: "It cost God plenty to get you out of that dead-end, empty-headed life you grew up in. He paid with Christ's sacred blood, you know. He died like an unblemished, sacrificial lamb. And *this was no afterthought.* Even though it has only lately—at the end of the ages—become public knowledge, *God always knew he was going to do this for you.* It's because of this sacrificed Messiah, whom God then raised from the dead and glorified, that you trust God, that you know you have a future in God" (1 Peter 1:18-21, Message).

We serve a God who knows the end from the beginning. He knew that sin and death would enter the universe through the rebellion of Lucifer and He realized that it would spread to earth through the fall of Adam and Eve. The Lord understood the destructiveness of sin and that it would bring about eternal death (Rom. 6:23).

But God also knew that He would not stand idly by as His earthly children suffered and died. As a result, the heavenly Trinity "predestined" one of its own members "before the foundation of the world" to descend to earth and become altogether human to solve the sin problem and its results.

The Lord provided a glimpse of that predestined role to the shattered Adam and Eve in Genesis 3:15. Speaking to the devil, God proclaimed that He would "put enmity between you and the woman, and between your seed and her seed; he shall bruise your head, and you shall bruise his heel" (RSV).

The repeated slaying of sacrificial lambs foreshadowed that promise all through Jewish history, but it was not put into effect until the incarnation, ministry, and death of Jesus, "the Lamb of God, which taketh away the sin of the world" (John 1:29).

The message of that life is that the Godhead cares. They are never caught off guard, and They predestined one of Their own number for my salvation.

Both Divine and Human

Have this mind among yourselves, which is yours in Christ Jesus, who, though he was in the form of God, did not count equality with God a thing to be grasped, but emptied himself, taking the form of a servant, being born in the likeness of men. And being found in human form he humbled himself and became obedient unto death, even death on a cross. Phil. 2:5-8, RSV.

Mysteries of all mysteries. God becoming a human being. God giving up the power that created the universe to become a lowly person on a sin-sick planet of little significance in galactic terms. God abandoning the glory of heaven to come to the dingy little village of Nazareth. Here is something that the human mind cannot even begin to grasp, let alone understand. And Paul doesn't even attempt to explain it. He merely states the bold and brutal facts of the case.

William Barclay writes that "in many ways this is the greatest and the most moving passage that Paul ever wrote about Jesus." In 2 Corinthians 8:9 the apostle noted that though Jesus "was rich, yet for your sake he became poor, so that by his poverty you might become rich" (RSV). But in Philippians 2 he expands upon that idea and fills out its meaning.

We should note several things about today's passage. The first is that nothing was forced upon Christ. It was all His initiative: "he humbled himself," "[he] emptied himself." He consciously and willfully chose to leave His heavenly place for me.

A second thing that we should recognize is that when Paul says Christ was in the "form" of God, he does not mean to imply that He was kind of like God. The word the apostle uses *(morphē)* means not merely outward appearance but an essential characteristic that never alters. Thus the New International Version renders the phrase as "being in very nature God." That idea verse 6 reinforces later when it points out that Christ had "equality with God." "Form" also appears when Paul discusses Christ's humanity. He truly became human.

The key thought in the passage is that Christ "emptied himself" to become human. It does not mean that He exchanged His divinity for humanity, but rather that He displayed the nature (or form) of God in the nature (or form) of a servant.

The divine Christ not only became human for us, He became obedient unto death, the ultimate extension of obedience. But His was not merely a death, but death on a cross—one reserved for criminals and society's lowest.

Father, help me in my own feeble thoughts to begin to grasp what Christ did for me. And help me to have His sacrificial mind-set.

Parting Thoughts
on the Divine Christ

He [Jesus Christ] is before all things, and in him all things hold together.
Col. 1:17, NIV.

Our passage for today makes two astounding claims about Jesus. The first is that He existed "before all things." He existed as far back in time as we can possibly imagine. There was never a time in which He did not exist. His existence is coextensive with that of the Father and the Spirit. Jesus may have lived only 33 years as a human being, but that short period is hardly a blip on the timeline of His eternal being.

The second claim is equally amazing. Jesus not only existed "before *all* things," but "in him *all* things hold together." We must read that thought in the context of the previous verse, which states that "in him *all* things were created, in heaven and on earth, visible and invisible, whether thrones or dominions or principalities or authorities—*all* things were created through him and for him" (Col. 1:16, RSV).

Note the forceful *alls* in verses 16 and 17.
1. "In him *all* things were created."
2. Jesus existed "before *all* things."
3. "*All* things were created through him and for him."
4. "In him *all* things hold together."

The implication of that fourth point is that Christ is not merely the Creator of all that exists, but also its sustainer. Not only did He bring everything into being, but He maintains it each moment.

Paul couldn't have painted a picture of the divine Christ in more forceful words. "But," some might be asking, "What about verse 15, which distinctly and clearly claims that Christ is "the first-born of all creation" (RSV)?

That is an excellent question, especially since many throughout Christian history have used that verse in an attempt to demonstrate that Christ was a created being and not fully divine, thereby undercutting the doctrine of the Trinity.

Here we need to examine the biblical concept of firstborn. While it can refer to line of birth, that is obviously not its meaning in the context of verse 17, John 1:1, and many other passages speaking to the divinity of Christ. Rather, firstborn throughout the Bible means *first in rank*. We see it illustrated repeatedly by the dignity and office held by the firstborn in both regular and royal families. Thus it is that Paul is claiming for Christ the highest position. He then goes on to illustrate that primacy in Colossians 1:16 and 17.

Part 2

Turn Your Eyes Upon Jesus as the Incarnate Christ

An Earthly Beginning

The record of the genealogy of Jesus the Messiah, the son of David,
the son of Abraham. Matt. 1:1, NASB.

What a way to begin a book. For a twentieth-century author to start a biography with a long list of names would guarantee the manuscript ending up in the editor's scrap heap.

To a Jew, however, commencing the story of a person's life with his or her genealogy was the most natural and interesting way. When Josephus, the first-century Jewish historian, wrote his autobiography, he began it with his genealogy, which he most likely found in the public records kept by the Sanhedrin.

The Jews placed great store on the purity of one's lineage. A priest who could not demonstrate his pedigree back to Aaron could not function in the priesthood (see Ezra 2:62).

A first-century Jew would not only find a genealogy at the beginning of a biography to be natural and interesting, but would consider it essential. That would especially be true for a book claiming that its subject was the Christ (the Greek word for the Hebrew "Messiah"). And Matthew makes that claim in his first verse: "A record of the genealogy of Jesus Christ the Messiah, the son of David, the son of Abraham." If Matthew could not prove the purity of Jesus' ancestry, he might as well not write the rest of his Gospel, because no Jew would read it.

Matthew's task was not only to demonstrate Jesus' racial purity, but also that He had particular ancestors. First, the Messiah would have to come from the line of David. "Your house and your kingdom," God had told David through Nathan the prophet, "will endure forever before me; your throne will be established forever" (2 Sam. 7:16, NIV). The Jews widely held that promise to be pointing to the coming Messiah. As a result, the New Testament repeatedly asserts that Jesus was a descendant of David.

It is also important to Matthew that he prove that Jesus was a son of Abraham. Not only is Abraham the father of the Jewish race, but God promised that He would bless all the people of the earth through him (Gen. 12:1-3).

Because Jesus is of the lineage of both David and Abraham, He qualifies for the role of Messiah.

One lesson of Matthew's genealogy is that God meets people where they are. When the divine Christ became the incarnate Jesus, He did so in a particular time and place. And just as He met the first-century Jews in their context, so He ministers to us today in our time and place.

A Troubled Mary

The angel Gabriel was sent by God to a city of Galilee named Nazareth, to a virgin betrothed to a man whose name was Joseph, of the house of David. The virgin's name was Mary. And having come in, the angel said to her, "Rejoice, highly favored one, the Lord is with you; blessed are you among women!" But when she saw him, she was troubled. . . . Then the angel said to her, "Do not be afraid, Mary, for you have found favor with God." Luke 1:26-30, NKJV.

Have you spent much time thinking about Mary? Here is a girl probably about 14 or 15 years of age who was engaged to an older man, as was the custom of the times.

That wasn't so bad. But then an angel shows up in her room and tells her she is going to be pregnant. Put yourself in her place. To say the least, this situation will be difficult to explain. After all, you can't exactly hide a protruding abdomen. Then there will be the baby. And what will Joseph think?

No wonder the Bible says she was troubled. You would be too.

But to get the full impact we need to mentally move back to the first century. Modern promiscuous culture has blunted our thinking on the topic. Let's face it, with 1 million teenage girls each year in the United States getting pregnant out of wedlock, we may not feel the full force of Mary's predicament. It is one thing to have a "problem" in New York City, but in a closely knit Jewish village in the first century the news brought by the angel must have been disconcerting in the extreme. After all, Jewish law regarded a betrothed woman who became pregnant as an adulteress, subject to death by stoning.

When we read the gospel story we need to remember that these were real people like you and me. They lived in communities with the same kinds of gossip mills and social dynamics as we have today. When Jesus left heaven for earth, He came to the mess that we call society.

As I think of Mary, I imagine my own daughters if they had been in a similar situation and my heart shudders.

No wonder Mary trembled. But, the God who knows each of us knew her. And the angel noted that she should "rejoice" because she was "highly favored" and "blessed."

There is a lesson here for me. In my day-to-day challenges I don't see the big picture clearly. I easily get discouraged. But God views the larger whole. He knows that I am at times being blessed when all I can discern is the sky caving in on my life.

Lord, give me the eyes of faith so that I might truly see.

No Ordinary Child

"And behold, you will conceive in your womb and bear a son, and you shall call his name Jesus. He will be great, and will be called the Son of the Most High; and the Lord God will give to him the throne of his father David, and he will reign over the house of Jacob for ever; and of his kingdom there will be no end." Luke 1:31-33, RSV.

While Mary may have been troubled (Luke 1:29) and afraid (verse 30) at the appearance of the angel Gabriel and his announcement of an unexpected birth, she must also have been totally astounded at the nature of the promised child. Mostly she was probably perplexed in the face of the information overload she received in a few short moments—information that would not only transform her life irrevocably but also change the course of world history.

Gabriel tells Mary at least five important things in verses 31-33 about the child she will conceive. First, it would be a boy. That was always good news in a Jewish home. While girls were welcome, the birth of a son meant that the family name would be carried on and that there would eventually be one more strong back to help support the family in a subsistence economy. In a patriarchal family the birth of a son was the highlight of a mother's life.

But what a son this one would be! A second point in the angel's announcement is that His name would be Jesus, the Greek form of the Hebrew name Joshua, which means "Yahweh saves" or "God saves." And, of course, all Jews were aware of the historic role of Joshua in being God's agent in conquering Palestine and establishing their people there.

Thus the very name assigned to the boy would be pregnant with important overtones. And Gabriel will fill out those overtones in a way scarcely conceivable to the human mind. He goes on to proclaim that this Jesus (1) will be "the Son of the Most High," (2) that "the Lord God will give to him the throne of his father David," and (3) that His kingdom would last forever and never end.

With those short phrases Gabriel told Mary that she would not only be the mother of the long-awaited Messiah, but that the Messiah would be divine. Here was a new idea. The Jews had viewed the Messiah as a great man like David, but not as God.

All in all, the announcement was of stupendous proportions. How would you feel if you had such an experience?

A side issue related to Mary's story is that God used such a humble girl for His purposes. And that is important news for you and me. God can also involve us in His great plan if we allow Him to do so.

An Improbable Explanation

Then said Mary unto the angel, How shall this be, seeing I know not a man?
And the angel answered and said unto her, The Holy Ghost shall come upon thee,
and the power of the Highest shall overshadow thee: therefore also that holy
thing which shall be born of thee shall be called the Son of God. . . .
With God nothing shall be impossible. Luke 1:34-37.

Mary might have been young and innocent and probably a bit naïve, but she knew the facts of life. And she also realized that babies did not come out of thin air, that it took a man and a woman to conceive one. As a result, her question is quite appropriate: "How can I have a baby? I'm a virgin" (Luke 1:34, TLB); "I am not married" (Phillips); "I've never slept with a man" (Message).

The question was normal enough—an expected response. Gabriel's answer, however, must have blown this young woman clear out of the water: "The Holy Spirit will come upon you, and the power of the Most High will overshadow you" (verse 35, RSV). Here we have an explanation that is unique and incomprehensible. It is a part of the Incarnation. By this time Mary's head must have been whirling with all kinds of powerful emotions. But the plain fact of the situation is that the child would be fathered by God the Holy Spirit. Here we have a mystery that we can't even begin to understand. The Bible doesn't seek to explain it but merely states it as fact.

The child that will be born of that improbable union is called "that holy thing," "holy child" (NASB), "holy" (RSV). The basic idea under the word "holy" *(hagios)* is "separate" or "different." That which is holy is separated from the sinful ways of the world and set apart for God and dedicated to Him. The point here is that unlike all the rest of humanity Jesus was born holy. All other human beings might become holy in their second birth when they accept Christianity (John 3:3, 5), but Jesus was born that way in His natural birth. He entered the world in a born-again state. Thus He had a desire for goodness from His birth onward.

We hear a great deal of discussion in some circles about the human nature of Christ. It is difficult to follow all of the arguments. But the Bible right up front in the gospel story tells us that Jesus was different in that He was born holy. No one said that about me (or you) at my birth. But then I was not born of a virgin with the Holy Spirit as my father. If I had been, then, and only then, would I be just like Jesus. He was born holy, while I was born under the effect of Adam's sin (Rom. 5:12).

Father, as we meditate upon the mystery of the Incarnation, help us to grasp more of the majesty and the wonder of it all.

An Abnormal Response

"I am the Lord's servant," said Mary; "may it happen to me as you have said."
And the angel left her. Luke 1:38, TEV.

Mary could have made many possible responses to her short conversation with the angel. A quite normal one would have been, "Do you think I'm nuts? Do you really expect me to go around with an obviously bulging stomach telling the legalistic people in my cramped community that the Holy Spirit made me pregnant?"

Here we need to get inside the skins of the Bible characters. It is all too easy to just read the story as something that happened to people who are essentially different from us. But that is wrong. It is unbiblical. We need to put ourselves into the story to get its true import. How would you feel if it happened to you or your daughter? What would be your response?

Philip Yancey asks, "How many times did Mary review the angel's words as she felt the Son of God kicking against the walls of her uterus? How many times did Joseph second-guess his own encounter with an angel—*just a dream?*—as he endured the hot shame of living among villagers who could plainly see the changing shape of his fiancée?"

And Malcolm Muggeridge states that in our day, with its family-planning clinics that provide convenient ways to correct "mistakes" that disgrace the family, "It is, in point of fact, extremely improbable, under existing conditions, that Jesus would have been permitted to be born at all. Mary's pregnancy, in poor circumstances, and with the father unknown, would have been an obvious case for an abortion; and her talk of having conceived as a result of the intervention of the Holy Ghost would have pointed to the need for psychiatric treatment, and made the case for terminating her pregnancy even stronger. Thus our generation, needing a Savior more, perhaps, than any that has ever existed, would be too humane to allow one to be born."

These would have been normal responses. But we can be forever grateful that Mary by faith declared herself to be God's servant who was ready to suffer the consequences to serve her Lord.

And she set the pattern for all those who would accept her Son and live by faith in Him. They are abnormal from the ways of the world but normal in those of God. Like their Lord, they are different.

January 16

The "Gospel" Before the Gospel

And Mary Said, My soul magnifies the Lord, And my spirit rejoices in God my Savior, for he has looked on the humble estate of his servant. For behold, from now on all generations will call me blessed; for he who is mighty has done great things for me, and holy is his name. And his mercy is for those who fear him from generation to generation. He has shown strength with his arm; he has scattered the proud in the thoughts of their hearts; he has brought down the mighty from their thrones and exalted those of humble estate; he has filled the hungry with good things, and the rich he has sent away empty. He has helped his servant Israel, in remembrance of his mercy, as he spoke to our fathers, to Abraham and to his offspring forever."
Luke 1:46-55, ESV.

In Mary's song we have what N. T. Wright calls "the 'gospel' before the gospel, a fierce bright shout of triumph thirty weeks before Bethlehem, thirty years before Calvary and Easter. . . . It's all about God, and it's all about revolution. And it's all because of Jesus—Jesus who's only just been conceived, not yet born, but who has made Elisabeth's baby leap for joy in her womb and has made Mary giddy with excitement and hope and triumph." Mary's song (often called the *Magnificat*) has been set to music with trumpets and kettledrums by Johann Sebastian Bach, whispered in the prayer closets of humble Christians around the world, and recited in countless church Christmas pageants. It is one of Christianity's most famous songs.

It is a song of God's power and the victory that He will achieve through the unborn child. Yet it doesn't tell the whole story. Mary has viewed the glory of the gospel but she has yet many things to learn as her child matures. He will be like a sword who pierces her soul (Luke 2:35). She will lose Him for three days when He is 12. Then she will question His mental balance when He is 30 and will utterly despair for three dark days in Jerusalem, perhaps wondering what went wrong and if she had been deceived. But beyond the fog and darkness of her clouded fears and thoughts will come Resurrection and Pentecost. Only then will she begin to see the whole picture of the baby she has conceived.

But for now her song echoes the Old Testament promises in nearly each of its words. Those covenant promises speak of a Savior who will make all things right, who will rescue His covenant people and turn this world upside down.

Oh God, like Mary of old, we do not see everything clearly. But like her, we rejoice in Your power and our salvation. We praise You today for what You have done, are doing, and will do in the future.

The Forgotten Partner

Now the birth of Jesus Christ took place in this way. When his mother Mary had been betrothed to Joseph, before they came together she was found to be with child of the Holy Spirit; and her husband Joseph, being a just man and unwilling to put her to shame, resolved to divorce her quietly. But as he considered this, behold, an angel of the Lord appeared to him in a dream, saying, "Joseph, son of David, do not fear to take Mary your wife, for that which is conceived in her is of the Holy Spirit."
Matt. 1:18-20, RSV.

And then there was Joseph! Not in a good situation.
Most of us never give much thought to him or the anguish he must have felt in his role in God's plan. He is just there, kind of like a house down the street that we are aware of but don't know anything about even though we pass it every day. Because of our lack of interest in him, I almost decided to skip over him in this devotional. After all, "he is only the husband of Mary." But, we need to remember, that the neglected partners of highly visible people are individuals who support and enable the celebrated ones to perform their functions.

So it was with behind-the-scenes Joseph. Not merely "the husband of Mary," he also functioned as the earthly father of Jesus. Of course, most of their neighbors considered him to be the father, given the rather scandalous circumstances of Jesus' birth. It was Joseph who took Mary and Baby Jesus to the Temple to dedicate Him to the Lord, it was Joseph who led the family to Egypt to escape the machinations of Herod, it was Joseph who brought the family back to settle in Nazareth, it was Joseph who accompanied the 12-year-old Jesus to the feast for His Bar Mitzvah, and it was Joseph the carpenter who taught Jesus the same trade. And during that teaching they spent countless hours together as the older man helped guide and shape the younger. To put it bluntly, Joseph is a crucial character in the story of redemption. Invisible to us, but quite visible and important in the life of our Lord and Savior.

Joseph faced the crisis of his life when he discovered that Mary was pregnant. He knew for certain it wasn't by him. But who then? She had that story about the angel and the Spirit, but that was far-fetched to say the least.

As a man with rights he could have made a scene. But being a good man who loved the "wayward" teenager, he decided to put her away silently. Then the angel visited him also and changed the course of his life—and ours.

There is a lesson here. We are all too prone to overlook the person or persons who sacrifice to make possible the public work of more visible individuals. Today is the day to stop that injustice. Think of the sacrificing but "invisible" people in your world and go out of your way to drop them a card or make a phone call of appreciation—today.

January 18

A Revolutionary Proclamation

"She will bear a son, and you shall call his name Jesus, for he will save his people from their sins." Matt. 1:21, RSV.

Here we have a revolutionary proclamation of the Messiah's mission. Matthew had plainly set forth Jesus from the first verse of his Gospel as the Messiah and the Son of David. In the Jewish mind, both titles had political overtones. The two came together in the vision of an earthly king. David had been an illustrious conquering warrior, and first-century Jews expected their Messiah-King to carry out the same program. The Messiah, or Christ, was to be a national deliverer.

For example, in the Psalms of Solomon (written in the period between the Old and New Testaments), the anointed Son of David is a king who will arise from among the people to deliver Israel from its enemies. That Davidic king would be endowed with supernatural gifts. "With a rod of iron he shall break in pieces all their substance, He shall destroy the godless nations with the word of his mouth" (Ps. of Sol. 17:24).

Israel's history had experienced three great bondages: the Egyptian, the Babylonian, and now the Roman. The first two had had political solutions, and the Jews expected the same for the third. For first-century Jews, a Messiah who did not at least deliver the nation politically could hardly be considered genuine. The Messianic hope of the Jews rested upon a king of David's line who would free them from the oppressor.

It is in that light that we need to see the revolutionary significance of Matthew 1:21. With one inspired sentence Matthew overturns the whole Jewish concept of the Messiah. *The Christ*, he asserts, *would not save His people from their Roman overlords, but from their sins.*

The fact that Jesus, as the anointed Son of David, would not deliver people from their enemies came as a terrible disappointment to the Jews of Christ's day, including the disciples. One of Jesus' most difficult tasks was to teach a people, who preferred the conquering-king model, the true nature of His Messianic kingdom.

If we look into our hearts we will probably find that we are very much like those Jews. It is much more pleasant to get rid of an enemy ("Let them have it, Lord; give them what they deserve.") than our pet vices, which are so tempting and beguiling. Yet the proclamation of Matthew 1:21 is that Jesus came to save *me* from *my* sins.

The Conquering Christ

She will bring a son to birth, and when she does, you, Joseph, will name him
Jesus—God Saves—because he will save his people from their sins.
Matt. 1:21, Message.

In spite of yesterday's reading, in one sense Jesus did act as a conquering king. He would "save his people from their sins." Here we must understand the word "sins" not only in terms of their guilt and penalty but also their power and consequences.

In other words, Jesus would not save people *in* their sins, but *from* them. A prominent function of Christ's ministry was to liberate His people from the imperialism of their personal sins, from the control of sin over their daily actions.

That liberation takes place at three levels. First, through His sinless life and His death on the cross, Jesus rescues His people from the penalty of sin. *The Desire of Ages* puts it nicely when it notes that "Christ was treated as we deserve, that we might be treated as He deserves. He was condemned for our sins, in which He had no share, that we might be justified by His righteousness, in which we had no share. He suffered the death which was ours, that we might receive the life which was His. 'With His stripes we are healed'" (p. 25).

Second, Jesus delivers His people, as we noted above, from the power of sin over their lives. And He provides them with the gift of the Holy Spirit to achieve that task.

Third, Jesus will eventually save His people from the presence of sin when He returns in the clouds of heaven to give them their eternal reward. All three of those "salvations" from sin are evident in the Gospels. Truly, Matthew's revolutionary Son of David/Messiah is a conquering king who will "save his people *from* their sins."

And His people includes you and me today. God not only wants to save me (each of us) from condemnation, but He desires to transform (Rom. 12:2) my life so that I might be more like Him day by day. There is power (the Greek is *dynamis* from which we get "dynamite" in English) in the gospel (Rom. 1:16) for me each and every day. Jesus wants each of us to take hold of that power right now.

Thank You, Father, for the gift of salvation through Jesus. Help me right now as I grasp Your saving power in a fuller way.

Jesus: "God With Us"

All this happened in order to fulfill what the Lord declared through the prophet:
"A virgin will conceive and bear a son, and he shall be called Emmanuel," a name
which means "God is with us." When he woke Joseph did as the angel of the Lord
had directed him; he took Mary home to be his wife, but had no intercourse with her
until her son was born. And he named the child Jesus. Matt. 1:22-25, REB.

The first Gospel proclaims Jesus as the ultimate fulfillment of Isaiah 7:14. He is Emmanuel or "God with us" (Matt. 1:23). That is perhaps the greatest claim in the New Testament. And the recognition that Jesus is truly the Son of God is a central point in each of the four Gospels.

Matthew 1:23 does not present Jesus as merely a great teacher. For Matthew, Jesus is no guru or seer, nor is He God's messenger in the sense that Islamic believers view Muhammed as the spokesperson of Allah. No! Matthew is emphatic: Jesus is "God with us." Christianity is built upon that essential claim. It cannot be discarded without totally abandoning the faith.

Nor does Matthew present Jesus as the God above us. The Old Testament often pictures God as above humanity. He is the God of the unapproachable Most Holy Place. But from the very first chapter of the New Testament, we begin to get another view, a fuller revelation, of the Old Testament God. He is no longer the Deity *above* us but is present, through Jesus, as "God *with* us."

Jesus, through His preaching, teaching, and healing acts of kindness, becomes the fullest revelation of God's character. "Anyone," Jesus claimed, "who has seen me has seen the Father" (John 14:9, NIV). And the book of Hebrews tells us that Jesus "reflects the glory of God and bears the very stamp of his nature" (Heb. 1:3, RSV). The fourth Gospel fills out the picture when it notes that "God so loved the world that he gave his one and only Son" (John 3:16, RSV).

In that only Son we have "God with us," the Son of David and the heir of David's throne and of God's promises to David and Abraham. We have the Messiah of God, the child born of the Holy Spirit and the virgin Mary, One whose mission is to "save his people from their sins" (Matt. 1:21). That divine Person is the theme of all the New Testament.

And He ought to be the theme and center of our lives. Through Jesus we need to be *with* God just as much as He is God with us. Today is the day to reorder our priorities. Today is the day for me to get *with* God and let Him be the center of my life in a new way.

A Strange Agent of Providence

And it came to pass in those days that a decree went out from Caesar Augustus that all the world should be registered. . . . So all went to be registered, everyone to his own city. Joseph also went up from Galilee, out of the city of Nazareth, into Judea, to the city of David, which is called Bethlehem, because he was of the house and lineage of David, to be registered with Mary, his betrothed wife, who was with child. So it was, that while they were there, the days were completed for her to be delivered.
Luke 2:1-6, NKJV.

God's providence works in strange ways. Throughout the Roman Empire periodic censuses took place with the double object of assessing taxation and identifying those liable for compulsory military service. We know from the historical record that in Egypt such censuses occurred every 14 years. And from A.D. 20 until about A.D. 270 the exact documents for each census are extant. Interestingly enough, a government edict from Egypt states that "it is necessary to compel all those who for any cause whatsoever are residing outside their districts to return to their own homes" for the census.

Thus it is that we find in the birth of Jesus the initial contact between the most powerful emperor in the world at that time and the future King of kings. We have in Luke's passage a premonition of kingdoms in conflict. Of course, we can be absolutely certain that Caesar Augustus had not the slightest notion of the existence of Joseph and Mary or the promised Christ child. In fact, he probably had no knowledge of even Nazareth or Bethlehem.

But Luke is making it clear that the birth of the boy called Jesus is the beginning of a confrontation between the kingdom of God and the kingdoms of this world. Within a century or so the successors of Augustus would not only have heard of the birth of the child, but would be seeking to obliterate His followers. And in just a little more than three centuries the Roman emperor himself would become a Christian. The story of kingdoms in conflict was already in progress on the road to Bethlehem.

Careful students of the Hebrew Bible would not have been surprised at the Bethlehem connection. Seven hundred years before, the prophet Micah had written:
"But you, O Bethlehem Ephrathah, . . .
from you shall come forth for me
one who is to be ruler in Israel,
whose origin is from of old,
from ancient of days" (Micah 5:2, RSV).
God in the past has used strange methods and people to work out His providence. My guess is that He does the same in our day.

Humble Beginning
With a Capital H

And she gave birth to her first-born son and wrapped him in swaddling cloths, and laid him in a manger, because there was no place for them in the inn. Luke 2:7, RSV.

The journey from Nazareth to Bethlehem was about 80 miles. But the over-crowded conditions because of the massive influx of people who needed to register for the census left little room for Joseph's family. They were probably happy for even the stable.

It was there in the manger, history's most famous animal feeding trough, that the Lord of glory entered the world as a human person. Like other infants of the day, His mother "wrapped him in swaddling cloths," which consisted of a square cloth with a long, bandage-like strip attached. Jesus was first wrapped in the cloth square and then the strip was wound around Him a few times to hold the "garment" in place. Such was the introduction of the Creator of all into human existence.

J. B. Phillips has written a rendition of the Incarnation that helps us visu-alize the gap between what Jesus left behind and what He came to here. Phil-lips imagines a senior angel showing a very young angel the splendors of the universe. They visit a multitude of blazing suns and whirling galaxies, finally entering one with more than a billion stars.

"As the two of them drew near to the star we call our sun and to its circling planets, the senior angel pointed to a small and rather insignificant sphere turning slowly on its axis. It looked as dull as a dirty tennis ball to the little angel, whose mind was filled with the size and glory of what he had seen.

"'I want you to watch that particular one,' said the angel. . . .

"'Well, it looks very small and rather dirty to me,' said the little angel. 'What's special about that one?'"

After being told of the Incarnation, the little angel asked, "'Do you mean that our great and glorious Prince . . . went down in Person to this fifth-rate little ball'" and "'stooped so low as to become one of those creepy, crawling creatures . . . ?'"

To think about the incarnation of the Christ into the baby Jesus is almost beyond our imagination. And our comprehension gets further stretched when we realize that He began His story in this world not in a mansion but in a manger in a fourth-rate village.

When I think of what He gave up for me, it makes me wonder what I should give up for Him.

Meeting Jesus:
A Life-changing Experience

And there were shepherds living out in the fields nearby, keeping watch over their flocks at night. An angel of the Lord appeared to them, and the glory of the Lord shone around them, and they were terrified. But the angel said to them, "Do not be afraid. I bring you good news that will cause great joy for all the people. Today in the town of David a Savior has been born to you; he is the Messiah, the Lord. . . ."
Suddenly a great company of the heavenly host appeared with the angel, praising God and saying,
"Glory to God in the highest heaven,
and on earth peace to those on
whom his favor rests." Luke 2:8-14, NIV.

There was plenty of fanfare when Jesus was born. But it seemed to be to the wrong people. After all, Israel had lots of really important individuals who were learned and upright and who had access to those with power and influence. So why begin the gospel proclamation with shepherds, men despised and largely ignored by the pillars of society? Such people couldn't read or write. Beyond that, their lowly work kept them dirty—both physically and ceremonially. They were quite unable to keep the details of the ceremonial law as interpreted by the Pharisees. Their flocks made constant demands. Thus they had no time for the meticulous hand washings and rules and regulations prescribed by their social betters. But their hearts were open in a way that those of the self-satisfied religious leaders were not.

One of the most revealing aspects of Jesus' birth narratives is that God selected such humble individuals to be first to tell the Christmas story to. But while the men may have been humble, the presentation came with power and glory, so much so that they trembled in fear. But their terror turned to joy at the announcement of the angel that the Christ had been born in nearby Bethlehem. At that point their senses were shocked again as "a great company of the heavenly host" burst out in a song of praise. One can only wonder at the impact the experience had on the shepherds. First they had only the dark, star-studded sky. Then they had the glory of one angel who turned the darkness of night into light. And last the multiplied, blinding glory of a host of heavenly beings.

The impact of the glory and the message delivered to them transformed their lives forever. After visiting the manger they returned to their fields "praising God for all they had heard and seen" (Luke 2:20, RSV) and spreading the good news to others (verse 18).

For them meeting Jesus was a life-changing experience. And so it is for you and me as we respond to the mystery of God's love in Jesus.

Jesus' Birth From
the Perspective of Heaven

And a great portent appeared in heaven, a woman clothed with the sun, with the moon under her feet, and on her head a crown of twelve stars; she was with child and she cried out in her pangs of birth, in anguish for delivery. And another portent appeared in heaven; behold, a great red dragon, with seven heads and ten horns, and seven diadems upon his heads. His tail swept down a third of the stars of heaven, and cast them to the earth. And the dragon stood before the woman who was about to bear a child, that he might devour her child when she brought it forth.
Rev. 12:1-4, RSV.

Here we have a birth narrative of a different type. In it we find no mention of adoring shepherds or glorifying angels. Revelation presents a picture radically different from the birth stories in the Gospels. It is a vision of the significance of Jesus' birth that pulls back the curtain to provide us with a glimpse of the Incarnation from the perspective of God's heavenly throne.

That point of view pictures a savage struggle that spreads to the earth as an enormous red dragon enters the picture, sweeping a third of the stars out of the sky and casting them to the earth. Subsequently the dragon (identified as "the Devil and Satan" in verse 9 [RSV]) crouches before the woman "that he might devour her child when she brought it forth."

What we find in Revelation 12:1-4 is the beginning of a cosmic conflict that commences in heaven and then moves to the earth. The ongoing battle will echo through the corridors of history until the end of time (verse 17). The rest of the book of Revelation indicates that the struggle pictured so graphically in chapter 12 will not reach its climax until the victorious Christ finally puts an end to the dragon and the forces of evil (Rev. 19; 20:11-15).

Some have viewed the Revelation perspective on the significance of Jesus as a "great controversy between Christ and Satan." Philip Yancey graphically captures the same picture when he writes: "On earth a baby was born, a king got wind of it, a chase ensued. In heaven the Great Invasion had begun, a daring raid by the ruler of the forces of good into the universe's seat of evil." The king, of course, was Herod and the initial chase took Jesus to Egypt, topics that we will view through the eyes of Matthew in the next couple days.

Lord, help us to see the larger issues as we read Your Word. Help us to be able to recognize more clearly the context in which our daily struggles take place.

God Is Not the Possession of Church Members

Now after Jesus was born in Bethlehem of Judea in the days of Herod the king, behold, wise men from the East came to Jerusalem, saying, "Where is He who has been born King of the Jews? For we have seen His star in the East and have come to worship Him." Matt. 2:1, 2, NKJV.

An important truth of the Bible is that God works with all people, not just those in the "church." So it was with the "Magi from the east" (NIV). Those men probably came from Persia, where they formed a priestly class learned in such areas as philosophy, medicine, and natural science. One of the main interests of such people was astrology, a "science" prevalent throughout the ancient world as a way of discerning the purposes of the gods. Thus when the Magi saw the supernatural star they set out to discover its significance.

We do not know exactly how they came to connect that special star with the birth of the "King of the Jews," but there are several possibilities. For one thing, as a result of the Babylonian captivity Jewish communities had scattered throughout the Near East. And since the second century B.C. those exiled Jews had a translation of the Bible in the universal Greek language. Thus learned individuals of the priestly type would have had access to the Old Testament.

Of special note to the astrological interest of the Magi would have been the words of another Gentile Magi in Numbers 24:17, in which Balaam declared: "A star will come out of Jacob; a scepter will rise out of Israel" (NIV). Many Jews about the time of Jesus' birth viewed that very text as a prediction of the coming Messiah.

That specific expectation and the more general Jewish one of the coming Messiah-King led to a widespread belief in the Roman Empire that a world ruler would arise in Palestine. Thus the Roman historian Suetonius (c. A.D. 100) could write: "There had spread over all the Orient an old and established belief, that it was fated at that time for men coming from Judea to rule the world" (*Life of Vespasian* 4:5). Similarly, Tacitus (c. A.D. 55-120), another Roman historian, reported that "there was a firm persuasion . . . that at this very time the East was to grow powerful, and rulers coming from Judea were to acquire a universal empire" (*Histories* 5:13). With those thoughts in mind, it is not too unusual that the Magi followed the star in their search for "He who has been born King of the Jews." Then again, the God who warned them in a dream not to go back to Herod (Matt. 2:12) may also have given them dreams concerning the star. Our God is able and willing to utilize a multitude of ways and people to set forth His saving truth.

A Positive Response to Jesus

When they heard the king they went their way; and lo, the star which they had seen in the East went before them, till it came to rest over the place where the child was. When they saw the star, they rejoiced exceedingly with great joy; and going into the house they saw the child with Mary his mother, and they fell down and worshiped him. Then, opening their treasures, they offered him gifts, gold and frankincense and myrrh. And being warned in a dream not to return to Herod, they departed to their own country by another way. Matt. 2:9-12, RSV.

It was quite a star. Not only was it bright, but, unlike other stars, it moved as it guided the Magi to the young Jesus. With the mobility of the star in mind, it is slight wonder that some have suggested that in actuality it was a band of angels—perhaps the same ones who serenaded the shepherds.

And, of course, those stargazers of the ancient East would be especially fascinated by a traveling star. Thus it was that they located the "King of the Jews."

After finding Jesus, "they fell down and worshiped him." That fact is crucial in Matthew's Gospel, because, according to the Ten Commandments, God had commanded the Jews not to "bow down" or "worship" anything but Himself (Ex. 20:3-5). By emphasizing the Magi's bowing down in a book written for Jews, Matthew is forcefully claiming that Jesus the Christ is none other than "God with us" (Matt. 1:23).

The Magi's interchange with Jesus did not end with their bowing down in adoration, but extended to the more tangible presentation of their gifts of wealth to Him. Worship never takes place just in our minds. To the contrary, it spills over into the world of everyday life as men and women, following the example of the Magi, give themselves and their wealth in response to Him who "so loved the world that he gave his one and only Son" (John 3:16, NIV).

The Magi's gift-giving was as much an act of worship as was their bowing. Beyond that, it provided the much-needed means for Joseph to take the young King to Egypt, where He would be safe from the evil intentions of Herod the Great.

There is a meaning in all of this for us. The Magi provide an example for us in offering their worship and gifts. "If we have given our hearts to Jesus, we also shall bring our gifts to Him. Our gold and silver, our most precious possessions, our highest mental and spiritual endowments, will be freely devoted to Him who loved us, and gave Himself for us" (*The Desire of Ages*, p. 65).

Today, Lord, I dedicate myself anew to You.

A Negative Response to Jesus

When Herod the king heard this, he was troubled . . . ; and assembling all the chief
priests and scribes of the people, he inquired of them where the Christ was to be
born. . . . Then Herod summoned the wise men secretly and ascertained from them
what time the star appeared; and he sent them to Bethlehem, saying,
"Go and search diligently for the child, and when you have found him
bring me word, that I too may come and worship him." . . .
Herod, when he saw that he had been tricked by the wise men, was in a
furious rage, and he sent and killed all the male children in Bethlehem and
in all that region who were two years old or under. Matt. 2:3-16, RSV.

H erod was "disturbed." But then any king would have been so by a report
about the birth of a child who would occupy his throne. But Herod the
Great had more reasons to be upset than most, partially because he was not
Jewish by birth, but an Idumean (a branch of the ancient Edomites). He was
Jewish, however, by religious profession and citizenship. Beyond that, Rome
had appointed him to be king of the Jews in 37 B.C. In order to make himself
more acceptable to the Jews he ruled, Herod married Mariamne, heiress of the
Jewish royal line.

All in all, Herod was a volatile mix of insecurity, with an inordinate desire
for power, and with an almost insane suspicion of others—all of which made
him ruthless when he sensed any challenge to his position.

Anyone who threatened him Herod would promptly eliminate. Thus
soon after making his brother-in-law high priest, Herod had him "acciden-
tally" drowned in the palace pool. Mariamne, his favorite wife, soon shared
her brother's fate when Herod suspected her of plotting against him. That same
fear led to the death of two of his sons. And five days before his death (about
the time Jesus was born), he had a third son, his oldest and thus his heir, executed. Roman Emperor Augustus claimed that it was safer to be Herod's pig
than his son.

Here was a king who would brook no challenge or threat to his authority.
And it was in Herod's territory that Jesus was born. It is little wonder that the
ruler was "disturbed" at the Wise Men's question "Where is he who has been
born king of the Jews?" (Matt. 2:2, RSV). Nor should we be surprised to find
him killing all the male children in Bethlehem under 2 years of age in an attempt to eliminate a potential rival.

While we can take the positive attitude of the Magi toward Jesus, we can
also make the negative decision of Herod. After all, there is a Herod in each of
us who wants to be the king or queen of our life.

A Third Response to Jesus

[Herod] was troubled, and all Jerusalem with him; and assembling all the chief priests and scribes of the people, he inquired of them where the Christ was to be born. They told him, "In Bethlehem of Judea; for so it is written by the prophet."
Matt. 2:3-5, RSV.

There exists a third possible response to Jesus in the Magi episode of Matthew 2—that of the Jewish leaders. Matthew tells us that "all Jerusalem" was "troubled" by the arrival of the Magi and their statements and questions regarding the birth of the "king of the Jews." The Jewish leaders understood the import of the Magi's mission and were able to pinpoint the fact that according to Micah 5:2 the Messiah would be born in Bethlehem. They knew their Bibles and its Messianic predictions. Ignorance was not one of their faults.

But the great tragedy of the Magi story is that the Jewish leaders were apparently "disturbed" because of their fear of what Herod might do, rather than being excited about the possible arrival of the Messiah. Matthew paints their response to Christ Himself as one of utter indifference. They made no trips to Bethlehem, although it is only about eight miles from Jerusalem; they gave no evidence of Herod's fear and hate; nor did they display the interest of the worshipping Magi. *They just didn't care.*

Thus in the Magi story Matthew presents three possible responses to Jesus: violent rejection, worship, and indifference. Those possibilities didn't cease in Matthew 2. To the contrary, how to respond to Jesus becomes a theme of all four Gospels. An associated motif is that the arrival of Jesus always divides people and brings conflict. Confronted by His life, teachings, and claims, every one of us finds ourselves forced into responding in terms of (1) praise and welcome, (2) hatred and opposition, or (3) cold indifference. One of the paradoxes of the coming of the Prince of Peace is that His claims have continued to separate people into these categories as the great controversy between Christ and Satan works itself out in the lives of individuals around the world in every generation.

These are issues that we need to take seriously. After all, the experience of the Jewish leaders demonstrates that church membership or even leadership does not mean that we are right with God. He gives each of us the freedom to do what we want with "the king of the Jews."

First Temple Visit

And when the time came for their purification according to the law of Moses, they brought him up to Jerusalem to present him to the Lord . . . and to offer a sacrifice. . . . Now there was a man in Jerusalem, whose name was Simeon, and this man was righteous and devout, waiting for the consolation of Israel, and the Holy Spirit was upon him. And it had been revealed to him by the Holy Spirit that he would not see death before he had seen the Lord's Christ. Luke 2:22-26, ESV.

Jesus and His family were Jewish. As a result, the family obeyed the cultural laws that He Himself had given to Moses 1,500 years earlier. About a month after His circumcision (performed on the eighth day of His life, Luke 2:21), the family took Him to the Temple in Jerusalem for the ceremonies connected with the purification of His mother and the dedication of her firstborn son.

The Temple visit undoubtedly occurred before the arrival of the Magi, since the parents would not have come to Jerusalem to tempt fate once Herod had been aroused. And, furthermore, they left Bethlehem for Egypt almost immediately after the Magi departed.

During their visit they met Simeon in the Temple, a godly man who belonged to a remnant of the Jews who were faithfully studying the prophecies regarding the Messiah ("the consolation of Israel"). Another student was Anna the prophetess who spent most of her waking hours in the Temple, speaking of the coming deliverer to all who would listen (verses 36-38).

Simeon was unique in that God had told him that he would not die until he had seen the Christ child. And when he discovered Jesus, he blessed Him, noting that he had now seen the salvation of God (verse 30), who would be "a light for revelation to the Gentiles, and for [the] glory" of Israel (verse 32, RSV). In that proclamation the aged Simeon moved beyond the general parochialism of the Jews. They all too often were looking for their own deliverer, not the Savior of all people. But in the inspired words of Simeon we discover even in Jesus' infancy that His incarnation would provide atonement for all people—both Jew and Gentile.

Here we have an important lesson. As members of a certain sector of God's family we can hold Jesus too close to ourselves and to those who think and believe just like us. We tend to see Him as *our* Savior. But Simeon's words remind us that Jesus is the Savior of all who accept Him and His work on the cross.

Simeon noted that all people will fall or rise (verse 34) in terms of their relationship to Jesus. Here we have a hard saying. William Barclay enlightens it by pointing out that "it is not so much God who judges a man; a man judges himself; and his judgment is his reaction to Jesus Christ."

Born With a Price on His Head

Now when [the Magi] had departed, behold, an angel of the Lord appeared to Joseph in a dream, saying, "Arise, take the young Child and His mother, flee to Egypt, and stay there until I bring you word; for Herod will seek the young Child to destroy Him.
Matt. 2:13, NKJV.

The shadow of the cross dominates the story of Jesus from this point forward. Jesus came into the world with a price on His head. His family escapes from Bethlehem in time to avoid Herod's hit men. A man who thought nothing of slaying members of his own family if he felt threatened by them, and gave orders on his deathbed that the leading citizens of Jerusalem were to be slaughtered so that there would be weeping at his funeral, would not think twice of killing a few dozen babies just in case one of them should be regarded as future royalty.

Some people have it easy in their early years. Not Jesus. He was born into a difficult part of the world at a time of trouble, fear, and violence. As N. T. Wright points out, "before the Prince of Peace had learned to walk and talk, he was a homeless refugee with a price on his head."

That is how God set about to liberate His people and bring eventual justice to the world. "There is no point," Wright continues, "in arriving in comfort, when the world is in misery; no point having an easy life, when the world suffers violence and injustice! If he is to be Emmanuel, God-with-us, he must be with us where the pain is."

Fleeing to Egypt in times of trouble had a long tradition among the Israelites, as illustrated by the stories of Abraham and Joseph. Egypt was the safest place to go. As a result, by the time of Jesus colonies of Jews had sprung up throughout Egypt, with Alexandria alone having upward of 1 million Jews. Thus when the family reached Egypt they would not find themselves altogether among strangers.

After Herod died, Joseph took his family back to Israel, but to Nazareth because of angel-inspired fear of Herod's son (Matt. 2:19-23).

Dirty little Nazareth. What a place for the King of kings to grow up in. It was not a notable place as was Jerusalem or even a Messianic location as was Bethlehem. Nathanael once wondered out loud if any good thing could come out of Nazareth (John 1:46).

Often we may be tempted to complain about the stack of cards that life has dealt us. Sometimes we feel sorry for ourselves because of life's injustices. In such times turn your eyes upon Jesus, who became you that you might someday inherit a heavenly kingdom.

The Silent Years

And the child grew, and waxed strong in spirit, filled with wisdom: and the grace of God was upon him. Luke 2:40.

Fast-forward 12 years. Verse 39 features the young Jesus returning from Egypt (after a brief stay) to Nazareth with His family. And verse 41 has Him traveling to Jerusalem at age 12 for His Bar Mitzvah. Today's verse (Luke 2:40) provides our sum total of biblical knowledge about the intervening years.

Then verses 41-51 describe His trip to Jerusalem, closing with the observation that He returned with His parents to Nazareth "and was obedient to them" (verse 51, NIV). Verse 52 adds that "Jesus increased in wisdom and in stature, and in favor with God and man" (RSV). After those few verses the story of His life fast-forwards another 18 years to the arrival of John the Baptist and the beginning of Jesus' ministry at about the age of 30. Thus after the events surrounding the birth narratives and the glimpse of His trip to the Temple at age 12 we have only three verses on the first 30 years of the most important individual in earth's history. Silence is what we have—nearly total silence.

What I would give to be able to fill out the picture! Just think if I discovered five pages of text or one "photograph" of those missing years. I would be instantly wealthy. But God in His wisdom just tells us that Jesus was normal in His growth patterns. Beyond that, we find nothing.

But not everybody was happy with that lack. As a result, from the second century on we find several birth and infancy gospels that fill out the blanks. The Infancy Gospel of Thomas, for example, has the 5-year-old Jesus fashioning sparrows out of soft clay. That was OK with His neighbors, but it was the Sabbath. As a result, certain Jews complained to Joseph. Joseph, in turn, rebuked Jesus, who "clapped his hands and cried to the sparrows: 'Off with you!' And the sparrows took flight and went away chirping." The Jews, as we might expect, "were amazed." Other stories picture the young Jesus healing the injured, raising the dead, cursing His enemies so that they die, and so on. Those glimpses into the developing years of Jesus were extremely popular for the next few centuries, so much so that the clay sparrow sequence found its way into the Koran in the seventh century.

What a contrast we find in the inspired Gospels, which present Jesus as one whom we and our children can identify with. He was obedient to His parents and developed mentally, physically, spiritually, socially, and vocationally as He lived in Nazareth and worked with Joseph in his carpenter's shop. He was truly one of us.

Jesus Begins to Get the Picture

After three days they found him in the temple, sitting among the teachers, listening to them and asking them questions; and all who heard him were amazed at his understanding and his answers. And when they saw him they were astonished; and his mother said to him, "Son, why have you treated us so? Behold, your father and I have been looking for you anxiously." And he said to them, "How is it that you sought me? Did you not know that I must be in my Father's house?" Luke 2:46-49, RSV.

The scene is understandable enough. A Jewish boy entered manhood when he was 12 years of age. At that time he became "a son of the law" (what would later be called *bar* [son of] *mitzvah* [the commandment]). After his Bar Mitzvah a Jewish youth is morally responsible for his actions and is eligible to participate in public worship.

As a result, we find Jesus traveling to Jerusalem with His parents for the ceremony. But the story takes an unexpected twist when they depart without Him and had to return to find their "lost" Son.

But Jesus wasn't lost. To the contrary, on that short trip He had discovered His real "home." The Temple ceremonies as He viewed them for the first time led to an understanding of His mission in life. *The Desire of Ages* notes that day by day He saw the meaning of the Temple services more clearly, especially through the sacrificing of the Passover lamb. "Every act seemed to be bound up with His own life. New impulses were awakening within Him. Silent and absorbed, He seemed to be studying out a great problem. The mystery of His mission was opening to the Saviour" (p. 78).

Meanwhile, Mary and Joseph were in a state of panic. No one likes to lose a child, but to lose the promised Savior must have been a jolt to their hearts.

Two things stand out upon their discovery of their growing Son. First, He subtly disowned Joseph as His father. Mary had called Joseph "your father." But Jesus responded that He had all the while been in "my Father's house," indicating that He had grasped the fact that He was the Son of God in a unique way. A second point to note is the amazement of the nation's foremost teachers as this young man asked them penetrating questions about the meaning of the Temple system and set forth profound answers in the mutual discussion.

Inspiration includes these few verses in the story of Christ's life because they represent a major turning point: Jesus now knows more fully who He is and the nature of His life's mission as the sacrificial Lamb of God. Yet that recognition did not make Him proud or haughty to Mary and Joseph. He returned with them and remained "obedient to them" (Luke 2:51, RSV).

The Call to Be Ponderers

But Mary treasured up all these things and pondered them in her heart.
Luke 2:19, NIV.

"Didn't you know that I had to be in my Father's house?" But [Mary and Joseph]
did not understand what he was saying to them. Then he went down to Nazareth
with them and was obedient to them. But his mother treasured all these things in
her heart. Verses 49-51, NIV.

Pondering! That's what mothers do best. Well, it may not be what they do best, but it does seem to be what they do all the time. They are wired differently than men. The typical father might be concerned about his children from time to time, especially when they are having a difficult time or have taken a wrong turn. But a mother's concern has a constancy that bewilders most males.

Mothers are ponderers. My mother was. She kept a little book for each of her four children. In it she placed the first lock of hair sheared from my head, noted the dates when I began to crawl and then walk, kept a record of my growth in terms of height and weight, and wrote out verbatim my first words and my memorable sayings.

Mary was like that. She kept a notebook in her heart. And what a notebook it must have been. On the positive side, she had an angel announcing to her that she would give birth as a virgin and that her child would be the Son of God and the Messiah. Then there were the angel-inspired shepherds praising God for His birth and mission. And, of course, she could not forget the Magi from the East who followed a star that wasn't a star and also came and worshipped the newborn as the king of Israel. Such occurrences would have led any mother to ponder.

But then there was the downside, the shadowy aspect, of His early years that would send shudders into any mother's heart. Not only did His birth lead to Herod's massacre of the babies of Bethlehem that they had barely escaped by fleeing to Egypt, but there was also that mixed message of Simeon, who recognized Jesus as the Savior, while also noting that He would be like a sword that would pierce Mary's soul.

And now this boy was disclaiming Joseph and telling His mother that His Father was God. And yet He was their Child. He lived in their home and ate their food like any other youngster. It is little wonder that Mary pondered all these things and hid them in her heart.

We need to do the same thing. Every day we must turn our eyes upon Jesus and ponder the meaning of His life and death for us as individuals. Today and every day we need to meditate upon Him and His significance. In short, God wants us all to be ponderers.

Countercultural John

As it is written in the Prophets:
"Behold, I send My messenger before Your face, Who will prepare Your way before You."
"The voice of one crying in the wilderness: 'Prepare the way of the Lord; Make His
paths straight.'"
John came baptizing in the wilderness and preaching the baptism of repentance for
the remission of sins. Then all the land of Judea, and those from Jerusalem, went out
to him and were all baptized by him in the Jordan River, confessing their sins.
Now John was clothed with camel's hair and with a leather belt around his waist,
and he ate locusts and wild honey. Mark 1:2-6. NKJV.

Not an average person, this John the Baptist. The very description of him portrays him as a person in protest of the status quo. Avoiding the luxury of the city for the brutal desert near the Dead Sea, he had given up fine clothes and ate a diet of locusts and wild honey. We are not exactly sure what the locusts were, since the Greek word has two possible meanings. It was either a grasshopper-like insect that Leviticus 11:22, 23 declared clean or it could have been a kind of bean (carob) that served as food for the very poorest people. But no matter what the word's meaning, Scripture introduces John the Baptist as a countercultural revolutionary.

In spite of his oddness, or perhaps because of it, he could draw a crowd to hear his message of repentance, confession, the arrival of the kingdom, and the need to be baptized. Mark tells us that "*all* the land of Judea, and those from Jerusalem, went out to him." "All," of course, does not mean every last person. But it does signify that this rugged man from the desert had a major impact on not only the people but also the Jewish leadership. First-century Jewish historian Josephus tells us that John's influence was even felt by Herod, "who feared lest the great influence John had over the people might put it into his power and inclination to raise a rebellion" (*Antiquities* 18.5.2).

The prophet, however, was not after Herod's throne. He desired his soul. No one could see or hear John the Baptist and view him as anything but countercultural. He not only looked the part but he had a countercultural message—one just as needed in the twenty-first century as in the first.

Before exploring that message, we should note that Mark introduces this powerful preacher who hails the new age of the kingdom of God with an Old Testament quotation, thereby signaling that Christianity is not a new religion but a development from within Judaism. Jesus and His message are not an afterthought of a failed plan for the Jewish nation, but they are the fulfillment of the law and the prophets. He is the Messiah predicted from the earliest pages of Scripture. God's plan has moved orderly in the past. And it will do so in the future.

A Message for "Dirty Little Rats"

In those days came John the Baptist, preaching in the wilderness of Judea, "Repent, for the kingdom of heaven is at hand." Matt. 3:1, 2, RSV.

Yesterday we met the "uncouth" John the Baptist; a revolutionary who didn't even honor the dress code for ministers; a preacher who apparently didn't understand the rules of religious etiquette. After all, he went so far as to thunder that even church members and leaders in high places should repent. And that God didn't even need them—that He could make good Jews (and Adventists) out of rocks if they didn't shape up.

John's message centers on the central requirement of each and every one of us every day: repent "for the forgiveness of sins" (Mark 1:4, RSV).

Repentance is one of those religious words that is easy for us to throw around without really coming to grips with its meaning. Most people confuse feeling sorry for their sins with repentance. As *Steps to Christ* points out, "multitudes sorrow that they have sinned and even make an outward reformation because they fear that their wrongdoing will bring suffering upon themselves. But this is not repentance in the Bible sense. They lament the suffering rather than the sin" (p. 23).

Halford Luccock has it right when he writes that "repentance, in John's preaching, was a thoroughgoing change." The word "calls for a right-about face, a will turned in a new direction. . . . It is more even than being sorry for one's sins. It is a moral and spiritual revolution. For that reason to repent genuinely is one of the hardest things in the world; yet it is basic to all spiritual change and progress. It calls for the complete breakdown of pride, of self-assurance, of the prestige that comes from success, and of that inmost citadel which is self-will."

Repentance in John's message led to confession. And here we need to be clear that confession does not begin with saying to God that we are sorry. The initial step in true confession is to come to grips with ourselves. Someone noted that we find the first step to saving grace illustrated by a man shaving one morning. As he looked at his own face in the mirror, he suddenly cried out, "You dirty little rat!" From that admission flows confession to God and other people whom we have wronged.

John's message is for all of us "dirty little rats" to stop justifying our actions and get on our knees. It makes no difference if our sins are of the nasty or vegetarian (e.g., pride in goodness or religious pedigree) type. All of us this day need to heed John's call.

More Lessons for "Dirty Little Rats"

After me comes he who is mightier than I, the thong of whose sandals I am not worthy to stoop down and untie. I have baptized you with water; but he will baptize you with the Holy Spirit. Mark 1:7, 8, RSV.

He must increase, but I must decrease. John 3:30.

In spite of all his peculiarities and forceful ways, John the Baptist was truly a great man. Not only did the common people travel long distances to hear him, but even the exalted religious leaders of the nation. And they not only listened, but they put up with his "insults" to their positions and characters. Eventually even the head of state would call for a meeting with him. John was truly a person of influence and prestige.

While that is true, it is also true that he never fell into the same pit as most of the rest of us "dirty little rats." Let me explain. I once knew a great evangelist who was a genuine success. He had brought thousands of people into the church. But he had succumbed to the habit of believing in his own greatness. We could say the same thing, of course, of great pastors, local church leaders, and even church members. There seems to be enough "ratness" in the world to go around.

One of the serious problems of human success in any line is its proximity to failure. And failure dominates when human beings begin to take the credit for success for themselves, when their vision of themselves becomes exalted, when they in essence point to themselves rather than to Jesus by their manners and subtle ways of saying things. That is the essence of "ratness."

The Baptist saw the problem clearly. And I imagine that he faced the same temptations to greatness as you and I. But he had discovered the most important lesson any of us can learn. Namely, that our self-centeredness is the root of our sin and the problems that flow from it.

John himself set forth the solution when his followers realized that the ministry of Jesus was overshadowing his own (John 3:26). But that was no big deal to John. He had learned the most important lesson in life: "He must increase, but I must decrease."

Dear friend, it is time to join John. Today we need to stop pointing to ourselves, to stop feeling that we are better than other people, and to let Jesus have His rightful place.

Help us, Father.

The True Significance of Jesus

Behold the Lamb of God, which taketh away the sin of the world. John 1:29.

People have said many things about Jesus, but none have been more insightful or important than the short sentence of the Baptist as he saw Jesus coming over a rise: "Behold, the Lamb of God, who takes away the sin of the world!" (RSV). The next day he again called Him "the Lamb of God" (verse 36).

That phrase may not mean much to those of us in the twenty-first century. Many of us have never even seen a real lamb. And none of us has ever sacrificed one. But for John's listeners it was a phrase pregnant with meaning.

Their minds would have gone back to the Jerusalem Temple, the tabernacle in the wilderness, and the book of Leviticus, which sets forth the centrality of the sacrifice of innocent lambs to foreshadow the events that would eventually transpire on Calvary where Jesus would die "once for all" (Heb. 10:10, 14) as the real Lamb of God for the salvation of all humanity.

The Old Testament sacrificial system was essentially substitutionary. Sinners brought their sacrificial animals before the Lord, laid their hands on the animals' heads, and confessed their sins, thereby symbolically transferring them to the animals that were to die as offerings in their place.

It appears that through time the Israelites lost the full impact of the significance of the sacrificial system as the multitude of repetitions dulled their sensitivity to what was taking place. But for Adam and Eve, who had never seen death, the impact must have been crushing. With every pulsation of the cut arteries in the lamb's neck would come the powerful message that "the wages of sin is death," that the lamb had died in their place and for their sins.

If we moderns are disgusted by such a teaching, just think how much more so is the teaching of the New Testament that Jesus, the eternal God, is the Lamb of God who died to take "away the sins of the world." The reality of that shed blood stands at the foundation of all the metaphors of salvation in the New Testament, including redemption (Eph. 1:7), justification (Rom. 5:9), reconciliation (Col. 1:20), propitiation (Rom. 3:25), and cleansing (Heb. 9:23).

John's teaching that Jesus is "the Lamb of God, which taketh away the sin of the world" provides the very foundation of the gospel and Christianity.

Without that Lamb we would still be lost in our sins and subject to the death that He took on Himself. Praise God for the Lamb!

Jesus Shocks John

Then Jesus came from Galilee to the Jordan to John, to be baptized by him. John would have prevented him, saying, "I need to be baptized by you, and do you come to me?" But Jesus answered him, "Let it be so now, for thus it is fitting for us to fulfill all righteousness." Then he consented. Matt. 3:13-15, ESV.

One of the most shocking things in John the Baptist's ministry is that Jesus came to him to be baptized. After all, hadn't he already publicly announced Jesus as the one who will baptize with a baptism superior to his own (Matt. 3:11)? And now Jesus shows up as a recipient of baptism as His first adult action in the Gospel story. No wonder John is shocked.

Here we have an act of Jesus that could easily have been misunderstood. After all, John's baptism was one of repentance, accompanied by confession. Yet the entire redemption story hinges on Jesus' sinless nature. Is this request for baptism an admission that He is wedged in the bog of sin like the rest of us? Given the facts, it is little wonder that John remonstrates with Jesus, claiming that He should baptize him.

But Jesus won't take no for an answer. He directs John to "let it be so *now*," thereby implying that their relationship will change in the future as Jesus' Lordship comes more into the open. In the meantime, He tells the Baptist, "It is proper for us to do this to fulfill all righteousness" (verse 15, NIV).

Part of the implication of that statement is that through His baptism Jesus became an example that His followers were to emulate. Thus Ellen White claims that "Jesus did not receive baptism as a confession of guilt on His own account. He identified Himself with sinners, taking the steps that we are to take, and doing the work that we must do" (*The Desire of Ages*, p. 111).

We should never forget that though He was personally sinless, Jesus identified with sinners throughout His life. Not only did He end His ministry on a cross between two thieves, but He began His public work in a river among penitent sinners. He was truly "God with us" (Matt. 1:23).

But that is only part of the story. Just as Jesus was baptized in the Jordan by descending into the river and came "up out of it" (Mark 1:10; cf. Acts 8:38, 39), so His followers are to be immersed in the watery grave, symbolizing that each has died to the old way of life and been raised to a new way that "we too might walk in newness of life" (Rom. 6:1-4, RSV).

Baptism for us, as it was for Jesus, is a visible sign of a conscious choice that we have decided to dedicate our lives totally to God and His kingdom.

A Beginning With a Double Message

And when Jesus was baptized, he went up immediately from the water, and behold, the heavens were opened and he saw the Spirit of God descending like a dove, and alighting on him; and lo, a voice from heaven, saying, "This is my beloved Son, with whom I am well pleased." Matt. 3:16, 17, RSV.

Jesus' baptism represented the official announcement of the Messiah's arrival and the beginning of His ministry. Not only did it give John the opportunity to openly proclaim Jesus as Messiah and Savior (John 1:29-34), but it also provided God the Father with the opportunity for a public validation.

The Gospels present three events related to the baptism. First, the heavens opened, symbolizing the restoration of communication between heaven and earth. Since the death of the last of the Hebrew prophets (Haggai, Zechariah, and Malachi) some 400 years before, Israel had had no direct visions from the Holy Spirit. The opening of heaven indicated that the period of prophetic barrenness had ended.

Second, "the Spirit of God descending like a dove, and alighting on him." We should not interpret that event as implying that Jesus did not have the Holy Spirit before. After all, He was the Son of Mary "through the Holy Spirit" (Matt. 1:18, NIV). Rather, it marks a turning point in the plan of salvation, for only after the Spirit comes does the Messiah's ministry begin. Beyond that, the reception of the Spirit places Jesus in line with several Old Testament heroes, including Gideon (Judges 6:34), Samson (Judges 15:14), and Saul (1 Sam. 10:6). Time after time in the Old Testament, individuals began their work for God *after* the Spirit rested upon them. So it was with Jesus.

The third post-baptismal event was the voice from heaven saying, "This is my beloved Son, with whom I am well pleased."

That heavenly proclamation had a profound message embedded in it. The words from heaven were a fusion of two Old Testament verses—Psalm 2:7 and Isaiah 42:1. All Jews accepted Psalm 2 as a description of the Messianic ruler who was to come. The quotation from Isaiah ("with whom I am well pleased") begins a passage on God's Servant, whose destiny was to suffer abuse and opposition that climaxes in the great Messianic passage of Isaiah 53, in which the Servant is "wounded for . . . the iniquity of us all" (verses 5, 6, RSV).

Thus Jesus left His baptism with two certainties. (1) That He was indeed the chosen One of God. And (2) that the way in front of Him was that of the cross. He might be King, but His throne would be a cross.

The Core of Temptation

Then Jesus was led up by the Spirit into the wilderness to be tempted by the devil.
Matt. 4:1, NASB.

Here for the first time the Gospels introduce us to Christ's major antago-
nist in the conflict between good and evil. Matthew calls him "the devil"
in verse 1, "the tempter" in verse 3, and in verse 10 "Satan" (adversary)—his
proper name since the Genesis fall. Prior to chapter 4, the devil has been active
behind the scenes, as with Herod, but now he comes out in the open and to the
forefront.

We should also recognize that neither God nor the Holy Spirit is the active
agent in temptation. Matthew is quite careful in his wording: "Then Jesus was
led up by the Spirit into the wilderness to be *tempted by the devil.*" James plainly
teaches us that God tempts no one (James 1:13). But God does allow His followers to encounter temptation for the strengthening and development of their
characters. As a result, we should not feel that we are out of harmony with God
when we find ourselves in difficult places. After all, Christ's temptations came
right after His spiritual high at His baptism. God's followers are not exempt
from the pressures of the world. Rather, they are given strength to resist those
forces (1 Cor. 10:13). So it was with Jesus. He faced the common temptations
of other humans. Yet He found victory (Heb. 4:15).

With Christ's temptations we meet the essential nature of temptation itself.
Earlier we noted that the incarnate Christ had "emptied Himself" when He
came to earth (Phil. 2:5-8). That is, He voluntarily gave up His divine attributes
and submitted to the conditions of life that we also face. While on earth, God
the Son lived in dependence upon God the Father, just as we do (John 5:19, 30;
8:28; 14:10). He truly became one of us.

Please note that His self-emptying was voluntary. No one forced Him to
become human. He chose to do so. It is at the point of Christ's voluntary self-
emptying that we find the focus and strength of His temptations. If the enemy
had been able to get Jesus to "unempty" Himself one time and get Him to
use His "hidden" power, the war would have been over, with Satan the victor.
Ellen White points out that "it was as difficult for him to keep [to] the level of
humanity as it is for men to rise above the low level of their depraved natures,
and be partakers of the divine nature" (*Review and Herald*, Apr. 1, 1875).

In Christ's temptations we find the center of ours also. The core of my
personal temptation every day is to stop relying on God and to become self-
sufficient, to be the god of my life.

Temptation Number 1:
God's Will or Mine?

And he fasted forty days and forty nights, and afterward he was hungry. And the tempter came and said to him, "If you are the Son of God, command these stones to become loaves of bread." But he answered, "It is written, 'Man shall not live by bread alone, but by every word that proceeds from the mouth of God.'" Matt. 4:2-4, RSV.

I have never been tempted to turn rocks into bread. Not even once in all of my life. In fact, that is no temptation for me at all for the simple fact that I can't do it. I could spend the next three years in the rock garden behind the church parking lot commanding stones to become bread and never have a single loaf to show for it.

But Jesus could. As the agent of creation (John 1:3), He could make bread out of stones, or even out of nothing. To do so, however, He would have to "unempty" Himself and take up His divine power. The temptation to transform rocks into bread was a Messianic temptation, aimed at One who not only had the power to carry out the act but who also knows that He has it.

While Jesus was undoubtedly hungry, and while the suggestion to produce bread from stones must have been attractive, we miss the point if we see the first temptation as merely one to satisfy His appetite. At its core, it was an attempt to get Jesus to use His divine power to satisfy His own needs, a course of action fatal to the plan of redemption in which He was to rely on God like other human beings.

Even more central was its implications for avoiding the all-important cross. By creating bread out of stones, Jesus could have set up an immediate economic/political kingdom, and the Jews would have followed Him gladly.

That is clear from John 6, when Jesus fed the 5,000. In that miracle the Jews saw the predicted prophet who would be like Moses (Deut. 18:18). After all, hadn't Jesus performed an equivalent to the manna miracle? The populace got so worked up that they sought to "make him king by force" (John 6:14, 15, NIV). Even the disciples got caught up in the move to make Jesus into a political Messiah at that time (Matt. 14:22).

But Jesus rejected the initiative. He knew that the way of the cross would be infinitely more difficult in setting up His kingdom than feeding the poor in a hungry land. Also, He realized that the way of the cross was the only way to solve the sin problem.

Lord, this day as I travel through life help me to seek Your will rather than the route of expediency.

Temptation Number 2:
Sensationalism or Faithfulness?

Then the devil took Him up into the holy city, set Him on the pinnacle of the temple,
and said to Him, "If You are the Son of God, throw Yourself down. For it is written:
'He shall give His angels charge over you,' and, 'In their hands they shall bear you
up, lest you dash your foot against a stone.'" Jesus said to him, "It is written again,
'You shall not tempt the Lord your God.'" Matt. 4:5-7, NKJV.

The devil can quote the Bible and sound impressive. Never forget that crucial fact. If Jesus' first temptation came at His greatest point of immediate weakness (hunger), the second aimed at His greatest point of strength—His familiarity with the Bible and God's promises.

Quoting from Psalm 91:11, 12, Satan suggests that Jesus should jump to fame. Absurd as it may seem to us, that wasn't a bad idea. After all, weren't the Jews always looking for a "sign" (Matt. 12:38; 1 Cor. 1:22) by which to identify the Messiah when He arrived? Here is the perfect one. A jump from the top of the Temple, towering more than 400 feet above the Valley of Hinnon, would be impressive indeed. Malachi had predicted that "the Lord whom you seek will suddenly come to his temple" (Mal. 3:1, RSV), and certain rabbis had predicted that "when the king Messiah appears, he will come stand on the roof of the Temple."

For the Jews, there was nothing like fulfilling a Bible prophecy. The people would easily line up behind that type of Messiah. They wanted a spectacular Messiah. To Jesus, that would be an easier way to win a following than a crucifixion. And its results would have been immediate.

But He once again answers Satan from the Bible. This time He pits scripture against scripture ("It is *also* written," NIV), which is particularly appropriate in this instance, since Satan has misapplied the passage from Psalm 91.

In His answer, Jesus teaches us that mere quotations from inspired writings are not enough. Those quotations must be accurately interpreted for meaning within their specific context and within the overall framework of the character of God. To run with quotations out of context may or may not make a person into a fanatic, but such a practice definitely cannot transform individuals into followers of Jesus.

In Jesus' second temptation we have an important lesson for our lives. The devil has a thousand ways to lead us astray, even through the use of the Bible. With that in mind, how important it is that we become Bible students who read God's Word faithfully so that we will be protected from that Satan who pursues us like a "roaring lion" (1 Peter 5:8).

Temptation Number 3:
Sell Out or Persevere?

Again, the devil took him to a very high mountain and showed him all the kingdoms of the world and their glory. And he said to him, "All these I will give you, if you will fall down and worship me." Then Jesus said to him, "Be gone, Satan! For it is written, 'You shall worship the Lord your God and him only shall you serve.'" Matt. 4:8-10, ESV.

What is your price? At what point are you willing to sell out to the devil? Satan understands us one and all. He knows that some people will cave in if he offers them $5. For others it might be $500. But for others he needs to offer $5,000, or $5 million, or even $5 billion. After all, he suggests, you have to do it only once. And you can always repent later. "Why not?" our minds tell us. If you don't take the offer, someone else will.

What is your cave-in point? What is your price? People spend a great deal of time discussing how Christ could be tempted just like we are. I would like to suggest that He was tempted far beyond what we will ever face. For one thing, we never feel the full impact of temptation, since when the devil reaches our price we fold up and sell out and opt for his bargain.

But more important, Christ had capabilities way beyond ours. He was tempted far beyond what ordinary human beings can ever possibly be, since Jesus actually had the power of God *in* His fingertips rather than *at* them.

In his final temptation for Jesus, the devil pulls out all the stops. He aims at the very purpose for which He came to the earth. He can become World Ruler *if* He will only bow down and worship Satan—now, and without the cross.

But Jesus has made up His mind to worship and obey God alone. He will not feel the full force of temptation again until Gethsemane, when He will once again struggle to stay surrendered to the Father's will.

Jesus went into the temptations with the tensions between the modes of conquering King and Suffering Servant ringing in His ears (Matt. 3:17). But He comes out of the experience with His mind made up. He will follow God's way of the Suffering Servant, the path that will eventually lead to a distasteful cross. Now He is ready to enter His formal ministry.

On a far lower level, temptation takes the same course in our life that it did in Christ's. Temptation is not merely being enticed to this sin or that. No! At its bottom, temptation has to do with whom we will follow as the lord of our life.

Kingdom Arrival

Then the devil left him, and behold, angels came and ministered to him. . . . From that time Jesus began to preach, saying, "Repent, for the kingdom of heaven is at hand." Matt. 4:11-17, RSV.

The devil left him."

Don't get your hopes up, though. Satan never quits. Luke tells us that "he departed from him until an opportune time" (Luke 4:13, RSV).

The devil had lost this round with the very human Jesus. But time was on his side. He would return when Jesus was down and more vulnerable. Satan works the same way with us. When it looks as if the coast is clear and we are safe at last, we trip over him "hiding in the grass" waiting for an "opportune time." And that time will come, generally when we are least able to resist. How important then that we stay tuned in to God in our daily walk.

A second thing to note in today's verses is that "angels came and ministered to him." Actually, they had never left Him, but now their ministry is more visible.

Here we have a crucial truth to remember in our daily lives. No matter how bad it gets, no matter how down we feel, God never forsakes us. Whether we are conscious of it or not, His angels are always at our side strengthening and encouraging us to face life's challenges.

With Matthew 4:17 we come to the beginning of Jesus' formal ministry. He has passed the crucial test and is now ready to preach the kingdom of God on the Father's terms rather than on Satan's.

His initial message, "Repent, for the kingdom of heaven has come near" (NIV) is identical with that of John the Baptist (Matt. 3:2). Like John, He urges people to turn away from their sins and toward God.

When Jesus says that the kingdom is near, we wonder how near. After all, He spoke those words 2,000 years ago, and earthly kingdoms still roll on.

But Jesus knew what He was talking about. There is a sense in which the arrival of King Jesus on earth ushered in the kingdom, and another sense in which its consummation is still future. The fullness of the kingdom will occur only at the second coming of Christ. The inauguration of the kingdom took place at the First Advent, but it does not exist in completeness until the Second.

Thus it is that even in our day I enter the kingdom the very moment that I accept Jesus' Lordship in my life. He is already my King. Praise God! I am already a child of the King.

Part 3

Turn Your Eyes Upon Jesus at the Beginning of His Ministry

Jesus the Caller

As he walked by the Sea of Galilee, he saw two brothers, Simon who is called Peter and Andrew his brother, casting a net into the sea; for they were fishermen. And he said to them, "Follow me, and I will make you fishers of men." Immediately they left their nets and followed him. Matt. 4:18-20, RSV.

The day began with two fishermen casting their nets. It was hard work, but satisfying. Though they would never get rich, by the standards of the day they were quite a bit above average in their level of living. After all, they owned a boat and had a steady income. Comparing their relative social position to successful small business owners in our day, we could consider them upper middle class.

And then *that Man* entered their lives and things would never be the same. "Follow me" were His words. And they did, putting their financial security behind them to accompany a homeless wanderer who claimed He would make them "fishers of men." They must have wondered what that meant.

Why did they give it all up?

People today face that same question. Why did some of my students abandon lucrative positions as practicing physicians or lawyers or businesspeople with high earnings to go back to school to live on a modest minister's salary many times lower than what they had been used to? Why did others opt to teach children and thereby both remain out of the public eye and out of many of the "good things" a lucrative career brings? The questions go on. Why did some decide to serve in foreign missions? And why have countless millions of Christians in all walks of life suffered losses in order to maintain honesty and integrity in their business practices?

The answer is found in the Man named Jesus and His powerful message. He still beckons individuals today. For some the call is immediate, like a flash of lightning in their lives. For others it takes place across weeks, months, and even years. Still the calling goes on as people make decisions to leave whatever kinds of nets they are casting.

But like Peter and Andrew, they don't know where it will all lead. And that is probably good, since Peter ended up on a cross and his business partner James Zebedee would find death at the hands of one of the Herods in a few short years.

Yet neither did those early disciples understand the bright side of the future—how they would change the world in their day and that every generation after them would be affected by their giving up their nets.

Jesus is still calling, my friend. Today He still asks men and women to become "fishers of men."

Calling Is a Process

Again, the next day, John stood with two of his disciples. And looking at Jesus as He walked, he said, "Behold the Lamb of God!" The two disciples heard him speak, and they followed Jesus. John 1:35-37, NKJV.

We often forget that some of Jesus' leading disciples had first been followers of John the Baptist. That was so of Andrew.

Now there is an obscure disciple. A glimpse at my concordance indicates that the Bible mentions his name only 13 times, usually in lists of disciples or as Peter's brother—Andrew is that "other guy" who had the famous sibling.

Yet it was the nearly invisible Andrew who led Peter to Christ. That resulted, of course, in Jesus immediately sizing Simon Peter up for special recognition. And here we find a point to note—Jesus never sees us merely as we are but as what we can become through His grace.

Peter, along with James and John Zebedee, would turn into one of Christ's most important and visible followers. That never seemed to bother Andrew. He was apparently willing from the beginning to take second place as someone who introduced people to Jesus.

The fourth Gospel does not indicate who the second disciple of the Baptist was who followed after Jesus with Andrew. But given his style, it was probably the author himself. John generally identifies himself as "that other disciple." Decades later the aged John has many memories of those early years. Writing the final Gospel, he seeks to fill in some of the blanks that Matthew, Mark, and Luke left out of the story. Some of those gaps had to do with the first calling of himself, Andrew, Peter, Philip, and Nathanael. Those events were so precious to the old man that he even remembered the exact words that took place and cited them in John 1:35-51. He will do so from time to time throughout his Gospel, thereby providing his readers down through the ages with intimate recollections that only a participant could have known.

One of those recollections is that the calling of the disciples was a process rather than the all-at-once event suggested by Matthew, in which they seemingly give up all at their first meeting with Jesus.

Not so, says John. First, some of them were disciples of the Baptist. Then some of those disciples questioned Jesus. Next they introduced other future disciples to Him. And only later did Jesus tell them to give up their businesses and follow Him.

The same is true in our day. Jesus still calls disciples step by step. My only question is what step He has in mind for me today.

Not All the Disciples
Were "Vegetarians"

*Jesus summoned His twelve disciples and gave them authority over unclean spirits, to
cast them out, and to heal every kind of disease and every kind of sickness.
Now the names of the twelve apostles are these: The first, Simon, who is called Peter,
and Andrew his brother; and James the son of Zebedee, and John his brother; Philip
and Bartholomew; Thomas and Matthew the tax collector; James the son of Alphaeus,
and Thaddaeus; Simon the Zealot, and Judas Iscariot, the one who betrayed Him.*
Matt. 10:1-4, NASB.

That is quite a list. Have you ever examined it carefully? Some of them
actually have tags to their names. Such was the case of Judas, who would
eventually betray Jesus to the authorities who put Him to death.

But more interesting in some ways are the labels attached to Matthew and Simon. While the first is identified as a tax collector ("publican" in the King James
Version), the second is labeled a Zealot. Neither is what we call middle of the
road. Nor is either the kind of person that we would nominate for the ministry.

Jewish tax collectors were generally far from upright in their business dealings. In fact, they served as puppets for the hated Roman government—Jews
who collected taxes for the enemy. But worse than that, any "extra" money they
managed to collect went into their oversized pockets. And they made sure they
obtained plenty of the extra kind. If a person didn't want to pay, there was always the ever-present Roman army, which had mastered all the techniques of
helping people to cooperate.

At the other end of the political spectrum of the day was Simon the Zealot.
The Zealots stood against Rome as terrorists in an effort to overthrow Israel's
hated rulers. It was a good day for a Zealot when he could step into a crowd and
leave his dagger in a Roman or a Roman collaborator, such as Matthew.

The miracle of Jesus' small group is that it contained both a Zealot and a
publican. But the greater miracle is that the four Gospels record no contention
between them, as they do among Peter, John, and some of the others.

History demonstrates again and again that Christ's message truly changes
people's hearts and lives. Genuine repentance brings conversion and a new life
in Jesus, even among deadly enemies.

A side lesson here is that you don't always have to agree with everybody in
the church to work with them. In fact, the opposite is true. The more perspectives in the group, the more ways it will discover to reach out to a world in need.

Jesus Announces the Principles
of His Kingdom

Seeing the crowds, he went up on the mountain, and when he sat down his disciples came to him. Matt. 5:1, RSV.

Jesus knew that the time for His ministry to take a firmer, more visible form had come. John the Baptist had announced His arrival, at His baptism He had been filled in a fuller way by the Holy Spirit for ministry and blessed by the Father, and at the temptation in the wilderness He had met Satan face-to-face and set His boundaries.

Subsequently He had begun His ministry in Galilee, announcing that the kingdom of heaven was at hand. Then came the calling of His students, understudies, disciples—those individuals who would eventually take over His mission. Jesus would spend much of His energy and time and patience during the next three years in preparing those young men for the task ahead of them.

His early ministry in Galilee was one of "preaching the gospel [good news] of the kingdom and healing every disease and every infirmity among the people." As a result, "his fame spread. . . . And great crowds followed him from Galilee and the Decapolis and Jerusalem and Judea and from beyond the Jordan" (Matt. 4:23-25, RSV). His ministry had become a sensation almost overnight as the people sensed that something great was happening.

The time had come for this popular teacher, this healer of disease, this unique person in the history of Israel to announce the principles of His kingdom. He will do so in what would become the most well-known sermon in world history—the Sermon on the Mount (Matt. 5-7).

In that inaugural sermon Jesus set forth the principles of His kingdom—He announced how its citizens were to think and live. It would cover every aspect of their lives.

He began by highlighting the ideal character of the citizens of His kingdom in the Beatitudes (Matt. 5:3-12). Then He followed it with treatments on a Christian's influence (verses 13-16), their righteousness (verses 17-48), their piety (Matt. 6:1-18), their goals and priorities in relation to their daily needs and desires (verses 19-34), their relationships with others (Matt. 7:1-12), and their commitment to Him and the Father (verses 13-29). By the time He was finished He had set forth principles of His kingdom for every aspect of the lives of those who would follow Him.

As a result, we need to listen carefully as the King speaks. His message is for me.

February 18

Blessed or Happy?

And he opened his mouth, and taught them, saying,
Blessed are the poor in spirit: for theirs is the kingdom of heaven. Matt. 5:2, 3.

In Matthew 5-7 we find the most famous sermon ever preached. The Sermon on the Mount begins with eight sayings that we have come to know as the Beatitudes. Each of them begins with the Greek word *makarios*, which we can translate in several ways, including "blessed" (NIV, KJV, RSV) and "happy" (Phillips and TLB).

But we have a problem if we render it "happy." After all, we all have our unhappy days in spite of our faith in Jesus. Of course, there is a sense in which believers are always happy and have a right to be so, because they are already members of God's kingdom. But even citizens of the kingdom still have some miserable days when "dumpy" is the only adequate way to describe their feelings.

And "feelings" is the key word in that sentence. I would like to suggest that "happy" is an inadequate translation of *makarios* because most of us view happiness as a subjective state. That is, happiness is how we feel. We feel either sad or happy.

But the Christian life is not based on a subjective feeling. I once had a young student come to my office saying that he was upset because he didn't feel happy. Those feelings had led to deep spiritual discouragement. After all, didn't Jesus repeatedly say that if people were Christians they would be happy? Therefore, since he wasn't happy he must not be a Christian. Something must be wrong with his life, but he couldn't figure out what it was. He had arrived at the pit of despair.

I explained to him that he had it all wrong—that our acceptance with God does not rest on subjective feelings of happiness or sadness, but in the *objective fact* that Jesus died for our sins and that all who accept His sacrifice in faith have *already* been forgiven and become citizens of the kingdom of heaven. In other words, my student friend was blessed by God no matter how he felt.

Thus even though I may not feel happy about being "persecuted for righteousness' sake" (Matt. 5:10), I can still have peace because I have been blessed by Jesus. That is a fact. And while there is a sense in which I can be happy about that peace of heart, blessedness is more than happiness. Blessedness is a reality that no dumpy day can take away from me.

The Upside-down Kingdom

Blessed are the poor in spirit,
For theirs is the kingdom of heaven.
Blessed are those who mourn,
For they shall be comforted. Matt. 5:3, 4, NKJV.

Not a good way to begin a sermon. The preacher hasn't got it figured out yet. He certainly isn't very astute politically or in tune with the times. Definitely He lacks the insight of a public-relations expert.

After all, who wants to hear about poverty of spirit and mourning? To be "successful" a preacher needs to give people what they want, to present them with the words and ideas they desire to hear.

And anyone who has been around for a while knows that people really tune in to such messages as "Blessed are the rich" or even "Blessed are the rich in spirit."

Now, if Jesus really intends to draw a crowd, He will have to wise up to the ways of the world. With a message that begins with "Blessed are the poor in spirit" and "Blessed are those who mourn" He will never even get to first base with most people. Jesus will never achieve the kind of success that the larger culture will respect.

But that's precisely where the rub comes between conventional values and Jesus. He is not concerned with the admiration of the world around Him. Rather He wants to be in tune with God.

As a result, His message is the opposite of that of the larger culture. It is counter to the world's wisdom. In effect, *the Beatitudes set the world's value system on its head.* They turn it upside down.

Jesus announced His kingdom as being radical from the beginning of His ministry. Thus its citizens would be radical also. That is the starting point of the Beatitudes, the Sermon on the Mount, and the entire New Testament.

"Blessed are the poor in spirit" and "those who mourn" are some of the world's most revolutionary statements. Yet they stand at the foundation of Jesus' message.

And that message is for me personally. It is for you. We have to make a choice between Jesus and the world—between His values and the world's.

Father God, why is it that the church in my community is so "normal"? Help me to become "abnormal" from the perspective of the world so that I might be among Your "blessed."

The Ideal Christian Character Profile

And he came . . . and stood on a level place, with a great crowd of his disciples and a great multitude of people . . . who came to hear him and to be healed of their diseases. . . . And all the crowd sought to touch him, for power came forth from him and healed them all. And he lifted up his eyes on his disciples, and said: "Blessed are you poor, for yours is the kingdom of God." Luke 6:17-20, RSV.

Luke puts the Sermon on the Mount in context, with massive crowds thronging Jesus for healing and spiritual blessing. And here we discover a basic principle of His life and ministry. Jesus knew that hurting people do not hear well. Therefore, He did not separate the physical and the spiritual. First, He healed their bodies, and then He offered spiritual blessing.

In the Beatitudes the Lord provides His followers with the ideal Christian character. Unlike the gifts of the Spirit, of which some go to one person and others to another, each Christian will have all eight characteristics. Thus a follower of Christ is not either meek *or* pure in heart, but one who is both meek *and* pure in heart. The eight characteristics are to form the moral profile of every Christian. They are the essential traits of kingdom citizens.

The second half of each beatitude describes the eight blessings that God desires to shower upon His people. Like the kingdom itself, the blessings are partly a present experience and partly future. Thus, for example, those comforted by the gospel message in their present daily life will find exceedingly more comfort at the Second Advent. The consummation of the kingdom will bring to fullness the present foretaste of each promised blessing.

The simplest division of the Beatitudes is to separate them in the same manner as the two tables of the law. Thus we can see the first four as describing a Christian's relationship to God, while the second four focus on a person's attitude toward other people. Unlike some church people, Jesus never separated a healthy relationship with God from a wholesome one with people.

The last thing to note about the Beatitudes is that they are progressive. Each characteristic leads to the next. As a result, those who recognize their spiritual poverty mourn over that fact, are humbled in the process, are led to hunger after righteousness, and after being filled are sent out into their communities to be merciful and pure in heart.

Help me this day, Lord, to internalize more fully each of the characteristics You set forth in the Beatitudes. I crave Your blessings.

Mourning Over Poverty

Blessed are the poor in spirit, for theirs is the kingdom of heaven.
Blessed are those who mourn, for they shall be comforted.
Matt. 5:3, 4, NASB.

At the very beginning of Jesus' profile of Christian characteristics is poverty of spirit. In the Old Testament poverty had spiritual overtones that Scripture identified with humble dependence upon God. Whereas the rich and self-sufficient tended to rely on their own strength, the poor could only look to the Lord for salvation and help in time of trouble.

In the New Testament it is the "poor in spirit" who stand with the publican in Jesus' parable, crying in their humbleness, "God be merciful to me a sinner" (Luke 18:13). The man felt the unbearable poverty of what he had to offer God. *The New English Bible* helps us grasp the meaning of the first beatitude, rendering it as "blest are those who know their need of God."

John R. W. Stott writes that it was the "publicans and prostitutes, the rejects of human society, who knew they were so poor they could offer nothing and achieve nothing," who received the kingdom in the gospel story. "All they could do was to cry to God for mercy; and he heard their cry." "Theirs," promised Jesus, "is the kingdom of heaven."

After recognizing one's helplessness and spiritual poverty, the next step is the sorrow of repentance, described in the second beatitude as mourning. It is one thing to acknowledge our spiritual poverty but quite another to mourn over it. "The mourning here brought to view is true heart sorrow for sin" (*Thoughts From the Mount of Blessing*, p. 9).

Thus the Christian life is not one of constant lighthearted joy and laughter, as some would have us believe. Christians weep over their shortcomings, the lacks in their lives that put Christ on the cross.

The good news of the first two beatitudes is not only that Christ's followers inherit the kingdom but that they will also be comforted. That comfort comes in two flavors—present and future.

On one level Christians are already comforted by forgiveness and assurance of salvation. But the best of all comfort is yet to come when Jesus arrives in the clouds of heaven to take His people home. At that time those who have died in Christ He will raise from death while "we who are still alive and remain on the earth will be caught up with them in the clouds to meet the Lord in the air and remain with him forever" (1 Thess. 4:16, 17, TLB). Now there is true comfort!

Jesus Gets It Backward Again

Blessed are the meek: for they shall inherit the earth. Matt. 5:5.

Jesus' teaching in the third beatitude once again stands over against the acceptable wisdom of our world. According to Him, it is not the pushy, the violent, the aggressive, or the selfish who inherit the earth. Rather, it is the meek—people who have seen their helplessness and poverty of spirit and have mourned over their shortcomings. Such individuals have little room for pride, but plenty of space for meekness.

The Greek word for "meek" can also be translated as "gentle," "humble," "considerate," and "unassuming."

We should not confuse meekness with weakness. The meek may have great authority and strength, but they choose not to use it for their own selfish ends. Humility and a genuine dependence on God always accompany the strength of the meek. Leon Morris suggests that "the strong who qualify for this blessing are the strong who decline to domineer."

Jesus describes Himself as meek in Matthew 11:29. Although He had all power, He entered Jerusalem and went to the cross peacefully. That was the opposite of the Zealot party, who expected the Messiah to overthrow the Romans by force.

Whether they be strong or weak, the meek are those who exhibit the virtues of humility and gentleness. For sinful humans, meekness flows out of the sense of helplessness and sin they feel when they attempt to live apart from the grace of God.

It is such people who will inherit the earth.

Earthly economics is based upon security and power. Unfortunately there is not an infinite amount of wealth. As a result, men and women everywhere struggle to obtain their share—or to put it more honestly, more than their share.

We see the results of human selfishness and aggression everywhere. Nation strives against nation on the international scene, while individuals struggle for position on the corporate ladder.

It hardly looks as though the meek will inherit much of anything worth having according to the world's standards. Jesus' final reward was a cross. And many of His faithful followers have endured persecution and lived in poverty.

But the promise of the third beatitude and the whole of the New Testament is that a change is coming. The meek in God's upside-down kingdom will inherit the earth. And not merely this old beat-up one, but one not broken with sorrow, sickness, and death.

The Gospel Unveiled

Blessed are those who hunger and thirst for righteousness,
for they shall be satisfied. Matt. 5:6, RSV.

With the fourth beatitude we have reached a major turning point. The first two exemplified a *turning away from* our human weakness and sin, while the third expressed the Christian's humility in light of that weakness. The fourth, by way of contrast, is a *turning toward* the positive aspect of Christianity. It is a hungering and thirsting to be right with God and to be like Him.

Thus the Christian life is more than a mourning over past sins. It is also an intense desire for present and future righteousness.

The fourth beatitude is one of the great promises of the Bible. Those who hunger and thirst after righteousness "shall be filled" (KJV). It does not promise "may be" filled, but "shall be." That is the good news that stands at the focal point of the New Testament.

Righteousness is a word with more than one meaning. In the fourth beatitude it implies both the lofty height of being right with God in relationship and of being like Him in character.

Humans have failed dismally in both endeavors. Paul puts it succinctly when he notes that "all have sinned, and come short of the glory of God" (Rom. 3:23). Recognition of that fact in our personal journey is what poverty of spirit and mourning are all about. Those whom the Spirit leads will have a deep sense of unworthiness that they are powerless to do anything about. It is in the light of that utter hopelessness that Paul rejoiced that we "are justified [or counted righteous] by his grace as a gift" (verse 24, RSV).

But the positioning of the fourth beatitude between those dealing with people's relationship to God (Matt. 5:3-5) and those highlighting their responsibility to other individuals indicates that righteousness in the Beatitudes is more than mere justification by faith. It also implies being right with God in character, as indicated by the fact that those who receive His justifying grace God then immediately sends out to serve the world by being merciful (verse 7).

Thus being filled with righteousness relates to both justification and sanctification. The gospel of Christ not only saves us from the penalty of sin but also from its ruling power in our daily life. And in place of being a gossiper and hateful, God wants to make me a peacemaker (verse 9). In place of lust, He desires to infuse me with purity of heart (verse 8). God wants me to be like Him in character. As a result, the word "righteousness" in the fourth blessing spans both halves of the Beatitudes.

The Best Day to Become
More Like Jesus

Blessed are the merciful: for they shall obtain mercy. Matt. 5:7.

Our Lord chose the sequence of the Beatitudes carefully to represent the order of salvation. Each beatitude follows logically from the previous one. Thus when I realize that I have no righteousness of my own and am truly poor in spirit, I mourn over my utter helplessness. I cry out for deliverance, and my understanding of my true state makes me genuinely meek rather than high and mighty. Having seen my desperate condition, I naturally hunger and thirst after God's forgiving and empowering righteousness.

At that point the God of all mercies jumps in and accepts my repentance, declares me forgiven, and implants a new heart within me. I have been redeemed, saved by His mercy toward me. That is the promise of the first four beatitudes.

The question then arises: How shall I respond? That is the topic of the "second table" of the Beatitudes. I will be merciful, pure of heart, a maker of peace, and patient when treated unjustly. In short, through God's power I will become more and more like Jesus.

The fifth beatitude illustrates the shift from the Godward to the humanward side of the Beatitudes nicely. I have just received the mercy of grace in the fourth one. And as I rise from my knees God sends me out to share that same mercy with my neighbor, my wife, my workmate. God wants me by His empowering grace to treat others as He has treated me. He desires that I will also be merciful when others fall short or have a need.

And here we need to remember that being merciful is more than an attitude. It is also an action.

A story tells of Jacob Bright coming home from town and finding a poor neighbor in great trouble. His horse had met with an accident and had to be killed. People were crowding around the man, saying how sorry they were. To one who kept on repeating this most loudly, Jacob said, "I am sorry $50. How much are you sorry?" He then passed around the hat to buy the man another horse.

Mercy is outgoing love. But before love can be *outgoing* it must be *outlooking*. It implies a change of heart. As William Barclay puts it, "Mercy is the reverse of self-centeredness. . . . It is the antithesis of selfishness."

Today is the best day to begin being merciful in a fuller way. Why put it off? Why not do an unexpected kindness to your husband, wife, or neighbor. *Today* is the time to pass on God's mercy.

The Importance of Priorities

Blessed are the pure in heart: for they shall see God. Matt. 5:8.

When guards led Sir Walter Raleigh to the execution block, his executioner asked him if his head lay right. Raleigh replied that "it matters little, my friend, how the head lies, provided the heart is right."

In like manner, when I go to my physician to have an operation on my leg, the first thing my doctor does is to check my heart. After all, if my heart is not right, there is no use getting my leg fixed. Without a functional heart, the best leg in the world will do me no good.

In the physical realm the heart is at the center of life. It is the pumping of that muscle that spreads life to the rest of the body.

It is the same in the spiritual realm. The biblical emphasis is on the importance of having our hearts right with God.

Jesus pronounces His blessing on those who are "pure in heart." Significantly, He does not commend those who are intellectual. He does not say, as some would, "Blessed are those who understand correct doctrine, for they shall see God." His focus is on the heart.

Now, don't get me wrong. Correct doctrine is important, but it is not at the center of the matter. You can have a correct doctrinal understanding and be meaner than the devil. A person can be "straight" on doctrine, yet be a curse to the church and a false representative of the Lord in daily life, in the family, and workplace.

In the Bible the heart stands for a person's whole inner state. The natural heart is self-centered and unclean (see Jer. 17:9), but Jesus calls for a transformed heart (Rom. 12:2; 2 Cor. 5:17). That is crucial to Christian living, for "out of the heart come evil thoughts—murder, adultery, sexual immorality, theft, false testimony, slander" (Matt. 15:19, NIV).

As in the physical realm, the core of Christian existence is the heart. A heart right with both God and other people sets the stage for both a correct understanding of doctrine and a correct expression of one's faith in daily living. Without a healthy spiritual heart, I am spiritually dead, no matter how well I understand theology or how much of the Bible I have committed to memory.

It is the pure of heart who shall see God.

Lord, help me today to get my priorities right. Help me today to surrender my heart to You. Help me today to start seeing You better.

Church Members
Come in Two Flavors

Blessed are the peacemakers: for they shall be called the children of God. Matt. 5:9.

B eing a church member is not the same as being a Christian. Some church members are nothing but trouble to their spouse, children, neighborhood, and congregation.

The first warning sign of such people is their critical attitude and harsh manner. They always have something to say about what's wrong.

Of course, they garb their nastiness in sanctity by saying that they are only out to correct the wrongs in the church or other people. While that motivation may be commendable, such people would do well to start cleaning up their warlike ways first and putting on the attributes of peacefulness.

Peacemaking, we need to recognize, is more than merely not living in the realm of criticism and faultfinding. It has a positive, active aspect nicely set forth in the following prayer:

"Lord, make me an instrument of Your peace. Where there is hatred let me sow love; where there is injury, pardon; where there is doubt, faith; where there is despair, hope; where there is darkness, light; and where there is sadness, joy. O divine Master, grant that I may not so much seek to be consoled as to console; to be understood as to understand; to be loved as to love. For it is in giving that we receive; it is in pardoning that we are pardoned; and it is in dying that we are born to eternal life."

Church members come in two flavors: children of God and children of the devil. If I were the devil I would make certain to plant the latter in each congregation. Needless to say, it is only the peacemakers who fall in the first category.

Peacemaking is a many-faceted activity. To be a peacemaker I need to evaluate every situation in the light of the gospel. I must ask, What are the implications of this action? After all, more individuals are involved than just me. How will what I do affect them? What effect will my actions have on the good name of Christ? or the church? or my community? A peacemaker walks in the light of the gospel message.

There is a quip that goes:

"To live with the saints in heaven is bliss and glory,
But to live with the saints on earth is often another story."

God is calling you today to make the church different from the world. He is summoning you as an individual to become a peacemaker in the likeness of Jesus.

Leaping for Joy in Hard Times

Blessed are they which are persecuted for righteousness' sake: for theirs is the king-
dom of heaven. Blessed are ye, when men shall revile you, and persecute you, and
shall say all manner of evil against you falsely, for my sake. Rejoice, and be exceeding
glad: for great is your reward in heaven: for so persecuted they the prophets which
were before you. Matt. 5:10-12.

With verses 10-12 we come to the last of Christ's eight blessings. It is also the longest, with verses 11 and 12 providing a commentary on verse 10.

Christianity as Jesus presented it is something less than a peaceful picnic. Of all the world's great teachers, perhaps He is the most brutally honest. Again and again He emphasized the fact that His followers would be persecuted *be-cause* they were like Him, *because* they would live according to principles diametrically opposed to those of the larger culture.

Christianity has resulted in persecution in every area of Christians' lives: in the workplace because of such issues as unwillingness to promote a less than honest deal or to work on Sabbath; in families because of new priorities and allegiances; in social life because of new lifestyles.

The plain fact is that true Christianity changes people. It makes them out of harmony with "normal" (spelled "sinful") human culture. The result is persecution.

Some of that persecution is gentle and almost invisible (except to the recipient), such as failure to receive a raise or a promotion or being snubbed at a social event.

Oftentimes it is brutal. The Roman emperor Nero, for example, wrapped believers in pitch and set them afire to serve as living torches to light his gardens. Others he sewed in animal skins, then set his hunting dogs upon them to tear them to shreds.

The list of atrocities goes on and on. Even Jesus was not exempt. He died the excruciating and humiliating death of the cross.

And the persecutions are not at an end yet. Revelation 13 has plenty to say on the topic. Persecution will continue to the end of time.

But please note, the persecution that Jesus is speaking about is "for righteousness' sake." All persecution does not lead to blessing.

But when people suffer for their fidelity to Christ, they should "leap for joy," for their "reward is great in heaven," Luke 6:23, RSV.

February 28

Salt Can Never Lose Its Flavor

You are the salt of the earth; but if salt has lost its taste, how shall its saltness be restored? It is no longer good for anything except to be thrown out and trodden under foot. Matt. 5:13, RSV.

With verse 13 Jesus shifts from His exposition of Christian character to a short section on a Christian's influence. But the two are closely related. After all, a Christian's influence depends upon character. Without a "Christian" character, there can be no "Christian" influence. The salt must be salty to be effective.

Salt has many functions. Societies without refrigeration use it as a preservative. But in order to be effective, salt must penetrate the food. Salt left a fraction of an inch away from food can neither preserve nor flavor.

Jesus describes Christians as "the salt of the earth." He has not commanded us to *become* salt, but has stated a fact—"You *are* the salt." Christians function as salt by intermingling with the surrounding culture. Only then can they carry out their God-given role of preserving and flavoring their society. Although Christians often do not realize it, their daily lives moderate the people and society around them as they live out the Beatitudes. They "flavor" the world through the little kindnesses they show, the humility they demonstrate, and so on. Even proud and hardened people often find it difficult not to respect true Christians, although they may not choose to emulate them. Thus one effect of Christian influence is to slow down the personal and social degeneracy Paul so aptly describes in Romans 1:18-32.

Salt is salt! Salt is salty! Without saltiness it is not salt!

How, therefore, can salt lose its saltiness? It can't. If it's not salty, it's not salt.

"So what?" you may be asking at this point. "What does this mean for my life?"

It means everything. Since Christians cannot choose not to be salt, the only thing that they can do is to elect not to function as salt, to reject the God-given role of salt.

And how can I do that? By not being like Jesus, who lived and died for the good of others. By failing to mix with the world and contributing a preserving influence.

With such choices individuals lose their saltiness. They are no longer salt (i.e., Christians). Such have become a part of the problem rather than the solution.

The moral of the story is simple. It makes a difference what principles we accept in our lives and how we relate to people in daily life.

Light Shines

You are the light of the world. A city set on a hill cannot be hid. Nor do men light a lamp and put it under a bushel, but on a stand, and it gives light to all in the house. Let your light so shine before men, that they may see your good works and give glory to your Father who is in heaven. Matt. 5:14-16, RSV.

Y ou *are* the light of the world." That is an outstanding statement when you consider whom Jesus was talking to. He was not addressing the religious leaders—was not encouraging preachers or theologians. Instead He was speaking to the common people—those who were entirely unimportant from the world's perspective.

Such a statement should cause us to stand up and take note. It is a remarkable thing to be a Christian. Jesus did not say that the world's learned philosophers or political strategists were the light of the world, but *you*—Mr. or Mrs. or Miss Average Christian. A remarkable claim, to say the least.

Note once again the *"you are."* Christians are the light of the world by the very fact that they are Christians.

How is that so? Because a Christian by definition is one who knows Jesus. A Christian is one who understands the plan of salvation in Jesus, the very message the world needs to hear.

Every Christian is a light to help others find salvation in Jesus. And every Christian is a missionary to tell others of God's love and of His forgiveness in Jesus.

That means *you. You are* the light of the world—every day.

There are two ways we can go wrong in our light privilege. One is to hide our light. The other is to think that we are the real light. We can afford to be humble here. Jesus is the real light, the source of all light. He Himself is clear on the topic when He claims that "I am the light of the world" (John 8:12).

But we, in turn, are light because we reflect His light and are connected to the source of power. When we become disconnected, we lose our ability to shine and thereby slip outside the realm of Christianity. Our only safety is moment by moment to stay connected to our source of spiritual power.

The metaphors of salt and light share the missionary enterprise, but in differing manners. Salt works silently as it lives God's love in the community, while light is a visible force as it openly proclaims the gospel.

Lord, help me today to be Your light in a dark world. Bring someone into my life today who needs a glimpse of Your love.

Filling Up the Law

Think not that I have come to abolish the law and the prophets; I have come not to abolish them but to fulfil them. Matt. 5:17, RSV.

With this verse Jesus has come to the third section of His great sermon in which He sets out the principles of His kingdom at the beginning of His earthly ministry. The first section dealt with a Christian's character in the Beatitudes (Matt. 5:3-12), and the second treated a Christian's influence (verses 13-16). Verses 17-48 highlight a Christian's righteousness (verse 20) and how it must be superior to that taught by the religious leaders of Jesus' day.

The preamble to His discussion appears in verses 17-20, with verse 17 indicating that Jesus had not come to abolish the law and the prophets but to fulfill them. The first thing to note about that verse is that the law and the prophets were the Bible of Jesus' day, what we call the Old Testament.

His teaching that He did not seek to destroy the law but to fulfill it has confused a lot of people. In spite of His plain words, they still read it to mean that He did away with God's law.

But "fulfill" does not mean to do away with—rather to fill full, to fill it up, to full-fill. We can interpret the word "fulfill" in at least three ways: (1) Jesus obeyed the requirements of the Old Testament law through His obedient life, (2) He fulfilled the predictive elements of the Old Testament, and (3) He brought out the full meaning of the Jewish Scriptures through His teachings. In one sense Jesus fulfilled the Old Testament in all three ways, but in the context in verses 21-48 we find Jesus filling out the *meaning* of the law.

Thus starting in verse 21, Jesus focuses on several Jewish teachings, beginning with the sixth and seventh commandments of the Decalogue. He prefaces each of His six teachings with "You have heard that it was said" and then goes on to explain the depth and breadth of the law or practice and its deeper meaning.

That is how Jesus is fulfilling the law. He is endowing it with meaning. As Ellen White puts it, "His mission was to 'magnify the law, and make it honorable' Isaiah 42:21. He was to show the spiritual nature of the law, to present its far reaching principles and to make plain its eternal obligation" (*Thoughts From the Mount of Blessing*, p. 49). In the process, He helps us come to grips with the spirit of the law—the spirit of love, which makes lawkeeping and obedient Christians.

Lord, help me today to listen to what the Master has to say.

The Permanence of Law

For verily I say unto you, Till heaven and earth pass, one jot or one tittle shall in no wise pass from the law, till all be fulfilled. Matt. 5:18.

J esus couldn't have said it stronger. Nothing can ever change God's law in the slightest degree. Its demands are permanent.

Just as heaven and earth are signs of stability in the sense that they are always there, so is God's law unending. It is not something that He alters from time to time because He might feel the urge to do something different. No, its principles are built into the very fabric of the universe.

I like the way *The Message* renders the first part of our verse: "God's Law is more real and lasting than the stars in the sky and the ground at your feet. Long after the stars burn out and earth wears out, God's law will be alive and working."

Now, that is permanent!

But why? Doesn't God have a free will? Can't He choose to do what He wants?

Of course He can do as He pleases. But the questions miss the point. The way of God's basic law is the way of health and life. Anything contrary to the law is death, destruction, and disorder. Take the Ten Commandments, for example. You can't have a healthy society in which people are killing one another and in which you can never trust anyone.

God's law cannot be changed because it is an outward representation of His character of love. Its very principles are for our eternal good.

Thus not even the smallest part of God's law—not a "jot or a tittle" (the smallest letter and the smallest point in the Hebrew alphabet)—will be altered. It is for our good.

And while that is true for the Ten Commandments, it is also the case of the entire Old Testament—the law and the prophets. The Old Testament still has validity for Christians.

Even the ceremonial law has meaning for us. What was nailed to the cross was the penalty for breaking the law rather than any part of the law itself. The ceremonial law is being fulfilled in the ministry of Christ. He was the Lamb who died for us (John 1:29), He is our Passover (1 Cor. 5:7), and He is currently functioning in the heavenly sanctuary as our great High Priest, as described extensively in the book of Hebrews. The action of the ceremonial law has shifted from earth to heaven, where the loving Christ is interceding for me today.

March 4

Taking God Seriously

Whosoever therefore shall break one of these least commandments, and shall teach men so, he shall be called the least in the kingdom of heaven: but whosoever shall do and teach them, the same shall be called great in the kingdom of heaven. Matt. 5:19.

N o human being will be justified in his sight by works of the law, since through the law comes knowledge of sin" (Rom. 3:20, RSV). "For by grace you have been saved through faith; and this is not your own doing, it is the gift of God—not because of works, lest any man should boast" (Eph. 2:8, 9, RSV).

Because we believe in grace and forgiveness and love, it is all too easy to think that God is so easygoing that it doesn't matter how we live or what we do. That is not so. Because He cares about us He wants us to be as whole as possible in a sick world.

Above all things, God wants our happiness, both now and eternally. And because He desires for us to be happy, He takes our needs seriously. We are important to Him.

As a result, God is doing all He can to guide His people through life. In the process He sets forth principles of life so that we can be healthier in our spiritual, physical, social, mental, and even vocational aspects.

He gave many such principles to His ancient people in the Old Testament. Then in the New Testament He provided additional insight into the happy and healthy life, and He has continued to guide His people in modern times through the gifts of His Spirit.

Jesus desires that we take God's counsels in the utmost seriousness, even those that may seem "least" or unimportant to us. It will not do to explain away this or that biblical instruction because it doesn't fit into our agenda.

And Jesus tells us that we are not only to practice God's principles in our lives but we are also to teach them to others. That instruction includes our responsibility as parents and family members, our opportunities in church, and our opportunities in the community and workplace.

We are representatives of the King of the universe. And He desires us to take Him just as seriously as He does us and our needs and problems.

Thus as Christians we will be faithful in both the "least" and the great things in God's Book. And we will do it in the sweet spirit of Jesus.

Help us, Father, is our prayer.

Pharisees Were Good People,
but Not Good Enough

For I tell you, unless your righteousness exceeds that of the scribes and Pharisees, you will never enter the kingdom of heaven. Matt. 5:20, RSV.

One of Jesus' most astounding statements, it must have all but knocked the disciples and other hearers off their feet. How could anyone have more righteousness than the scribes and Pharisees?

At this point we need to let Jesus speak and not try to collapse Him into Paul. His concern is not that His followers needed His righteousness or righteousness by faith to be superior to the Pharisees. To the contrary, He is explicit that it is "your righteousness" (mine and yours) that must exceed that of the scribes and Pharisees.

But how could that be? After all, the scribes were a class that spent all their time in teaching and expounding God's law. They had a superabundance of dedication to God's Word. And the Pharisees were not merely good men—they were the best of men. They were a select class of some 6,000 individuals who had totally dedicated their lives to bringing about the coming of the Christ through living sinless lives.

Who could have more righteousness than a Pharisee? Look at them. First, they were lovers and protectors of the Bible as the Word of God. They had developed their massive oral tradition to preserve the true meaning of Scripture.

Second, Pharisees were completely devoted to God's law. They loved it with all their heart. Their dedication to keeping it inspired them to formulate thousands of guidelines so that they wouldn't even come close to the appearance of evil. Thus they had some 1,521 oral rules on how to keep the Sabbath. Such laws touched every aspect of their lives.

Beyond those qualities, the Pharisees were filled with missionary and evangelistic zeal and they were good "adventists." That is, they awaited the coming of the Messiah with anticipation. Many of them believed that the Messiah (Christ) would come if the Torah (law) were kept perfectly for one day.

The Pharisees were like some of us church members. They believed all the right things and desired to do good.

But here is the tragedy: they fell short of the kingdom. We need to take stock of ourselves so that we don't end up like the Pharisees of old. They may have been the best people in the church—but somehow they weren't good enough.

Jesus knocked His hearers flat when He announced that their righteousness must exceed that of the religious athletes of the day. How?

Filling Up the Law, Part 1

Ye have heard that it was said by them of old time, Thou shalt not kill; and whosoever shall kill shall be in danger of the judgment: But I say unto you, That whosoever is angry with His brother without a cause shall be in danger of the judgment. Matt. 5:21, 22.

With Matthew 5:21 we have come to the first of six illustrations of how our righteousness must exceed that of the scribes and Pharisees (verse 20). In those six examples we find Jesus filling up the meaning of the law (verse 17).

Common to each illustration are the words "you have heard that it was said" and "I say unto you." Those who had done the initial saying were such Jewish leaders as the scribes and Pharisees, who had taken God's Old Testament law and created oral tradition to protect that law and to apply it to the life of the people. Such Jewish leaders were generally sincere in their attempts to make the law meaningful. But their sincerity did not protect them from error.

That is why Jesus comes in with His "but *I say*." Those words are of crucial importance in understanding both Matthew 5:21-48 and the entire Sermon on the Mount. In them Jesus is pronouncing Himself to be the authority on the meaning of the law. But He was not basing His teaching on the judgment of others. To the contrary, *He was the authority on the law.* He approaches it not as a mere teacher, but as the lawgiver, the One who knows the height and depth of the law because He is the God who gave it in the first place.

In the process, He overturns pharisaic approaches to the law. The Pharisees, as Jesus will demonstrate, were excellent on the letter of the law, but poor in its spirit. They were perfectionists at heart, and all perfectionists need a list of do's and don'ts. To make the law manageable if they are going to obey it perfectly, they need to cut it down in size. Pharisees of all ages have done that by being careful in how they define sin. For them sin tended to be actions.

But Jesus overturns all such attempts. Refusing to play the pharisaic game, He moved beyond the outward letter of the law to its inward spiritual intent. Thus He pointed out that the root problem is not the act but the thought and attitude behind it. In that way Jesus shattered the easy perfectionism of the Pharisees of both His day and ours.

Lord in heaven, help me to grasp in my heart the full meaning of the law and not merely its outward shell.

Filling Up the Law, Part 2

Ye have heard that it was said by them of old time, Thou shalt not commit adultery:
But I say unto you, That whosoever looketh upon a woman [or man] to lust after her
[or him] hath committed adultery with her [or him] already in his [or her] heart.
Matt. 5:27, 28.

This is serious.

I remember the first time I came to grips with this passage. I was 19 years old and had been baptized from an agnostic background a few months before. There I was in a local store gawking at a woman while waiting for my wife. Of course, I wasn't just gawking; I was thinking the same sort of thoughts I had delighted in before I became a Christian.

Suddenly it hit me like a ton of bricks. The Holy Spirit spoke to my conscience loud and clear: "You can't do that. It is wrong to lust after a woman, to think the kind of thoughts you are doing." I didn't care much for the lesson. After all, I had been "innocently" enjoying myself, and then He had to break into my meditations. I felt like telling the Holy Spirit to take a hike.

In actuality I had begun to realize that sin was more than an act—that it was a mind-set. I had started to recognize the truth Jesus set forth when He taught that sin "proceeds from the heart" (Matt. 15:18, RSV). Jesus made the same point when He moved the meaning of the sixth commandment from killing to anger (Matt. 5:21, 22).

I had been quite comfortable before He did that. After all, I have never killed anyone. And in all probability I won't murder anyone in my entire life. That is a thought that makes me feel good. But it's better than that. Not only have I never murdered anyone; no one has ever accused me of such an act. I guess I am a pretty good guy, a person who at least has part of his act together.

But such self-righteousness shatters when I begin to read Jesus in His filling up of the law. He tells me that I can't even be angry in the sense of a person who holds on to anger, refuses to let it die, and seeks revenge. Here Jesus hits me square. While I don't murder, I do become angry with some of the people with whom I have to deal.

I don't like this new theology. I am more comfortable with my own definitions. They make me feel good.

But Jesus' purpose isn't to make me feel good. It is to help me see the nature of sin and my great need of His forgiving and empowering grace.

Lord in heaven, help me to live in my life the full meaning of the law and not merely its outward shell.

Following Jesus Isn't Normal

You have heard that it was said, "You shall love your neighbor and hate your en-
emy." But I say to you, Love your enemies and pray for those who persecute you, so
that you may be sons of your Father who is in heaven; for he makes his sun rise on
the evil and on the good, and sends rain on the just and on the unjust.

Matt. 5:43-45, RSV.

So you want to be like God? If so, read verses 43-45 through thoughtfully several times.

Just how much does our righteousness need to exceed that of the scribes and Pharisees (see Matt. 5:20)? From Matthew 5:21 onward Jesus has been illustrating that "exceeding" righteousness. And it has been exceeding in the extreme. He has told us that we can't have hateful thoughts, lustful desires, or easy divorces, and that our thoughts and speech must be pure.

Then in verses 38-42 Jesus appears to have topped it off by telling us we can't even retaliate toward those who do us wrong. But now in verses 43-45 He goes even further than that. It is one thing for me not to hit you back when you hit me. But it is quite another for me to love you when you do me wrong, to pray for you when you misuse me and persecute me.

Jesus has upped the ante to the highest possible amount in terms of what it means to have a righteousness that exceeds that of the scribes and Pharisees. How can anyone do such things? It's not normal.

That's right. Loving one's enemies isn't normal, but it is Christian, and the next few verses will tell us why it is Christian. The key words are "so that." We are to love our enemies and pray for those who spit upon us "so that [we] may be sons of [our] Father who is in heaven." That is what God is like. He sends the gifts of sunshine and rain on both those who love Him and those who hate Him. He even gave His Son to die for those who were His enemies (Rom. 5:8). And Jesus prayed for those who put Him on the cross.

We must do the same in our daily lives "so that" we will be like the Father. Ellen White helps us see the picture when she writes that God's "love received, will make us . . . kind and tender, not merely to those who please us, but to the most faulty and erring and sinful. . . . It is not earthly rank, nor birth, nor nationality, nor religious privilege, which proves that we are members of the family of God; it is love, a love that embraces all humanity. . . . To be kind to the unthankful and to the evil, to do good hoping for nothing again, is the insignia of the royalty of heaven, the sure token by which the children of the Highest reveal their high estate" (*Thoughts From the Mount of Blessing*, p. 75).

The Character of
Character Perfection

Be ye therefore perfect, even as your Father which is in heaven is perfect.
Matt. 5:48.

"Therefore" is a key word in verse 48. It implies a conclusion to what has gone before.

This verse, with its call for Godlike perfection, needs to be connected with its context from verse 20 onward, but most specifically to verses 43 through 47, as a comparison of verse 45 with verse 48 will clearly demonstrate. Those are the only two verses in the entire chapter that summon Christians to be like their Father in heaven. Verses 43 through 47 make explicit the essence of that likeness.

Jesus is not dealing with abstractions here. Being like the Father means loving one's enemies, just as God loves His enemies. After all, doesn't He provide sunshine and rain for evil people (verse 45)? Anybody, even tax collectors and other unsavory sorts, can love their friends (verses 46, 47). But God demands of His children supernatural love for *all* people. Just as the Father so loved the world that He gave His Son to die for people who were ungodly and His enemies, so are Christians to love even those who despitefully use them, "so that" they may be like the Father, "so that" they might be perfect, just as their heavenly Father is perfect.

That thought brings us to the word "perfect" in Matthew 5:48. Translated from the Greek word *teleios*, it has nothing to do with concepts of absolute sinlessness. To the contrary, *teleios* means "maturity," and in most instances most translations translate it as such.

In the Bible's use of the concept, people are *teleios* (perfect) when they are full-grown or have reached full stature. And for human beings that maturity means being restored to the likeness of God in whose image they were created. Thus it is only natural for Jesus to claim in Matthew 5:48 that the Christian should become *teleios* (perfect or mature) in love like the Father in heaven. After all, "God is love" (1 John 4:8). That is the essence of His perfection of character. Thus character perfection centers on acting in love like God rather than behaving like the devil.

Such an understanding of verse 48 lines up with its parallel in Luke, which reads: "Be merciful, even as your Father is merciful" (Luke 6:36, RSV). It also is in harmony with that forceful quotation in *Christ's Object Lessons* on perfectly reproducing the character of Christ (p. 69). The context makes it clear that such a reproduction centers on a "spirit of unselfish love and labor for others" (pp. 67, 68).

Father, help me today to be a loving person so that I might be like You.

79

March 10

Sin Followed Me to Church

Beware of practicing your piety before men in order to be seen by them; for then you will have no reward from your Father who is in heaven. Matt. 6:1, RSV.

With Matthew 6:1-18 Jesus shifts the center of His discussion of kingdom principles from a Christian's righteousness to a believer's piety. He selects almsgiving (verses 2-4), praying (verses 5, 6), and fasting (verses 16-18) to illustrate principles that we can apply to all acts of religious piety. It is frightening to believe that we can go off the track in such religious activities as prayer and giving to God, but Jesus says we can.

In essence, He is teaching that we didn't fully get rid of sin when we left our nasty way of life. To the contrary, sin is more than eager to follow us to church.

His pattern is the same in each illustration. First comes a description of the false way of piety, which focuses on public display of the "worshiper's" holiness. He uses the word "hypocrites" in each illustration. In Greek "hypocrite" means an actor on the stage. Applied to religious experience in Matthew 6, a hypocrite is one who wears a false face. He or she is pretending to honor God, while really glorifying self. Such people, Jesus asserts, have already had their reward. The second half of each illustration suggests a proper way to fulfill the obligation (e.g., pray in secret). In each case the central idea is that motivation for devotion should be grounded in a person's relationship with the Father rather than a desire to look good. All three illustrations close with a statement that God will reward the faithful.

In Matthew 6:1-18 Jesus brings us face-to-face with "vegetarian sins," sins that look so good because they are tied to religious practice, the sins of the Pharisees of every generation.

Such sins are deceptive and deadly because they capture us unaware—they make us feel so religious, so right. But that is where deceptiveness comes in. They lead us to think that we are clean when we are still filled with the rotten core of sin—prideful self-sufficiency and self-centeredness.

Jesus, dear friend, wants to save us even from our religious sins, even from our spiritual pride, even from feeling good about our prayer life.

And how does He propose to do this? The same way He does for prostitutes and drug dealers. He wants our prideful spirit to fall at the foot of the cross and be crucified.

But beyond crucifixion of our self-righteous pride, Jesus wants to engineer our rebirth through life in the Spirit. The good news is that He is able if we are willing.

Praying With Understanding

In this manner . . . pray:
> *Our Father in heaven, Hallowed be Your name. Your kingdom come. Your*
> *will be done On earth as it is in heaven. Give us this day our daily bread. And for-*
> *give us our debts, As we forgive our debtors. And do not lead us into temptation, But*
> *deliver us from the evil one. For Yours is the kingdom and the power and the glory*
> *forever. Amen.* Matt. 6:9-13, NKJV.

Jesus' disciples had a problem. The Master prayed a lot, but He had never taught them how to do it. They argued that John the Baptist had done that for his disciples, and they wanted the same (Luke 11:1). In response, Jesus provided two types of instruction. In the first He noted that they should not merely "heap up empty phrases" as did those who wanted to be heard "for their many words" (Matt. 6:7, RSV). He then went on to provide them with a sample prayer that was to provide them with a model for their own.

Prayer is not just a "bunch of words" that we mumble in a mindless or passionate sort of way. No, we find in Jesus' prayer both order and structure. It comes as a shock to some people that something as spiritual as prayer could have any system or structure to it. But Christ's prayer provides a model that has all the essential elements of prayer.

While it is not wrong to recite the Lord's Prayer *if* it is done with meaning and thought, it is better to see the Lord's Prayer as a pattern prayer that provides us with an outline of the essential elements that should be in both private and public prayers.

As such, Jesus' outline prayer is much like the outline used by many preachers. Each part of the outline provides a heading of things that we need to remember in the prayer. The prayer itself expounds and fills out each point.

The prayer is comprehensive in that it covers all the elements of both our relationship with God and with other people, as well as our personal needs. Even the order of the petitions is important. The first three have to do with God and His glory, whereas the second three petitions concern our human needs and necessities. Thus we must give God first and supreme place—then and only then should we turn to ourselves and our needs and desires. It is only when God receives His proper place that other things fall into line.

We thank You, Lord, for taking the time to teach us to pray, for taking our needs seriously. We want to learn from You, especially in our prayer life.

March 12

A Goal Survey

Do not lay up for yourselves treasures on earth, where moth and rust destroy and where thieves break in and steal; but lay up for yourselves treasures in heaven, where neither moth nor rust destroys and where thieves do not break in and steal. For where your treasure is, there will your heart be also. Matt. 6:19-21, NKJV.

With these verses in Christ's inaugural sermon on the principles of His kingdom the action shifts from strictly religious matters to a Christian's attitudes toward the things of our world.

Jesus first treats the negative side of the issue, noting that earthly things lack permanence. The plain fact of the matter is that earthly wealth at its best is transitory. Moths, rust, worms, rats, mice, stock-market crashes, currency fluctuations, inflation, and a host of other things whittle away at it. Then there are thieves, individual and corporate. And in the end you lose it all at death. When it comes right down to it, there isn't any solid reason to trust earthly wealth.

In the second part of today's verses our Lord begins to focus on the positive—laying up our treasures in heaven. And He puts forth the general principle that "where your treasure is, there will your heart be also."

In examining this teaching it is helpful to go back to the first commandment, which reads, "Thou shalt have no other gods before me" (Ex. 20:3). That command is basic to the Old Testament. It not only shaped the history of the Jews, but also that of the life of Jesus' followers.

When applied to Matthew 6:19-24, we might helpfully paraphrase it as "Thou shalt have no other goals before me." Then, suggests F. D. Bruner, we can paraphrase the intent of Matthew 6:21 to be: "Where your goal is, there will your heart be also."

Here is a crucial insight, because our goals determine our actions as well as everything else in our life. Thus where our heart is, or that on which we have set our heart, is all-important. Whatever it is will determine both how we live our lives and where we will spend eternity.

What is it that I love? What truly captivates my imagination, my spare time, my highest allegiance? Such questions can help me determine both the location of my heart and the shape of my goals. They are questions that we ought to meditate upon today.

Today Jesus is offering me a choice. Today He is appealing to my heart. What is my response? How shall I answer Him this day?

Whose Slave Are We?

No man can serve two masters: for either he will hate the one, and love the other; or else he will hold to the one, and despise the other. Ye cannot serve God and mammon.
Matt. 6:24.

That verse was undoubtedly more forceful in the ancient world than it is to us. The verb translated as "serve" is from *doulos*, the word for "slave." The Greek word behind "master" is *kurios*, denoting absolute ownership and nearly always rendered as "lord" in the New Testament. Thus the idea of Matthew 6:24 is that no one can be enslaved to two owners or lords at the same time.

To catch the full impact of this statement we need to realize that the ancient world did not regard a slave as a person but as a living tool. Slaves had no rights of their own. They were completely under the control of their masters, who could do with them as they wanted. Masters could sell slaves, beat them, throw them out, or even kill them.

A second thing to note is that in the ancient world slaves had no time of their own. All of it belonged to their master. In modern culture each worker has time off for personal needs. During that time they can have hobbies or even hold a second job. But that was not so in the ancient world of slavery. A slave's time belonged wholly to the master.

Jesus is saying that Christians must let God be the undisputed master of their lives. Paul makes the same point in Romans 6:16, in which he says we are slaves to either sin or righteousness, Satan or Christ.

Thus Christians, being enslaved to Jesus, always take God's will into consideration in all they do. They daily ask themselves, "What does God wish me to do?" Every moment of their time they live for Him. God has no part-time devotees who largely serve Him but then moonlight for some other master in their time off.

When Jesus said no person can serve two masters, He meant it.

Still, some of us try anyway, in spite of the impossibility. But in that attempt, whether we recognize it or not, we have really opted for Satan. "He who does not give himself wholly to God is under the control of another power, listening to another voice. . . . Half-and-half service places the human agent on the side of the enemy as a successful ally of the host of darkness" (*Thoughts From the Mount of Blessing*, p. 94).

March 14

Strategies for Overcoming Worry

Seek ye first the kingdom of God, and his righteousness; and all these things shall be added unto you. Take therefore no thought for the morrow: for the morrow shall take thought for the things of itself. Sufficient unto the day is the evil thereof.
Matt. 6:33, 34.

Jesus meets His followers where they are on the track of life. He realizes that we really don't have our acts together, that we might not be headed in the right direction in our Christian lives, that we are all messed up.

With that realistic understanding, He counsels His followers not to worry about material things, because it is both useless (Matt. 6:28-30) and pagan, in the sense of acting as if they did not have a heavenly Father who cares for them (verses 31, 32).

But Jesus' primary aim was not to discuss our problems but to point to their solution. Along that line, He set forth two strategies. One is to seek God's kingdom first. Most of our worries stem from the fact that we are headed in the wrong direction. We desire and worry about material things, when what Jesus is really telling us is that if we must be concerned about something, it needs to be about our relationship to God. Get that straight, and all else will fall into perspective in the lives of those who trust in faith.

Living one day at a time is Jesus' second suggestion for defeating worry. "Do not be anxious about tomorrow; tomorrow will look after itself. Each day has troubles enough of its own" (Matt. 6:34, NEB).

In 1871 a worried young medical student read 21 words that changed his life: "Our main business is not to see what lies dimly at a distance, but to do what lies clearly at hand." Putting those words into action daily made Sir William Osler one of the most honored physicians of his generation.

Each of us stands at the edge of two vast eternities—the past and the future. We dwell, however, only in the present. If we are going to live successfully in the present, then we must handle each moment and each day as it arrives. That is not to denigrate the value of intelligent planning for the future, but it does suggest the futility of worrying about events not under our control. Another way of putting Jesus' message is not to fret about crossing the possibly flooded rivers of our life until we get to them.

Thank You, Lord, that You are not only concerned about our spiritual life, but that You care enough to help us live the life of faith in the realm of this world.

Practical Advice for Me

Judge not, that you be not judged. . . . Why do you see the speck that is in your brother's eye, but do not notice the log that is in your own eye? . . . You hypocrite, first take the log out of your own eye, and then you will see clearly to take the speck out of your brother's eye. Matt. 7:1-5, RSV.

No one can accuse Jesus of not having a sense of humor as He looked out at His disciples and the rest of His "church" or audience. He knew them just as He does us. And He recognized that some of His followers would possess a critical spirit and would be perpetually seeking to expound upon the sawdust specks in the eyes of other church members, all the while running around with a two-by-four hanging out of their eye socket.

Why is it that those who seem to have such obvious problems in their own lives have such a burden to straighten out others? It happens in families, in churches, and all other areas of life.

Once again in His inaugural sermon Jesus sets forth important principles on how to live in His kingdom. Now, however, He has shifted the focus to a Christian's relationship to others.

Here we see Jesus at His practical, down-to-earth best in dealing with us as human beings in our everyday life. His illustrations are not only powerful and memorable but also true to life. Who hasn't had the dubious "privilege" of receiving advice from some person who has the problem 10 times worse?

When all is said and done about specks and logs, it is important to note that we really do have a responsibility to others with their *genuine* specks (rather than those based upon our biased thinking).

But never forget that we are not commanded to be speck removers until after we have become successful beam extractors. In other words, we need to seek the Lord to help us see ourselves clearly and to aid us in caring for our own issues before we humbly attempt to help others. *Thoughts From the Mount of Blessing* puts it nicely: "You cannot exert an influence that will transform others until your own heart has been humbled and refined and made tender by the grace of Christ. When this change has been wrought in you, it will be as natural for you to live to bless others as it is for the rosebush to yield the fragrant bloom or the vine its purple clusters" (p. 127).

Lord, I need help with my logs, beams, and two-by-fours.

The Blank Checkness of Prayer

*Ask, and it shall be given you; seek, and ye shall find; knock, and it shall be opened
unto you: For every one that asketh receiveth; and he that seeketh findeth; and to
him that knocketh it shall be opened.* Matt. 7:7, 8.

I s that really true? Is prayer a blank check upon which we merely inscribe our
requests? Does God always give believers everything they ask for?

Be careful here. We get into a great deal of trouble by proof-texting, by taking statements out of context and then generalizing them in irresponsible ways to fit our personal desires.

Let's also be honest here. Has God given you everything you have asked for? Why not? How has it affected your faith?

To be sure, Jesus' statement on prayer is in itself an absolute promise of what God will do for us, but it has a very definite context of judgment—a theme that runs throughout Matthew 7. The first six verses of the chapter have dealt with the problem of judging other people and thinking of them more harshly than we do ourselves. In the process, Jesus tells us that we will get unjust judgment back in full measure. Realizing our weakness, we cry out, "Who is sufficient for these things? How can I live up to God's standard?" Christ's answer is that He will give us what we need if we ask, seek, and knock.

What is true of Matthew 7:1-6 is also of the entire Sermon on the Mount. We feel hopeless when we see the demands of true righteousness. It is in the context of those requirements that Jesus offers us His grace to forgive and overcome so that we can live the Christian life.

We need to see our earthly life as a school in which we build a character like Christ's for the life beyond. God is preparing us for eternal life. Thus He is willing to give us everything we need for well-rounded Christian development. In that context the message of our Lord is "Ask, and it shall be given you; seek, and ye shall find; knock, and it shall be opened to you."

We do indeed have a blank check in Matthew 7:7, 8—for God's grace. A reading of the Sermon on the Mount in the light of our fractured lives helps us see how impossibly mixed up we are. Those who take seriously the terrifying demands of the Sermon must always take seriously God's willingness to assist them. God *always* answers our prayers for forgiveness, grace, love for others, and strength to make it through the day.

The Core Principle
of Christ's Kingdom

So whatever you wish that others would do to you, do also to them, for this is the Law and the Prophets. Matt. 7:12, ESV.

I don't like that verse because it interferes with the way I run my life. And that's irritating.

Behind our distaste for the golden rule is our dislike of God's law, which plainly states that love to God and others is what true living is all about. And behind our hostility toward the law is an aversion to the God who gave it. Why doesn't He just mind His business and let us do our thing?

That question brings us to the real root of the issue. The reason we don't like the golden rule, the law, and even God, is that they interfere with the natural course of our self life, our sinful life outside of Christ. We must never forget that love of self is the center of sin. The sinful nature is entirely self-centered, whereas the golden rule and the law and God are other-centered. Those things interfere with our self-centered life. And that puts us at enmity with them.

The self-centered life says that if you like something, take it; if you desire someone else's spouse, use them; if it serves your purpose, lie to get what you want. Then along come Jesus and God and Their meddlesome law and rule to frustrate our natural selves. It makes us feel downright hateful at times. That's what Jesus wants to put an end to. He wants to transform our hearts and minds so that we will be in harmony with God, His law, and His rule. He seeks to write the principles of His kingdom on our hearts. Then we will love the golden rule of Matthew 7:12.

With that rule, with its claim that doing the loving thing to others "*is the Law and the Prophets*," the Sermon on the Mount has come full circle from Matthew 5:17: "Think not that I am come to destroy the law, or the prophets: I am not come to destroy [them], but to fulfill [them]."

Both Matthew 5:17 and 7:12 highlight the law and the prophets. Those texts bracket the central core of Christ's inaugural sermon. As a result, we must view the golden rule as a summary of Christ's interpretation of the meaning of the law and the prophets (the Old Testament), with Matthew 5:21-7:11 being His expansion or filling out of several principles inherent in that one-verse summary.

Both in the summary and in the commentary we discover that *God's law is a way of living and thinking rather than a list of do's and don'ts.*

March 18

Christians Are Fruit Inspectors

Beware of false prophets, who come to you in sheep's clothing but inwardly are ravenous wolves. You will know them by their fruits. . . . Every sound tree bears good fruit, but the bad tree bears evil fruit. Matt. 7:15-17, RSV.

Jesus had both eyes open. He knew that His church would have problems, that there would be leaders who looked impressive and could preach captivatingly well, but who would take advantage of the naïve and gullible.

As a result, near the close of His inaugural sermon on kingdom principles He supplied us with two forceful illustrations of the need to keep both of our eyes open. In the process, He tells us that we will actually need to judge others in terms of the fruit of their work.

All the way through the Bible we find both true and false prophets, true and false teachers and preachers. The lesson for us is that not all who claim to be from God with a message from Him are actually what they pretend to be. Some religious teachers, Jesus notes, actually look like sheep on the outside, but inwardly are like ravenous wolves who desire to feed upon the flock of God.

The two creatures make a nice contrast. Sheep are among the most harmless of animals, whereas wolves have the reputation of being ruthless and bloodthirsty. Now, it is not difficult to distinguish a wolf from a sheep. But that's not the problem. The situation Jesus is describing is one in which the wolves arrive at church masquerading as sheep. That is, while they claim to speak for Jesus, they are actually under the employ of the devil.

Here is a problem that arises because of the subtlety of the situation. They are only inwardly wolves. To all outward appearances, such men and women are God's servants. And where accepted as such, they prey upon the souls and pocketbooks of the believers.

That brings us to Jesus' second illustration, the one about trees and fruit. A law in nature tells us that you don't get coconuts off of poison ivy plants. Nature is consistent and predictable. So are people. If you give them enough time and space, their true character will show through in the fruits of their lives and teachings—either for good or evil. Jesus' point is that we need to keep our eyes open.

Help us, Father, to have a spirit of discernment as we seek to hear Your voice.

A Sobering Verse

Not every one who says to me, "Lord, Lord," shall enter the kingdom of heaven, but he who does the will of my Father who is in heaven. Matt. 7:21, RSV.

Today's verse is one of the most frightening in the New Testament. It flatly states that I can be lost while claiming Jesus as my Savior; that I can be deceived; that I can think that all is well with my religious life when everything is actually wrong.

Matthew 7:21 is also one of the most serious passages in all of God's Word. Jesus is not playing games. He has spent a large portion of His inaugural sermon telling us how the scribes and Pharisees had deceived themselves. Now He is pointing at me and you. We can be just as confused and misled as those Jewish leaders unless we pay heed to His words. There is nothing more serious in all the teaching words of Jesus than His proclamation in Matthew 7:21-23. Our Savior is speaking to us with all the earnestness of His soul. It behooves us to listen carefully.

Not all who claim to be believers in Jesus as Lord and Savior will be saved according to verse 21. That is an amazing thought, given the fact that so many say that the totality of salvation is claiming Jesus as Savior. Here Jesus is warning us that being saved involves more than merely making such claims.

And what more is needed? Jesus answers that question in the same verse, when He states that we must be doers and not mere hearers of His Father's will. John reinforces that point when he writes that "we may be sure that we know him," if we keep His commandments and walk as Jesus did (1 John 2:3-6, RSV).

That's good news. It's true assurance of salvation. We can know! Praise God!

But what is "doing the Father's will"? Here we must remember that the context of Matthew 7:21-23 is the entire Sermon on the Mount. Jesus has just spent Matthew 5-7 setting forth God's will for His people. Doing God's will is living the Beatitudes; it means being salt and light as we witness; it means living out the height and depth of His law of love in our community; it is loving even our enemies and thus being like God; it is doing God's will in our prayer life and stewardship; it means having our priorities right and trusting Him in terms of our daily needs rather than being focused on material things; and it means refusing to judge others, while at the same time treating them as we would like them to treat us.

Doing God's will means being like Jesus.

March 20

"That Day"

Many will say to me in that day, Lord, Lord, have we not prophesied in thy name? and in thy name have cast out devils? and in thy name done many wonderful works? And then will I profess unto them, I never knew you: depart from me, ye that work iniquity. Matt. 7:22, 23.

"That day" is the day of judgment, the time when all accounts get settled and God hands out rewards and punishments.

A story tells of a young boy given the task of planting string beans in his mother's garden. The job started out quite well as he carefully broke up the clods and planted each seed every two inches down the rows. But the sun was getting hotter and his friends passed him, waving happily as they headed toward the swimming hole. Soon the job became less and less attractive. "Whoever," he asked himself, "would want so many string beans? What a waste of a summer day." Such thoughts put an end to his faithfulness. He had done enough, he concluded, and dumped the rest of the seeds in a hole partway down a row. His mother was pleased, though. All looked well. But then "that day" arrived. In his case it was when the seeds sprouted. It was plain to all what had happened. The day of reckoning had come.

"That day," Jesus tells us, will eventually happen for the entire world. Then our relationship to God's will will be evident to all. How we have lived our lives will make a difference. Our present is a part of our future. According to Jesus, it will determine our future. That is His teaching in Matthew 7:21-23.

The judgment decision of Jesus, "depart from me," "I never knew you," will be the hardest He will ever have to say. Some people have the idea that the final judgment is so that God can weed out as many people as possible. But that is Satan's interpretation, not God's intent.

The opposite position is the one in which the truth lies. God and Christ want to see as many people in heaven as possible. The judgment is not to keep them out, but to get them in. It certifies before all the universe that they have indeed accepted the sacrifice of Jesus on the cross as the atonement for their sins, and that they have allowed God to fill them with the principle of His love.

God and Christ have done Their part in this drama. The only question is, "Have we?" Have we allowed the Holy Spirit into our hearts to infuse God's loving principles? Have we allowed Him to live out those principles in our daily lives?

The Astonishing Jesus

And when Jesus finished these sayings, the crowds were astonished at his teaching,
for he taught them as one who had authority, and not as their scribes.
Matt. 7:28, 29, RSV.

Jesus is now ready for the next stage of His ministry. He has been filled with the Spirit at His baptism, has set His boundaries with Satan in the wilderness for the contest to come, has called His disciples, and now has finished preaching His inaugural sermon, in which He set forth in no uncertain terms the principles of His kingdom. Thus He is ready to move into a wider ministry. But before examining His more extensive work we should note that "the crowds were astonished at his teaching."

And why shouldn't they be? They knew Him as an unlearned carpenter from a little village called Nazareth in Galilee. He was not a scribe or a Pharisee, but a commoner, a laborer. Jesus had not sat at the feet of Gamaliel or any other learned teacher. Rather, He was nothing but a rustic and lowly carpenter. But suddenly He bursts upon the scene claiming the most astounding things from the beginning of His ministry. His arrival is a shock to the Jewish body politic.

Look at His audacity in the manner of His teaching. Unlike the scribes, He did not recite long lists of quotations to make a point. To the contrary, He claimed to be *The Authority*. "I say unto you" was His style rather than "so-and-so has said."

And did you hear some of His claims? He says "I am come," not "I was born." And where, His hearers are left to wonder, did He come from? Obviously from the One He so very personally calls "My Father."

But perhaps the most profound statement of the Sermon on the Mount regarding His personal sense of identity appears in Matthew 7:22, in which He says, "On that day many will say to me, 'Lord, Lord'" (RSV). He does not hesitate to declare that people will address Him as Lord, as a divine person. It is little wonder that the words of Jesus astounded the Jews. Not only did He teach in an authoritative manner, but by assuming the prerogatives of God He was claiming to be God.

They were stunned. And we should be, too. The problem is that He is not new to us. In the Western world He is like a piece of familiar furniture. We need to see Him with fresh eyes that we might also be amazed by our wonderful Lord.

March 22

Authority Beyond Words

When Jesus came down from the mountain, large crowds followed Him. And a leper came to Him and bowed down before Him, and said, "Lord, if You are willing, You can make me clean." Jesus stretched out His hand and touched him, saying, "I am willing; be cleansed." And immediately his leprosy was cleansed. Matt. 8:1-3, NASB.

Words are cheap. Anyone can make great statements or preach a powerful and insightful sermon. Some years ago a minister came through town proclaiming that if people had the right kind of faith they could leave his meetings and "never sin again." I had heard that one before. At one time I myself used to teach it. I would have been more impressed if the man had said that he had faith enough to leave the auditorium, go down to Lake Chapin, and walk on water. Real authority has demonstrable action, not mere verbiage.

Jesus had genuine authority not only in His words but also in what He was able to do. That is what Matthew 8 and 9 are all about. Chapters 5-7 set forth Jesus as an authoritative teacher (see Matt. 7:29), then immediately follow two chapters demonstrating that He has authority in deeds as well as words. And once again His authority would astonish the crowds (Matt. 7:28, 29; Matt. 9:33).

There is a plan to Jesus' life just as there is a plan to Matthew's Gospel. Between Matthew 8:1 and 9:33 the first Gospel has Jesus performing nine miracles that demonstrate His authority in a way that leaves no doubt about who He is. The first miracle finds Jesus healing a leper. Leprosy was the most dreaded disease in the ancient world. Beyond the physical deterioration of the victim was the social ostracism. Lepers were banished from human society immediately upon diagnosis. They had to leave family and friends, cover their faces, and cry "Unclean" wherever they went.

Yet Jesus could heal even a leper. He has authority even over such a dreaded disease. The eight subsequent miracles demonstrate that He has power not only over disease but also over the forces of nature and the demonic world. In the end of the demonstration of authority, Matthew writes that "the crowds marveled, saying, 'Never was anything like this seen in Israel'" (Matt. 9:33, RSV).

Jesus not only speaks as God, He acts as God. He has authority. And that authority is meant for our own cleansing just as much as it was for the unclean 2,000 years ago.

Authority Over Distance

When Jesus had entered Capernaum, a centurion came to him, asking for help.
"Lord," he said, "my servant lies at home paralyzed, suffering terribly."
Jesus said to him, "Shall I come and heal him?"
The centurion replied, "Lord . . . just say the word, and my servant
will be healed. For I myself am a man under authority, with soldiers under me. . . . I
say to my servant, 'Do this,' and he does it." Matt. 8:5-9, NIV.

The second miracle is the healing of the servant of a Gentile (Matt. 8:5-13). To the Jewish way of thinking, only a leper was more unclean than a Gentile. While lepers couldn't enter Jerusalem at all, Gentiles could not worship in the Jewish Temple, since they could go no farther into the Temple complex than the outermost court, fittingly called the "court of the Gentiles."

The centurion, recognizing his unworthiness in the eyes of a Jew, exemplifies remarkable faith. Comparing Jesus to himself as a military commander, he says that Jesus does not need to go to his house to perform the miracle. All He needs to do is issue a command, and the healing will take place.

The centurion is the first person in Matthew's Gospel to understand the scope of Jesus' authority—that He doesn't even need to be present for His word to be carried out. Thus He had authority, not only over disease, but also over distance.

Jesus not only commends the centurion for his faith, but He also utilizes the occasion to present a picture close to the Jewish heart. The Jews expected that at the coming of the Messiah a great banquet would take place, in which all Jews would sit down to a feast. Gentiles would not be present.

But Jesus puts a new twist on the story. According to Him, many Gentiles (those "from the east and west," verse 11) will be at the feast, but many of the Jews ("the children of the kingdom") "shall be cast out into outer darkness" (verses 11, 12).

Thus with one stroke Jesus put forth two themes that will run throughout His ministry: the salvation of the Gentiles and the precarious situation of the Jews if they reject the Messiah.

This second miracle is pregnant with meaning for us today. Nowhere do we find a better description of the authority of Jesus in relation to the angels whom He sends to care for the needs of those who have faith in Him. He still reaches across the distance of time and space to be with and bless His people. For that we can praise God daily.

Authority Over Nature

Suddenly a great tempest arose on the sea,
so that the boat was covered with waves. But He was asleep. Then His disciples
came to Him and awoke Him, saying, "Lord, save us! We are perishing!"
But He said to them, "Why are you fearful, O you of little faith?" Then He arose and
rebuked the winds and the sea, and there was a great calm. So the men marveled,
saying, "Who can this be, that even the winds and the sea obey Him?"
Matt. 8:24-27, NKJV.

"Who can this be?" "Who is this man?" That is the question that the disciples were struggling with as they began their walk with Jesus. It is still one that challenges us today.

Today's verses find Jesus and His followers caught in the midst of a fierce storm on the Sea of Galilee. Lying nearly 700 feet below sea level, it is surrounded by hills and mountains that are especially steep on the east side. And just 30 miles to the northeast is the 9,200-foot Mount Hermon. The interchange of the cold air from Mount Hermon and the warm air of the lowlands could produce unexpected fierce storms on even what appeared to be a clear day. Such is the situation in which the disciples find themselves.

And there is Jesus, sleeping. Like us, He did not come as a "superman" but one who became exhausted with the pressing of the crowds and the business of life. He was truly one of us and is therefore able to sympathize with our weaknesses (Heb. 4:15; 2:17).

But, while He was sleeping His disciples had whipped themselves up into a frenzy of fear and self-pity. Don't You even "care if we perish?" they shouted as they woke Him from a sound sleep (Mark 4:38, RSV).

He did care, rebuking the winds and the storm, and also the disciples for their lack of faith. The result: calmness in both the sea and their hearts.

But to these men the calming of the sea was astounding. Who can this be, who has power over nature? they were forced to ask. The experience was crucial to their developing understanding of who they were following, since in the Old Testament it is Yahweh (God) alone who has power to quell natural storms (Ps. 6:7; 89:9; 104:6, 7; Isa. 51:9, 10). Jesus' authority over nature helped the disciples begin to realize more fully that He was indeed "God with us," the Yahweh of the Old Testament.

The good news is that the Jesus who saved His disciples from the storm is still mighty. As His followers, we have nothing to fear in the long run, because we serve a Lord who has authority. We never face the trials of life alone. Even though He appears to be sleeping in some of the dangers that we face, He is still mighty to save.

Authority Over the Supernatural

When they arrived on the other side of the lake . . . two men with demons in them met him. They lived in a cemetery and were so dangerous that no one could go through that area. They began screaming at him. . . . [They] begged, "If you cast us out, send us into that herd of pigs." "All right," Jesus told them. "Begone."
Matt. 8:28-32, TLB.

Jesus has power not only over distance and the natural world, but also over the realm of the demonic, the supernatural. That is the next link in the chain of understanding that Matthew is unfolding regarding His identity.

With this miracle story we find Jesus' outreach ministry continuing to broaden. He is now in the Gentile territory of the Decapolis (a word meaning "ten cities") on the southeast shore of the Sea of Galilee. Two uncontrollable, naked (Matt. 8:28) madmen rush at the startled disciples and Himself. Here we find Jesus face-to-face with the demonic for the first time since His confrontation with Satan in the Wilderness of Temptation. There He had established His supremacy, and these possessed men acknowledge that fact, addressing Him as the "Son of God" and asking why He has come to torment them (Matt. 8:29). Recognizing the helplessness of their situation in the face of Jesus' authority and the fact that they are on the losing side of the battle, the demons entreat Him to cast them into a herd of swine feeding nearby. Upon receiving their request, they stampede the herd into the sea, where it perishes (verse 32).

At that point, the pigs' herders head for the city to testify about what they had seen. Soon the whole population is on the scene, where they find the healed men sitting on the ground, clothed, and in their right mind (Mark 5:15).

That change is a remarkable part of the story but not its most surprising aspect. One would have expected the thronging crowd to be filled with joy that the naked madmen had become sane and sensible. We might even assume that they would have Jesus exercise additional power in healing their sick. But all they wanted Him to do was to get out of their territory as soon as possible (Matt. 8:34).

And why? Because even though an undeniable miracle had taken place, it had led to the destruction of their pigs. They had been hit in the most tender part of their anatomy—their pocketbook.

Here we have a real situation as we come to Jesus. How will we relate to His authority if He threatens our wallet or other idols of our life?

March 26

Authority Over Sin

And behold, they brought to him a paralytic, lying on his bed; and when Jesus saw their faith he said to the paralytic, "Take heart, my son; your sins are forgiven."
Matt. 9:1, 2, RSV.

Here we find not merely another healing. To the contrary, the Technicolor aspect of this event is that Jesus had linked the healing with the forgiveness of the man's sins.

That connection would not escape some of the "visitors" in the crowd. Matthew 9:3 tells us that the scribes soon began muttering about Jesus' blaspheming. They, we should remember, belonged to the learned class. Experts in the study of the law of Moses, Scripture often refers to them as "teachers of the law," and they will later play a leading role in the arrest and trial of Jesus. But for the present they are merely accusing Him of blasphemy. Luke helps us get at their meaning when he adds their explanation: "Who can forgive sins, but God alone?" (Luke 5:21). In short, they had caught Jesus in the act of claiming a divine prerogative.

One of the unfortunate facts of church life is that every congregation seems to have its contingent of "scribes." These scowling brothers and sisters are always looking for what is wrong. And like the scribes of old, their attitude itself blinds them to the positive. Jesus' inquisitors appear to have missed altogether the significance of the amazing miracle. Obsessed with orthodoxy, they had no heart for a human being in need. Their focus on their traditions prevents them from seeing the spiritual realities being enacted before their eyes. All they saw and heard was that Jesus forgave the paralytic. That was enough for them. They now had a charge against Him that would eventually lead to His cross.

Jesus understood their theology. He was aware that they believed that no sick persons could be healed until their sins were forgiven, and that they held that only God could do so.

He could have avoided the problem by being discreet. Instead Jesus offered them both a claim and a challenge, asking, "Which is easier, to say, 'Your sins are forgiven' or to say, 'Rise and walk'?" (Matt. 9:5, RSV).

That question put the scribes on the spot. After all, any trickster can claim to forgive sins. No one could ever confirm it, however. But a healed paralytic was both verifiable and an assertion of divinity.

Jesus had made His point. But He had also signed His own death warrant.

Authority Over Death

Behold, a ruler came in and knelt before him, saying, "My daughter has just died;
but come and lay your hand on her, and she will live."... And when Jesus came to
the ruler's house, and saw the flute players, and the crowd making a tumult, he said,
"Depart; for the girl is not dead but sleeping." And they laughed at him. But when
the crowd had been put outside, he went in and took her by the hand, and the girl
arose. And the report of this went through all that district. Matt. 9:18-26, RSV.

People will do strange things when they are desperate. And Jairus, a synagogue ruler (Luke 8:41), was exactly that.

Normally he would have kept his dignity, walked with a measured tread, and spoken calmly with those he met. He had a social status to preserve.

But with the death of his daughter all that had changed. He has heard about a prophet in town healing people. Maybe, just maybe, He can do something about death. Throwing caution and dignity to the wind, he prostrates himself before Jesus on a dusty road with his neighbors looking on. As N. T. Wright observes, "Who cares about dignity when your daughter's life is at stake."

Recognizing his budding but trembling faith, Jesus tells him "Do not fear, only believe" (Mark 5:36, RSV). The present tense of the Greek imperative means to keep on believing, to hold on to faith rather than to give up in despair.

"Only believe." And Jairus did, following Jesus to his own home. There they came face-to-face with the "experts on death," hired professional mourners, who laughed with derision at Jesus' statement that "the girl is not dead but sleeping." The mourners recognized death when they saw it. And they knew that dead people don't come back to life.

But Jesus, practicing "the art of ignoring," does the impossible. Taking her hand and telling her to arise, He demonstrates that He has authority over death itself.

That teaching is one of the most important in the New Testament. It climaxes the gospel story when Jesus Himself gains victory over death and rises from the grave. And it becomes the centerpiece of world history when Jesus comes a second time to resurrect the dead (1 Thess. 4:13-18; 1 Cor. 15:51-54).

The raising of the synagogue ruler's daughter is Jesus' first demonstration that Christians have nothing to fear, even in death, but have every reason to believe in Him. Why? Because what He did for Jairus' daughter He will eventually do for each and every one of His followers.

Who Is This Jesus?

The true light that enlightens every man was coming into the world. John 1:9, RSV.

Jesus has demonstrated that He speaks with authority and that He possesses it over disease, distance, nature, the supernatural, sin, and even death.

But who is this Jesus? And what does He mean to me? His own answer was that He is one who "will draw *all* men to myself" (John 12:32, RSV). Another answer, supplied by the apostle John, pictures Jesus as "the true light that enlightens every man" (John 1:9, RSV). The "all" and "every" are important in those verses. Jesus never impacted only those who met Him face-to-face during His earthly sojourn. He never blessed only those who heard Him preach or experienced His healing power. No. He "draws" and enlightens "all" down through the corridors of history. And that means "every" one who has ever been born, whether they have ever heard the name of Jesus or not. Through the Holy Spirit He still enlightens the minds of individuals around the world, even though they have never listened to the gospel message from the lips of a human preacher.

"Wherever there is an impulse of love and sympathy, wherever the heart reaches out to bless and uplift others, there is revealed the working of God's Holy Spirit. In the depths of heathenism, men who have had no knowledge of the written law of God, who have never even heard the name of Christ, have been kind to His servants, protected them at the risk of their own lives. Their acts show the working of a divine power. The Holy Spirit has implanted the grace of Christ in the heart of the savage, quickening his sympathies contrary to his nature, contrary to his education. The 'Light, which lighteth every man that cometh into the world' (John 1:9), is shining in his soul; and this light, if heeded, will guide his feet to the kingdom of God" (*Christ's Object Lessons*, p. 385).

"Those whom Christ commends in the judgment may have known little of theology, but they have cherished His principles. Through the influence of the divine Spirit they have been a blessing to those about them. . . . Among the heathen are those who worship God ignorantly, those to whom the light is never brought by human instrumentality, yet they will not perish. . . . The Holy Spirit has touched their hearts, and they are recognized as the children of God" (*The Desire of Ages*, p. 638).

Who is Jesus? The light of the world, who has authority to enlighten and draw every human being who has ever lived.

Jesus: The Reader of Human Hearts

Now when He was in Jerusalem at the Passover, during the feast, many believed in His name when they saw the signs which He did. But Jesus did not commit Himself to them, because He knew all men, and had no need that anyone should testify of man, for He knew what was in man. John 2:23-25, NKJV.

The big problem with performing miracles and other "signs" is that people tend to follow for the wrong reason. Jesus realized that. Our Savior understood the human heart and that most people could not be trusted no matter what their outward profession of belief or allegiance. "He knew what was in man."

The scene in today's passage finds Jesus on His first visit to Jerusalem at the time of the Passover. He had made a great impression on all of Palestinian Judaism during His early ministry in Galilee. But now He had arrived in the capital of His people and "many believed in His name when they saw the signs which He did."

And it was Passover, the very time of year when Jesus later would give up His life for the sins of the world as the Lamb of God (John 1:29), or, more specifically, as our "Passover," who "was sacrificed for us" (1 Cor. 5:7, NKJV).

Seemingly everything was in place for Jesus to step forward and openly declare Himself to be the Messiah. Why didn't He? The answer is that He knew the human heart too well. He understood that many of those who believed were only attracted by the outward show of the things that they had seen and would abandon Him because of the fickleness of the human heart. "He knew what was in man." As a result, Jesus did not "commit Himself to them."

But because He knew the hearts of those He dealt with, there were some whom He was willing to open up to. It is no accident that the next two major stories in John's Gospel feature Nicodemus and the Samaritan woman at the well. Jesus could not only identify the hearts of would-be followers who were shallow and fickle, but He could see below the surface and appreciate people who were receptive to His message. And He was willing to commit Himself to such. In the stories of the Samaritan woman and the Jewish ruler we find unlikely candidates for Jesus' kingdom. But He saw below the surface and revealed Himself to them in a way that He could not with most people. And out of that opening up flow some of the most precious truths of His ministry.

This Jesus who knows us so well still wants to lead us today. He wants us to open up to Him so that He can more fully reveal Himself to us.

Coming at Night Is Better Than
Not Coming at All

Now there was a man of the Pharisees, named Nicodemus, a ruler of the Jews. This man came to Jesus by night and said to him, "Rabbi, we know that you are a teacher come from God; for no one can do these signs that you do, unless God is with him."
John 3:1, 2, RSV.

Here is another person impressed by the "signs" and miracles that Jesus had been performing. Jesus could have cautiously viewed Nicodemus as one more of that crowd fascinated with the possibilities they glimpsed in His wonder-working power and authority.

But Jesus, who "knew what was in man" (John 2:25), recognized that in Nicodemus He had found one who was a true seeker after God, not one merely attracted by the "bright lights" of His ministry.

But Jesus had to look below the surface to perceive that. After all, here was a person of a different class from the masses of those who generally followed Him. On the surface we know several things about Nicodemus. First, He was a Pharisee, one of that elite group of some 6,000 individuals who had dedicated their lives to being right with God through keeping the law in all of its thousands of details. The Pharisees of Jesus' day were a "religious aristocracy." They were people with pedigree.

Not only was that pedigree religious; it also was political and social. John describes Nicodemus as a "ruler of the Jews," meaning that he was a member of the Sanhedrin, that select group of 71 men that functioned as the highest governing power of the nation under Roman rule. Beyond that, he was rich, as demonstrated by the gift he later provided for Jesus' burial.

It was that prestigious individual who sought Jesus at night. Too often we fault the man for sneaking about in the dark, as if he were ashamed to be seen with Jesus. But the wonder is that, with his background, he came at all. Only a miracle of grace enabled Nicodemus to overcome his prejudices and his upbringing and the views of his class even to approach Jesus. Never forget, it is better to come to Jesus at night than not at all.

Here we have an individual of conviction and courage. And that Jesus who reads human hearts honored those characteristics.

Father in heaven, help me this day to break out of the mold of the world around me. Help me to have the courage of Nicodemus that I might receive the blessing of Nicodemus.

Too Many "Water" Christians

Jesus answered and said unto him, Verily, verily, I say unto thee, Except a man be born again, he cannot see the kingdom of God. Nicodemus saith unto him, How can a man be born when he is old? can he enter the second time into his mother's womb, and be born? Jesus answered, Verily, verily, I say unto thee, Except a man be born of water and of the Spirit, he cannot enter into the kingdom of God. That which is born of the flesh is flesh; and that which is born of the Spirit is spirit. John 3:3-6.

Jesus knew what was in Nicodemus' heart. And He knew what the rich, pharisaic ruler needed.

Nicodemus needed to be born again or born from above. It wasn't enough merely to be born as a child of Abraham into the covenant people of Israel. He somehow needed something more.

Here the fourth Gospel picks up on a theme it first introduced in John 1:12, 13. There we read that "to all who received him, who believed in his name, he gave power to become children of God; who were born, not of blood nor of the will of the flesh nor of the will of man, but of God" (RSV).

Many in our day seem to believe that all humans are automatically children of God—that God is the Father of all people. Not so. He may be their Creator, but that does not mean that He is their Father.

The Bible is clear on this point. It is only those born of the Spirit and who have responded in faith who belong to the family of God. They may have been born Jews, Catholics, Adventists, or Baptists, but that doesn't make them a part of God's family.

That is what Jesus is telling Nicodemus. He needs a double baptism—both of water and of Spirit so that he might be born from above as a part of God's kingdom.

In our day it is at the point of the double baptism that the problem enters the church. All church members have by definition been baptized with water. But that is only half of what they need. And it is by far the lesser half. More important, they must have a new heart and empowerment for Christlike living through the baptism of the Holy Spirit.

The problem is that there are too many "water" church members. They belong to the church but not to God's family in heaven. It is from the "water" group that come dissension, backbiting, and trouble of every kind within the visible church.

Lord, help me today to desire to move beyond the water and into the Spirit. I need Your help right now.

April 1

Christianity
Is Not a Discussion Group

"How can a man be born when he is old? . . ." "Do not marvel that I said to you,
'You must be born anew.' The wind blows where it wills, and you hear the sound of
it, but you do not know whence it comes or whither it goes; so it is with every one
who is born of the Spirit." Nicodemus said to him, "How can this be?"
John 3:4-9, RSV.

But how do I move from being a "water" Christian to being a genuine part of the family of God, a Spirit Christian? What is the process? How does it happen?

Those are the same questions that Nicodemus had. He also was perplexed. And he should have been. Here we stand face-to-face with one of the great mysteries of the faith, that of the new birth from above, the process through which people become Spirit-filled believers.

We could wish that Jesus' answer would have been more straightforward. But using the Greek word *pneuma*, He provides a play on words that still gets the point across. *Pneuma* means both "spirit" and "wind." The new birth, Jesus tells Nicodemus, is like the wind. You can hear and see the wind but you can't tell where it came from or where it is going. The wind has a mystery about it. And while there are many things about the wind that you do not understand, its effect is visible to all. The Spirit, Jesus continues, works in the same way. You may not understand how He does so, but you can see the effects of it in human lives.

In short, Jesus tells us that we really cannot comprehend the way the Spirit works, but we can understand the results. William Barclay tells the story of a converted drunk. His fellow workers did their best to ridicule the man's new faith. "'Surely,' they said to him, 'you can't believe in miracles and things like that. Surely, for instance, you don't believe that Jesus turned water into wine.' 'I don't know,' the man answered, 'whether He turned water into wine when He was in Palestine, but I do know that in my own house He has turned beer into furniture.'"

Jesus has made it plain that we cannot really understand conversion. And here is a point on which many church members get hung up. They think Christianity is an endless discussion group in which perpetual debating is what it's all about.

Not so, says Jesus. Christianity in the end is something that must be experienced. It is, in part, the Spirit filling our lives, transforming them, and using them for God's glory.

Jesus the Serpent

As Moses lifted up the serpent in the wilderness, so must the Son of Man be lifted up, that whoever believes in him may have eternal life. John 3:14, 15, ESV.

Here Jesus takes us back to a story recorded in Numbers 21:4-9. In it the children of Israel were up to their favorite "churchly" pastime—grumbling and complaining. They regretted ever having left Egypt.

In punishment for their lack of faith in the face of His miraculous leading, God sent them a plague of deadly fiery serpents. Repenting, the people cried for mercy. In response, the Lord instructed Moses to make an image of one of the serpents and to hold it up in the midst of the camp. All who followed God's instruction in faith and looked upon the serpent would be healed.

The Jewish people loved that story and were fond of retelling it. The major problem with it was that God had also told them never to make an idol or to worship one. But the Lord had commanded the manufacture of this one, in spite of the fact that the serpent had been a symbol of Satan since Eden. The Jews apparently stored the bronze serpent itself in the tabernacle and later the Temple as a sacred object until King Hezekiah, after discovering that people were worshipping it, had it broken in pieces (2 Kings 18:4). About the time of Jesus one Jewish writer found it necessary to point out that it wasn't the bronze serpent that had healed the people, but God (Wisdom of Solomon 16:7).

At any rate, Jesus used that rather peculiar Jewish story to make an important point in closing off His discussion with Nicodemus: Just "as Moses lifted up the serpent in the wilderness, so must the Son of Man be lifted up, that whoever believes in him may have eternal life."

Like other portions of the discussion with Nicodemus, we find a mystery here. After all, how can we possibly compare the crucifixion of Jesus to a snake on a pole? Isn't the snake in biblical history the problem rather than the solution?

While we might not understand all the ins and outs of what Jesus said, His meaning is absolutely clear: that a faith response on our part conditions spiritual healing, the new birth, and the working of the Spirit in our hearts and lives, just as it did among the ancient Israelites in the desert.

Individuals are not born saved for eternal life. It comes through looking at Jesus upon the cross in an attitude of profound faith in the power of God.

April 3

Needed: A Response
to the God Who Loves

For God so loved the world, that he gave his only begotten Son, that whosoever believeth in him should not perish, but have everlasting life. For God sent not his Son into the world to condemn the world; but that the world through him might be saved. He that believeth on him is not condemned: but he that believeth not is condemned already, because he hath not believed in the name of the only begotten Son of God.
John 3:16-18.

Here we have the heart of the gospel, the starting place for thinking "Christianly." The "for" of verse 16 reflects us back to verses 14 and 15 and the importance of having faith as we look upon Jesus on the cross.

But verse 16 carries our understanding a giant step forward. Jesus didn't get on that cross all by Himself. No, He had been sent by the Father who so loved the world that He gave His one and only Son (the real meaning of "begotten") to rescue the inhabitants of Planet Earth.

Here we find an important truth about God the Father: He took, and always takes, the initiative in our salvation. He is not some standoffish deity who must be pacified or who is stern and angry with sinful humans. To the contrary, He loved sinners so much that He took the lead in providing them with the solution to the problem of sin and death. It is time to move beyond the contrast between a condemning God and the sweet, loving, and gracious Jesus who needs to change the Father's attitude. John 3:16 tells us that They are in this together. It all started with the Father. In His love He sent the Son not to smash and punish sinners, but to save them.

John 3:16 tells us something else about God. Namely, that He "loved the world." All of it, not just some nation or social group, not merely a part who have been selected out of the masses of spiritually destitute for heavenly bliss, but all of it. He "loved [and loves] the world." That includes you and me.

And that thought leads to what John 3:16 teaches about us. The key ideas are two. One is that without God's rescue plan we will perish. The second is that we must respond to God's offer. We are born needing salvation. Thus "whosoever believeth" is the truth set forth by Jesus.

The good news is that the gracious God who loves the world also supplies each of us with the power to believe in that Jesus who was uplifted on the cross for us. Today is the day to take God's gift of belief and let Jesus into our hearts.

Believers Already Have Eternal Life

The Father loves the Son, and has given all things into his hand. He who believes in
the Son has eternal life; he who does not obey the Son shall not see life,
but the wrath of God rests upon him. John 3:35, 36, RSV

Eternal life" is the phrase that ties together today's reading with yesterday's. Verse 16 declares that whoever believes will have eternal life. And verse 36 claims that those who believe already have that gift.

Here we have a theme that runs across the first half of the fourth Gospel. John 5:24 finds Jesus saying "he who hears my word and believes him who sent me, has eternal life" (RSV) and in John 6:47 He tells His followers that "he who believes has eternal life" (RSV).

That gift is not for the future, but is a present possession of all who believe. What a promise! Every one who truly believes already has eternal life.

But then, you may be wondering, why do genuine Christians die? Here we need to recognize the biblical distinction between eternal life and immortality. The first we already possess, but immortality is something not given to any human until the second coming of Jesus. Paul tells us that at that time "the trumpet will sound, and the dead will be raised imperishable, and we shall be changed. For this perishable nature must put on the imperishable, and this mortal nature must put on immortality." Only then will death ultimately be defeated (1 Cor. 15:51-55, RSV).

The facts of the case are that eternal life is subject to the first death, in which people spend some time sleeping in their graves. On the other hand, immortality means that its possessors are not ever subject to death of any kind. Christians have eternal life now, but will not be immortal until God bestows the gift on them at the end of earthly history. The wicked, of course, will never receive it. Thus, being mortal, they will perish in hell fire rather than suffer throughout the ceaseless ages of eternity at the hands of the God of love (see 2 Thess. 1:9; Mal. 4:1; Rom. 6:23; Rev. 20:14).

Another important thing to note about John 3:36 is that God's wrath is not the same as uncontrollable anger, but His attitude of love that eventually brings to an end a world in which the innocent suffer. Revelation 6:16 describes it as "the wrath of the Lamb."

The best news in John 3:36 is that each of us has a choice to cast our vote for eternal life.

Bridge Building Par Excellence

A woman of Samaria came to draw water. Jesus said to her, "Give Me a drink." For His disciples had gone away into the city to buy food. Then the woman of Samaria said to Him, "How is it that You, being a Jew, ask a drink from me, a Samaritan woman?" For Jews have no dealings with Samaritans. John 4:7-9, NKJV.

The apostle John loves a good story. His first one was about Nicodemus, the rich ruler of the Jews. This one is about a Samaritan outcast. The individuals involved have almost nothing in common. What holds them together is the fact that Jesus "knew what was in man" (John 2:25, RSV). Both stories illustrate that truth.

The setting for John 4 is the province of Samaria, which in Jesus' day was wedged in between the Jewish lands of Judea to the south and Galilee to the north. Right in the midst of those two political entities so concerned with religious and racial purity was Samaria, a land anything but pure. Both its people and its religion were a mixture of the Jewish and the pagan. As a result, Jews had nothing to do with the Samaritans, who were more than willing to return the favor. In typical Near Eastern fashion, the Jews and Samaritans had been in a bitter quarrel for more than 400 years.

And then Jesus stops to rest while His disciples are off finding something to eat. While He waits, a Samaritan woman shows up at midday to get some water from Jacob's well. At that point Jesus does the unthinkable—He asks her for a favor.

That very act speaks volumes about Jesus. First, it demonstrates His humanity. Like us, He got hungry and thirsty. That is important in the Gospel that most emphasizes His divinity. Second, it indicates that something about Him led the woman not to just ignore or flee from Him. She sensed that here was a person who was warm and sympathetic.

Third, Jesus was a bridge builder who was willing to transcend the hatreds and prejudices of His time and place. That breaking down of barriers, however, was not merely between races but also barriers of social custom sanctified by age. Jewish teachers were not allowed to talk to women in public, let alone one with a notorious character. That is evident in her reply to Him: "You are asking a favor from me, a Samaritan woman!" Unheard of. But here we find our Lord demonstrating that God loves the world not merely in theory, but also in practice.

How is it with me? Am I a bridge builder like my Lord? If not, why not?

Evangelist Par Excellence

Jesus answered her, "If you knew the gift of God, and who it is that is saying to you, 'Give me a drink,' you would have asked him and he would have given you living water. . . . Every one who drinks of this water will thirst again, but whoever drinks of the water that I shall give him will never thirst; the water that I shall give him will become in him a spring of water welling up to eternal life. John 4:10-14, RSV.

We should notice something in the dialogue between Jesus and the Samaritan woman. Namely, He refused to argue with her. Several times she attempted to draw Him into a debate: "Are you greater than our father Jacob" (verse 12, RSV)? Where is the proper place to worship God? On this mountain or in Jerusalem (verse 20)? Did you know that Jacob is our father (verse 12)? Other Jewish teachers would have hotly disputed those last two items.

But Jesus didn't take the bait. Rather, He calmly kept on track as He revealed gospel truth to her. And in the end, by not arguing over side issues and by keeping to His evangelistic message, He won her over.

The core of His offer is living water. Living water is from a running source and generally preferable to still water from the bottom of a well. But the woman could obviously see that there were no such streams available. Beyond that, she could tell that He didn't even have a bucket to get still water out of the well. Who do you think you are? she threw at Him. Do you think that you are better than our Father Jacob?

Jesus didn't get emotional at that not-so-subtle attack. He merely reiterated His offer of something better than she had ever had before.

And in the process He was making a Messianic claim. Living water in the Jewish mind was not only water from a stream; it was also a phrase linked to the coming Messianic age in which "they shall not hunger nor thirst" (Isa. 49:10), a time when the parched ground would become a pool and the thirsty land springs of water (Isa. 35:7). It was God Himself who was "the fountain of living waters" (Jer. 17:13).

The message was beginning to dawn on the Samaritan woman. She wanted what Jesus had (John 4:15), even though she wasn't sure exactly what it was.

Meanwhile, we should recognize that our Savior knew the business of how to get His message out. Be accepting, don't argue, and keep coming back to the truth of the gospel.

April 7

Facing the Truth

The woman said to Him, "I know that Messiah is coming" (who is called Christ). "When He comes, He will tell us all things." Jesus said to her, "I who speak to you am He."
John 4:25, 26, NKJV.

"Go, call your husband" (John 4:16, NKJV). Now that was a bomb! It completely caught the Samaritan woman off guard.

A perceptive command, it completely blindsided her. "I have no husband," she blurted out (verse 17). Jesus agreed with that, pointing out that she had had five husbands and was currently "shacked up" with a man she wasn't married to (verse 18).

That hurt. It may have been the truth but it was uncomfortable. The best thing to do from her perspective was to change the topic to something more neutral: "I perceive that you are a prophet" (verse 19). And in case that didn't work, she could always start an argument about where one should worship (verse 20). Anything but more conversation about her personal life.

Here we are not much different from that Samaritan woman. We will do anything to escape dealing with our cherished shortcomings and sins. As soon as a possible revelation of them comes up we immediately seek an escape route. And any old one will do. The main thing is to put distance between ourselves and our conscience. Change the subject, argue, attack, flee. It doesn't matter. We will do anything rather than face up.

But it is facing up that leads to the kingdom. When Jesus confronted her in His gentle way she might try to play escape games, but her whole sordid situation was now in the open.

Christ's revelation forced her to come to grips with the total inadequacy of her life. Here is an important spiritual dynamic. We never truly see ourselves until we are in the presence of Christ, until we see who we are in relation to God. Then and only then do we feel a need for Him and cry out for the living water that will truly satisfy (verse 15) and the Messiah who "will tell us all things" (verse 25).

A conviction of our personal sin is always the beginning of salvation. After that comes the cry for help. At that point Christ can offer Himself more fully: "I who speak to you am He" (verse 26), the One who can truly reach out and help.

Help me today, my Father, to be honest with both myself and You that You might help me where I need it the most.

A Lesson for the Disciples

Just then the disciples came. They marveled that He was talking with a woman.
. . . [They] besought him, saying, "Rabbi, eat." But he said to them, "I have food to
eat of which you do not know." So the disciples said to one another, "Has any one
brought him food?" Jesus said to them, "My food is to do the will of him who sent
me, and to accomplish his work." John 4:27-34, RSV.

The disciples don't have the foggiest notion about what is going on. All they know is that Jesus is talking to a Samaritan woman. Against the background of the rabbinic precepts, that was shocking. "Let no one talk with a woman in the street, no, not even with his wife," ran one of their sayings. Women, rabbinic thought went, were incapable of receiving any real teaching. And here Jesus was speaking to a woman!

Naturally they were astonished. But by this time they knew Jesus well enough not to ask Him why. They only did what was foremost on their minds. After all, they were hungry, and Jesus must be also.

The woman, meanwhile, existed in a state of wonder also. Forgetting who she was, and why she had sneaked out to a well far from town to avoid people, she ran off without her water jar to tell people that she had found the Christ. Her hearers were at that very moment coming to see Jesus for themselves.

Here we have an interesting situation. A woman who had known Jesus for possibly no more than an hour was far in advance of the disciples in her understanding of Him. She had already seen her sin and had come to grips with her spiritual needs, while the disciples had yet to struggle with the pride and self-sufficiency that drove their lives. Beyond that, Jesus had plainly stated to the Samaritan woman that He was the Christ. That realization would not completely form in the disciples' minds until much later.

Jesus was excited in a way His followers only dimly comprehended, saying that He had lost His hunger because He was involved in doing His Father's will. The woman was excited too. In fact, even the townspeople who were on their way out to see Jesus were excited.

The only people not excited in this story are the 12 disciples, who had their minds on food. In that context Jesus quoted two proverbs about the readiness of the harvest.

It is still possible that those who have been longest with Jesus may be the ones with the least insight into the wonder of who He is. Even now "old time" saints might have their minds focused on "food" rather than on the Christ. Such can learn from the Samaritan woman.

An Unlikely Evangelist

From that city many of the Samaritans believed in Him because of the word of the woman who testified, "He told me all the things that I have done." So when the Samaritans came to Jesus, they were asking Him to stay with them; and He stayed there two days. Many more believed because of His word; and they were saying to the woman, "It is no longer because of what you said that we believe, for we have heard for ourselves and know that this One is indeed the Savior of the world."
John 4:39-42, NASB.

The woman was an unlikely evangelist. But then she had an exceptional message to match her exceptional (spelled "notorious" here) life. She had met a man, she announced to the villagers, who had told her everything that she had ever done. That had their ears. Because what she had done was much, and everybody knew it. As a result of her testimony, the center of the village shifted toward the well with the woman in the forefront.

We read in *The Desire of Ages* that "as soon as she had found the Saviour the Samaritan woman brought others to Him. She proved herself a more effective missionary than His own disciples. The disciples saw nothing in Samaria to indicate that it was an encouraging field. Their thoughts were fixed upon a great work to be done in the future. They did not see that right around them was a harvest to be gathered. But through the woman whom they despised, a whole cityful were brought to hear the Saviour. She carried the light at once to her own countrymen.

"This woman represents the working of a practical faith in Christ. Every true disciple is born into the kingdom of God as a missionary. He who drinks of the living water becomes a fountain of life. The receiver becomes a giver. The grace of Christ in the soul is like a spring in the desert, welling up to refresh all, and making those who are ready to perish eager to drink of the water of life" (p. 195).

The woman of Samaria might have been an unlikely evangelist, but she was a successful one. She had a message about *her* sin and *her* Savior that led others to investigate for themselves. In the process, they also found a personal Savior.

Before Jesus came into the woman's life both she and her neighbors considered her beyond hope. But Jesus performed two miracles in her life: He enabled her to break away from her past, and He opened up to her a new future.

From that perspective, there is nothing else that Jesus can be called but "Savior of the world."

Part 4

Turn Your Eyes Upon Jesus at the Height of His Ministry

April 10

A Revolutionary Message

And He came to Nazareth, where He had been brought up; and as was His custom, He entered the synagogue on the Sabbath, and stood up to read. And the book of the prophet Isaiah was handed to Him. And He opened the book and found the place where it was written,
"The Spirit of the Lord is upon Me, Because He anointed me to preach the gospel to the poor. He has sent Me to proclaim release to the captives, And recovery of sight to the blind, To set free those who are oppressed, To proclaim the favorable year of the Lord."
And He closed the book, gave it back to the attendant and sat down; and the eyes of all in the synagogue were fixed on Him. And He began to say to them, "Today this Scripture has been fulfilled in your hearing." Luke 4:16-21, NASB.

Nothing like returning home to have the honor of preaching to those who knew you as a child. They now viewed Him as an accomplished rabbi or teacher. As a result, they asked Him to take the Scripture reading and the homily on the text.

Probably known as the boy "who was a bit different," Jesus had come a long way since His boyhood days in that village. And He was different, but in ways that they did not suspect. He had in fact become the most famous person ever raised in Nazareth. Stories of His teachings and miracles had spread everywhere. He was truly a celebrity. It was only natural that He should have the honor of the Sabbath service.

His choice of a text is an interesting one. But how He treated it is even more so. Jesus considered the passage from Isaiah 61:1, 2 as Messianic. He read the first part of the verse and probably commented on it afterward as He explained its message.

In essence it set forth the Messianic role in terms of the cup-of-cold-water theology that we examined in the story of the woman at the well, a message that had formed a large aspect of His teaching and healing ministry up to that time. He had preached the gospel to the poor, set at liberty those who were oppressed by disease and sin, healed the blind, and proclaimed that the kingdom was at hand.

So far, so good. Then He did two things. First he failed to read the last part of the passage, which read: "to proclaim . . . the day of vengeance of our God" (RSV), thereby signaling that His mission would be divided into two parts: the arrival of the kingdom of grace during His first advent and the arrival of the kingdom of glory when all would be made right at His second coming.

His first words were that Isaiah's Messianic prophecy had been fulfilled. It was a claim that He was Himself the expected Messiah.

Not Everybody Likes Faithful Preachers

"There were many in Israel with leprosy in the time of Elisha the prophet, yet not one of them was cleansed—only Naaman the Syrian."
All the people in the synagogue were furious when they heard this. They got up, drove him out of the town, and took him to the brow of the hill on which the town was built, in order to throw him off the cliff. But he walked right through the crowd and went on his way. Luke 4:27-30, NIV.

I have preached sermons that some people didn't like. But I have never faced the intensity of reaction that Jesus did as He spoke to His hometown people.

Interestingly enough, their initial response had been positive and supporting. "Great sermon!" And to think, He is Joseph's boy. And "all spoke well of him, and wondered at the gracious words which proceeded out of his mouth" (Luke 4:22, RSV).

Jesus would have been the hero of the day if He had just stopped right there and let the crowds go on and on about how proud they were of their home-grown product.

But Jesus just had to be Jesus. They wanted healings like those that had taken place in Capernaum. But He had something they needed to hear, knowing all the while that it would lead to His rejection: "Truly, I say to you, no prophet is acceptable in his own country. But in truth, I tell you, there were many widows in Israel in the days of Elijah, when the heaven was shut up three years and six months, when there came a great famine over all the land; and Elijah was sent to none of them but only to Zarephath, in the land of Sidon, to a woman who was a widow. And there were many lepers in Israel in the time of the prophet Elisha; and none of them were cleansed, but only Naaman the Syrian" (verses 24-27, RSV).

And for those words they decided to kill Him (verses 28, 29). Why, because He preached something they didn't want to hear. Both of His illustrations uplifted God's saving grace to Gentiles. He had been scripturally correct, but that made no difference to them. They were mad enough to murder.

The church still has such people 2,000 years later. Preach something they don't like, even if it is faithful to the Bible, and they are out to get the preacher. Of course, they may not attempt to kill preachers and others they disagree with, but they do roast them, boil them, and fry them in their conversations with others who share the same spiritual illness.

We do well to consider the full scope of Scripture and the lesson taught by the congregation at Nazareth.

April 12

True Learning

At that time Jesus declared, "I thank thee, Father, Lord of heaven and earth, that thou hast hidden these things from the wise and understanding and revealed them to babes; yea, Father, for such was thy gracious will. All things have been delivered to me by my Father; and no one knows the Son except the Father, and no one knows the Father except the Son and any one to whom the Son chooses to reveal him."
Matt. 11:25-27, RSV.

"At that time."

Times were changing. The powerful of this world had imprisoned John the Baptist, and those wise in the philosophies and the theologies of the day all too often rejected both the Lord Jesus and His teachings. In response, He highlighted the fact that it was the weak, the simple people, who often understood Him most clearly. All through the gospel story we discover that it is the poor, the sinners, the tax collectors, prostitutes, and ordinary folk who most readily responded to Him. On the other hand, the learned specialists, as they analyzed His work, claimed that what He was doing did not fit with their complicated theories.

While it is true that the intellectuals in general had no use for Jesus, while the humble welcomed Him, we need to be careful in what conclusions we draw from those facts. As William Barclay put it, "He is very far from condemning intellectual power; what He is condemning is *intellectual pride*. . . . 'The heart, not the head, is the throne of the gospel.' It is not cleverness which shuts out; it is pride. It is not stupidity which admits; it is humility. Jesus is not connecting ignorance and faith. A man may be as wise as Solomon, but if he has not the simplicity, the trust, the innocence of the childlike heart, he has shut himself out."

If you desire to truly know the Father you need to watch Jesus and listen to Him carefully, because "no one knows the Father except the Son." The book of Hebrews puts it a bit differently when it notes that "in many and various ways God spoke of old to our fathers by the prophets; but in these last days he has spoken to us by a Son. . . . He reflects the glory of God and bears the very stamp of his nature" (Heb. 1:1-3, RSV).

"Turn your eyes upon Jesus" is His own message, as well as that of the entire New Testament. Other knowledges are useful in life and some of them may help us see the glories of Jesus even more fully. But the essential knowledge becomes the context in which all other learning has meaning.

The Great Invitation

Come unto me, all ye that labour and are heavy laden, and I will give you rest. Take my yoke upon you, and learn of me; for I am meek and lowly in heart: and ye shall find rest unto your souls. For my yoke is easy, and my burden is light. Matt. 11:28-30.

How to find God is the question of the human heart down through the ages. It was certainly the quest of Jesus' hearers. In Matthew 11:27 He had told His audience that the way to discover God was through Himself. He follows that announcement with an invitation: "Come unto me, all ye that labour and are heavy laden, and I will give you rest."

The word "rest" is the key to understanding this passage. The Septuagint (Greek) translation of Exodus 33:14 uses the same word to signify the rest that God was to give Israel through Moses' leadership. Throughout the first Gospel, Matthew has been comparing Jesus to Moses, and its development parallels the Exodus experience. Jesus, in Matthew's eyes, is the prophet like Moses whom God said He would raise up (Deut. 18:15, 18).

But, the second Moses will succeed where the first failed. The second will give that "rest" promised through Moses but was never achieved (Matt. 11:28, 29). That argument dominates Hebrews 3 and 4, which argues that Christ is greater than Moses because He brings His people into true "rest."

Another key word in our passage today is "yoke." The rabbis spoke of "the yoke of the law" as a great blessing, but under their interpretation it had actually become a burden. Jesus later accused the scribes and Pharisees of making the people carry "heavy . . . loads" by their legalistic demands (Matt. 23:4, NIV). With their thousands of regulations and rules they had perverted God's intention in the law through Moses.

But Jesus seeks to bring His followers back to God's original plan: that the law be a blessing as people focus on its spirit and not merely the letter. With the multitude of extra baggage that the Jews had added to it, it had become massively heavy and impossible to bear.

Unfortunately, people are still in the business of making the yoke of the law heavier and heavier with this rule and that, with this restriction and that, until the law becomes something to escape from rather than to delight in, as it was for the psalmist (Ps. 119:47, 70, 77).

Keep your eyes on Jesus as He continues to expound on the spirit of the law, but even more so as He indicates how His death will lead to ultimate "rest."

April 14

Yoke Conflict

At that time Jesus went through the grainfields on the sabbath; his disciples were hungry, and they began to pluck heads of grain and to eat. But when the Pharisees saw it, they said to him, "Look, your disciples are doing what is not lawful to do on the Sabbath." Matt. 12:1, 2, RSV.

It didn't take long for yoke conflict to arise between Jesus and the Pharisees. In fact, it jumps in in the next verse after Jesus invited His followers to take His yoke, "for my yoke is easy, and my burden is light" (Matt. 11:30, RSV). The occasion for conflict finds Him and the disciples walking through a grain-field, with the disciples not only picking some of the grain but rubbing it between their palms so as to separate the kernels from the chaff. At that point the ever-present Pharisees cry out, "Look, your disciples are doing what is not lawful to do on the sabbath."

In our day we might think that they were upset because the disciples had taken grain that did not belong to them. But that was not the problem. In fact, in gathering and eating the grain as they passed through a field they were doing what the law of Moses explicitly allowed. Deuteronomy 23:25 tells us that it was permissible to pick a neighbor's grain with the hand but not with a sickle.

The problem was that the disciples did it on the Sabbath. Such was an act of harvesting, and harvesting was defined as work, and work on the Sabbath was sin. But they were not only harvesting; as they rubbed the grains in their hands they were also threshing. And threshing also represented a forbidden Sabbath activity. Then, of course, the Pharisees could also accuse them of traveling. Their tradition considered walking more than 1,999 paces to be taking a journey and thus a breach of the Sabbath.

The Pharisees may have expected Jesus immediately to put a stop to such unlawful activity, although they undoubtedly had a sneaking suspicion that He would not do so. Rather, to their surprise, He met them on their own ground by retelling a story from 1 Samuel 21:1-6, in which David in his hunger broke the letter of the law but God blessed him anyway.

Several truths flow out of that episode. One is that human need always takes precedence over the letter of the law. The second is that "the Son of Man is Lord of the Sabbath" (Matt. 12:8, NIV) and certainly knew what He meant when He gave the law in the first place.

In the end the story leaves us with a question. What is my approach to God's law? Do I see it as a blessing or an unbearable yoke?

Sabbath Confrontation

Again he entered the synagogue, and a man was there with a withered hand. And they watched Jesus, to see whether he would heal him on the Sabbath, so that they might accuse him. And he said to the man with the withered hand, "Come here." And he said to them, "Is it lawful on the Sabbath to do good or to do harm, to save life or to kill?" But they were silent. And he looked around at them with anger, grieved at their hardness of heart, and said to the man, "Stretch out your hand." He stretched it out, and his hand was restored. Mark 3:1-5, ESV.

Fast on the heels of the grainfield confrontation of Matthew 12:1-8 comes a second conflict over the Sabbath in verses 9-13 (also in Mark 3:1-5). The interesting thing about this one is that Jesus could easily have avoided it but chose not to.

The scene itself has three main characters: Jesus, a man who had had a crippled hand for a long time, and those "watching Jesus" to see if He would do something they considered wrong.

Obviously seeing His would-be accusers, Jesus didn't skirt the issue. After all, synagogues reserved the front seats for such dignitaries. Now, Jesus knew that the Pharisees were not against medical care on the Sabbath, so long as it involved a matter of life and death for the sick person. But the man with the crippled hand obviously didn't fit into that category. He had had the disability for some time, and his healing could have easily waited a day or two.

But for Jesus it was a test case. He called the man up front where everybody could see and asked the watching Pharisees whether it was lawful to do good or evil on the Sabbath.

That put them in a dilemma. No one could answer that it was permissible to do evil. Thus they had no choice but to answer that it was lawful to do good. And wasn't healing a person doing good?

That first question put the Pharisees on the spot, but why Jesus asked it was obvious. The second question, however, at first leaves us baffled: "Is it lawful . . . to save life or to kill?" After all, who was killing anybody? All that was in question was the healing of a man's hand. But Jesus once again indicates that He understands the human heart (John 2:25). At that very time the Pharisees were beginning to concoct a plan to kill Jesus because He didn't agree with their understanding of the law (Matt. 12:14).

Out of these conflict stories flow not only hatred in those who fail to understand the principle of the law and who are watching for faults, but important principles relating to the Sabbath for Jesus' followers.

Help us, Father, as we ponder these stories to gain a fuller understanding of the relation of law and mercy.

April 16

Sick "Churchly" Types

The Pharisees went out, and immediately held counsel with the Herodians against him, how to destroy him. Mark 3:6, RSV.

Some "churchly" types are real sick.

A case in point is the Pharisees of old. They had just witnessed a merciful act of God's power. But they were so upset that all they could think of was killing Jesus because He didn't keep the Sabbath correctly.

Religion often aggravates certain negative aspects of human nature. It makes some people eager to find faults when they could and should be alert for the power and mercy of God. Such sick watchers tend to focus on a misunderstanding of the purpose of God's law.

A hallmark of all legalism is that it puts law above human considerations and mercy. But, as in the Sermon on the Mount, Jesus in His healing on the Sabbath miracles attempts to help the religious leaders see the spiritual nature of the law, that outward obedience to it must be rooted in *agapē* (love) if it is to be understood correctly.

Unfortunately, the leaders did not understand the law they claimed to prize so highly. As a result, when Jesus pointed them to its foundation in *agapē*, they plotted "how they might destroy him" (Matt. 12:14).

That is the paradox of legalism. Legalists, in their purported love for God and His law, become angry with those who disagree with them over their particular theological interpretations—so angry that they are willing to murder their opponents or destroy their reputation. Even such anger itself, according to Jesus, is actually the equivalent of murder (Matt. 5:21-26).

Anybody who has been a church member very long knows that the spirit of Pharisaism is not dead. It is alive and well in the twenty-first century among those who would attack and criticize others over differences of opinion.

Indeed, most congregations have their contingent of Pharisees. More frightening yet, a Pharisee lurks within the skin of each of us. It seeks to impose its spirit on an unsuspecting church and an undeserving world. Every Christian needs to remember that mercy is better than sacrifice (Matt. 12:7) and that *agapē* is the heart of God's law.

Today is one for self-examination. I mean you and I, my friend. Is my religion sick or healthy? How do I know?

The Sabbath as a Means of Grace

And he said unto them, The sabbath was made for man, and not man for the sabbath.
Mark 2:27.

Two great truths flow out of Jesus' early confrontations with the Jews on how the Sabbath should be kept. The first appears in today's verse: "The sabbath was made for man, and not man for the sabbath."

One implication is that God established the Sabbath for all people and not just for the Jews. Jesus did not say "the Sabbath was made for the Jews." And even a cursory look at the Old Testament demonstrates the accuracy of Jesus' conclusion. After all, the first observance of the Sabbath was by God Himself at the end of Creation week thousands of years before any Jews existed. From beginning to end, the Bible supports the fact that God intended the Sabbath for all people—"man" or mankind.

But the context of Jesus' statement about the Sabbath being "made for man" helps us understand why God had set it apart in the first place. The Jews had made a real mess of the Sabbath. Focusing on what people could not do on the Sabbath, they had developed some 39 categories of forbidden work and more than 1,500 rules on how it should be kept, with an overwhelming emphasis on the negative. They acted as if God first created the Sabbath and then made people to observe it.

Jesus, the Creator of the Sabbath, turned that thinking on its head. And with good reason. The Jews acted as if the Sabbath were primary and first— that God had a Sabbath and needed someone to keep it and thus created humanity to fill that void. Not so, Jesus pointed out. The very order of creation demonstrates that "the sabbath was made for man, and not man for the sabbath." After all, the Lord created human beings on the sixth day, while He did not institute the Sabbath until the seventh. From the beginning God recognized that people would need the Sabbath. So He created it to meet their spiritual, physical, social, and mental requirements as they worship, fellowship, rest from work, and study His Word. God created the Sabbath as a means of grace for His people—all of them for all time.

With that in mind, it is of more than passing interest that the Sabbath commandment is the only one in the Ten Commandments that begins with "remember." He knew just how prone people would be to forget and neglect the one means of grace that He established to meet their needs at the very beginning of this earth's journey.

The Lord's Day

The Son of man is Lord even of the sabbath day. Matt. 12:8.

I was in the Spirit on the Lord's day. Rev. 1:10.

The second important truth that flows out of Jesus' early confrontations with the Jews on Sabbath observance is the fact that He "is Lord even of the sabbath day." That is quite a claim. It is either correct or false. But no matter what, it led directly to the cross. To the Jews it was the height of blasphemy. But from Jesus' perspective it was the very ground for His right to delineate how the Sabbath should be honored. After all, if He was truly Lord of the Sabbath He would have more understanding on why it was instituted than anyone else.

The claim itself takes us historically back even before God gave the Sabbath in the Ten Commandments through Moses. Genesis 2:1-3 reads: "Thus the heavens and the earth were finished, and all the host of them. And on the seventh day God finished his work which he had done, and he rested on the seventh day from all his work which he had done. So God blessed the seventh day and hallowed it, because on it God rested from all his work which he had done in creation" (RSV).

And who was that God who rested that first Sabbath and blessed and hallowed the seventh day? It probably included the entire Godhead. But we know for a certainty that Jesus observed that first Sabbath and was at the forefront of establishing the seventh-day Sabbath in human history.

And how do we know that? Because of the testimony of the New Testament, which plainly states that "all things were made through him [Jesus the Word], and without him was not anything made that was made" (John 1:3, RSV); "in him all things were created, in heaven and on earth . . . all things were created through him and for him" (Col. 1:16, RSV); and through Jesus God "created the world" (Heb. 1:2, RSV).

There is absolutely no doubt that Christ was the active agent in Creation week and that He instituted history's first Sabbath. Thus He can claim that He is Lord of the Sabbath (Mark 2:28). The seventh-day Sabbath is the only day in the Bible that identifies "the Lord's day" (Rev. 1:10).

In giving it at Sinai the "I am" Lord of the Exodus (Ex. 3:14; John 8:58) made it plain that He intended to make the seventh-day Sabbath a weekly reminder of two facts: That He created (Ex. 20:8-11) and that He redeems (Deut. 5:12-15).

How thankful we can be as Christians that we can honor the Lord on His special day.

Jesus: A Person of Courage

The man went away and told the Jews that it was Jesus who had healed him. And this was why the Jews persecuted Jesus, because he did this on the sabbath. But Jesus answered them, "My Father is working still, and I am working." This was why the Jews sought all the more to kill him, because he not only broke the sabbath but also called God his own Father, making himself equal with God. John 5:15-18, RSV.

The conflict between Jesus and the Jewish leaders goes on and on. Not merely because of the Sabbath, but because He was taking on the prerogatives of God in defining lawful activity on the holy day. And here we need to be very clear. Jesus never once in the New Testament ever rejects the seventh-day Sabbath. What He does discard is the Jewish way of observing it—their making a means of joy and grace into a burden and a yoke so heavy that no one could carry it.

All the way through the Sabbath conflict in John 5 Jesus is claiming to be the Messiah and divine, both implicitly and explicitly. On the implicit level the very miracle of healing a person who had been unable to walk for 38 years was a messianic sign. Isaiah's picture of the new age brought about by the Messiah indicates that "then shall the lame man leap like a hart" (Isa. 35:6, RSV). On the explicit level Jesus was not backward in identifying God as His Father in a special sense (John 5:17). His Jewish listeners had no problem discerning what He meant—that He was "making himself equal with God" (verse 18). That would become even clearer in the following verses, in which Jesus attributes to Himself the prerogatives of raising the dead and judgment—attributes in Jewish thinking of no one but God.

It was those claims that led Jesus step-by-step toward the cross. The Sabbath was merely an outward aspect of the struggle between Jesus and the religious leaders. The heart of the issue was that by asserting to be divine He was in their eyes committing blasphemy, the very charge they would lay against Him during the various trials that resulted in His crucifixion.

In all of His actions we find Jesus to be a person of extraordinary and unique courage. He knew that to speak and act as He did was courting death. But He understood His mission and moved forward.

Lord, today help me to have the same kind of faith in Jesus as He had in Himself. And strengthen me to have more of His courage.

I Am My Own Judge

The Father judges no one, but has given all judgment to the Son. John 5:22, RSV.

Now there is a thought pregnant with meaning: Jesus as our judge.
Many of us have seen pictures of the judgment in which a somewhat apathetic (if not fearsome) Father sits upon the judgment throne with Jesus prostrate before Him pleading for the salvation of His followers.

Wrong on both counts. First, the Father is not indifferent, let alone fearsome. He is not someone who has to be persuaded by Jesus or anyone else. The plain fact of the case is that He "so loved the world, that he gave his only begotten Son, that whosoever believeth in him should not perish, but have everlasting life. For God sent not his Son into the world to condemn the world; but that the world through him might be saved" (John 3:16, 17).

Banish all thought of God as the stern judge who needs to be convinced by a soft-hearted Christ. No! It was the Father Himself who out of a warm and caring heart initiated the plan of salvation.

Not only did the Father begin the plan, but, according to Jesus, the Father has even handed the responsibility for judgment over to Him. And that is just the beginning of an interesting part of the story. Because Jesus tells us in John 12 that He is turning over our judgment to us.

Do you find that one hard to believe? Well, listen to Him: "If any one hears my sayings and does not keep them, I do not judge him; for I did not come to judge the world but to save the world. He who rejects me and does not receive my sayings has a judge; the word that I have spoken will be his judge on the last day" (John 12:47, 48, RSV).

Now, I know that Jesus said that it will be His words that finally judge. But think about the implications of that statement. It is you and I as individuals who make decisions about accepting or rejecting that judgmental word. We have the final decision-making authority as to where we will spend eternity. The hinge is how we relate to Him through His Word. In that sense we are our own judges.

The same basic truth shines forth in John 3:36: "He that believeth on the Son hath everlasting life: and he that believeth not the Son shall not see life; but the wrath of God abideth on him."

We need to take more seriously the great opportunities and responsibilities that God has granted to each of us through Jesus.

Resurrection Hope

Verily, verily, I say unto you, The hour is coming, and now is, when the dead shall hear the voice of the Son of God: and they that hear shall live. For as the Father hath life in himself; so hath he given to the Son to have life in himself. . . . Marvel not at this: for the hour is coming, in the which all that are in the graves shall hear his voice, and shall come forth; they that have done good, unto the resurrection of life; and they that have done evil, unto the resurrection of damnation. John 5:25-29.

Here we find another topic that runs throughout John's telling of the story of Jesus. Resurrection is absolutely central to his understanding of the good news that we call the gospel. And that aspect of the good news begins with the resurrection of Jesus Himself, who rose from the grave and achieved victory over death.

But from our perspective an important part of that narrative is that Jesus did not gain victory over death for Himself, but for each of His followers. As He put it when explaining His future resurrection to His disciples shortly before His death, "Because I live, ye shall live also" (John 14:19). Or as the same writer put it in the book of Revelation when addressed by the already risen Christ: "I am he that liveth, and was dead; and, behold, I am alive for evermore, Amen; and have the keys of hell and of death" (Rev. 1:18). Those keys, of course, point to our own resurrections.

John 5:28 doesn't tell us when the resurrection will take place—only that it "is coming." Jesus is more explicit in John 6, in which we read, "No one can come to me unless the Father who sent me draws him; and I will raise him up at the last day" (verse 44, RSV). Again, "he who eats my flesh and drinks my blood has eternal life, and I will raise him up at the last day" (verse 54, RSV).

Thus from John's Gospel we realize that that blessed event will take place at the end of time. But to read John 5:29 alone one would end up with the idea that the resurrection of life and the resurrection of damnation take place at the same time. But John corrects that part when he explains in Revelation 20 that the two resurrections will be separated by 1,000 years (the millennium), with Christ's followers arising at the Second Advent and the wicked sleeping in their graves until after the millennium.

All will hear His voice; all will be resurrected; but what a difference in their destinies.

Lord, help me today to put my life in the perspective of eternity. I desire with all my heart to meet You face-to-face at Your second advent.

April 22

How Do You See?

The Pharisees again asked him how he had received his sight. And he said to them, "He put clay on my eyes, and I washed, and I see." Some of the Pharisees said, "This man is not from God, for he does not keep the sabbath." But others said, "How can a man who is a sinner do such signs?" There was a division among them. So they again said to the blind man, "What do you say about him, since he has opened your eyes?" He said, "He is a prophet." John 9:15-17, RSV.

Seeing, for most of us, is an extremely important part of life. We cannot imagine what it is like to be blind, let alone to be born that way. Thus we are careful throughout life to protect our eyes. They are precious to us.

In John 9 we find the story of Jesus healing a man born blind. Not exactly an everyday occasion in most neighborhoods. It wasn't in that one either. Everybody was shocked.

The miracle was astounding. The only problem in the Jewish mind was that it happened on the weekly Sabbath. That brought the Pharisees into play.

The best way that we can describe their spiritual vision after questioning the healed man is fuzzy and blurred. As a group they didn't know what to think. Some doubted that it had even happened until they questioned the man's parents. With that escape route to denial blocked, they faced a conundrum. Some said nobody is of God who does such things on the Sabbath. But others pointed out that sinners couldn't possibly do such a miracle. All in all, we can only consider them as confused.

Then there were the parents. They had no doubt that their son had been born blind and now saw clearly. But in the end they let fear of getting put out of the synagogue, and possibly losing their social standing in the community, distort their own vision. As a result, they saw through eyes of fear.

Last, there was the man himself. The most important thing to him was that he saw at all, something he had never been able to do in his entire life. He knew he had experienced a first-class miracle.

When asked who Jesus was, he at first called Him a prophet (John 9:17). But he will eventually see Him as Lord and worship Him (verse 38). The healed man saw through the eyes of faith.

How is it with me today? How do I see? How is my spiritual eyesight?

Father, please help me see You more clearly. Help me to put away distorting fear. Enable me to see ever more vividly through eyes of faith.

More on Seeing

For the second time they called the man who had been blind, and said to him, "Give God the praise; we know that this man is a sinner." He answered, "Whether he is a sinner, I do not know; one thing I know, that though I was blind, now I see." They said to him, "What did he do to you? How did he open your eyes?" He answered them, "I have told you already, and you would not listen. Why do you want to hear it again? Do you too want to become his disciples?" John 9:24-27, RSV.

A gutsy response to be sure. Although born blind, the man had nothing wrong with his brain or his courage or his faith.

He had experienced the miracle of Jesus in his life and was ready to stand up for what he believed. Even in the face of powerful people. Even in the face of being ostrasized.

While he didn't understand how Jesus had done it, he knew he had been healed. And that had become the turning point in his life. No matter what the cost he would follow Jesus.

That disgusted the authorities, who replied that they were disciples of Moses. "We know," they retorted, "that God has spoken to Moses, but as for this man, we do not know where he comes from" (John 9:29, RSV).

The ever-perceptive healed man replied with a voice bolstered by faith, experience, and insight: "'Why, this is a marvel! You do not know where he comes from, and yet he opened my eyes. We know that God does not listen to sinners, but if any one is a worshiper of God and does his will, God listens to him. Never since the world began has it been heard that any one opened the eyes of a man born blind. If this man were not from God, he could do nothing.' They answered him, 'You were born in utter sin, and would you teach us?' And they cast him out" (verses 30-34, RSV).

One lesson this experience teaches us is that vision is directly connected to the heart. In the face of an obvious act of God, we can do one of two things. We can deny that we have seen a miracle and head in the direction of doubt. Or we can confess that we have indeed viewed the working of the Divine and enter the path of faith.

The interesting thing about how we see is that it leads us ever more firmly in the direction in which we first responded to God's obvious work. Faith and doubt are two ways of life that solidify over time.

Final Thoughts on Seeing

Jesus heard that they had cast him out; and when He had found him, He said to him, "Do you believe in the Son of God?" He answered and said, "Who is He, Lord, that I may believe in Him?" And Jesus said to him, "You have both seen Him and it is He who is talking with you." Then he said, "Lord, I believe!" And he worshiped Him. And Jesus said, "For judgment I have come into this world, that those who do not see may see, and that those who see may be made blind." John 9:35-39, NKJV.

Jesus never forsakes those who have taken their stand for Him. They may have been "cast out" as this healed man was (John 9:34), they may have had family difficulties because of their decision to follow Jesus, or they may even have lost their job. But the good news is that Jesus always sticks with us when we have decided to stick with Him.

Thus it is that we find Jesus searching out the man who had been ostracized and guiding him further into the life of faith. To that humble individual Jesus revealed Himself to be the Son of God, and he accepted Jesus ever more fully. Loyalty to Jesus brings revelation—it results in clearer and clearer spiritual vision.

John concludes the story of the man born blind with some of his favorite themes. First, that Jesus came into the world for judgment. Whenever Jesus confronts people, they pass judgment on themselves.

Those who think they know it all are those who fail to recognize that they are blind indeed. It is those who are unaware of their blindness who are beyond help and hope.

On the other hand, it is only those who realize their blindness and who desire to see better who can have their eyes opened. Only those who acknowledge their weakness can become strong. Only those who confess their blindness can learn to see. And those who recognize their own sin can be forgiven.

Like the Pharisees of Jesus' day, it is those who feel no need who receive no help. It is those born blind and weak who gain healing.

When confronted by Jesus we either see more clearly or become blinder than ever. Meeting Jesus is a judgment call. We can either confess our blindness and receive healing, or we can claim that we already see perfectly and be left in darkness.

Here is a priceless opportunity. And it is yours and mine as we walk through this day.

An Illustration of Blindness and Salvation

*He stood up and said to them, "Let him who is without sin among you be the first
to throw a stone at her." And once more he bent down and wrote on the ground. But
when they heard it, they went away one by one, beginning with the older ones, and
Jesus was left alone with the woman standing before him. Jesus stood up and said to
her, "Woman, where are they? Has no one condemned you?" She said, "No one, Lord."
And Jesus said, "Neither do I condemn you; go, and from now on sin no more."*
John 8:7-11, ESV.

Caught in the "very act" of adultery.

That is a Technicolor phrase. It is difficult not to see the picture. And it is
not a nice one. This woman was obviously problematic.

Of course, there is a missing part to the story. Even holy perfectionists such
as the Pharisees had to know that adultery is not a solitary pastime. Where is
the man? Did they free him because he was a friend? Or was the whole thing
arranged to trap Jesus? After all, if He lets the woman loose they can accuse
Him of not accepting the law of Moses. But if He follows the law and advocates
stoning according to the law, they can then report Him to the Romans, since
He would have broken their law in issuing a death sentence. It looked like a no-
lose situation to the Pharisees. No matter which way Jesus went on this case,
they had Him.

It is at that point that the Jesus who "knew what was in man" (John 2:25)
stood up. His invitation was exquisite and insightful: the one without sin should
throw the first stone. That unexpected move caught the scribes off guard because they knew that their Bible told them repeatedly that all had sinned.

But in case they didn't get the point, Jesus "bent down and wrote on the
ground." Many have wondered what He wrote, but the woman's accusers had
no question as they saw Him writing. To their shame, He briefly "traced before
them . . . the guilty secrets of their own lives" (*The Desire of Ages*, p. 461), "beginning with the older men."

One by one they slinked away, leaving Jesus alone with the obviously problematic woman. Unlike her "churchly" accusers, He did not tell her about her
sins. She knew her faults all too well. So to this woman caught in the "very act"
Jesus gave the gospel in two parts:

(1) He did not condemn her, and

(2) He instructed the forgiven woman to go out to a new way of life.

That is His message to me this day.

April 26

The Ultimate End
of Willful Blindness

Wherefore I say unto you, All manner of sin and blasphemy shall be forgiven unto men: but the blasphemy against the Holy Ghost shall not be forgiven unto men. And whosoever speaketh a word against the Son of man, it shall be forgiven him: but whosoever speaketh against the Holy Ghost, it shall not be forgiven him, neither in this world, neither in the world to come. Matt. 12:31, 32.

The unforgivable sin!

That is quite a thought in the light of Jesus' ministry. How could there even be such a thing as a sin that He cannot forgive? After all, yesterday we noted that Jesus forgave a woman caught in the "very act" of adultery. And the New Testament expresses full and complete forgiveness for all sorts of sins. How could there be one so serious as to be unforgivable either in this life or in eternity?

Here we need to look a little more carefully at today's Scripture reading, which says that the unforgivable sin is blasphemy against the Holy Spirit. What does that mean?

To get a fuller perspective we need to go to John 16:8, in which Jesus tells us that a major function of the Holy Spirit is to convict us of our sin. And when He does so, I can respond in one of two ways. First, I can drop to my knees, confess, and be forgiven (1 John 1:9). Or, I can tell the Spirit to "bug off," to leave me alone, that I am happy without His interfering in my life.

The function of the Spirit is to bring me to conviction of sin through the avenue of my conscience. Those with a healthy conscience repent, but those who consistently refuse the Spirit's ministry develop what Paul calls a "seared" (1 Tim. 4:2) or "defiled" (Titus 1:15) conscience. That is, their conscience is no longer functional. As a result, the Holy Spirit can no longer reach them. Thus they do not repent and cannot be forgiven. It is no accident that Jesus brought up this teaching in the context of the Jewish leaders labeling His ministry as from Satan (Matt. 12:27). Although they had plenty of evidence to the contrary, by ignoring the Spirit's testimony they were passing judgment on themselves and hardening their hearts. They were in the process of sealing themselves off from the only channel through which God could reach them.

If you are worried about committing this sin, it is a good sign that you haven't done so. On the other hand, as N. T. Wright puts it, "once you declare that the only remaining bottle of water is poisoned, you condemn yourself to dying of thirst."

The Danger of Negative Religion

When the unclean spirit has gone out of a man, he passes through waterless places seeking rest, but he finds none. Then he says, "I will return to my house from which I came." And when he comes he finds it empty, swept, and put in order. Then he goes and brings with him seven other spirits more evil than himself, and they enter and dwell there; and the last state of that man becomes worse than the first. So shall it be also with this evil generation. Matt. 12:43-45, RSV.

Christianity is not a negative.

No one will ever be saved by what they stopped doing.

That is the lesson Jesus teaches in Matthew 12:43-45. His closing words refer to the wayward Jewish leaders of His time. By all counts those individuals, from a human perspective, were good people. For their religion they were willing to give up almost any pleasure. They had huge lists of forbidden things that they followed in order to clean up their lives.

In a sense they had swept their house clean and put it in order. Yet a few verses earlier we learned that they were plotting the death of Jesus (verse 14). By claiming that He was inspired by the devil (verse 27), they were committing the unpardonable sin (verses 31, 32).

Yet they were good people. Went to church every Sabbath. Gave tithes fanatically. And kept away from bad things to eat. Their problem, Jesus points out, is that they had gotten rid of the nasty things in their life, but hadn't let God fill it with the positive. As a result, they now had a religious devil (or seven of them) and were worse off than ever, because there is no sin so deceptive as the sin of goodness and pride in one's religious achievements.

Those kinds of people are still with us today. I once met a sanctimonious church member who was meaner than the devil. And I even encountered a vegan that could outdo the devil.

The focal point of Christianity is not so much getting rid of the evil (although that is certainly important, even if it is only preparatory) as it is letting God's Spirit into our lives with His fruit. Not emptiness, but fullness is God's goal for each of us. Not the negative but the positive. "The fruit of the Spirit is love, joy, peace, patience, kindness, goodness, faithfulness, gentleness, self-control" (Gal. 5:22, 23, RSV).

Christianity is a positive rather than a negative. It is fullness of the Spirit rather than a mere emptiness of evil.

April 28

Jesus: Sane or Insane

Then he went home; and the crowd came together again, so that they could not even eat. And when his family heard it, they went out to seize him, for people were saying, "He is beside himself." Mark 3:19-21, RSV.

It must be getting pretty bad when even your family thinks you are crazy. How is it, we may be wondering, that Jesus' family could reach such a conclusion?

If we think about it, possible reasons aren't too difficult to discover. For one, Jesus had left what was apparently a prosperous carpenter's business in Nazareth. And for what? To become a wandering teacher with no visible means of support?

Second, Jesus wasn't coming across as politically astute. In fact, He was obviously on a collision course with both the religious and secular leaders of the nation. And He didn't even seem to care.

Third, Jesus had formed His own little religious society—a strange one at that: fishermen, a reformed tax collector, a fanatical nationalist—riffraff. Those are not the kind of people you gather around yourself if you want to make an impact on society.

The family could only conclude that Jesus, for all His good qualities, was losing touch with reality. Beyond that, His course of action not only endangered Himself, but might eventually put the entire family at risk. Thus their attempt to take custody of Him so that they could keep Him away from trouble. From Jesus' perspective, we can only wonder if such experiences lie behind His saying that "a man's foes will be those of his own household" (Matt. 10:36, RSV).

What meaning does this episode have for us? Much, in every way. Madness is the verdict of the secular and even the religious world for all those who enthusiastically give their entire lives to a religious or philanthropic cause. J. D. Jones writes that "the world honours the man who for the sake of fame risks his life in battle; but if a man risks his life for souls for whom Christ died, it counts him a fool." And Halford Luccock adds, "'He is mad' has always been an ultimate tribute in Christian history to those who served, not two masters, but One. Paul won that distinguished service decoration. Festus cried, 'Paul, you are mad' (Acts 26:24)."

How is it with me?

Am I mad or just a plain old normal church member?

More Family Matters

Then His brothers and His mother came, and standing outside they sent to Him,
calling Him. And a multitude was sitting around Him; and they said to Him, "Look,
Your mother and Your brothers are outside seeking You." But He answered them,
saying, "Who is My mother, or My brothers?" Mark 3:31-33, NKJV.

Other than Mary and Joseph (to a lesser extent) we don't find much about Jesus' family in the New Testament. Matthew names His brothers as James, Joseph, Simon, and Judas and mentions sisters in passing (Matt. 13:55, 56).

John tells us that His "brothers did not believe in him" and that He couldn't be straightforward about His plans with them (John 7:5, 3; cf. 10, RSV). On the other hand, the birth and early childhood narratives of Matthew and Luke leave no doubt that Mary understood and believed in her Son's forthcoming mission.

The events of Mark 3:31-35, in which Jesus redefines His family, began in verse 21 when His brothers and mother show up to take custody of Him, fearing that He was losing His bearings. Thus the two family passages form a sandwich around the opposition of the Jerusalem scribes who believed that a devil possessed Him (verses 22-27).

The overall pattern of verses 21-35 finds unity in that both groups oppose Jesus and believe that He is under the control of an evil power. It is impossible to say if Mary shared that attitude, or if she was merely under the domineering influence of Jesus' brothers, who had no doubts about His problems. On the other hand, she may have become discouraged. After all, things weren't turning out as she probably imagined they would. Instead of Jesus acting like the promised Messiah, as far as she could see, He was merely making a mess out of His life and heading for catastrophe.

We can be thankful that Mark 3 is not the end of what we know about Jesus' family. Some, if not all, of His brothers eventually came to believe in Him, probably after His death and resurrection (Acts 1:14). After that, Jesus appeared to James (1 Cor. 15:7), who later became the leader of the Jerusalem church (Gal. 1:19; 2:9; Acts 12:17; 15:13; 21:18). He would also write the book that carries his name, while Jesus' brother Jude would write the letter that bears that title (James 1:1; Jude 1).

The moral of the story: Never give up on your family, even if they think you are nuts and try to block your walk with Jesus.

April 30

Redefining Family

And He looked around in a circle at those who sat about Him, and said, "Here are My mother and My brothers! For whoever does the will of God is My brother and My sister and mother." Mark 3:34, 35, NKJV.

It was His family's attempt to control Him that led Him to redefine the meaning of family. An underlying thought behind His reinterpretation of family is that certain relationships are actually closer than those of blood. It took such ties to bind together such men as Matthew the tax collector and Simon the Zealot. In their previous experience they would have welcomed each other's death. But now they belonged to the brotherhood of Jesus' inner circle. Their shared faith, dedication, goals, and experiences had welded them together with the other disciples as a family in Jesus that was infinitely more intimate for Him than His birth family.

Two basic ideas flow out of Jesus' interactions on the issue of family in Mark 3. The first is that those who follow God will eventually find themselves in conflict with those who live by the principles of the prince of this world.

That had certainly been the case with Jesus. In His desire to fulfill God's principles wholeheartedly, He had not only run into conflict with the religious and secular authorities but also with His flesh-and-blood family.

Jesus' teaching must have meant a great deal to Mark's first readers. Because of their Christianity, they also had faced rejection by their families, persecution, and even brutal deaths. But now they had a new family, brothers and sisters in the faith who shared their values.

The dynamic of both family rejection and inclusion in the family of God is still with the church in the twenty-first century. And it is still just as precious.

A second fundamental idea that emerges from Mark 3:34, 35 is that the basis for building God's new family in Jesus is following God's will: "Whoever does the will of God is My brother and My sister and mother."

In such dedication Jesus recognized genuine kinship; He identified a bond of union that transcended earthly relationships and would last throughout all eternity.

Praise God that I can belong to the family of God!

Teaching in Parables

That same day Jesus went out of the house and sat beside the sea. And great crowds gathered about him, so that he got into a boat and sat there; and the whole crowd stood on the beach. And he told them many things in parables. Matt. 13:1-3, RSV.

Midway through Jesus' ministry we find two major transitions. One had to do with location and the second with His method of teaching.

His early teaching had largely taken place in the synagogue. That was understandable, because it was the place where the Jewish people expected to hear God's Word expounded. But the opposition to Jesus' teaching made it prudent to avoid what for Him had become places of confrontation. Beyond that, His popularity with the people had so increased that no synagogue could hold the crowds. Thus in Matthew 13 we find Him teaching by the lakeside.

Not only did He have a new venue for His teaching, but also a new methodology: "He taught them many things in parables." It isn't that He hadn't ever used parables before, but as opposition increased He began to employ them more.

Jesus wasn't the first Jewish teacher to use parables, but writes Klyne R. Snodgrass, "there is no evidence of anyone prior to Jesus using parables as consistently, creatively and effectively as he did."

Someone has aptly described a parable as "an earthly story with a heavenly meaning." It employs an illustration of something familiar on earth to help people grasp a heavenly or spiritual reality.

Parable teaching had several advantages. For one thing, it was safe. With some out to destroy Him, by the use of parables Jesus could teach in a manner that did not unduly alienate His enemies or provide them with concrete words that they could use against Him.

A second advantage is that people love stories, and the Jews of old were no exception. Every preacher knows the power of a story to hold attention.

But perhaps their greatest value is their ongoing teaching function. Ellen White put it nicely when she wrote that "afterward, as they looked upon the objects that illustrated His lessons, they recalled the words of the divine Teacher. To minds that were open to the Holy Spirit, the significance of the Saviour's teaching unfolded more and more. Mysteries grew clear, and that which had been hard to grasp became evident" (*Christ's Object Lessons*, p. 21).

May 2

A Lesson in Evangelism, Part 1

A sower went out to sow. And as he sowed, some seeds fell along the path, and the birds came and devoured them. Other seeds fell on rocky ground, where they had not much soil, and immediately they sprang up, since they had no depth of soil, but when the sun rose they were scorched; and since they had no root they withered away. Other seeds fell upon thorns, and the thorns grew up and choked them. Other seeds fell on good soil and brought forth grain, some a hundredfold, some sixty, some thirty.
Matt. 13:3-8, RSV.

Parables always have a context. The rejection of Jesus by so many in Matthew 11 and 12 not only led to a radical shift in His teaching methodology in chapter 13, but also dictated the content of the parables. After all, Matthew faces a dilemma as he writes his Gospel several decades after Christ's death. How is it that so many spurned the Messiah? That rejection seems to go against Jewish eschatological expectations. Why do some respond to Jesus, while most do not?

Jesus' answer begins with the parable of the four types of soil. In essence, He teaches that the root of the trouble does not lie with God. After all, He has made provision for the preaching of the gospel to all types of people (soils), but all do not respond in the same way.

Two constants continue throughout the parable. First the sowing seems to be the same for all types of soil. They all get the same treatment, the same Word. Second, all four types hear the message. Where they differ is not in hearing but in responding. One point the four types share is that they are all *potential* disciples in the sense of being followers of Christ's message. Whether potentiality advances to actuality is not in hearing the Word but in responding to it.

In the parable Jesus sets forth four types of soil, three of which fail in developing to maturity and one in which the Word succeeds. We are left with two impressions after reading this parable. First, those who receive the Word and remain faithful are definitely in the minority. That insight lines up with the experience of Jesus' first hearers and with the reality of evangelism in our day. Second, fruition depends upon human response.

The overall message of the parable of the sower to those early disciples and to us is not to give up just because evangelistic results look so meager. Our responsibility is to sow the Word. And if we do so consistently there will be results.

The end lesson: Keep on sowing in spite of the level of outward success.

A Lesson in Evangelism, Part 2

Hear ye therefore the parable of the sower. Matt. 13:18.

In Matthew 13:18-23 we find something quite rare in the Gospels: Jesus explaining each part of His parable of the sower found in verses 3-8. The lesson is of crucial importance both to those disciples and to us because it is all too easy to get discouraged in evangelistic outreach and give up, thinking that the problem must be in something we are doing wrong. No, says Jesus. The fault is in the soil.

Some individuals are pathway hearers or no-growth people. The fields of Palestine tended to consist of long, narrow strips divided by pathways. Anybody who has ever had a vegetable garden knows that such pathways soon come to be packed soil in which even weeds have a difficult time growing. Similarly, some hearers' hearts and minds have been hardened. They have an impenetrable shell of emotional and intellectual defenses that refuse entrance of the gospel message. Satan is all too willing to snatch it away before it has a chance to take root.

Other people are shallow-growth people, represented by shallow soil underlaid by a sheet of rock. Such hearers have some good soil, some hope. They look like a successful plant at first, but have no adequate possibility for root growth. Such individuals, Jesus says, are shallow-soil people. They have potential, but they don't allow God's Word to enter deeply into their emotions and intellect. It doesn't become the controlling force in their life. As a result, when trouble comes they just fade away like an inadequately rooted plant in the full glare of the summer sun.

Still other people are stunted-growth hearers. Any gardener knows that weeds grow faster than vegetables. And if not controlled, they will crowd out the good stuff. Such people first respond to the gospel message, then get strangled by the things of this world. Jesus noted that it is the love of things that crowds out and eventually kills their religious experience.

It is only after that dismal catalog of potential Christians who fail in one way or another that Jesus comes to the full-growth people who bear fruit for the kingdom. They may not be as consistent or as plentiful as the sower may desire, but they will emerge. Failure in evangelism should not cause us to become discouraged. As long as there is sowing, there will be reaping.

The end lesson: keep on sowing in spite of whatever the level of apparent success.

May 4

Parables: A Probing
Teaching Technique

Then the disciples came and said to him, "Why do you speak to them in parables?"
And he answered them, "To you it is given to know the secrets of the kingdom of
heaven, but to them it has not been given. For to the one who has, more will be
given, and he will have an abundance, but from the one who has not, even what he
has will be taken away. This is why I speak to them in parables, because seeing they
do not see, and hearing they do not hear, nor do they understand. . . . But blessed are
your eyes, for they see, and your ears, for they hear." Matt. 13:10-16, ESV.

Now here is a perplexing statement. Was Jesus really saying that He taught in parables to hide the truth rather than make it clear to all His hearers? What did He mean when He told His disciples, "To you has been given the secret of the kingdom of God, but for those outside everything is in parables; so that they may indeed see but not perceive, and may indeed hear but not understand; lest they should turn again, and be forgiven" (Mark 4:11, 12, RSV)?

Mark's version is even more mystifying than Matthew's. After all, both John and Jesus brought their ministries into the public with calls to repentance. Did Jesus speak in parables to make ideas clearer or to muddle truth in such a way that people wouldn't be able to understand and repent? Did He really desire them to remain in their lost state?

His statements have troubled people across time. They seem to contradict the very reason that He used parables.

One way of resolving the problem is to remember that Jesus was simultaneously speaking to at least four groups of people in the same audience: (1) the 12 disciples, (2) a believing but fluctuating larger group of followers, (3) the "crowd," which included many who were curious but did not necessarily believe, and (4) His adversaries.

In that context parables had the function of dividing the audience between those who were really interested and those seeking entertainment. Jesus used parables as a method to get His hearers to take hold of the topic and wrestle with it in their minds so that they could arrive at a fuller understanding. He wanted them to think through the implications of the story.

Conversely, as William Barclay puts it, "the parable *conceals truth from those who are either too lazy to think or too blind through prejudice to see.*" This method of teaching became a kind of judgment as it sifted out the tares from the wheat, those whose thoughts were of this world and those who were spiritually minded.

The end lesson: God wants me to wrestle with the great truths of His Word.

Why Is the Church Messed Up?

Another parable He put forth to them, saying: "The kingdom of heaven is like a man who sowed good seed in his field; but while men slept, his enemy came and sowed tares among the wheat and went his way. But when the grain had sprouted and produced a crop, then the tares also appeared. So the servants of the owner came and said to him, 'Sir, did you not sow good seed in your field? How then does it have tares?' He said to them, 'An enemy has done this.' The servants said to him, 'Do you want us then to go and gather them up?' But he said, 'No, lest while you gather up the tares you also uproot the wheat with them. Let both grow together until the harvest, and at the time of harvest I will say to the reapers, "First gather together the tares and bind them in bundles to burn them, but gather the wheat into my barn."'"
Matt. 13:24-30, NKJV.

Have you ever noticed that the church is all messed up? That it has some members who are less than they should be? That some of them are downright hypocrites?

The parable of the weeds (tares) helps us understand the problem from God's perspective. It carries the explanation of the rejection of Jesus a bit further than the parable of the four soils. While the soils emphasize the perversity of human reaction, the weeds parable points beyond the human realm to the supernatural activity of the devil, to the cosmic conflict between Christ and Satan. Thus the rejection of Jesus results not only from human irresponsibility, but also the work of the devil (the enemy of verses 28, 39).

The weeds parable also moves the activity of the devil and the rejection of Christ and His principles right into the church. Jesus provided the parable to help Christians down through the ages to understand that the church is not perfect. It is a mixture of weeds (apparent Christians) and wheat (genuine Christians), a condition that will continue to exist until the Second Advent harvest. That does not imply that some weeds should not be removed through excommunication (see Matt. 18:15-20), but rather that in most cases human discernment will not be adequate to carry out the weeding process.

And that brings us to a final lesson in the parable of the weeds: God did not make us judges of our brothers and sisters in the church, except in cases of open sin. Congregations across history have found themselves torn up and destroyed by those who take over the prerogatives of God in condemning and judging others. Don't worry, Jesus says, God will make things right in the end. Meanwhile, we need to accept the church as what Christ told us it would be— less than perfect.

May 6

The Mystery of It All

The kingdom of God is like a man who casts seed upon the soil; and he goes to bed at night and gets up by day, and the seed sprouts and grows—how, he himself does not know. The soil produces crops by itself; first the blade, then the head, then the mature grain in the head. Mark 4:26-28, NASB.

The miracle of it all! One day you have dirt and a dead-looking little seed. A week later you have a growing plant!

We should see the parable of the growing seed as an extension of the parable of the sower (Matt. 13:3-8; Mark 4:1-20), especially the last part, which deals with the fruitfulness of good soil. All in all, the parable of the sower was rather discouraging, since it predominantly spoke of failure for the person sowing the gospel seed, with only one fourth of the hearers truly accepting the Word.

The parable of the growing seed is in one sense a correction provided by Jesus as an encouragement to those tempted to feel discouraged with the amount of fruitless labor they are expending on those with "hearing" problems. The bottom line in the parable of the growing seed is that things are happening, even when it doesn't look that way—that God is growing His kingdom in the hearts of people even as we sleep. It is a process that we don't understand, but one that is evident in germination and the developing fruit.

Ellen White sets forth that truth in a way that I have found encouraging throughout the years. Speaking of the resurrection day, she writes, "All the perplexities of life's experience will then be made plain. Where to us have appeared only confusion and disappointment, broken purposes and thwarted plans, will be seen a grand, overruling, victorious purpose, a divine harmony.

"There all who have wrought with unselfish spirit will behold the fruit of their labors. . . . How little of the result of the world's noblest work is in this life manifest to the doer! How many toil unselfishly and unweariedly for those who pass beyond their reach and knowledge! Parents and teachers lie down in their last sleep, their lifework seeming to have been wrought in vain; they know not that their faithfulness has unsealed springs of blessing that can never cease to flow. . . . Men sow the seed from which, above their graves, others reap blessed harvests. . . . They are content here to know that they have set in motion agencies for good. In the hereafter the action and reaction of all these will be seen" (*Education*, p. 305).

The bottom line: don't be discouraged by what you see. The Holy Spirit is working in ways we do not understand.

Small Beginnings Make a Big Difference

The kingdom of heaven is like a grain of mustard seed which a man took and sowed in his field; it is the smallest of all seeds, but when it has grown it is the greatest of shrubs and becomes a tree, so that the birds of the air come and make nests in its branches. . . . The kingdom of heaven is like leaven which a woman took and hid in three measures of flour, till it was all leavened. Matt. 13:31-33, RSV.

Have you ever felt insignificant? Have you ever concluded that your church is too small and puny to make a difference?

I suffer from both kinds of insignificances as I drive through a great city. It makes me wonder, "What is the use in even trying?"

Christ's earliest disciples must have felt that way. The Jewish leadership must have helped them in their insecurity by pointing out what a motley little crew they were—unlearned peasants and fishermen. And they intimated that Jesus couldn't possibly be the Messiah. His kingdom would never amount to anything.

By outward appearances the Jews were right.

It is in the face of all that smallness that Jesus gave the parable of the mustard seed. It wasn't actually the tiniest seed in Palestine, but it was the smallest one cultivated. Yet it became the largest of the cultivated shrubs, reaching a height of from 10-12 feet.

That little beginnings can make a difference is the lesson of the mustard seed. They can change the world. Outwardly the church of Jesus' day was miserably insignificant. Yet by the end of His life Jesus was telling the disciples to take Christianity to all the world (Matt. 28:19, 20). And they did, thereby illustrating the truth of the mustard seed.

The lesson: we can make a difference—both as a group and as individuals. Don't be put off by small beginnings, but put your heart and soul into God's work. It is by such dedication that Christ's message has spread to all corners of the earth.

The parable of the leaven is also about kingdom growth, but this time in the hearts and lives of individuals. Just as a bit of yeast or leaven transforms the flour into which it is kneaded, so the gospel transforms every part of a person's life.

The interesting thing about leaven is that it is a symbol of evil in the Old Testament. Hardly looks like one for righteousness. But the truth is that there are two leavens in the world—that of Christ and that of the devil. Therefore choose your yeast carefully.

Christianity Is No Bargain

The kingdom of heaven is like treasure hidden in a field, which a man found and covered up; then in his joy he goes and sells all that he has and buys that field. Again, the kingdom of heaven is like a merchant in search of fine pearls, who, on finding one pearl of great value, went and sold all that he had and bought it.

Matt. 13:44-46, RSV.

We all love a bargain. Some people will stand outside a store for hours, waiting until it opens, just to get a good deal. In short, they want to pay less for something than it is worth.

From the perspective of the bargain hunter Christianity is a really bad deal.

The parables of the hidden treasure and the pearl of great price bring us back to the human response factor in the rejection of Jesus that He presented in the parable of the four soils. It is little wonder that Jesus' kingdom was not popular with the majority, including religious leaders. And it's still not.

Why? Because the cost of accepting Jesus as Christ and Lord is nothing less than all we have and all we are. He will later tell His disciples that the price of the kingdom is the crucifixion of their very selves (Matt. 16:24, 25).

Thus Dietrich Bonhoeffer, whose life ended when he was executed for seeking to put an end to Hitler's madness, writes that "when Christ calls a man, he bids him come and die." There is no cheap grace—no bargains in this store. True Christians are those who see the value of what Christ offers and willingly give up all that they have and are to become a part of it. That is no bargain.

But there are bargain hunters hanging around the church. They want the pearl—the treasure—but only at a discounted price. That perspective goes a long way toward helping us understand the church. Only some of its members have given *all*. Others are merely weeds masquerading as wheat in the Lord's garden. To become genuine wheat a person must be willing to abandon *all* for the kingdom.

Of course, the lack of bargainhood also explains why true Christianity has always been and will always be a minority religion.

But if we really see what Christ has to offer, perhaps we will recognize that it actually is a bargain indeed. What do I give up? One short little life that will end in death and is beset by trouble throughout. For what? Eternal life in a world that knows no sickness or pain or sorrow (Rev. 21:1-4).

Not a bad bargain after all.

The Parable That Brought Me
Back to the Church

Once again, the kingdom of heaven is like a net that was let down into the lake and caught all kinds of fish. When it was full, the fishermen pulled it up on the shore. Then they sat down and collected the good fish in baskets, but threw the bad away. This is how it will be at the end of the age. The angels will come and separate the wicked from the righteous. Matt. 13:47-49, NIV.

I am a perfectionist at heart. I not only desired to live a perfect (defined as sinless) life, but I wanted to pastor the perfect church. Converted from agnosticism at the age of 19, I had ideals that were of the highest order. That was OK, but mine were not plugged into biblical reality.

After several years in the pastorate I could only conclude that the churches I was serving were really messed up. They weren't perfect! And I was beginning to have some doubts about myself. My solution: quit. Not only quit but study philosophy to find the real meaning of life. Mine was to be a progressive journey away from the church and what I perceived as Christianity.

There was only one problem—the escape hatch didn't work. At the end of six years of study I had come to the conclusion that philosophy held no ultimate answers on the meaning of life. And since I had already explored the Eastern religions for possible hope and had found them wanting, I was somewhat perplexed.

The only answer that I could envision was a return to the happy hedonism that I had left behind at age 19. At least that held short-term meaning. "Eat, drink and be merry, for tomorrow we die." "If it feels good, do it!" But from experience I already knew the emptiness of that solution. I really wanted meaning.

To put it mildly, I was extremely frustrated. It was at that point in my journey that three things happened at about the same time. One of them led me back to Matthew 13:47-49 and the parable of the net. My secular Jewish mentor by accident helped me see that every religious movement is made up of true believers and those just along for the ride, including cultural "Christians."

Suddenly the "net" sprang into my mind. Why didn't I see it sooner? Jesus had clarified part of my problem 2,000 years earlier. The church has always been, and until the end will be, a mixed bag of those who really believe and have given up all for the kingdom and those masquerading.

That, I thought, is the kind of congregations I had known. And with that thought I was on my way back to the church.

May 10

When Disciples Become Apostles

These twelve Jesus sent out with the following instructions: "Do not go among the Gentiles or enter any town of the Samaritans. Go rather to the lost sheep of Israel. As you go, proclaim this message: 'The kingdom of heaven has come near.' Heal the sick, raise the dead, cleanse those who have leprosy, drive out demons. Freely you have received, freely give." Matt. 10:5-8, NIV.

The first four verses of Matthew 10 list the names of the 12 disciples, whom Jesus now calls "apostles." Here we have a shift in terminology that points to a change in the role of the twelve. Up to then they had been "disciples," learners or followers. But now Jesus identifies them as "apostles," from the Greek *apostolos*, meaning "one sent as a messenger." It is one thing to be a follower of a person with a message, but quite another to receive the responsibility of being the messenger.

Prior to this time the twelve have been like passengers in a car. Now Jesus is handing them the keys. And just as riders often don't pay much attention to exactly how things are done in varying circumstances—when to make this turn and that—and thus need a bit of careful instruction by their parents before they set out on their maiden voyage, so it is that Jesus has some very definite counsel on how the twelve should carry out their mission.

First, He counsels, stick with Jewish audiences. Don't even attempt to go to the Samaritans or Gentiles.

That sounds like a strange command from a Man who came as Savior of the whole world. But Jesus had His reasons. For one thing, the disciples weren't ready mentally to deal with the Gentiles. Even years later, Peter in Acts 10 would find it almost impossible to enter the house of a Gentile until God gave him a revelation that it was all right. And afterward he still had to repeatedly defend his actions.

A more important reason for not going to the Gentiles was because of Jewish prejudice itself. If Jesus' followers had aggressively begun working among the Gentiles, no self-respecting Jew would have paid them any attention. It would have confirmed Jesus' enemies' suspicions that He was in league with the devil.

The widening of mission will come, as demonstrated by the book of Acts. But meanwhile, Jesus has provided us with an important evangelistic hint. Namely, always start by putting your first energies into that which is close at hand rather than indulging in useless dreams about future "glory" in some far-off land.

The Downside of Apostleship

Behold, I send you forth as sheep in the midst of wolves: be ye therefore wise as serpents, and harmless as doves. But beware of men. Matt. 10:16, 17.

Some have felt that Jesus got it all backward. They have met some church members who have been harmless as serpents and wise as doves. There may be some like that in your congregation. And with a little Spirit-guided introspection we might discover those characteristics in ourselves.

But Jesus didn't have it backward. He knew what He was talking about. Matthew 10 is the second of His recorded sermons in the first Gospel. The initial one was the Sermon on the Mount, in which He set forth the principles of His kingdom. This one finds Jesus instructing His disciples to preach those principles as He sends them out on their first independent evangelistic tour.

So far the instruction has been very encouraging. Not only were they to preach the message, but, like Jesus, they were to "heal the sick, cleanse the lepers, raise the dead, [and] cast out devils" (Matt. 10:8). It sounded like a great deal. They were going to get to do some really neat things. If all went well, they would have power and authority. People, they must have thought, would seek them out. Everything would be wonderful.

But! And "but" is one of the most important words in our vocabulary. "But" that wasn't the whole story. The reason that they needed to be wise as serpents and harmless as doves soon showed up in Jesus' sermon in the words "but beware of men."

The disciples would have notoriety all right, but it wouldn't all be positive. After all, it hadn't been thus far in the experience of Jesus. He preached a countercultural message that the individuals already running things in the Jewish world—the high priests, Pharisees, scribes, and the Sanhedrin—would view as an outright challenge to their position.

He had not made friends by shouting out in public, "You have been told in the past, but I say unto you." His message confronted the powers that be. And they would react, eventually putting Jesus on the cross.

And now Jesus is telling His followers to do and say the same things. They also would be resisted. As a result, they would need the wisdom of a serpent and the tranquil personality of a dove as they navigated through a complex world.

May 12

The Upside of Persecution

Beware of men; for they will deliver you up to councils, and flog you in their syna-
gogues. . . . When they deliver you up, do not be anxious how you are to speak or
what you are to say; for what you are to say will be given to you in that hour; for it
is not you who speak, but the Spirit of your Father speaking through you. . . . You
will be hated by all for my name's sake. But he who endures to the end will be saved.
Matt. 10:17-22, RSV.

Not a particularly happy message! You will preach peace, but end up receiving violent treatment.

Those disciples with ears to hear must have thought that they were experiencing echoes of the final beatitude. "Blessed are those who are persecuted for
righteousness' sake, for theirs is the kingdom of heaven. Blessed are you when
men revile you and persecute you and utter all kinds of evil against you falsely
on my account. Rejoice and be glad, for your reward is great in heaven, for
so men persecuted the prophets who were before you" (Matt. 5:10, 11, RSV).
Luke's version of those statements tells us that we should "leap for joy" when all
those evil things happen to us because of our stand for Jesus (Luke 6:23).

One thing you may never have noticed about that beatitude is that it is the
only one repeated. Jesus gives a double dose of the "blessed are you when persecuted" message, undoubtedly because it was so distasteful and difficult to grasp.

But the blessing is there. Most readers of this page are probably not being persecuted today. But some will encounter it from their families as they
take their stand for Jesus. Others are feeling the brunt of the evil one's power
because they have decided to live for Jesus in the workplace. And still others
because they live under political forces that oppose the principles of Christianity. And if you are safe now, Revelation 13 is a clear prophecy that things will
get more lively in the persecution realm as earth nears the end of its course and
the forces of evil make their final attempts to crush Christ's followers.

Meanwhile, according to Jesus in Matthew 10, those followers will have no
need to fear. Jesus will be at their side, even giving them words to say in time
of crises. And when they have endured "to the end" they "will be saved." That
is the upside of persecution.

Dear Lord, help me to be a faithful messenger of Your Word. Help me in
times of peace and in times of trouble. Thank You.

No Fear

A disciple is not above his teacher, nor a servant above his master. It is enough for the disciple to be like his teacher, and the servant like his master. If they have called the master of the house Beelzebul, how much more will they malign those of his household. So have no fear. Matt. 10:24-26, ESV.

No fear! Really? Does Jesus know what He is talking about? Has He gone off the track? After all, He had just listed all kinds of things that would happen to them in verses 17-23. In verses 24 and 25 He noted that they would not be above Him but would be persecuted like He was. And He already knew that His life was heading toward a Roman cross. Yet He instructs His disciples to have "no fear."

"No fear" and the reasons for it will dominate this part of Jesus' sermon on mission, being specifically mentioned three times in verses 26, 28, and 31. The obvious fact is that from a human perspective the followers of Jesus have a great deal they could fear, since they will face rejection, persecution, and even death. But still He tells them to have "no fear."

Here all of us who have accepted Christ need to listen up. We often get cold feet and exuberant intestines (signs of fear) at the slightest rejection because of our faith or when we need to speak up for it in difficult contexts. And if what Jesus says is true, then it could get a lot worse. Yet He says "no fear" or "fear not." How can He be so sure of that command? How can He say "have no fear" in the face of things inherently filled with fear?

In verses 26-31 He will provide three forceful answers to those crucial questions. First, we are not to fear "for nothing is covered that will not be revealed, or hidden that will not be known" (Matt. 10:26, RSV).

In other words, things will not always be as they are now. We see things through a cloud here, but in the future we will perceive them as they really are. Then truth will triumph and God and His people will stand vindicated. At that point in time the principles of the persecutor and the Christian heroism of the believing witness will manifest their true value, and each will receive their due reward.

Witnesses for Christ can have "no fear" because they know that the judgments of eternity will correct the judgments of time.

More No Fear

Fear not them which kill the body, but are not able to kill the soul: but rather fear him which is able to destroy both soul and body in hell. Matt. 10:28.

N o fear again! "Fear not them which kill the body, but are not able to kill the soul." Taken in the context in Matthew 10, those who can "kill the body" are those persecutors who will eventually put several of the disciples to death (see verses 17-23). Those oppressors may be able to put people to death, but they are unable to destroy the person eternally. Following death and sleep in the grave (Dan. 12:2) there comes a resurrection (see 1 Thess. 4:13-18).

It is that hope of resurrection that made the cowardly disciples fearless. After they met the resurrected Christ who claimed to have the keys to death and the grave (Rev. 1:18) and realized that because He had risen, they would also, they were absolutely unafraid.

Their gospel became that Jesus not only died, but that He resurrected on the third day (1 Cor. 15:1-4). His resurrection served as a guarantee of their own at the end of time (verses 51-53). The resurrected Christ became the theme of apostolic preaching (Acts 2:24; 3:15; 5:30). That hope made the apostles "fearless." They had "no fear" because their enemies could kill their bodies but could not destroy them as individuals. Thus they had "no fear" because of the resurrection hope.

On the other hand, there is someone whom we should fear. That is "him which is able to destroy both soul and body in hell"—God Himself. Here we need to take a look at the word "soul." The Bible does not hold to the Greek belief that individuals consist of a material body and an immortal soul. To the contrary, immortality is a characteristic of God Himself (1 Tim. 6:16) that will not be bestowed on Christ's followers until the resurrection at the Second Advent (1 Cor. 15:51-53).

The soul, meanwhile, is merely the whole person. Thus we find in Genesis 2:7 that "the Lord God formed man of the dust of the ground [the material aspect], and breathed into his nostrils the breath [or spirit] of life; and man became a living soul." The Revised Standard Version and most other versions translate the Hebrew word for "soul" as "a living being." The soul is nothing less and nothing more than a living being or person. And it is only God who can eradicate a person eternally, a task called the "second death," the punishment of the wicked in the lake of fire that totally destroys them at the end of the millennium.

Because they serve God, Christians can have "no fear," even in the midst of trouble.

Still More No Fear

Are not two sparrows sold for a penny? And not one of them will fall to the ground without your Father's will. But even the hairs of your head are all numbered. Fear not, therefore; you are of more value than many sparrows. Matt. 10:29-31, RSV.

I have been making God's job easier for the past few years in the hair-counting arena. A bad hair day for me is now "hair" in the singular. But still I have never taken the time to count what's left.

In fact, I don't know of anyone who has ever numbered the hairs they have attached to their cranium. And here we come to Jesus' point. Namely, that the Creator-God knows us far more intimately than we ever will ourselves. In short, He cares.

Christ's main illustration in today's reading is just as illuminating about the concern of the Father. "Are not two sparrows sold for a penny?" He asks. Now a penny was about the smallest coin in a Jewish wallet. Being one sixteenth of a denarius, it wasn't worth much. And you could buy two sparrows with only one penny.

Luke's Gospel puts it a bit differently, noting that five of the little birds sold for two pennies (Luke 12:6). That tidbit of information makes the illustration even more powerful. Apparently the sparrow market operated on the same principle as many stores do today. If you were willing to spend a penny you got two birds, but if you spent two pennies you could get double the birds with an extra one thrown in for free. What a bargain! If we combine Matthew's and Luke's accounts we realize that God cares even for the sparrow that had no value at all. Or as one writer has pointed out, "even the forgotten sparrow is dear to God."

So why should Christ's followers have no fear? Because they are of infinitely more value than many sparrows and hairs, and if God cares for them we can be sure that He has far more concern for us.

So there we have it. As Christians we should have no fear because:

1. The judgments of eternity will set things straight and correct those of time (Matt. 10:26, 27).
2. People really can't do anything to harm us permanently (verse 28).
3. And God cares for each of us, including those who seem to be forgotten by the world and even the church (verses 29-31).

We can rejoice today that we have a God who cares, a God who is powerful, a God who will make all things right in the end.

May 16

More on Fear

Therefore whoever confesses Me before men, him I will also confess before My Father who is in heaven. But whoever denies Me before men, him I will also deny before My Father who is in heaven. Matt. 10:32, 33, NKJV.

It doesn't look as if we are through with fear yet. Now, I know that today's passage does not use the word "fear," but fear is in the context and underlies the only reason that a believer would not "confess" or "acknowledge" or "stand up" for Jesus. *The Message* vividly brings out the dynamic of fear undergirding the passage: "Stand up for me against world opinion and I'll stand up for you before my Father in heaven. If you turn tail and run, do you think I'll cover for you?"

While Jesus has pounded home three times that His followers don't need to fear, we still find ourselves tempted that way. I am. Of course, there is no one who is out to take my life right now or to do me physical harm. But if I really say what I think they might make fun of me or consider me unsophisticated, some kind of hayseed who should have been born 200 years ago. It is hard for us humans not to fear—it seems to be in our very bones.

But if we let Christ handle our fears about our precious selves, the rewards are great. Those who stand up for Christ have an advocate in heaven. That's good news on the days we are strong, but frightening on those that we fail.

And here the good news gets even better. The Jesus of grace is even willing to stand up for us when we have denied Him if we confess our sin and rededicate ourselves to His "no fear" agenda. Peter discovered that grace when he fell flat on his face the evening before the Crucifixion. He not only denied Jesus in the face of fear, but cursed and swore that he didn't know Him. That forceful testimony convinced his hearers.

The good news is that Peter eventually found his knees and was restored again. For the rest of his life he confessed his Lord (although not perfectly) until he finally met crucifixion himself.

And further good news is that Christ willingly confesses us before the Father when we acknowledge Him in our words and lives. But the bad news is that if we persistently choose to deny Him in our daily walk, we only hurt ourselves in the long run.

I suppose the only question I need to ask myself is "Whom should I fear most—other people or God?"

Fearful Decisions

Do not think that I have come to bring peace on earth; I have not come to bring peace, but a sword. For I have come to set a man against his father, and a daughter against her mother, and a daughter-in-law against her mother-in-law; and a man's foes will be those of his own household. He who loves father or mother more than me is not worthy of me. Matt. 10:34-37, RSV.

That is quite a statement from One called the "Prince of Peace" (Isa. 9:6). Here we find Jesus at His realistic best. His followers may not need to fear, but there is plenty about which to be fearful, including in one's own family when some decide to walk with Him in line with His principles, while others choose to go against Him and His principles, each with strong views on the topic.

His statement that "I have come to set a man against his father, and a daughter against her mother, and a daughter-in-law against her mother-in-law" probably impacted His hearers at two levels at the same time. On level one Jesus was using language familiar to His Jewish audience. The prophet Micah had written: "The son treats the father with contempt, the daughter rises up against her mother, the daughter-in-law against her mother-in-law; a man's enemies are the men of his own house" (Micah 7:6, RSV).

The rabbis took that verse and applied it to the time of the Messiah (*m. Sotah* 9:15). Again, they taught that one of the events to take place at the coming of the Messiah would be division within families. Thus we read: "When Messiah comes" "daughters will rise up against their mothers, and daughters-in-law against their mothers-in-law" (*b. Sanhedrin* 97:a).

With that background in mind, Jesus may have been making a Messianic claim in a place and a manner that the modern casual reader doesn't see. But a first-century Jew may have easily made the connection.

More on the surface is Jesus' teaching that He will be absolutely first in the life of every true follower. He will be more important than even life's closest human relationships, more important than anything.

Jesus is setting forth no abstract theoretical problem. All through time individuals have had to make excruciating decisions to follow Him in the face of the objection of a spouse, or of children, or of the larger community. Such choices are among the most painful we ever have to make. Yet they are just as important for eternal life as they are painful.

Lord, give me grace to get my priorities right. Amen.

Fear's Solution

He who does not take his cross and follow me is not worthy of me. He who finds his life will lose it, and he who loses his life for my sake will find it. Matt. 10:38, 39, RSV.

A cross was no laughing matter or casual symbol in the time of Jesus. He and His disciples knew what it stood for. In A.D. 7 Judas of Galilee had led a revolt against Rome. After the general Varus had broken the revolt, he had crucified some 2,000 Jews. So that the Jews would get the message, Varus placed their crosses along the roadsides of Galilee.

The idea of being crucified doesn't do much to our twenty-first-century imaginations.

We have never seen a crucifixion. But not the disciples. When they saw a knot of Roman soldiers escorting a person through town carrying or dragging part of a cross, they recognized it as a one-way trip. They knew the cross to be the cruelest and most humiliating of deaths—and one that the ruling Romans were more than willing to use frequently to keep troublesome areas such as Palestine under control.

Yet here was Jesus telling His uncomprehending disciples that every Christian would have a cross. They must have wondered what He was talking about. After all, they were expecting to hold high level positions in His government, not be criminals suffering crucifixion. While at the moment they didn't understand, they would in the years ahead.

More incomprehensible yet was Jesus telling them that taking up their cross would lead to life, that "he who finds his life will lose it, and he who loses his life for my sake will find it."

But what was puzzling then would become clearer after Jesus experienced His own cross and the apostles began teaching the message of the cross. It declares not that all of us will die on literal crosses, but that our self-centered way of living and thinking will come to an end and we will live for God's kingdom rather than for our self-centered and selfish goals. Paul put it succinctly when he penned: "I am crucified with Christ: nevertheless I live; yet not I, but Christ liveth in me: and the life which I now live in the flesh I live by the faith of the Son of God, who loved me, and gave himself for me" (Gal. 2:20).

One of the paradoxes of life is that by clinging to our selfish goals we lose out in the end. But by living the way of the cross we find life eternal. And it is when we recognize that fact that the despicable cross puts an end to (crucifies) all fear.

Cup-of-Water Religion

Whoever gives to one of these little ones even a cup of cold water because he is a disciple, truly, I say to you, he shall not lose his reward. Matt. 10:42, RSV.

Too many of us have it all backward. We think of greatness in the kingdom as doing some strenuous thing for the Lord. Perhaps we consider it as having the most amount of inspired writings stored up in our heads so that we have a Bible answer for every question that comes up. Or we might regard it as correct worship in church or spending our thoughtful hour with Jesus each day or making great exertions in missionary outreach.

We have all kinds of theories on the topic. But most of them not only put our "selves" at the center of the "great" venture, but they miss the point. True Christianity, as we noted earlier, is letting Jesus live out His heart of love in our lives every day. The items listed above may or may not be significant, depending on how we relate to them, but something as simple as passing out a cup of cold water to the thirsty is always important.

Our religious ideas get into trouble when we take the initiative of separating Jesus' two great commandments. We get all worked up about honoring God with all our hearts, minds, and souls (Matt. 22:37), but then sail through life not loving our neighbors as ourselves (verse 39). Sometimes we are even hard and cruel to them in the name of Christ if they are not doing what we think is right.

And here we make the mistake of religionists down through the ages. The ancient Jews were like us. They got all excited about the outward focus of religion, but forgot what it was supposed to accomplish in their lives. Thus Micah asks, "With what shall I come before the Lord, and bow down myself before God on high?" The answer was not some great offering. Rather, "He has showed you, O man, what is good; and what does the Lord require of you but to do justice, and to love kindness, and to walk humbly with your God?" (Micah 6:6, 8, RSV). And James writes that "religion that is pure and undefiled before God and the Father is this: to visit orphans and widows in their affliction, and to keep oneself unstained from the world" (James 1:27, RSV).

All too many are excellent on the "unstained" part of that text but miss the rest of it. Jesus didn't. He had to deal with "unstained" Pharisees daily. It is in that context that He set forth His cup-of-cold water theology. People who live His life of love will find their reward in God's kingdom.

May 20

Spiritual Nearsightedness

*And he told them a parable, saying, "The land of a rich man brought forth plenti-
fully; and he thought to himself, 'What shall I do, for I have nowhere to store my
crops?' And he said, 'I will do this: I will pull down my barns, and build larger ones;
and there I will store all my grain and my goods. And I will say to my soul, Soul, you
have ample goods laid up for many years; take your ease, eat, drink, be merry.' But
God said to him, 'Fool! This night your soul is required of you; and the things you
have prepared, whose will they be?' So is he who lays up treasure for himself, and is
not rich toward God." Luke 12:16-21, RSV.*

Nothing like having a conversation with yourself. The good news in that
approach is that at last you have found someone who agrees with you.
The bad news is that "both of you" might be wrong. Conversations with ourselves have no room for a reality check. They just might be based on nearsight-
edness.

Jesus is the ultimate reality checker. He is the ultimate optometrist and
ophthalmologist to fix our eyes for better vision.

Someone has said that money is like seawater: the more you drink, the
thirstier you become. That is certainly the case with the man talking to himself
in today's passage. Never once did it seem to come to his mind that he might
share some of his "bounty" with others less fortunate than himself. Helping
others transcended his mental world. The really important thing was taking
care of himself. And that meant getting more and more and more so that he
could build better and better and bigger and bigger barns so that he could get
still more and more and more.

He never saw beyond this world. And he made all his plans accordingly. In
that he was a "normal" human being.

William Barclay tells the story of a young man conversing with one who
had been around longer. "I will learn my trade," said the younger. "And then?"
asked the older. "I will make my fortune." "And then?" "I suppose that I shall
grow old and retire and live on my money?" "And then?" "Well, I suppose that
someday I will die." "*And then?*" came the question that hit him hard. The person "who never remembers that there is another world is destined some day
for the grimmest of grim shocks."

Jesus put it right when He set the stage for the parable of the rich fool with
its theme text: "Take heed, and beware of all covetousness; for a man's life does
not consist in the abundance of his possessions" (Luke 12:15, RSV). Here is a
real pair of spectacles.

Try them on today.

The Cost of Discipleship

Now great multitudes went with Him. And He turned and said to them, "If anyone comes to Me and does not hate his father and mother, wife and children, brothers and sisters, yes, and his own life also, he cannot be My disciple. And whoever does not bear his cross and come after Me cannot be My disciple. For which of you, intending to build a tower, does not sit down first and count the cost, whether he has enough to finish it. Luke 14:25-28, NKJV.

Jesus didn't lack for disciples. Gaining followers was apparently one of the easiest things for Him to do. After all, He could heal their illnesses, miraculously feed them if the need arose, and He had great stories. All in all, Jesus was wonderful entertainment.

Many of those following Him had not the slightest idea about what it meant. As a result, Jesus stops, turns to the crowd, and gives them the brutal facts of life regarding true discipleship. It means "hating" your family and even your own life.

Here Jesus is speaking in hyperbole (an extravagant statement used as a figure of speech) to get their attention. The core meaning of what He is trying to get across is that nothing in all the world can come before God in our lives— that no love in life (not even love for our selves) can compare with the love we have for Him. Becoming a follower of Jesus means being willing to give up all for Him, even life itself.

Undoubtedly Jesus caught their attention with His forthright statements about hating their families and their lives. And now that He has their notice He pushes on with the fact that following Him is not a casual choice.

That brings Him to His sermonette on the cost of discipleship, which concludes in Luke 14:33 with the dictum: "Whoever of you does not renounce *all* that he has cannot be my disciple" (RSV).

Counting the cost is crucial for would-be disciples. Thus it is important for me.

And what is that cost? It is not merely my tithe (10 percent of my income) and offerings. It means to let Him be Lord of *all* of my money.

Nor does it merely mean one seventh of my time on the Sabbath during which I worship Him. No! It means to let Him be Lord of *all* my time.

So what is the cost of following Jesus? Nothing less than total dedication of all that I am and have to His kingdom and glory.

Help me today, dear Lord, not only to count the cost, but be willing to pay it.

Introducing the Parable
of the Prodigal God

Then drew near unto him all the publicans and sinners for to hear him. And the Pharisees and scribes murmured, saying, This man receiveth sinners, and eateth with them. Luke 15:1, 2.

We have now arrived at what might be my favorite chapter in the Bible, Luke 15, with its graphic portrayal of lostness and foundness in several flavors. The lost sheep, the lost coin, and the lost son feature largely. But we miss the point of the chapter if we fail to see its central character: the great "Finder," whom Timothy Keller calls "the prodigal God," the God who risks Himself and lavishes grace on stupid sheep, senseless coins, and rebellious sons; the God who loves and gives of Himself beyond measure.

The central person in Luke 15 is God, and the key word in unlocking its meaning is "murmured." Jesus introduces the three parables in the chapter with the scribes and Pharisees murmuring about Jesus receiving sinners and eating with them (verse 2), and its last scene features the older brother murmuring and complaining about the grace the father has shown to his younger, wayward sibling.

Murmuring, by the way, is an important word in the gospel story. In Luke 5:30, for example, we find the Jewish leaders murmuring about the disciples and Jesus because they fellowshipped with people who needed to be saved. And in Luke 19:7 they murmured because Jesus was going to the house of Zacchaeus. Then, of course, there is that well-known passage in Revelation 12:10, which identifies the devil as the accuser, the father of all murmurers.

While the idea of murmurings frames the stage in Luke 15, the central theme of the chapter is three parables that each feature rejoicing.

In the end we find a chapter featuring three kinds of lostness, two kinds of searching, and two kinds of responding to God's grace. We will let the parables unlock the various lostnesses and findings. But here we need to look at the two types of responders. According to Jesus, church members fall into two basic kinds: the rejoicers and the murmurers. In the latter category are those who are always complaining about the other members, the sermon, the pastor, and about each other. They can't see God because they are focused on what's wrong. Then there are the rejoicers, who sing with enthusiasm and pray with exuberance. Why? Because they recognize the prodigal God of grace working in their midst. Perspective determines what we see.

A Revolutionary Picture of God

Which one of you, having a hundred sheep and losing one of them, does not leave the ninety-nine in the wilderness and go after the one that is lost until he finds it? When he has found it, he lays it on his shoulders and rejoices. And when he comes home, he calls together his friends and neighbors, saying to them, "Rejoice with me, for I have found my sheep that was lost." Just so, I tell you, there will be more joy in heaven over a sinner who repents than over ninety-nine righteous persons who need no repentance. Luke 15:4-7, NRSV.

I wish Jesus hadn't called us sheep. Sheep are about the stupidest animals on the face of the earth. They are so dense that they can practically get lost in their own backyard.

Jesus' first parable in Luke 15 is about a sheep gone astray—not a rare occasion in Palestine. But it is more than about a lost sheep. More important, it is about a shepherd, really God, who cares enough to "go after" the lost one and rejoice when He finds it.

Here is not a God the Jews in Christ's audience would have recognized. While they believed that He might accept a sinner coming back to Him on hands and knees doing penance, the concept of a Deity who risked Himself to seek out sinners was beyond their ideas.

But here we have a crucial point. Salvation never starts with us. God makes the first move to help us in our lostness, as He did with Adam in the garden (Gen. 3:8-10). As *Christ's Object Lessons* puts it, "in the parable of the lost sheep, Christ teaches that salvation does not come through our seeking after God but through God's seeking after us. . . . We do not repent in order that God may love us, but He reveals to us His love in order that we might repent" (p. 189).

The central words in the parable are "joy" and "rejoicing," used three times in four verses. The climax comes in verse 7, in which Jesus reports that there is "joy in heaven over one sinner who repents" (RSV).

Here is another point of the parable that flew in the face of the teachings of the scribes and the Pharisees. They had a saying that "there is joy in heaven over one sinner who is obliterated before God." We find the disciples sharing that mentality in Luke 9:54, 55, in which they thought Jesus might be delighted if a few ungrateful Samaritans got wiped off the face of the earth.

Not so, said Jesus, as He pictures the God who risks Himself in searching for the lost and throwing a party when they are found.

Praise God for the revelation of His care.

Another Look at the Prodigal God

Or again, if a woman has ten silver coins and loses one of them, does she not light the lamp, sweep out the house, and look in every corner till she finds it? And when she does, she calls her friends and neighbours together, and says, "Rejoice with me! I have found the coin that I lost." In the same way, I tell you, there is joy among the angels of God over one sinner who repents. Luke 15:8-10, REB.

I still remember the day that my mother lost her wedding ring. I must have been about 7 or 8 years old. The search was stupendous. The whole family looked everywhere, at everything, under everything, behind everything, and in everything. And when that didn't come up with results we moved everything. And still not finding it, we did it again. I can assure you that great rejoicing filled the Knight household when the lost was found.

Jesus, in telling us about the lost coin, once again reminds us that that is what God is like—one who searches and rejoices because He has been able to rescue one more sick sinner.

It is not difficult to imagine losing a coin in a first-century Palestinian peasant's house. For one thing, they were very dark, with one 18-inch window for lighting. But that is the good part of the story. The real difficulty was the floor: dirt with a layer of straw or dried reeds covering it. And, of course, a lot of other things had gotten mixed in with that covering, including old pieces of food that may have fallen into it. Altogether it would be a difficult place to find a small coin. But the coin was needed. It had an important monetary place in a subsistence economy, and it may have had emotional value.

The picture is of a woman. . . . No, the picture is of God come into a peasant's world, getting down on His knees in the rubble, holding an oil lamp in one hand and sifting through the "stuff" on the floor with the other.

And when the proverbial search for the lost pin in the haystack has been successful, there is an outburst of joy. So, said Jesus, is there joy among the angels in heaven when one sinner is found and repents.

God loves a party. He loves to rejoice. And Jesus does also, even as the complaining, murmuring Jewish leaders look on, shocked and offended by His picture of God.

What they needed to know is that it was a major purpose of His life to help people gain a better understanding of what God is like. Some of us still need to catch the meaning of His demonstration and incorporate it into our own lives.

The Flavors of Lostness

*And he said, "There was a man who had two sons; and the younger of them said to
his father, 'Father, give me the share of property that falls to me.' And he divided his
living between them. Not many days later, the younger son gathered all he had and
took his journey into a far country, and there he squandered his property in loose
living." Luke 15:11-13, RSV.*

Not the kind of kid I would have wanted. Couldn't even wait for the old boy
to die, but demanded his share while his father still lived.

While the older son as the firstborn would have received a double portion,
the younger's portion was apparently quite a nest egg. And he knew exactly
what he was going to do with it. For one thing there would be wine and dancing. There would be freedom to do what he wanted, whenever he wanted. He
would never have to work with the kind of bankroll he had. And then there
were the ladies. Don't forget them. Lots of them for his every need.

Only one problem. He couldn't do the things he had in mind too close to
home. No, he would have to go to a "far country." After all, he knew his father's
principles.

The interesting thing about this third parable of lostness in Luke 15 is that
it presents no search. Why? is the question that faces us, especially since a son
is more valuable than a sheep or a coin. And there were searches for them.

The answer is in his type of lostness. A coin has no spiritual sense at all.
Such people don't even know they are lost. Thus the search. A sheep has some
spiritual sense, enough to know it is lost, even if it doesn't have the foggiest notion how to get home. Thus the search.

But the son had a lot of spiritual sense. He knew he was lost and he knew how
to get home. But the last thing he wanted was to go there. In a state of rebellion, he is
glad to be lost and planned to live it up. A search would have been useless.

In his wisdom the father knows that love cannot be forced. It was such in
my own case. I still remember the day the Marine Corps recruiter phoned and
my father discovered I was quitting college. It was quite a scene, but what can
you do with a know-it-all 18-year-old.

The father in the parable did the only thing he could do. In his love he let
the boy go, realizing in his heart that his son would have to learn through the
hard knocks of life.

Meanwhile, God the prodigal Father is waiting for His chance. He never
gives up on us, even as He watches us blow our inheritance.

Never!

Where My Rope Ends
and God's Starts

But when he had spent all, there arose a severe famine in that land, and he began to be in want. Then he went and joined himself to a citizen of that country, and he sent him into his fields to feed swine. And he would gladly have filled his stomach with the pods that the swine ate, and no one gave him anything. But when he came to himself, he said, "How many of my father's hired servants have bread enough to spare, and I perish with hunger." Luke 15:14-17, NKJV.

I used to wonder why Jesus had this poor young man lusting after pig food. After all, he was Jewish.

Much better, I thought, to have him feeding chickens. Quite a pleasant pastime. Or, better yet, sheep. I remember as a boy in northern California the sheep romping around on the green hills of spring. A fond memory.

But Jesus has the young rebel feeding swine, the dirtiest of domesticated animals and unclean to a Jew. But it's worse than that. The kid is pictured drooling over hog food. I don't know if you have seen what pigs on a traditional farm eat. I can assure you, you wouldn't want to put it in your mouth.

What Jesus is really telling us with the swine food story is that this young guy had come to the end of his rope. His money was gone. And with it went the friends—women first, I imagine, and then the males. No more good times with him.

And then this young man actually had to work for a living. Spoiled all his life, the whole thing must have come as a shock. And the kind of work—detestable in the extreme. He was at the end of his rope.

But the end of our rope for many of us is when the prodigal God can most easily reach us. The end of our rope is the beginning of His.

The ever-searching Holy Spirit found the young fellow in a pigsty. The Bible tells us that when he hit bottom "he came to himself." That is, he saw what it is like to live without the Father. He saw at last where a life of rebellion had carried him.

Having come to his existential moment, he realized as never before his need of the Father. And with that Spirit-guided insight he made a decision to turn his life around and head for home.

Father, help me to realize how much I need You. Please never let me forget or neglect my dependence on You.

The Human Way of Salvation

I will arise and go to my father, and will say unto him, Father, I have sinned against heaven, and before thee, and am no more worthy to be called thy son: make me as one of thy hired servants. Luke 15:18, 19.

At least part of the lost son's theology is correct. Truly unworthy to be called a son, he had lived in a state of rebellion, beginning with his command to his father to give him his share of the inheritance. "I want mine now, old man. I can't wait forever for you to die. I've got a life to live. And I want to do it while I'm young. So cough it up because you can't take it with you."

Nice kid! Just the kind most of us never want. Disrespectful and selfish.

And then he got his wish. And with the wish came dissipation in the form of substance abuse, sex on the go, and all the other pleasures of the world. And he really had no desire for the father as long as he had money to support his habit. He turns to the father only when he is desperate. Not much love there, only driving desperation. Yes, he is truly unworthy of being a son. But at last he is willing to admit it.

And he's right on another point: "I have sinned against heaven, and before thee." Sin is not merely against other people. It is primarily against God, the Father of us all. David expressed that truth after his own "far country" experience of adultery with Bathsheba and the murder of Uriah to cover his tracks. In the end, in repentance he cried out to God, "Against thee, thee only, have I sinned" (Ps. 51:4, RSV).

Good theology so far. But then the younger son goes off the track. "Treat me as one of your hired servants" is his plea.

To understand the implications of that request, we need to remember that there were three levels of young men in a prosperous household. At the top of the social heap were the sons. They had rights and privileges that no one else had. Beyond that, they were heirs. But the returning boy knew that he had forfeited that position.

Then there were the slaves. They had some security. After all, the family owned the slaves and thus they belonged to the household. At the bottom of the pile were the hired servants. Here today, gone tomorrow, depending on the need for workers. The most insecure position.

In effect, the son is going to request that the father give him exactly what he deserves. Apparently he desired to work his way back into good favor. By taking the absolutely lowest spot, perhaps through years of hard work he could make himself "worthy" of sonship again.

But in that "salvation by works" approach, he totally misunderstood the Father.

The Father's Way of Salvation

And he arose and came to his father. But while he was yet at a distance, his father saw him and had compassion, and ran and embraced him and kissed him. And the son said to him, "Father, I have sinned . . . and . . . am no longer worthy to be called your son." But the father said to his servants, "Bring quickly the best robe, and put it on him; and put a ring on his hand, and shoes on his feet; and bring the fatted calf and kill it, and let us eat and make merry; for this my son was dead, and is alive again; he was lost, and is found." And they began to make merry. Luke 15:20-24, RSV.

The son may have understood his sin and his needs, but he totally miscalculated the father's love. He based his understanding on human logic: I will get what I deserve. The father's understanding reflected divine logic: I will give him what he needs. What he deserves is the grinding punishment of endless work with little reward. But what he needs is love, care, forgiveness, and restoration.

In choosing to offer the rebel what he did not deserve the father fully illustrates the Father. Giving people what they don't deserve is what Paul will call grace. Jesus didn't use the word, but no one could have more graphically illustrated its meaning.

The undeserving son is fully restored in a flash. "Quick," shouts the joyous father, "bring the *best* robe." Not any old robe. Only the top for *my* son. "And put a signet ring on his hand," one that has the family seal that he can stamp in the moist clay of financial and legal agreements—the family checkbooks and credit cards of his day. And put shoes on his feet, the symbol of a free person.

But, best yet, "let's have a party second to none. Let's even kill the prime calf we have been saving for a special occasion and pull out all the stops. We should hold nothing back on this high day. My son has returned."

Such is the prodigal God's grace to us. Timothy Keller points out that "prodigal" does not mean "wayward," as most suppose, but "recklessly spendthrift." Thus "the father's welcome to the repentant son was literally reckless, because he refused to 'reckon' or count his sin against him or demand payment." Just the best for my "son."

Party time again, the third joyous party thus far in Luke 15. It gives us the impression that God loves parties and that the church ought to be the most cheerful place on earth.

There may be degrees of holiness, but there are no degrees of forgiveness. At the very moment that we respond to the urging of the Spirit to return to the Father we are fully and without conditions restored as children of God. That's grace. And grace deserves a party.

A Lifelong Church Member's View of Salvation

Now his elder son was in the field; and as he came and drew near to the house, he heard music and dancing. . . . He was angry and refused to go in. His father came out and entreated him, but he answered his father, "Lo, these many years I have served you, and I never disobeyed your command; yet you never gave me a kid, that I might make merry with my friends. But when this son of yours came, who has devoured your living with harlots, you killed for him the fatted calf." Luke 15:25-30, RSV.

Not everybody likes a party!

The older son was one of those. And as a 19-year-old convert when I first read this parable I agreed with him. After all, he did have an excellent argument. Why rejoice at his brother's return? After all, he has recklessly spent his share of the inheritance. And now he wants to come home and spend mine. Why rejoice about that?

Good point! And don't forget the brother's reason for the trip home. Please remember that he was destitute and starving. What else could he do? There is little wonder that the older son was angry. I would have been so also.

Why the party? he cries. Give him what he deserves. Let him work his fingers down to the bone and then maybe he should have a few scraps off the (spelled "my") table.

That, my friends, is an excellent description of human justice. Give him what he deserves. And that's human logic. Give people what they deserve. But the Father's logic says give them what they need, give them what they don't deserve, give them grace.

But that is one thing that this good churchgoing son never really understood. Just listen to his outburst: "I kept all your stinking commandments, yet you never gave me a party. Do you really think I like all that holy stuff? I went to church every Sabbath, but I hated every minute of it. But I did it anyway. That ought to count for something."

And look where his heart really was. "And there is that so-called son of yours. He was out living it up with prostitutes while I was cleaning the sheep manure from under my fingernails after a hard day in the field. I really wanted to do what he did. But instead I slaved away on your stupid farm. I deserved a party and never got one."

The tragedy of the story is that the good boy—the boy who never left the father's house or the church, the boy who had all of the privileges—never understood the father. What a terrible waste—to spend one's life in the Father's house with the heart and mind of a hired servant rather than those of a son or daughter.

Extending Hope
to Church Members

And he said to him, "Son, you are always with me, and all that I have is yours. It was right that we should make merry and be glad, for your brother was dead and is alive again, and was lost and is found." Luke 15:31, 32, NKJV.

What a tragedy to spend all your life in the father's house while never understanding his heart. Even worse, what a travesty to spend all one's life in the church and never coming to grips with the Father's love and grace.

With the older son we have returned to the parable of the coin earlier in Luke 15. Shiny and nice, the coin looks good on the outside. But it is lost. And being a coin it doesn't have any spiritual sense. Impressed with its own outward appearance, it doesn't even know that it is lost. But it is still in the house, the church, the synagogue.

Here Jesus returns to the Pharisees in His audience of verses 1 and 2. Speaking to all those listening to Him, He provided the parable of the lost sheep for the commoners (average sinners) who knew they were lost but didn't know what to do about it. He presented the story of the lost son to represent the listening tax collectors, rebels at heart who were living it up on their ill-gotten gain. But the scribes and Pharisees and other "good" church members get two doses: the parable of the senseless coin and the parable of the church-going, hardworking person who appears to have everything in order, but who is totally lost, yet doesn't know it.

The parable closes with the older son, who doesn't have the slightest idea why God loves a party. He is feeling critical of others and sorry for himself. Yet he could have had a party. All he had to do was ask. The tragedy of the older sons of life is that they never understand the Father. They just sit in church and grumble—even about grace.

The story closes with the father going out into the dark to see if he can't reach the heart of the older son, searching for him just as the woman did for her coin.

The most frustrating part of the parable is that we don't know what happened. That's because it hasn't ended. It's me and you who are out there on that dark evening. And God is asking us if we are going to continue to have the mind of a hired servant or are finally going to become genuine sons and daughters.

Paying Attention to the Word

There was a rich man who was clothed in purple and fine linen and who feasted sumptuously every day. And at his gate was laid a poor man named Lazarus, covered with sores, who desired to be fed with what fell from the rich man's table. Moreover, the dogs came and licked his sores. Luke 16:19-21, ESV.

H ere is Jesus at His graphic best as a storyteller. The thing to note is the absolute contrast, with the rich person having it all in luxurious profusion and the poor individual being about as destitute as one can imagine. Notice the "nice" touches, with dogs licking his sores and his just wanting a few scraps from the table. With Lazarus we have the only person Jesus ever gave a name to in all of His parables. Interestingly enough, his name means "the one who God helps."

In due time "the poor man died and was carried by the angels to Abraham's bosom," while the rich man died and ended up being tormented in "Hades," from which he spotted Lazarus. "And he called out, 'Father Abraham, have mercy upon me, and send Lazarus to dip the end of his finger in water and cool my tongue; for I am in anguish in this flame.'" But Abraham merely told him to remember the past, in which he had had all the good things and Lazarus the worst. Well, then, he requests, at least send him to warn my five brothers, "lest they also come into this place of torment" (see Luke 16:22-28, RSV).

And then comes the punch line: "Abraham said, 'They have Moses and the prophets; let them hear them.' And he said, 'No, father Abraham; but if some one goes to them from the dead, they will repent.' He said to him, 'If they do not hear Moses and the prophets, neither will they be convinced if some one should rise from the dead'" (verses 29-31, RSV).

Some have viewed the details of this parable as literal. But think about it for a moment. Is heaven so close to hell that you can converse between the two? Beyond that, it is based on a Greek view of life after death and of Hades rather than the Jewish idea of sleep in the grave (Dan. 12:2).

Jesus put together some interesting folklore and mythology of the day to make three points: (1) being rich is not a sign of God's blessing or eternal reward, (2) we need to remember those less fortunate than ourselves, and (3) even a miracle as a sign will not change a person unwilling to learn from the Word of God as presented in the Bible.

Help me, Father, to let Your Word shape my life today. Help me to appreciate it more while it can still do me some good.

June 1

Beware of Praying
to Yourself About Yourself

Two men went up into the temple to pray, one a Pharisee and the other a tax col-
lector. The Pharisee stood and was praying this to himself: "God, I thank You that I
am not like other people: swindlers, unjust, adulterers, or even like this tax collector.
I fast twice a week; I pay tithes of all that I get." But the tax collector, standing some
distance away, was even unwilling to lift up his eyes to heaven, but was beating
his breast, saying, "God, be merciful to me, the sinner!" I tell you, this man went
to his house justified rather than the other; for everyone who exalts himself will be
humbled, but he who humbles himself will be exalted. Luke 18:10-14, NASB.

Nothing like praying to yourself about yourself! Of course, everything he
said about himself was true. He did fast. He did meticulously give tithes.
He was not like other men. And he certainly wasn't like that miserable, lowly
tax collector.

All in all, the Pharisee was a good man. And he knew it. In his prayer he wanted
to make sure that God also recognized it. So he offered a testimonial to his righteousness, his faithfulness to the church, and so on. He reminds one of Rabbi Simeon ben
Jochai, who once said, "If there are only two righteous men in the world, I and my
son are these two; and if there is only one, I am he!" In actuality, the Pharisee in the
parable did not really go to pray but to inform God how good he was.

"But," William Barclay writes, "the question is not, 'Am I as good as my
fellow men?' The question is, 'Am I as good as God?'" When we see ourselves
next to God all a person can do is cry "God, be merciful to me—the sinner!"

That was the prayer of the tax collector. And note that he said "*the* sinner,"
rather than *a* sinner. He was acutely aware of his personal shortcomings and rebel-
lions. From the depths of his fractured heart he gasped out his confession to God.

And here is the miracle of grace. It is not pride in our goodness, or even
goodness itself, that counts with God. But rather an honest facing up to our
lives in the light of His Word and character.

"If we confess *our* sins, he is faithful and just to forgive us our sins" (1 John
1:9). "By grace are ye saved through faith; and that not of yourselves: it is the
gift of God: not of works lest any man should boast" (Eph. 2:8, 9).

Take heed: "He also told this parable to some who trusted in themselves
that they were righteous and despised others" (Luke 18:9, RSV).

A Real Scuzzball

He entered Jericho. . . . And there was a man named Zacchaeus; he was a chief tax collector, and rich. And he sought to see who Jesus was, but could not, on account of the crowd, because he was small of stature. So he ran on ahead and climbed up into a sycamore tree to see him, for he was to pass that way. And when Jesus came to the place, he looked up and said to him, "Zacchaeus, make haste and come down; for I must stay at your house today.". . . And when they saw it they all murmured, "He has gone in to be the guest of a man who is a sinner." Luke 19:1-7, RSV.

Zacchaeus was the most hated man in town. And for good reason. He was not merely a tax collector but a chief tax collector. To put it another way, he was very rich. As a result, he had one of the biggest houses in town, he had fine clothes, and he had a full house of servants. And the people knew that he was wealthy only because he had unjustly taken their money.

Jericho was a wonderful place for a tax collector to get rich. Located in the Jordan Valley, the town served as a crossroads for trade from east to west and from north to south. But even more important were the huge number of palms and a balsam grove that perfumed the country for miles around. Josephus called Jericho "the fattest in Palestine." And the Romans carried its dates and balsam to the ends of their empire.

It was a great place to be a tax collector, especially given the way taxes were collected. Unfortunately, the system lent itself to abuse. Romans at that time farmed out the business of collecting taxes in a region. They assessed a region to be worth so much, then sold the right to gather taxes within that area to the highest bidder. Any extra that the collector could obtain was his to keep. And if people didn't like the taxes he set, he always had the Roman soldiers to back up his demands. Pay up or else.

Zacchaeus had risen to the top of his field. A chief tax collector, he had others under him, raking off a percentage of their gains also. A good racket to be sure. But one that made him the most hated man in town.

And when Jesus came to Jericho we find the most disliked man in town meeting the most popular one. Zacchaeus may have been rich, but he was also lonely and knew that something was desperately wrong. He wasn't sure what his problem was, but he had heard about a new prophet who even had a tax collector among His disciples.

As with all who feel their need, Zacchaeus wanted to see Jesus.

Scuzzball Meets Jesus

When Jesus got to the tree, he looked up and said, "Zacchaeus, hurry down. Today is my day to be a guest in your home." Zacchaeus scrambled out of the tree, hardly believing his good luck, delighted to take Jesus home with him. Everyone who saw the incident was indignant and grumped, "What business does he have getting cozy with this crook?" Luke 19:5-7, Message.

The most hated man in town being forced up into a tree must have been an entertainment that day for the citizens of Jericho almost as interesting as the passing of Jesus. After all, it's not every day that you find a super-rich guy like Zacchaeus hoisting up his fine clothes and climbing into a tree.

Zacchaeus really didn't have much choice if he wanted to see Jesus. I imagine that he had already tried to get a viewpoint on the road. Being short, he had probably tried to worm his way through the crowd to get up front. For someone else that may have worked, but for Zacchaeus it was an experience of elbows in the ribs and kicks from people in the pushing crowd who could do it without getting marked for higher taxes in the future. A great day for an angry crowd, but one of bruises for Zacchaeus. He was getting what he deserved.

But he also had his needs. And one of them was at least to view Jesus, although he realized that seeing was all he would get. After all, the Jews held tax collectors to be unclean. Not only did they work for the hated Romans; they extorted. They could hit you up for more of your hard-earned money at will. Such men were not even allowed into a synagogue.

Up the tree was the only solution. And then the wonder of wonders. Jesus stopped right in front of the tree and invited Himself to dinner at the little sinner's home.

Everybody was shocked, but nobody more than Zacchaeus. But the crowd wasn't only shocked—it was scandalized, grumbling (murmuring) that this so-called prophet would cozy up to a blatant crook.

Here, as in Luke 15, we have the murmuring of the scribes and Pharisees once again. But this time Jesus is not dealing in parables but in real life. He sensed need wherever it was. The purpose of His life was to meet those lacks. Zacchaeus was not only the richest man in town, but also the loneliest. And in Jesus he found a friend.

The good news is that Jesus wants to be friends with each of us if we will humble ourselves and let Him in.

Jesus Transforms Scuzzballs

And Zacchaeus stood and said to the Lord, "Behold, Lord, the half of my goods I give to the poor; and if I have defrauded any one of anything, I restore it fourfold." And Jesus said to him, "Today salvation has come to this house, since he also is a son of Abraham." Luke 19:8, 9, RSV.

Meeting Jesus changes your life. Repeatedly throughout the four Gospels we discover that when people encounter Jesus they are never the same afterward. Not merely a nice man with some kind and wise words, He was a transformer of lives.

So it was with Zacchaeus, the money-grubbing tax collector who had been gouging everybody in town financially. A genuine experience with Jesus changed his life forever. And all the community knew it.

Committing half of his goods to the poor, the other half got whittled down by his decision to restore fourfold anything he had unjustly taken. In that pledge he exceeded the requirements of Jewish law, which stipulated a double-the-value restoration (Ex. 22:7). A transformed person, he was determined to do more than the law demanded.

The Desire of Ages, in commenting upon this story, notes that "no repentance is genuine that does not work reformation. The righteousness of Christ is not a cloak to cover unconfessed and unforsaken sin; it is a principle of life that transforms the character and controls the conduct. Holiness is wholeness for God; it is the entire surrender of heart and life to the indwelling of the principles of heaven. . . .

"If we have injured others through any unjust business transaction, if we have overreached in trade, or defrauded any man, even though it be within the pale of the law, we should confess our wrong, and make restitution as far as lies in our power" (pp. 555, 556).

I still remember the day I read those words as a young Christian. They hit me between the eyes and lodged in my conscience. At first I tried to get rid of them and move on with my life.

But I could get no peace. For the six years that I had worked in a grocery store I had helped myself to candy bars and whatever else I wanted. Bit by bit it added up.

And now I was convicted that I should meet with the store's manager, confess, and plop a fair piece of money on his desk. But I was broke and trying to earn my way through college. I had lots of "buts."

But I was also a Christian. The Zacchaeus path was my only option.

God Always Takes the Initiative

The Son of man is come to seek and to save the lost. Luke 19:10.

Lost!

Here is a Technicolor word, especially to anyone who has ever actually been lost.

Have you ever been lost? I remember once as a teenager I got lost while hiking in the redwood forests of northern California. At first I remained fairly calm. I knew that if I tried hard enough and long enough I would find my way out. But the farther I went, the more lost I became, as I no longer saw anything that even looked familiar. It was then that panic set in.

Lost is not a good feeling. But it is an impressive one. A person who is lost has only one goal and hope—to become unlost.

When reading the Bible, we need to pay close attention to the meaning of "lost." The word does not mean damned or doomed. Rather it indicates being in the wrong place. People are lost when they have wandered away from God, when they have rebelled against His will and struck out on their own path in life.

Some lost people are totally oblivious to the fact, as were the Pharisees of Jesus' day and the "holy" types of all generations. They managed to get lost in the church. But other types know that they are spiritually lost and desire to be rescued. Such are the Zacchaeuses of the world.

One of the most important truths ever uttered by Jesus is that He came to seek and save that which is lost. And He doesn't care if you are lost in the church or in a house of prostitution. He has a mission.

That mission we see reflected in Scripture from one end to the other. No sooner do we find Adam and Eve sinning than we find God searching them out in the garden. So it was with the lost coin and the lost sheep of Luke 15. Salvation is never a matter of us approaching God. It is always Him coming after us. God so loved the world that He sent His one and only Son into the world to search out that which has been lost. His love and grace is always proactive. He does not wait for us to make a move. Instead, He seeks us out.

Thank You, Father, for the dynamics and richness of Your grace. Thank You for searching me out. And now, please help me to keep hold of Your hand.

A Shadow of the Future

At that time Herod the tetrarch heard the reports about Jesus, and he said to his attendants, "This is John the Baptist; he has risen from the dead! That is why miraculous powers are at work in him." Matt. 14:1, 2, NIV.

When Jesus heard what had happened, he withdrew by boat privately to a solitary place. Hearing of this, the crowds followed him on foot. Verse 13, NIV.

A new threat to Jesus arises in Matthew 14:1, this time in the person of Herod Antipas, the ruler of Galilee. Although Herod was quite familiar with John the Baptist's ministry, he seems to be relatively ignorant of Jesus. Thus, probably as a result of both superstition and an overwrought conscience, Herod confuses the two men and fears that perhaps Jesus is a resurrected John.

And he had good reason for an inflamed conscience. Some time earlier the prophet of repentance had confronted Herod regarding his unlawful liaison with his brother's wife. The upshot was that the ruler had John arrested and would have put him to death had he not feared the people, who held the Baptist to be a prophet (verse 5).

A weak man, Herod not only feared the people but also his lover, who maneuvered him into beheading John against Herod's better judgment. Because he also feared the opinions of his guests, he allowed himself to be manipulated (verses 6-11).

The story shows Herod Antipas to be an irresolute person who more than once in a short period goes against his conscience. As a result, his imagination gets the best of him when he learns about Jesus' ministry.

Herod is hardly a man to be trusted. Thus it is little wonder that Jesus "withdrew . . . to a solitary place" after John's disciples report his death to Jesus (verses 12, 13). But the crowds follow Him. He soon feeds some 5,000 of them, which results in a desire to make Him king.

Meanwhile, we need to return to the significance of John's death. There is a reason that Matthew and Mark spend so much precious space on it. Namely, the telling of John's end is integrally linked to Jesus' own forthcoming death. The death of John foreshadows that of Jesus. Just as John had been Jesus' forerunner in ministry (Matt. 3:1-11), so will he be His forerunner in death. Jesus understands that and begins to withdraw so that He can more fully prepare His disciples for what is to come.

Invisible People Make a Difference

A large crowd followed Him, because they saw the signs which He was performing on those who were sick. . . . Jesus, lifting up His eyes and seeing that a large crowd was coming to Him, said to Philip, "Where are we to buy bread, so that these may eat?" This He was saying to test him, for He himself knew what He was intending to do. Philip answered Him, "Two hundred denarii worth of bread is not sufficient for them. . . ." Andrew, Simon Peter's brother, said to Him, "There is a lad here who has five barley loaves and two fish, but what are these for so many people?" John 6:2-9, NASB.

Too often we overlook the common people in the Bible story, those quiet individuals, who are "just there." Largely ignored in their own time, and probably by most Bible readers today, those individuals made a difference. We find a lesson for us here. You don't have to be a Peter or a Billy Graham for God to use you as a blessing to other people.

Central to today's passage are three individuals whom we don't hear much about in the Bible, even though two of them are disciples. The first of the "hidden" figures in the feeding of the 5,000 is Philip. Outside of listings of the 12 disciples, none of the Gospels except the fourth even mention his name. In John 6 Jesus asks him how much food it would take to feed the crowd. Philip's answer was about six months' wages (200 denarii). The only thing he contributes to the miracle story is to highlight its magnitude. But his approach is basically pessimistic: "There is nothing we can do. The situation looks hopeless."

Then there is Andrew, another of the hidden disciples. He is best known as the brother of Peter. The world is full of such types. The introductions of, "Meet so-and-so, he is the brother of, wife of, husband of, son of so-and-so." There are the "really important people" and there are the Andrews.

But Jesus teaches us in John 6 that the Andrews of life make a difference. Moving beyond the pessimism of Philip, Andrew is the one who said, "I will see what I can do." Andrew may not have been the star of the show, but he functioned as the spark plug who got things off of dead center.

His part in ministry was doing something simple. In this case, finding a boy, two dried-up sardine-sized fish, and five barley loaves, the cheapest of all bread.

And then there is the boy himself. Probably clueless as to what he was doing in salvation history. But he was willing to give the little he had.

Help us today, Lord, to give what little we have, realizing that no matter how humble our person or our gift, we make a difference.

The Need of Prayer
in the Midst of Success

Jesus said, "Make the people sit down." Now there was much grass in the place; so the men sat down, in number about five thousand. . . . When the people saw the sign which he had done, they said, "This is indeed the prophet who is to come into the world!" Perceiving then that they were about to come and take him by force to make him king, Jesus withdrew again to the mountain by himself. John 6:10-15, RSV.

Ever feed a large crowd? Even a couple dozen guests can drive a host to distraction in the planning and the supplying.

Try 5,000! Or, better yet, 20,000, since the count in those days was males only. Wives and children need to be added in. But even feeding 5,000 is a pretty good achievement if you can do it with two small fish and five diminutive barley loaves.

The crowd did not miss the significance of the miracle. Immediately energized, they identified Jesus as "the prophet who is to come," a reference to Deuteronomy 18, in which Moses proclaimed: "The Lord your God will raise up for you a prophet like me from among you, from your brethren—him you shall heed" (verses 15, 18, RSV).

"Here is the promised one" flashed through the minds of the crowd. Here is the second Moses. Just as Moses provided miraculous manna in the wilderness, so Jesus supplies us with bread from heaven (John 6:5-14). And just as Moses delivered us from our oppressors, the chain of logic ran, so his successor will rescue us from the Romans. They determined to make Jesus king on the spot. Even the disciples got carried away with the possibility. Mark tells us that Jesus had to "make" or "compel" them to get into their boat and leave Him, while He dismissed the crowds (Mark 6:45, 46).

We miss an important point of the story if we fail to see Jesus here being enticed to obtain the kingdom without a cross. He is facing His ultimate temptation. Here we have a repetition of His first wilderness temptation, but with greater forcefulness. Now He had demonstrated that He could indeed make bread out of "stones," and it profoundly impressed the people. "Build the kingdom on bread. Make it the first point in Your program to abolish hunger. Multiply loaves and fishes all the time, and the people will love You."

We sense the seriousness of the temptation for Jesus reflected by the fact that immediately after dismissing the crowds, "he went up on the mountain to pray" (verse 46, RSV).

Doing God's will in the accomplishment of His mission remained central in His life. And doing God's will is always a matter of prayer, even for me this day.

June 9

Faith Develops

He was there alone, but the boat by this time was many furlongs distant from the land. . . . In the fourth watch of the night he came to them, walking on the sea. . . . And Peter [asked] him, "Lord, if it is you, bid me come to you on the water." He said, "Come." So Peter got out of the boat and walked on the water.
Matt. 14:23-29, RSV.

Peter could walk on water! Great stuff! Look at me, guys!

And that's when the trouble began. The most adventurous of Jesus' disciples did fine with water walking as long as he kept his eyes on Jesus. But then, in good Peter style, he began to focus on himself and how well he was doing. It is at that point that he noticed the wind and the fierceness of the storm and his walking-on-water life of victory began to fall apart. And it didn't take much time.

As soon as he took his eyes off of Jesus, the source of his power, he began to sink. In desperation, he shouted out, "Lord, save me."

And He did! He would do so time after time as the great apostle struggled between the poles of faith and doubt. Jesus does the same thing in our lives as we move forward rather haltingly in our spiritual journey. There are days when even I "can walk on water." But other times I find myself sinking fast. The one constant is the availability of Jesus, who is ready to "save" at our request.

The scene in which Peter walks on water takes place after Jesus had sent the disciples away after the feeding of the 5,000. When He finished praying He went to meet His disciples, who were at that time battling a fierce storm. That is when Peter did his water-walking thing and learned the importance of keeping his eyes on Jesus.

But there is another, and even more important, truth in this storm incident. When Jesus and Peter got into the boat, the storm miraculously stopped, and the disciples "worshipped him, saying, 'Truly you are the Son of God'" (Matt. 14:33, RSV).

That is the first time that the disciples give that title to Jesus, but it will not be the last. And with each repetition the title will have greater meaning as they ever more fully understand the identity of their Lord.

Their experience foreshadows ours as day by day we gain a fuller understanding of that Jesus who is the object of our worship and the source of our power.

Where Else Can I Go?

After this many of his disciples drew back and no longer went about with him.
Jesus said to the twelve, "Do you also wish to go away?" Simon Peter answered
him, "Lord, to whom shall we go? You have the words of eternal life; and we have
believed, and have come to know, that you are the Holy One of God." Jesus answered
them, "Did I not choose you, the twelve, and one of you is a devil?" He spoke of
Judas the son of Simon Iscariot, for he, one of the twelve, was to betray him.
John 6:66-71, RSV.

All good things on earth come to an end sooner or later. For a time the multitudes flocked after Jesus. They couldn't get enough of Him. Many were excited at His miracles. Others had come to be baptized by His disciples—so many that it had been an embarrassment (John 4:1-3). Jesus could hardly escape the press of the people. And it merely got worse after the feeding of the 5,000 in John 6:1-15. At that time they attempted to make Him king.

But Jesus had different ideas and dismissed the crowds. And then He gave that talk about eating His flesh and drinking His blood, claiming to be the bread of life.

That was too much. The beginning of the end was already in sight as many of His followers "drew back and no longer went about with him." Some of them had begun to see more clearly where Jesus was headed. After all, you can't challenge the authorities time after time and expect to get away with it. They could recognize that He was destined for disaster.

They followed Him willingly as long as the loaves and the fishes were plentiful. Seeking what they could get out of it, they had gone after Him for purely selfish reasons. But, they were not interested in following a person who didn't have enough sense to take the kingship when it was offered to Him.

And then there was the first foreshadowing of the dark side of Judas. He had his own ideas about helping Jesus move in what he considered the right direction.

In the light of the changing times, Jesus asked the 12 if they would forsake Him also. Peter's response is a classic: "Lord, to whom shall we go? You have the words of eternal life."

That answer has sustained me many times as things have gotten difficult and even the church looked like a mess. Like Peter, I did not understand everything, I was not happy with things, and I couldn't see into the future. But I did know one thing for certain: that Jesus and faith in Him made more sense than anything else. Where else could I go? I have never been sorry that I stuck with Jesus through the bad times as well as the good.

June 11

God Leads Us One Step at a Time

The officers then went back to the chief priests and Pharisees, who said to them, "Why did you not bring him?" The officers answered, "No man ever spoke like this man!" The Pharisees answered them, "Are you led astray, you also? Have any of the authorities or of the Pharisees believed in him? . . ." Nicodemus . . . said to them, "Does our law judge a man without first giving him a hearing and learning what he does?" They replied, "Are you from Galilee too?" John 7:45-52, RSV.

Jesus' world continued to crumble as He entered into what seemed to be an endless round of confrontations with the Jewish authorities. He knew what was happening, yet did not back down in the face of encroaching pressure, speaking openly in the Temple and challenging the nation's religious leadership.

The problem got to be so obvious that the common people began to discuss why the leaders weren't taking action against Him. "Can it be," they asked, "that the authorities really know that this is the Christ?" (John 7:27, RSV).

That was too much. It was the last straw. The leadership sent a delegation to arrest Jesus and put an end to the trouble. But that too backfired. Amazed by Jesus, those very officers of the law returned empty-handed, claiming that they had never heard anything like His words.

That event could have provided the religious authorities with a wake-up call. But all they could reply was that it was only ignorant peasants who had believed in Jesus. None of the Sanhedrin or Temple officials or the Pharisees had accepted Him.

It was in that context that one of the rulers of the Sanhedrin did speak up. Nicodemus, who had cautiously come to Jesus at night in John 3, suggested that Jewish law did not judge a person without a hearing. For that he received scorn.

Note that Nicodemus was still cautious. He didn't exactly defend Jesus. Nor did he come out in the open as a follower. But he carefully expressed a few words that indicated that the mysterious wind of the Spirit was operating in his heart and life (see John 3:7, 8).

Nicodemus did not carry his protest any further. Apparently, as one author puts it, his heart told him to defend Jesus but his head told him not to take the risk.

But he had taken another step on a pathway that would lead into full openness when he and Joseph of Arimathea buried the crucified Christ (John 19:38-42).

God had guided him step by step. That is the same way that He is leading you and me.

The Mystery of Providence

"It is also written in your law that the testimony of two men is true. I am One who bears witness to Myself, and the Father who sent Me bears witness to Me." Then they said to Him, "Where is Your Father?" Jesus answered, "You know neither Me nor My Father. If you had known Me, you would have known My Father also." These words Jesus spoke in the treasury, as He taught in the temple; and no one laid hands on Him, for His hour had not yet come. John 8:17-20, NKJV.

One gets the impression in reading John 8 that something like a court trial is taking place. On the other hand, one wonders who is being tried. First impressions are that the Jewish leaders are sitting in judgment on Jesus. But the more one meditates on the chapter, the more it looks as if it's the leaders who are on the defense.

That was certainly so in the case of the woman caught in the very act of adultery (John 8:1-11). The Jewish leaders had come out strong in not only condemning the woman but also in seeking grounds on which to find Jesus guilty. Yet after He wrote a bit on the ground they all slunk off in shame. Jesus had the evidence, and there was no one left to cast the first stone except Him. He was in control. They had been judged.

Beginning with verse 12, the Jewish leaders entered yet another round of judgment and sparring. This time it centered on Jesus' claim to be "the light of the world" and that those who followed Him were in the light. That left the Pharisees, by implication, in the darkness.

At that point the Pharisees launched into an attack on Jesus that was in essence a defense move rather than one of prosecution. They argued that He was out of bounds in His claims, because He was witnessing to Himself to be the light, which in Jewish thought was tantamount to ascribing to Himself the functions of God and the Messiah. Jesus didn't back down, claiming not only that His witness was true but that His Father joined Him as a second witness. Jesus had His opponents on the defensive. Yet, remarkably, they did nothing to "lock Him up," even though it was becoming more and more obvious that it was what they desired to do.

And why didn't they arrest Him? Because "His hour had not yet come." Here we have a phrase that John uses repeatedly. All through his Gospel Jesus is moving toward His "hour." And that hour will finally come. But only after everything is ready.

There is something important here. We as humans will never fully understand God's activity in human history. Yet He in His providence is always carrying out His plan. And that providential working is taking place daily in each of our lives.

Religion Out of Focus

There came to Jesus scribes and Pharisees, which were of Jerusalem, saying,
Why do thy disciples transgress the tradition of the elders? for they wash not their
hands when they eat bread. But he answered and said unto them, Why do ye also
transgress the commandment of God by your tradition? Matt. 15:1-3.

We have to congratulate the scribes and Pharisees on their persistence. No matter how far they have to travel to attack Jesus they will do it. It is unfortunate that they couldn't find a better purpose for their dedication.

The conflict between Jesus and the Jewish leaders recorded in Matthew 15 and Mark 7 centers outwardly around ceremonial defilement. But at a more profound level, it involves the very nature of religion and the depth of human sinfulness.

The Pharisaic party had a purpose: to question Jesus about why His disciples broke the tradition of the elders. Note, they were not accusing Him of doing so, but of teaching His disciples to disrespect the traditions. And in that accusation they were quite right.

According to Matthew's Gospel, the problem had to do with the washing of hands. Here it is important to note that the issue wasn't sanitation but ceremonial uncleanliness. In their genuine and sincere desire to honor God, the Pharisees had picked up on His instruction on priestly washing in the sanctuary (Ex. 30:17-21) and expanded the idea to everyday life. In addition, they multiplied the number of things causing defilement and ritualized the cleansing process. So important did ceremonial washing become to them that they eventually devoted an entire book of the Mishnah (the written version of the oral tradition) to it (called *Yadaim*, or "Hands"). The faithful were required to wash their hands in the prescribed manner, or their food, and by extension their whole person, would be unclean and unfit for worshipping God. Meanwhile, Jesus illustrated in Matthew 15:3-6 that some of their traditions led them to transgress the Ten Commandments, notably the one directed at loving and caring for their parents.

Here we have a case of *the sin of devotion*—a sin of religious people trying hard to be religious and manufacturing rules in the process. That is not a pharisaic disease, but is also found among Catholics, Baptists, and Adventists. It shows up in the angry deacon, the Inquisition, and those who blow up when someone does not eat as they think they should.

Jesus on True Religion

What comes out of the mouth proceeds from the heart, and this defiles a person. For out of the heart come evil thoughts, murder, adultery, sexual immorality, theft, false witness, slander. These are what defile a person. But to eat with unwashed hands does not defile anyone. Matt. 15:18-20, ESV.

The second half of the conflict over uncleanliness finds Jesus turning His back on the Pharisees and speaking first to the crowd, who have apparently been standing out of the line of fire, and then to the disciples.

He tells the crowd that the Pharisees don't really understand true defilement, and by extension, true religion (Matt. 15:10, 11). Then the disciples come to Jesus, pointing out that He had offended the Pharisees in His teaching on the subject. To which Jesus replied that they were merely blind leaders leading other blind leaders, and that following them would only result in disaster (verses 12-14).

But Peter, and probably the other disciples, isn't satisfied, so he presses Jesus for more explanation. Apparently the teaching on ceremonial uncleanness was so pervasive in Judaism that even the disciples were having a difficult time understanding Jesus' perspective.

That explains His exasperated words to them in verses 16 and 17. In essence He says, "How can you be so dull? After all the time you have listened to Me, can't you see what I mean?"

Jesus continues to explain to His slow-witted disciples that genuine defilement is not a matter of externals—what goes into a person. Rather, it is rooted in the heart (a person's inner being), and it is out of a sinful heart that sinful acts proceed (verses 17-20).

In short, true religion is not a matter of externals. Rather, it finds its source in an attitude of love toward God and other people. That mind-set becomes the source for all a person's actions. Later Jesus will become even more specific on this point, noting that all of God's commandments are built upon *agapē* (love) to God and other people (Matt. 22:36-40).

In Matthew 15 we have the very core of Jesus' definition of true religion. What a pity it is that so many of us remain focused on the items of do and don't while missing the real thing. While some of those do's and don'ts may be important, they are so only when the heart is right.

June 15

Seeing Beneath the Surface

His disciples came and begged him, saying, "Send her away, for she is crying after us." He answered, "I was sent only to the lost sheep of the house of Israel." But she came and knelt before him, saying, "Lord, help me." And he answered, "It is not fair to take the children's bread and throw it to the dogs." She said, "Yes, Lord, yet even the dogs eat the crumbs that fall from the masters' table." Then Jesus answered her, "O woman, great is your faith! Be it done for you as you desire." And her daughter was healed instantly. Matt. 15:23-28, RSV.

Northern Galilee wasn't distant enough from Jerusalem. The Pharisees had followed Him that far. Yet Jesus needed time to instruct His disciples in the face of the coming crisis. The only solution was to enter Gentile territory, including Tyre, Sidon, and Caesarea Philippi. That would also put Him beyond the reach of Herod Antipas.

As we might expect, Jesus soon encountered non-Jews. One was a Canaanite woman who came to Him begging for mercy for her demon-possessed daughter. In response, He does something that seems offensive to us, but which His Jewish disciples certainly expected. He ignores the woman. The disciples, sensing what they perceive to be Jesus' attitude, ask Him to turn her away.

Jesus responds by telling the woman that He had been sent to the Jews. But, undeterred, she keeps imploring Him for help. He then tells her that it is not right to toss the children's food to the dogs. At that point she sees a glimmer of hope, pressing her claim by admitting she is willing to be a dog if she can only receive the blessings of the kingdom.

Jesus rewards her profusely. Not only does He commend her faith, but He heals her daughter. This unnamed Canaanite woman has grasped what the disciples have failed to understand—that a person must be willing to become nothing in order to enter the kingdom.

While that is true, Jesus' apparent harshness to the woman still offends most modern readers of the Bible. Here we need to remember that facial expressions and body language accompanied His words. By the twinkle in His eye, in the slight smile at the corner of His mouth, she saw a sign of hope. Ellen White notes that "beneath the apparent refusal of Jesus, she saw a compassion that He could not hide" (*The Desire of Ages*, p. 401).

Help me, Father, to be as sensitive to You and desire You as much as the Canaanite woman did.

Whose Leaven?

When His disciples had come to the other side, they had forgotten to take bread. Then Jesus said to them, "Take heed and beware of the leaven of the Pharisees and the Sadducees." Matt. 16:5, 6, NKJV.

Somebody is always messing up. This time no one had brought any bread. That worried the disciples greatly, and Jesus knew it. So while they had their minds on bread, He told them to beware of the leaven of the Pharisees and Sadducees, referring to their false ideas about true religion, including their erroneous ideas of the mission of the Messiah. After all, all of them were looking for a powerful earthly king rather than a suffering servant. That teaching, as we saw at the feeding of the 5,000, posed a genuine temptation to the disciples. Such thought could easily continue to permeate their minds, much as yeast spreads through dough.

Yet that view of Messiah's function would soon be shattered as Jesus became the Lamb of God. He needed to implant the true leaven in their minds to prepare them for that event and their own future work.

Jesus had a message for them, but all they could think about was their stomachs. That brought forth what may be Jesus' harshest comment on their dullness: "O men of little faith, why do you discuss among yourselves the fact that you have no bread? Do you not yet perceive? Do you not remember the five loaves of the five thousand, and how many baskets you gathered? . . . How is it that you fail to perceive that I did not speak about bread?" (Matt. 16:8-11, RSV). At that point, they finally realized that He had in mind the leaven of the false teachings that they had grown up with and with which they had filled their minds.

One significant fact to note is that Jesus links the Pharisees and Sadducees together. They were opponents in Jewish religious and political life, standing for radically different ideas. But in Jesus they had found a common enemy who threatened the status quo. A powerful enemy makes strange bedfellows. Their unity will last up to the Crucifixion.

As we meditate today, we need to remember the lesson of the leaven and how powerful extra-biblical philosophies are in distorting our beliefs. Above all, we need to keep our eyes turned to Jesus and His Word.

Crisis Point

When Jesus came into the region of Caesarea Philippi, He asked His disciples, say-ing, "Who do men say that I, the Son of Man, am?" So they said, "Some say John the Baptist, some Elijah, and others Jeremiah or one of the prophets." He said to them, "But who do you say that I am?" Simon Peter answered and said, "You are the Christ, the Son of the living God." Matt. 16:13-16, NKJV.

With these verses we have come to what is in many ways the most critical episode in the life of Jesus. As William Barclay points out, it occurs at "the crisis of Jesus' life. Whatever His disciples might be thinking, He knew for certain that ahead there lay an inescapable cross. Things could not go on much longer. The opposition was gathering itself to strike. Now the problem and the ques-tion confronting Jesus was this—had He had any effect at all? Had He achieved anything? Or, to put it another way, had anyone discovered who He really was?"

The only way to find out was to ask those closest to Him, those who would soon, unbeknownst to them, take over His movement as true apostles. The question at this point was whether they had learned the basic thing they needed to know as disciples, since without the understanding that Jesus had sought to give them as disciples they could never be apostles.

Jesus really didn't care what others thought of Him, but He desperately needed to know the opinion of the disciples. He had reached the critical point of His ministry.

So He asked them the fundamental question that underlies everything: "Who do you say that I am?" Everything rode on their answer. With relief Jesus heard Peter respond, "You are the Christ, the Son of the living God." At that point He knew that He had not failed. The eyes of the disciples had at last opened.

But while they understood *who* Jesus was, they had no idea of *what* that meant. As a result, we find Jesus commanding the disciples that they should "tell no one that He was Jesus the Christ" (verse 20, NKJV). That seems like a strange command, but it was a necessary one, since Peter and the other dis-ciples did not yet understand what His true office was. They still had the con-quering-king perspective. And that is normal, since there is no evidence in pre-Christian times that any Jews thought of a suffering Messiah.

Sometimes we have just enough knowledge to be dangerous. Balanced un-derstanding is crucial before we open our mouths too wide.

Two Rocks

Jesus answered him, "Blessed are you, Simon Bar-Jona! For flesh and blood has not revealed this to you, but my Father who is in heaven. And I tell you, you are Peter, and on this rock I will build my church, and the powers of death shall not prevail against it." Matt. 16:17, 18, RSV.

Peter's sensitive ears must have been overjoyed to hear such a promise coming from Jesus. A real blessing indeed. Simon Bar-Jona translates as Simon son of Jona, Peter's formal name. And Jesus has no doubt that the Father through the Holy Spirit had revealed Jesus' true identity to His disciple.

At that point the blessing moves into one of the most contentious passages in Christian history: "You are Peter, and on this rock I will build my church, and the powers of death shall not prevail against it."

The question is, who or what is the rock that forms the foundation of the church? Was it Peter the man or Peter's confession that Jesus is truly the Christ?

In beginning to answer we need to realize that the text makes a play on words in the rock statement. The Greek text reads, "you are *petros*, and upon this *petra* I will build My church." Josephus uses *petra* to describe the massive stone blocks in the towers of Jerusalem (*Wars* 6.140). *Petros*, on the other hand, represents an ordinary rock that one can carry. That understanding lines up with Ephesians 2:20, in which Paul describes Christ as the "corner stone" and the prophets and apostles forming the rest of the foundation of the church.

Then again, if Jesus had made Peter the chief disciple, that would have put an end to the ongoing argument about which of them was the greatest. That may have been what Peter *wanted* to hear, but as we shall soon see, Peter *wanted* to hear a whole lot of things that Christ never intended.

What he *did hear* is that his confession that Jesus is the divine Christ is the very foundation on which the Christian church is built.

And even the powers of death would not be able to stop Christ's church. His power over death in the Resurrection (first introduced in Matt. 16:21) would make even shaky little rocks strong as they realized that as long as they were with God, people could do nothing to harm them. They (and we) have nothing to fear. We serve a risen Lord.

The Keys of the Kingdom

I will give you the keys of the kingdom of heaven; and whatever you bind on earth
shall have been bound in heaven, and whatever you loose on earth shall have been
loosed in heaven. Matt. 16:19, NASB.

Here we have another verse that has ripped through Christian history. Just what is it that Jesus promised Peter? What are the keys and the binding power of the church?

A key is an obvious metaphor for admitting people through a door. A hint to understanding the "key" symbol appears in Luke 11:52, in which Jesus condemns the scribes for misusing "the key of knowledge" and thereby hindering people from "entering" the kingdom. And in Matthew 23:13 we find Him berating the scribes and Pharisees because they "shut the door of the kingdom of heaven in people's faces" and refuse to "let those enter who are trying to" (NIV). We should couple those verses with Jesus' saying in John 17:3 that to know Him is eternal life.

In their work, the scribes and Pharisees have been misusing the key and blocking people from knowledge of Jesus. Peter, by contrast, is to open the way. That is exactly what we find him doing in Acts 2 and 3, in which his preaching brings many Jews into the kingdom, and in Acts 10, in which he opens the door for Gentiles to enter. That role, of course, is not restricted to Peter. All true disciples proclaim the central key: that Jesus is the divine Christ. In Matthew 28:18-20 we find Him commanding all disciples to carry His message to the ends of the earth through the use of the teaching key so that many can come to a knowledge of Him and be baptized.

Peter's blessing also includes binding and loosing—a responsibility extended to all the disciples in Matthew 18:18. Most translations seem to infer that whatever the church decides on earth will get ratified in heaven. But that is not what Jesus said. The Greek verb tenses make it clear that the church on earth will carry out heaven's decisions, rather than heaven confirming the church's decisions.

With Matthew 16:16 and Peter's confession that Jesus is the divine Christ, we have come to a turning point in the gospel story. The disciples at last know *who* Jesus is, but not *what* that means. The *what* will provide the thread we need to follow as we turn our eyes upon Jesus as He moves toward the cross.

Part 5

Turn Your Eyes Upon Jesus as He Moves Toward the Cross

The Meaning of Messiahship

From that time Jesus began to show his disciples that he must go to Jerusalem and suffer many things from the elders and chief priests and scribes, and be killed, and on the third day be raised. Matt. 16:21, RSV.

B y now it had become evident that Israel as a corporate body was not going to accept Jesus as the Messiah. That left a major task for Jesus to accomplish: to prepare the disciples for His death.

Matthew 16:21 is the first explicit announcement of that fact. We should be aware of each of its elements. He

1. "*must go* to Jerusalem,"
2. "*suffer many things* from the elders and chief priests,"
3. "*be killed,*"
4. "and on the third day *be raised.*"

It wasn't as if He hadn't alluded to some of those events before. But now it was time for straight talk. Thus the significance of "Jesus began." He must teach those things openly and explicitly.

And why, we need to ask, did Jesus choose this precise time to set forth such important teachings? Because Peter's confession that He was the divine Christ indicated that he and the other disciples had begun to gain insight. They now knew who Jesus was. But it was one thing for them to confess that Jesus was the Messiah, but quite another for them to understand the nature of that Messiahship. The disciples had visions of glory and triumph in their heads, but Jesus knew that His end would be death and rejection. As He saw the plotting of the religious powers, He realized that it was vital to instruct His followers on the true reality of His mission.

Why the urgent necessity? Without the knowledge of His forthcoming death, it would have completely shattered their faith. And even with it their faith bordered on being wiped out. But He told them before it came to pass, so that when it did they might believe (John 13:19).

Earlier on, Jesus could not have given such information. Had He done so, because of the universal conception the Jews had of a kingly Messiah, the disciples would have rejected Him outright. They would have refused to believe because, as far as they were concerned, Jesus didn't even know what Messiahship was all about. But now, because they knew who He was, He could explain to them *what* His mission was.

"Must" Means Necessary

Then Jesus began to teach his disciples: "The Son of Man must suffer much and be rejected by the elders, the chief priests, and the teachers of the Law. He will be put to death, but three days later he will rise to life." Mark 8:31, TEV.

"Must" means necessary. Jesus was telling His disciples that He "must . . . be put to death." From His perspective, the cross was not an option but mandatory. He had come to earth not only to live a sinless life as our example, but "to give his life as a ransom for many" (Mark 10:45, RSV). "This is my blood of the covenant," He told His disciples at the Last Supper, "which is poured out for many" (Mark 14:24, RSV).

Christ's death was central to the plan of salvation. Without His substitutionary death there would be no salvation at all. Because of that necessity He began to teach the disciples plainly. But as the events related to His first attempt make plain, it would be a difficult task.

Why? Because everything in the disciples' background went against it. Their understanding of Messiahship taught plainly that the Messiah would "arise from the posterity of David" to "deliver in mercy the remnant" of God's people and at the same time destroy their enemies (4 Ezra 12:32-34). He would come "to smash the arrogance of sinners like a potter's jar; to shatter all their substance with an iron rod; to destroy the unlawful nations with the word of his mouth" (Ps. of Sol. 17:23, 24).

The Jews knew nothing of a suffering Messiah. As a result, Jesus' proclamation that He must suffer and die caught the disciples totally off guard. No line of reasoning could have led them to conclude that Jesus must die. A suffering Messiah was an impossibility. They were not ready for a Messiah who would perish to save them from their sins. They expected one who would rescue them from their Roman oppressors.

And not understanding the role of the Messiah, they certainly were in no position to capture the meaning of His resurrection—a lack that would later cause them great anguish.

The preconceived ideas they had brought to Scripture blinded the earliest disciples. The same dynamic threatens all of us.

Help us, Lord, to have eyes to see and hearts to believe.

The Struggling Christ

And Peter took him and began to rebuke him, saying, "God forbid, Lord! This
shall never happen to you." But he turned and said to Peter, "Get behind me,
Satan! You are a hindrance to me; for you are not on the side of God, but of men."
Matt. 16:22, 23, RSV.

What a fall! All the way from being inspired by God in verse 17 to being Satan in verse 23.

Peter may have correctly identified Jesus as the divine Messiah, but he had not the slightest idea what that involved. Thus the strenuous education program Jesus begins in verse 21 and extends up through His death on Calvary.

But why the forcefulness of the rebuke? Because Peter had usurped the role that Satan had earlier taken in the wilderness of temptation. Both of them had suggested that Jesus could fulfill His mission without His death on the cross. And to both Jesus exclaimed, "Get behind me, Satan!" (Mark 8:33, RSV).

We miss the point if we imagine that Jesus thought Peter was Satan. Rather, He saw Satan speaking through His chief disciple. Peter was playing the part of the tempter. And the temptation was the central one in Jesus' life. In fact, He undoubtedly found the thought of His forthcoming death to be even more distasteful than did Peter.

Jesus had seen crucifixions in His travels, and like any normal human being, He had no desire to exit the world by the excruciating death of the cross. He would have found it much easier to become the political Messiah that the Jews and the disciples expected.

But even more important, He had no wish to bear the judgment of the world by becoming sin for all humanity in the sacrifice on Calvary (John 12:31-33; 2 Cor. 5:21). The thought of separation from God while bearing the sins of the world on the cross was abhorrent to Him in the extreme.

The lure to do His own will by avoiding the cross was the *great temptation* of Jesus' life. He had conquered it after feeding the 5,000 when they tried to make Him king, and He would face it again in Gethsemane, where He would repeatedly pray, "If this cannot pass unless I drink it, thy will be done" (Matt. 26:42, RSV).

Here is a fruitful thought. We too often picture Jesus as above the daily problems that we contend with. Not so! He struggled also as He passed through life one step at a time. And He had to constantly resort to His knees. So do I.

Avoid Being Peter

He then began explaining things to them: "It is necessary that the Son of Man proceed to an ordeal of suffering, be tried, and after three days rise up alive." He said this simply and clearly so they couldn't miss it.
But Peter grabbed him in protest. Turning and seeing his disciples wavering, wondering what to believe, Jesus confronted Peter. "Peter, get out of my way! Satan, get lost! You have no idea how God works." Mark 8:31-33, Message.

The proud Peter got it right between the eyes. He was sincere enough, but had hit the most sensitive nerve ending in Jesus' being. The forcefulness of His rebuke to Peter implies the importance of the cross to His ministry and the need to educate the future leaders of His church on its centrality.

Not only had the temptation come, but it had emerged from the mouth of a friend. It is a sad fact of life that Satan can use Jesus' followers—even His ministers—to do his own work.

As Christians we have not only the potential of betraying Jesus, but also one another. We too can guide fellow Christians in the wrong direction and discourage them from doing God's will by advising them to avoid all dangers to themselves and inconveniences to ourselves. Lest we unwittingly play the role of Satan, we need to be more aware than was Peter.

Peter's experience can teach us yet other lessons. One is that we as Christians are a mixed bag. In one moment I can have a divine insight, then in the next I can be a tool of the devil. At our best we are fallible creatures partly controlled by knowledge and partly by ignorance. All of us have one foot in the kingdom. We have been saved in the sense that we have accepted Jesus, but the plain fact is that He has a lot more to do in us.

Another lesson is that we need to be careful not to cast off people because of their stupidity and errors. Jesus, in the days and weeks to come, would demonstrate almost infinite patience in working with His erring disciples. One writer has pointed out that "only a massive stupidity could keep them from understanding," but they managed to do exactly that until after the Resurrection. Jesus, however, did not abandon them as a lost cause. Our Savior had begun to teach them about the meaning of being the Christ. Just as He didn't give up on them, so He hasn't given up on me. And I shouldn't give up on you.

The Meaning
of Discipleship: Number 1

Then Jesus said to His disciples, "If anyone desires to come after Me, let him deny himself, and take up his cross, and follow Me." Matt. 16:24, NKJV.

When Jesus "began to teach them that the Son of man must suffer many things . . . and be killed" (Mark 8:31, RSV), He was truly only commencing His instruction, because *a new understanding of Messiahship dictates a new perspective of discipleship*. And if the new interpretation of Messiahship was distasteful to Peter and the others, the new concept of discipleship would be equally abhorrent. "If anyone desires to come after Me, let him deny himself, and take up his cross, and follow Me."

That verse contains two of the most difficult words that a person will ever have to face—"deny" and "cross." When we think of self-denial we imagine abstinence from certain luxuries for a certain period of time, while at the same time, perhaps, congratulating ourselves on how well we are doing in being self-controlled and/or generous.

But that is far from what Jesus meant by "deny." It is a sharp and demanding word. One scholar suggests that in verse 24 it means "to forget one's self, lose sight of one's self and one's interests."

Another writer points out that "the denial of *self* is something deeper" than mere self-denial. "It is making ourselves not an end, but a means, in the kingdom of God. It is subordinating the clamoring ego, with its shrill claim for priority, its preoccupation with 'I,' 'me,' and 'mine,' its concern for self-assertion, its insistence on comfort and prestige; denying self, not for the sake of denial as a sort of moral athletics, but for Christ's sake, for the sake of putting the self into his cause."

Thus *there is a massive difference between self-denial and denying one's self*. The first is a minor surface operation, while the second is a matter of the heart—or, more specifically, a change of heart.

Here is a place where each of us followers of Jesus needs to become more transparent, more honest. Jeremiah tells us that "the heart is deceitful above all things, and desperately corrupt" (Jer. 17:9, RSV). The last thing that my heart wants to do is to realize that denial of the self stands at the center of being a genuine Christian.

The Meaning
of Discipleship: Number 2

If anyone wants to follow in my footsteps, he must give up all right to himself, take up his cross and follow me. Mark 8:34, Phillips.

The second difficult word in Jesus' description of discipleship is "cross." The bad news to Peter and the rest of the disciples (including us) is that Jesus' cross is not the only one. He goes on to say that each of His followers will have his or her own cross.

To fully understand the statement that each person must take up the cross, we need to put ourselves in the place of those first disciples. The idea of a cross or of being crucified doesn't do much for our twenty-first-century imaginations. To us, "crucifixion" is a word that has lost most of its meaning. But that was not true for the disciples. They knew that bearing a cross was a one-way trip leading to nowhere but death.

It is with that realization that the word "deny" and the word "cross" intersect. The cross, like the concept of denial of self, has been trivialized by the Christian community. For some people, bearing the cross is wearing it as an ornament around their neck. For others it means putting up with some discomfort or inconvenience in life, such as a nagging husband or a sloppy wife, or even a physical impediment.

Jesus does not have in mind those caricatures of cross-bearing. He is speaking of the cross as an instrument of death—not physical for most of His hearers, but of the crucifixion of the self, the denial of the center of our life and our primary allegiance to our self. Ellen White points out that "the warfare against self is the greatest battle ever fought" (*Steps to Christ*, p. 43). And James Denney emphasizes that "though sin may have a natural birth it does not die a natural death; in every case it has to be morally sentenced and put to death." That sentencing is an act of the will under the impulse of the Holy Spirit. Jesus and Paul repeatedly refer to it as a crucifixion.

Paul is especially clear on that topic in Romans 6, in which he describes becoming a Christian as a crucifixion of the "old self" (verse 6, RSV) and a resurrection to a new way of life with a new center—Jesus and His will. It is that death that is implicit in His command to deny one's self and bear one's cross. Paul points out that baptism by immersion is the perfect symbol of spiritual death and resurrection to a new life centered on God (verses 1-11).

The Meaning
of Discipleship: Number 3

For whoever desires to save his life will lose it, but whoever loses his life for My sake will find it. For what profit is it to a man if he gains the whole world, and loses his soul? Or what will a man give in exchange for his soul? Matt. 16:25, 26, NKJV.

We have spent a disproportionate amount of time on Matthew 16:13-26. For 10 days we have meditated upon those verses. And for good reason. They provide the pivot point in the gospel story. Up to that point we focused on *who* Jesus is. After it the emphasis shifts to *what* Messiahship involves.

And central to that meaning are the two crosses—Christ's and ours. The teaching of the two crosses holds the core of the meaning of Christianity, in terms of both Messiahship and discipleship.

To understand Jesus' teaching related to my cross more fully, I need to remember that sin, in its most basic sense, is putting my self and my will, rather than God and His will, at the center of my life. Sin is rebellion against Him in the sense that I choose to become the ruler of my own life—saying "No" to God and "Yes" to self.

It is the self-centered life principle so natural to human beings that must die. Thus Dietrich Bonhoeffer speaks to the heart of what it means to be a Christian when he writes that "when Christ calls a man, he bids him come and die."

Jesus pointed to the essential human problem when He claimed that "no one can serve two masters" (Matt. 6:24, RSV). The bottom line is: Whom will I put on the throne of my life? My self or God? I cannot serve both at the same time. *When I come face-to-face with the claim of Christ, I must either crucify Him or let Him crucify me. There is no middle ground.*

It is in that context that losing one's life or gaining it and gaining the whole world or losing it takes on meaning. What, I need to ask myself, is my price? In what area and at what point would I be willing to sell out my soul in exchange for earthly rewards? Is it popularity, money, prestige, "love," "fun," or something else? In the end it doesn't make any difference, because I am still stuck with a choice that will not go away. The decision is always between something or Jesus.

Encouragement in Times of Need

After six days Jesus took with him Peter, James and John the brother of James, and led them up a high mountain by themselves. There he was transfigured before them. His face shone like the sun, and his clothes became as white as the light. Just then there appeared before them Moses and Elijah. . . . And a voice from the cloud said, "This is my Son, whom I love; with whom I am well pleased. Listen to him!" Matt. 17:1-5, NIV.

The Transfiguration is connected with what has gone before. That is, Peter's confession that Jesus is the Christ (Matt. 16:16) and Jesus' devastating prediction of His death and resurrection and His statement about His disciples' crosses (verses 21-28).

Matthew tells us that Jesus went up on the mountain six days after the events at Caesarea Philippi, but he doesn't tell us why. But Luke does. Luke 9:28 claims that He took three disciples "up on the mountain to pray" (RSV).

He certainly had plenty to pray about. By now He had fully committed Himself to go to Jerusalem and the cross that awaited Him there, a thought that horrified Him. He also had a burden to pray for His noncomprehending disciples, those whom He would soon leave behind to head up His church on earth.

And what weak individuals they were at this stage. Luke tells us that what they did on the Mount of Transfiguration they would later do in Gethsemane— they slept while Jesus prayed (verse 32). And these were His closest disciples— those whom He had for the first time selected from among the 12 for special instruction. If they were operating spiritually at such a low level, what must have been the condition of the other nine? No wonder Jesus felt the need to pray.

There upon the Mount the Transfiguration took place, a representation of the future kingdom of glory in miniature. Its purpose was to encourage both Jesus and the disciples, who were in a "tailspin of bewilderment" as a result of Jesus' redefining Messiahship and discipleship. But first and foremost, it strengthened Jesus Himself.

Especially important was the voice from heaven—the same voice that Jesus had heard at His baptism when He was just starting out on His mission. Now He hears it again at the very point His ministry turns its direction toward Jerusalem. God was putting His stamp of approval on Jesus' decision and His course of action. It was as if the Father were saying, "Go ahead, You have made the right choice. I will be with You."

We can be thankful that we have a God willing to encourage us when we need it most.

June 28

Not Every Day Is a Spiritual High

And when they came to the crowd, a man came up to him and kneeling before him said, "Lord, have mercy on my son, for he is an epileptic and he suffers terribly; for often he falls into the fire, and often into the water. And I brought him to your disciples, and they could not heal him." Matt. 17:14-16, RSV.

What a contrast! On the Mount of Transfiguration Jesus and the "three" had witnessed a bit of heaven. Now, coming off the mountain, they glimpse a fragment of hell in the life below. To say the least, they descend to find a difficult situation.

In fact, it was exactly the kind of circumstances that Peter had hoped to avoid when he had said on the mountain, "It is good for us to be here; let us make three tabernacles" (Mark 9:5, NASB). If Peter could have had it his way he would have stayed up there forever.

But Jesus had not forgotten His mission. The purpose of the Transfiguration was to strengthen Him for it. And He arrived just in time to face a serious problem. The nine disciples had publicly failed in healing a boy, and the scribes were having a great time of it, casting doubt not only on the ability of the disciples but, by extension, on Jesus.

The humiliation of the disciples was extreme. It was at that point that Jesus showed up and cured the boy. Why had they failed? the disciples asked Him later. That was a good question, since He had already given "them authority over the unclean spirits" (Mark 6:7, RSV). And upon returning from their first mission experience without Jesus they had reported that they had "cast out many demons" (verse 13, RSV). What was different now? A first suggestion is that Jesus' announcement a week earlier that He would be rejected and die had shattered their faith. They couldn't give what they didn't have. Beyond that, they may have had a bad attitude, grousing about the special privilege of Peter, John, and James in going with Jesus while they remained behind.

What we know for sure is that their prayer life was weak (Mark 9:29). Of course, their discouragement and lack of prayer were not unrelated. Most people stop praying when they become discouraged. Yet that is the very time we need to pray more than ever.

It would be nice if we could always remain on a spiritual high on the mount with Jesus. But the hard fact of life is that mountain highs of necessity are followed by "coming down" to the real world. And in that we need prayer to navigate successfully, even if we don't feel like praying.

The end point: Pray anyway.

Lessons From a Fish Story

*What thinkest thou, Simon? of whom do the kings of the earth take custom or trib-
ute? of their own children, or of strangers? Peter saith unto him, Of strangers. Jesus
saith unto him, Then are the children free. Notwithstanding, lest we should offend
them, go thou to the sea, and cast an hook, and take up the fish that first cometh up;
and when thou hast opened his mouth, thou shalt find a piece of money: that take,
and give unto them for me and thee.* Matt. 17:25-27.

Another example of the unpreparedness of the disciples is the Temple tax
episode. That event takes the form of an attempt by the Jewish leaders to
trap Jesus by creating a situation in which either answer to their question is
problematic.

The question "Does not your teacher pay the tax?" catches Peter off guard.
A negative answer will provide a pretext for charging Jesus with rejecting the
Temple service. Peter, wanting to avoid that horn of the dilemma, quickly an-
swers that Jesus will pay the tax.

But that hasty reply merely lands Peter (and Jesus) on the other horn. After
all, priests and others devoted solely to God's service could claim exemption.
As a result, Peter in effect denies Jesus' role as a prophet and teacher in Israel.
Thus the same apostle who a short time before had set forth Jesus as the Son
of God and the Messiah now stumbles over himself and sanctions the very
conception of Jesus put forth by the Jewish leaders.

Jesus does the best thing to disarm the situation, telling Peter that He is
exempt, but to pay anyway by catching a fish that would have the right amount
of money in its mouth.

At first glance that miracle seems out of harmony with what we read in the
biblical Gospels and more in line with the exotic miracles of the apocryphal
gospels. But a moment's reflection shows that the miracle of the fish with the
coin fits the very need of Jesus at the time. For one thing, it definitely proves to
Peter the true status of Jesus. Second, it is almost impossible to believe that the
disciple could keep his mouth shut about how they obtained the money. Third,
even though Jesus outwardly complied, technically it was not His money that
paid the tax. Thus the miracle made both horns of the dilemma disappear.

An overlooked point in this event is that Jesus acted as He did so as not to
give offense. The lesson we need to catch is that He avoided useless confrontation whenever possible. What a better place the church of today would be in if
all disciples followed Him in avoiding needless conflict.

June 30

The Disciples' Favorite Question

At that time the disciples came to Jesus, saying, "Who is the greatest in the kingdom of heaven?" And calling to him a child, he put him in the midst of them, and said, "Truly, I say to you, unless you turn and become like children, you will never enter the kingdom of heaven. Whoever humbles himself like this child, he is the greatest in the kingdom of heaven." Matt. 18:1-4, RSV.

With this passage we have come to the disciples' favorite question. They seem to be obsessed with it. Mark 9:33, 34 tells us they had been "arguing" on the road about who was the greatest.

Perhaps the stimulus for the problem was Jesus' blessing of Peter after his reply that Jesus was the divine Christ. It is almost impossible to believe that he hadn't gloated over that commendation. Then there was the selection of three of the disciples to go with Jesus on the Mount of Transfiguration.

But at a deeper level the question of greatness resides at the center of the sinful human heart. The desire for egocentric importance fuels both the world's greatest accomplishments and its greatest sins. The desire to stand out, to be superior, to have people look at and admire "me" is part of the great rebellion of human beings against God. It was also the root of Lucifer's sin in heaven. He had said in his heart, "I will raise my throne above the stars of God. . . . I will make myself like the Most High" (Isa. 14:13, 14, NIV). The desire to be the greatest, even to be the god of our own life, forms the very foundation of sin. And, as we noted earlier in discussing Matthew 16:24, the only solution to that problem is the cross—that is, the death of our selves and the born-again experience in Christ.

In Matthew 18:2-4 Jesus tells His disciples that the greatest in the kingdom will be like little children. Children were of little account in antiquity, and we find Jesus here turning the wisdom of the world on its head by proclaiming that true greatness does not lie in accomplishments and worldly sophistication but in the humility and transparency of children.

The disciples, as we might expect, didn't like that lesson and immediately forgot it. To be honest, I don't enjoy it either.

And with that realization it is back to the foot of the cross in humble repentance.

Get Off Your Holy High Horse

Whoever receives one such child in my name receives me, but whoever causes one of these little ones who believe in me to sin, it would be better to have a great millstone fastened around his neck and to be drowned in the depths of the sea. . . . See that you do not despise one of these little ones. For I tell you that in heaven their angels always see the face of my Father who is in heaven. Matt. 18:5-10, ESV.

One thing is clear from these verses: God cares for the weak ones in our congregation, whether they be young and innocent (the "child" in verse 5) or new or struggling members (the "little ones" of verses 6 and 10).

While verse 5 has a promise connected to the reception and caring of insignificant children, Jesus changes the tone in verse 6 from promise to warning. Meanwhile, the topic in the flow of His presentation moves from humility to the seriousness of causing "unimportant" believers (the "little ones") to stumble in their Christian walk.

The overall message of the passage is that it is better to have a millstone around one's neck and be drowned than to lead a weak Christian astray.

The warning is clear enough. Yet how easy it is to heap honors upon the visiting guest speaker while not even saying hello to those who look as if they can't afford proper clothes for church.

Endless stories tell about the deacon who speaks harshly to a person who doesn't seem to fit into the congregation; about the "saintly" matrons of the church who criticize new Christians in their hearing about something they brought to the potluck that wasn't up to their personal standards; about the better-than type who offend a person searching after meaning with comments about their jewelry; about those who have insulted teenagers who haven't quite got their act together.

It is no wonder that many never return to our church. But their "guardian angels" (Matt. 18:10, NEB) are working with them. And we should also.

Today is the time to get off of our holy high horse and take heed to the words of Jesus, extending our love to those "little ones" found in every congregation who are beloved of God. He wants to change our hearts and characters so that we might be a force for good in their lives.

July 2

So You're Offended!

If your brother sins against you, go and tell him his fault, between you and him alone. If he listens to you, you have gained your brother. But if he does not listen, take one or two others along with you, that every word may be confirmed by the evidence of two or three witnesses. If he refuses to listen to them, tell it to the church; and if he refuses to listen even to the church, let him be to you as a Gentile or a tax collector. Matt. 18:15-17, RSV.

How much misery we could avert if church members followed the counsel of Jesus set forth in these verses. All too often what happens is that individuals, whose overly sensitive selves think they have been offended, begin to shoot off their mouths to any who will listen. Possible reconciliation gets transformed into gossip and eventually the trash of bad feelings.

In considering "our" feelings and "our" selves we trounce on other "selves," whom we may or may not have even understood.

I remember as a pastor that people would come up to me and begin to complain about others in the church. Of course, they expected me to "do something about it," which usually meant that they wanted me to talk to the "offending party" or even have the church take action against them.

My answer was always the same: "Why have you come to me?" Most of the time I was met with a blank stare. At that point I would open the Bible to Matthew 18:15.

Jesus couldn't have said it more clearly. Don't make the problem public, but go to the person privately and keep it between the two of you if possible. It never helps to bring sin out in the open if we can solve the problem in private. Then again, in many cases we are dealing with misunderstanding rather than "sin" or true offense. Sometimes it is merely our own trumped-up vision of our own "dignity."

Whatever the problem, Jesus makes it clear that the offended one should take the initiative—"go." That is a command to be like the God who sent His own Son to make reconciliation with those who had "spit in His face."

If a personal conference doesn't solve the problem, invite a couple other mature Christians into the discussion to help bring in some objectivity. And, if that doesn't work, then, and only then, should you take the issue to the congregation.

Bottom line: Here is a Christian grace I can start living today.

Peter's Try at Greatness

Then came Peter to him, and said, Lord, how oft shall my brother sin against me, and I forgive him? till seven times? Matt. 18:21.

Now there is a practical question. One wonders why Peter even asked it. But, given the context, perhaps the reason is not difficult to discover. For one thing, Jesus had been speaking to the topic of problems between individuals. For another, the disciple had been hearing echoes of glory in his head ever since Jesus had commended him at Caesarea Philippi. And, third, since that time all of the disciples had been arguing about which of them was the greatest.

Peter was sure that it was him. And now he would demonstrate it before them all, including Jesus, who would undoubtedly have praise for his generosity.

"How often am I to forgive my brother . . . ? As many as seven times?" (Matt. 18:21, NEB). Peter had no doubt about the "greatness" of his statement. After all, seven forgivenesses is a lot, especially since the rabbis taught that one must not forgive more than three times.

Thus Rabbi Jose ben Hanina claimed that "he who begs forgiveness from his neighbour must not do so more than three times." And Rabbi Jose ben Jehuda said, "If a man commits an offense once, they forgive him; if he commits an offense a second time, they forgive him; if he commits an offense a third time, they forgive him; the fourth time they do not forgive."

The biblical base for that ruling appears in the opening chapters of Amos, from which the rabbis concluded from the oft-repeated "for three sins" of the various nations, "even for four," that the limit of God's forgiveness was three times. Thus Peter, in an act of exceptional generosity, doubled the accepted Jewish quota and added one for good measure. Not bad for a hard-fisted and probably short-tempered fisherman.

But behind Peter's outward question lies one that interested him far more. Namely, when have I reached the limit of forgiveness? When with a clear conscience can I cut loose and let people have it? Or when, after I have filled the obligatory limit, may I be my real self and with a clear conscience give people what they deserve?

Those are questions all of us would like to have answered. Christ's disgusting response is "never."

The Limits of Forgiveness, Part 1

Jesus replied, "I do not say seven times; I say seventy times seven." Matt. 18:22, NEB.

Yesterday we began to examine Peter's question about the limits of forgiveness. The disciple, of course, had not only asked the question, but had supplied a rather generous answer. Seven forgivenesses is a lot of forgiving, especially in an area of sensitivity.

Jesus answers Peter in two parts. First, He says, the correct number is not seven but "seventy times seven" (NEB, RSV, NIV margin) or 490. Now that is a lot of forgiveness (even if it is a mere 77 times, as suggested by the NIV)—so much that a person would lose count before transgression number 491 (or even 78) had arrived. However, Jesus is not teaching a lesson on the arithmetic of forgiveness, but rather that forgiveness has no limit.

That is not the answer Peter expected, for, as we noted yesterday, Peter, like you and me, is really more interested in the limit of Christian love and forbearance than in its extent. After all, it is reassuring to know at what point I can stop loving my neighbor with a good conscience, to know when I have fulfilled my quota of love and forgiveness, so that I can as a "good Christian" let people have what they deserve.

All too often I find myself standing with Peter and the all-too-human implication underlying his question: "When can I let go?" "When do I have a right to explode at these stupid yokels that I have to live with? work with? go to church with?"

Here are some real questions of practicality for daily living. Especially since those other people really are disgusting—really are deserving of a bit of my wrath, a good tongue-lashing, a piece of my mind. And they are. I have been so patient with them, but they don't seem to get the point. So if forgiveness doesn't seem to solve the problem, perhaps a bit of attack will wake them up.

That line of thought represents Peter's ideas on the topic and mine also. But Jesus frustrates both of us by stating that there is no limit to forgiveness.

That is not an answer that Peter can even begin to understand. So in the next few verses Jesus will illustrate His point.

Lord, give me ears to hear as my Lord tells me something that I really need to understand.

The Limits of Forgiveness, Part 2

Therefore the kingdom of heaven may be compared to a king who wished to settle accounts with his servants. When he began the reckoning, one was brought to him who owed him ten thousand talents; and as he could not pay, his lord ordered him to be sold, with his wife and children and all that he had, and payment to be made. So the servant fell on his knees, imploring him, "Lord, have patience with me, and I will pay you everything." And out of pity for him the lord of that servant released him and forgave him the debt. Matt. 18:23-27, RSV.

Jesus knew that Peter would not get the point of the 490 forgivenesses from a mere statement on the topic. As a result, part 2 of His reply to the apostle's question is a story that illustrates the point.

The parable of the unmerciful servant (Matt. 18:23-35) has three main characters: the king (God), a servant forgiven an unbelievably large debt (you and I), and a servant (our neighbor, wife, husband, children, fellow church member) who owes the first servant (you and I) a manageable debt.

The parable has three scenes. In scene number one the first servant is in the king's audience chamber, where the ruler forgives him a large debt. It was not merely large—it was a stupendous amount, a debt that could never be paid.

Ten thousand talents doesn't mean much to me because I don't think in those terms. But the figure begins to be understandable when I realize that the combined annual budget for Idumea, Judea, and Samaria was only 600 talents. And the budget for the relatively prosperous Galilee was 300 talents.

Thus when Jesus notes that "he could not pay," He was uttering a plain truth. No way an individual could even begin to pay such a 10,000-talent debt.

At that point the parable moves into human logic—give the debtor what he deserves. But in the face of that just punishment the servant falls on his knees, praying for the king to allow him time and he would repay everything, an impossibility that must have been evident even to him.

At that point in the parable divine logic takes over. The king forgives the penitent petitioner. Here is grace: giving people what they don't deserve, giving them what they need.

We Peters have no problem with the story thus far. After all, we love God's grace when bestowed upon us. Sleeping better in the light of grace, we praise God every day for that special gift. And we should.

July 6

The Limits of Forgiveness,
Part 2 Again

But that same servant, as he went out, came upon one of his fellow servants who owed him a hundred denarii; and seizing him by the throat he said, "Pay what you owe." So his fellow servant fell down and besought him, "Have patience with me, and I will pay you." He refused and went and put him in prison till he should pay the debt.
Matt. 18:28-30, RSV.

Scene two in the parable moves the action from the divine-human perspective of scene one to that of the relationship between two human beings. And it is at this level that we Peters get into trouble.

Let's catch the dynamics. Having just gotten off of my knees and left my place of prayer, I am truly in a good mood in the full assurance of God's forgiveness. So far, so good.

But 10 minutes later I run across a jerk who has been avoiding me for weeks. And for good reason. He owes me money, and I am the last person he wants to see.

And it is no small amount. After all, 100 denarii is 100 days' pay, approximately a third of a year's salary. Even at the modest minimum of $7.50 per hour for 100 eight-hour days the amount equals $6,000. That is a significant part of my yearly budget. I want my money, and I want it now. So I grab him by the throat and order him to pay up or else.

And what is the response? A falling on the knees and a request to have patience and a promise to pay what he owes.

That's not good enough for me. I have had to deal with this slick dude long enough. Now is the time for justice and to make things right. Gracious too long with this shifty character, I will give him exactly what he deserves.

In act two of Christ's parable on forgiveness we find the human perspective. This person has used up the quota of forgiveness. Having reached the limits of forgiveness, I can at last cut loose with my righteous fury. It is time for me to hand out the legal punishment.

Completely overlooked is the fact that his request for mercy from me almost exactly echoes my recent prayer to God on the same topic. Also, conveniently, I have "forgotten" that the money owed to me is really a part of my debt to God.

But why remember such technicalities when I am right and others are wrong? It is only just that I give them what they deserve. Or is it?

The Limits of Forgiveness, Part 2 Yet Again

When his fellow servants saw what had taken place, they were greatly distressed, and they went and reported to their lord all that had taken place. Then his lord summoned him and said to him, "You wicked servant! I forgave you all that debt because you besought me; and should not you have had mercy on your fellow servant, as I had mercy on you?" And in anger his lord delivered him to the jailers, till he should pay all his debt. So also my heavenly Father will do to every one of you, if you do not forgive your brother from your heart. Matt. 18:31-35, RSV.

Scene three brings Jesus' answer to Peter on the limits of forgiveness to a climax. The moral of the story: we need to be just as forgiving to others as God has been to us (verse 33). The same lesson appears in the Sermon on the Mount, in which Jesus said, "If you do not forgive others their sins, your Father will not forgive your sins" (Matt. 6:15, NIV).

Many have attempted to moderate the parable or explain why its sharp contrasts cannot be genuine. But it is those very contrasts that help us to understand not only the wideness of God's mercy but also the mercy He expects in us as Christians.

The 10,000-talent debt is unbelievably large. A talent equals 6,000 denarii. Thus the debt is 60,000,000 days' wages. One could work the 100-denarii debt off in 100 days, but it would take more than 164,383 years to erase the 10,000 talents if one labored seven days a week.

Alternately, one could carry the 100-denarii debt in one pocket. But the 10,000-talent debt would require an army of approximately 8,600 porters, each transporting a 60-pound bag of coins, forming a line five miles long if spaced a yard apart.

William Barclay sums up the meaning of the contrast nicely when he pens that "the point is that nothing that men can do to us can in any way compare with what we have done to God; and if God has forgiven us the debt we owe Him, we must forgive our fellow-men the debts they owe us. Nothing that we have to forgive can even faintly or remotely compare with that which we have been forgiven."

So Peter has the answer to his question regarding the limits of forgiveness. For both him and us today, the answer lies not in counting or in some sort of extreme moral exertion, but rather in tilting your head toward the cross and beholding the Christ who paid your debt that you might go free.

Help me, Father, to have Your heart and Your love as I deal with others today.

July 8

Jesus on Marriage

The Pharisees also came to Him, testing Him, and saying to Him, "Is it lawful for a man to divorce his wife for just any reason?" And He answered and said to them, "Have you not read that He who made them at the beginning made them male and female," and said, "For this reason a man shall leave his father and mother and be joined to his wife, and the two shall become one flesh"? So then, they are no longer two but one flesh. Therefore what God has joined together, let not man separate.
Matt. 19:3-6, NKJV.

Two of the greatest sources of Jesus' teachings are His responses to the questions of Peter and those to the queries of the Jewish leaders. It is in the context of an attempt by the Jews to trap Him that Jesus provides us with five central ideas on marriage.

First, God Himself designed marriage. It is a God-given institution, rather than a social contract. Second, marriage is an ordinance between the sexes. God "made them male and female." God's intention was not a unisex world. Michael Green notes that "there is a God-ordained difference and complementarity between the sexes. That is so obvious that it only needs to be stated in this late twentieth century when homosexuality has come to be seen as an equally valid alternative to marriage." Third, marriage is intended to be permanent: "the two shall become one flesh." The Creator never intended in His perfect creation that the marriage relationship should ever shatter. Unfortunately, in a less-than-perfect world every union does not fulfill God's goal. But divorce is never His ideal.

Fourth, marriage is exclusive. The two—not three, four, or five—are to become one flesh. One man and one woman form a marriage. That ideal rules out the convenient "affairs" of so many people today and the polygamy of the ancients. Apparently, God's allowance for polygamy in the Old Testament was a less-than-ideal concession to entrenched custom and human weakness. Fifth, marriage creates a nuclear family unit. It includes both leaving one's parents and uniting with a spouse. Thus marriage becomes the strongest and most important of all human relationships.

Today is a good moment to stop and thank God for marriage. It is also an excellent time for those who are married to renew their vows to each other and for those who are contemplating marriage to think seriously of the sacred implications of this divine gift. We have a God who desires to make good marriages even better, to heal broken relationships, and to forgive those who have fallen short of His ideal.

A Man With the Right Question

As He was setting out on a journey, a man ran up to Him and knelt before Him,
and asked Him, "Good Teacher, what shall I do to inherit eternal life?" And Jesus
said to him, "Why do you call Me good? No one is good except God alone."
Mark 10:17, 18, NASB.

The most remarkable thing about this individual is that he approached Jesus at all. Matthew tells us that he was young and rich (Matt. 19:20, 22,
23), while Luke says that he was a ruler (Luke 18:18). It is that very class that
Jesus had the most difficult time with. The poor and the prostitutes and the tax
collectors flocked to Him, but not the Jewish aristocracy of either the religious
or political realms.

The man not only came, but he "ran." And not only that, he knelt before
Jesus. Here was a person who defied his social class, someone willing to face
the scorn of his peers. Now other rich men of the ruling class found themselves drawn to Jesus. One thinks of Nicodemus and Joseph of Arimathea. But
they were discrete. Nicodemus, for example, came to Jesus secretly "by night"
(John 3:2). And Joseph quietly went to Pilate to request permission to bury
Him (Matt. 27:57, 58). One can hardly imagine them running up to Jesus and
publicly kneeling before Him in the dust. This young man had something special about him, a zeal that is refreshing.

The aristocrat also had a concern, one that blinded him to everything else.
He was in earnest about salvation. Addressing Jesus as "Good Teacher," he inquired what he had to "*do*" to inherit eternal life. Obviously he saw behavior as
the key to religion.

Before giving an answer, Jesus questioned him on why he had described
Him as good. After all, Jesus noted, "no one is good except God alone." Apparently Jesus was seeking to get the young man to be explicit as to where he stood
on His identity. Was He merely a teacher or was He God, as the use of the term
good implied? The rich young ruler had undoubtedly heard Jesus before. But
he was still in the valley of decision on His identity. Jesus' question was a gentle
nudge to force him to come to grips with the issue.

In the face of this remarkable young man I need to ask myself anew, "How is
my enthusiasm quotient for Jesus?" And beyond that, "Is my interest in eternal
life the dominating aspect of my life?" Good questions to meditate upon today.

Jesus Provides the "Correct" Answer

"What must I do to inherit eternal life?"
... Jesus answered, ... "You know the commandments: 'You shall not murder,
you shall not commit adultery, you shall not steal, you shall not give false testimony,
you shall not defraud, honor your father and your mother.'" Mark 10:17-19, NIV.

The rich young ruler expected a behavioral answer to his question about salvation, and Jesus gave him what he wanted, telling him that if he desired eternal life he should "keep the commandments" (Matt. 19:17). Then Jesus listed several of the Ten Commandments.

The list itself helps us begin to understand the young man's problem. We should note at least four things about the list. First, the commandments cited all come from the second table of the law and deal with the way people treat others. That selection provides a hint that his problem probably centered on his relationship to other people rather than on his dedication to God.

Second, Jesus lists the commandments in order: the sixth, seventh, eighth, and ninth. But then, to our surprise, he lists the fifth after the ninth. Why? Undoubtedly to call attention to it. The rich young ruler may have been among those Jesus condemned in Mark 7:11-13 for using the human tradition of *corban* to avoid caring for his parents' material needs in their old age.

Third, we find an injection that is not one of the Ten Commandments: "You shall not defraud." The term is used of keeping back wages from laborers. The implication is that he may have gained at least some of his wealth at the expense of the poor.

Fourth, Jesus does not mention the tenth commandment (dealing with covetousness) at all. It will soon be evident that covetousness stands at the very center of the man's spiritual problem.

In Matthew's account Jesus adds a quotation from Leviticus 19:18 ("love your neighbor as yourself"[RSV] to the commands that one should obey (Matt. 19:19, RSV). Once again, Jesus uses a text that was important in Judaism and at the core of the young man's problem.

In closing our reading today, let us use our imagination. Picture yourself talking with Jesus about the Ten Commandments. How would He arrange them to meet your special "issues" as you deal with God and other individuals? Your honest answer will be revealing.

Jesus Provides the "Real" Answer

"Teacher," he declared, "all these I have kept since I was a boy."
Jesus looked at him and loved him. "One thing you lack," he said. "Go, sell
everything you have and give to the poor, and you will have treasure in heaven.
Then come, follow me."
At this the man's face fell. He went away sad, because he had great wealth.
Mark 10:20-22, NIV.

Apparently not at all embarrassed by his claim, the young man confidently replies that he has kept all of the commands that Jesus had listed. He truly did seem to be a shining example of a certain type of moral person who prided himself in his obedience to God's stipulations. But he will soon discover that mere morality is not enough to gain entry into the kingdom of heaven. Jesus will probe a bit further, demonstrating that the individual's obedience was outward and legal rather than inward and spiritual.

Before moving to that examination, we should note that Mark tells us that Jesus "loved him." Obviously He saw something special in the young ruler. Perhaps it was a heartfelt appreciation of his evident sincerity, fearlessness, and enthusiasm. Here was a person, Jesus may have thought, who could truly do something for the kingdom.

It was at that point that He extended to the young man an invitation to become a disciple. "Come," He said, and "follow me."

But there was a condition: "Go, sell everything you have and give to the poor." With that unexpected command Jesus cut to the heart of the rich man's problem. Mark tells us that "he was saddened, and he went away grieving, for he was one who owned much property" (NASB). It would be just as true to say that his property owned him. The center of his life, his possessions were the one thing that he would not give up, even for the kingdom.

One of the most persistent memories of my experience at Pacific Union College is of a large painting of Jesus and the rich young ruler that hung on the wall behind the pulpit in the chapel. In a meditative mood, the young man was deciding what was really of most value to him.

We are each deciding that same question every day. Some of us, like the man confronted by Jesus, will opt to play church without total surrender and dedication. But Jesus is not interested in partial Christians. He desires all of me.

A Side Lesson on Wealth

Jesus said to him, "If you would be perfect, go, sell what you possess and give to the poor, and you will have treasure in heaven; and come, follow me." When the young man heard this he went away sorrowful; for he had great possessions.
Matt. 19:21, 22, RSV.

It is easy to draw the wrong conclusion from these verses. The rich young ruler's problem was not money itself but the *love* of money.

Jesus was not categorically condemning wealth in His confrontation with the ruler. After all, He did not make the same request of Nicodemus or Zacchaeus or other people of means that He dealt with. But wealth was the danger for this man. It was his idol, the thing that kept him from God.

Halford Luccock points out that "Jesus was not laying down poverty as either a requirement or an ideal for everyone. He was a Good Physician, and did not prescribe the same pill for every patient. He looked on this patient and loved him with an individual love, a love which saw him as a person with a specialized need. Then he prescribed the action that would free him from the thing that was holding him back. In this case, it was wealth."

For you or me it may be something different. But we all must meet the same requirement—total surrender of all that we are and all that we have to God's will so that He is truly Lord of our life.

When I read the story of the rich young ruler, another rich-young-ruler type comes to my mind. But what a difference in their responses. Both had power, prestige, and money. Both received the invitation to discipleship. Both had to make a decision to give up their past. But what a difference.

In Paul we get a glimpse of what the young ruler could have been like as he used his gifts for God. But the latter chose to use his gifts for himself.

With such individuals in mind, the apostle would later write that "the love of money is the root of all evils" (1 Tim. 6:10, RSV). But for those who have been able to put wealth in its right place, God has utilized their gifts across the history of the church to sustain His work and help those in need.

Wealth is tricky. It can be either a curse or a blessing. As with all gifts, it is up to each of us as to how we will use them.

Human Impossibilities =
God's Possibilities

Then Jesus said to His disciples, "Assuredly, I say to you that it is hard for a rich man to enter the kingdom of heaven. And again I say to you, it is easier for a camel to go through the eye of a needle than for a rich man to enter the kingdom of God."
When His disciples heard it, they were greatly astonished, saying,
"Who then can be saved?"
But Jesus looked at them and said to them, "With men this is impossible, but with God all things are possible." Matt. 19:23-26, NKJV.

After the rich young ruler turns from Jesus and His claim of total surrender, Jesus tells His disciples that "it is hard for a rich man to enter the kingdom of heaven," just as difficult as it is for a camel to go through the eye of a needle.

The camel going through the needle's eye imagery has had several interesting interpretations. One of them holds that walled cities had two gates. One was the great main gate through which all traffic moved. In addition, the wall often had a little low and narrow gate. The theory suggests that when the main gate was locked, the only way into the city was through the little gate through which even an adult person could hardly pass erect. It is said that this little gate was called "the needle's eye." Needless to say, if a person had to squeeze getting through, it would really be tough for a camel, the largest animal in Palestine.

According to that questionable understanding, it was difficult for the camel to make it through the gate, but not impossible if it expended a great deal of effort. Such an analogy would make entering the kingdom of heaven for a rich person possible if they worked hard enough at it.

But that is not what Jesus was teaching. By the camel and the needle's eye illustration He was not saying that it is difficult, but that it is impossible—just as impossible as for the largest of animals to go through the smallest of holes.

That teaching caught the disciples off guard. Like other Jews, they viewed the wealthy as blessed by God. Who, they ask, can make it into the kingdom if it is impossible for the blessed rich?

"With men," Jesus replies, "this is impossible, but with God all things are possible." And with those words Jesus sets the stage for His parable of grace in Matthew 20.

God, help me to move beyond my misconceptions of Your kingdom, including those related to our impossibilities and the possibilities of Your grace.

July 14

Another Pregnant Peter Question

Then Peter said to him, "We left everything to follow you.
What will we get out of it?"
And Jesus replied, "When I, the Messiah, shall sit upon my glorious throne
in the kingdom, you my disciples shall certainly sit on twelve thrones
judging the twelve tribes of Israel. And anyone who gives up his home, brothers,
sisters, father, mother, wife, children, or property, to follow me, shall receive a
hundred times as much in return, and shall have eternal life." Matt. 19:27-29, TLB.

What do I get out of this?" "What's in it for me and those who have given up everything and followed You?" If I had been Jesus I would have been tempted to tell Peter to shut up and get his act together, that he didn't have the slightest idea what following Me meant.

I guess we can be thankful that I am not Jesus. Our Lord used Peter's self-centered question to provide instruction needed by both those first disciples and His followers 20 centuries later.

Jesus' answer to Peter's question has two levels. The first is what he *wants* to hear (Matt. 19:27-29). The second illustrates what Peter *needs* to hear (Matt. 19:30-20:16). He used the same twofold approach to the rich young ruler. What the man wanted to hear was that entrance to the kingdom is based on obedience (Matt. 19:17). But what he needed to hear was that it took total dedication (verse 21).

We need to read Peter's question of what he will get in the context of the young ruler. He failed to give up everything, but Peter and the rest of the disciples had done so.

Jesus' answer in Matthew's Gospel is fourfold. First, those who have had to relinquish their earthly families receive the larger fellowship of God's family of believers here on earth. Second, they have the promise of eternal life. Third, they will be made prosperous. Along that line, Peter must have been all ears when Jesus told him that he and the other 11 would each get a throne to sit upon that would presumably be quite near to Jesus' own throne. Thrones were important to Peter. And, as we shall soon see, he wanted his as close to Christ's as possible.

Last, Jesus' answer contains a cryptic warning to Peter and the other disciples not to become overconfident in their position in the kingdom just because they were the first of His followers. It is that lesson that Peter *needs* to hear in a mind crowded with thrones.

Lord, help me to hear what I need to hear as I read Your Word and not merely what I want to hear.

A Disgusting Parable

And when evening came, the owner of the vineyard said to his steward,
"Call the laborers and pay them their wages, beginning with the last, up to the first."
And when those hired about the eleventh hour came, each of them received a
denarius. Now when the first came, they thought they would receive more; but
each of them also received a denarius. And on receiving it they grumbled at the
householder. Matt. 20:8-11, RSV.

Some of Jesus' parables are more disgusting than others. Near the top of the list in this category is the one about the farmer in Matthew 20:1-16. It tells about a householder (God) who goes out to hire day laborers for his vineyard. (Scripture often refers to Israel as God's vineyard—see Isa. 5:1-7). At the beginning of the 12-hour workday the landlord makes a formal agreement with the available workers to pay a denarius for a full day's labor.

But the farmer is desperate because when grapes ripen they must be harvested immediately or many of them will spoil. So he returns repeatedly to hire more laborers. His last trip is at the eleventh hour, when the day is almost over. The implication is that the later workers can't be too ambitious or they would have been employed earlier. But they must eat, so they show up for work anyway.

The story's irritating aspect begins in verse 8 when at the end of the day the landlord lines the workers up in the reverse order from which he hired them. Thus the last get paid first. Then, in plain view of the others, he pays those one-hour laborers one denarius—a full day's pay.

Now what do you think is going on in the minds of those who spent all day in the vineyard? Arithmetic! "If those guys got a full day's pay for one hour's work," the logic runs, "we deserve 12 days' pay—that is two weeks' earnings, if you subtract the Sabbaths. At last," they rejoice, "we have discovered an employer who will allow us to get ahead."

Then comes the bombshell. Everyone gets exactly the same pay! No wonder they complain. I was a young construction worker when I first read Matthew 20, and I grumbled with them. To me, it was a travesty of justice.

And Peter undoubtedly had the same reaction. We need to remember that Jesus gave the parable in response to his question of Matthew 19:27: "What do we get?" His mind had been on extra-special honors. He liked the first part of Christ's answer in which he and the other disciples were to have thrones and riches. That is what he wanted to hear. But in Matthew 20 he gets what he needs to hear. And that wasn't so pleasant.

Disgusting Parables Are for Peters

But many that are first will be last, and the last first. Matt. 19:30, RSV.

So the last will be first, and the first last. Matt. 20:16, RSV.

Yesterday we began to examine the parable of the farmer and the laborers. We left the scene with those hired first grumbling because they received the same amount as those brought in near the end of the day.

The farmer replies that he had done them no wrong. After all, he had paid them what they had agreed to. The problem in the laborers' eyes was that he had been generous with those hired later. "Am I not allowed to do what I choose with what belongs to me? Or do you begrudge my generosity?" the land owner asks (Matt. 20:15, RSV).

The issue at hand is one of grace—giving people more good things than they deserve. Thus the laborers hired first were really complaining about God's graciousness. They are upset because the farmer is generous.

In our Scripture reading for today we note that Jesus bracketed the parable with a repetition of the "first will be last." It is a subtle warning and rebuke to Peter and his fellows.

Jesus had already told them what they wanted to hear—that they would have thrones and riches and importance in the kingdom. Now He presents to them what they need to hear—that they shouldn't get puffed up with their importance just because they were the first disciples.

Here we have a highly practical teaching with implications for us modern-day disciples. A very real implication of the parable is that the first won't be in the kingdom at all unless they get over their grumbling about God's graciousness and move away from too much concern with their position and rewards.

Certainly Jesus aimed His first-shall-be-last statements at Peter and the disciples. But in our day they could apply to those who have served Jesus all their lives in contrast to those who are converted in old age, or longtime members of a congregation who helped finance and build the local church in contrast to later members who may be rising to positions of leadership.

In the end we need to see the message of the parable as universal. None of us are so good and holy that we can grumble about God's grace to others. Doing so may leave us in the unenviable position of being last, even if we started first.

More on What Disciples Need to Hear

Behold, we are going up to Jerusalem; and the Son of man will be delivered to the chief priests and scribes, and they will condemn him to death, and deliver him to the Gentiles to be mocked and scourged and crucified, and he will be raised on the third day. Matt. 20:18, 19, RSV.

They don't know it, but the disciples are totally unplugged when it comes to the essence of the kingdom and what was happening to Jesus. They were having visions of thrones (Matt. 19:27, 28) and personal greatness (Matt. 20:20-24) while Jesus struggles with forebodings of a cross and rejection. The disciples and Jesus are operating in two different worlds.

As a result, He supplies them more of what they need to hear rather than what they want to hear. This time it is a third replay of His predictions about His forthcoming death and resurrection. That is their greatest need at the moment. After all, they are now heading for Jerusalem and the cross of Calvary.

Jesus had first raised the topic immediately after Peter's confession that He was the Christ. They had at last identified Him as the Messiah, but they had no idea of what that meant. So Jesus first tells them of His forthcoming death and resurrection in Matthew 16:21. He returned to the topic in Matthew 17:22, 23. And now in Matthew 20:18, 19 He sets it forth again. But with each repetition He fills in more details. Now He informs the disciples that the Jewish leaders, after condemning Him to death, will "deliver him to the Gentiles." Other first-time details are the manner of His suffering—mocking and flogging—and the type of His death—crucifixion. "The effect," pens R. T. France, "is to emphasize not only the totality of the rejection (Jewish leaders and Gentiles), but also the humiliation and the harrowing pain; this is to be no glorious martyrdom, but an ugly, sordid butchery. It is thus all the more striking to read yet again here that *he will be raised on the third day*."

Yet the disciples heard none of it! They had their own concerns that were blocking them from grasping the clear word of God to them. Their own ambitions and daily struggles made them deaf to Jesus.

Here is a theme of the gospel story. And rightly so. A perverseness of human nature makes us alive to our self and our desires and dead to God and His will. And that, my friends, is not merely a first-century phenomenon.

July 18

A Firstness Argument

Then the mother of the sons of Zebedee came to Jesus with her sons, bowing down and making a request of Him. And He said to her, "What do you wish?" She said to Him, "Command that in Your kingdom these two sons of mine may sit one on Your right and one on Your left." Matt. 20:20, 21, NASB.

Just a little request. Only the two most important positions in the coming kingdom.

Nothing speaks more loudly as Jesus and the disciples advanced toward the cross than their differing perspectives regarding the nature of His kingdom. The threads of the cross and human firstness run parallel in this final journey.

And just as Jesus' predictions of His death become progressively more detailed, so does the struggle for supremacy scenes among the disciples. The one in Matthew 20:20, 21 is by far the most blatant attempt at a power takeover by any of the disciples. James, John, and their mother didn't beat around the bush. They wanted nothing less than the two most powerful positions in Jesus' forthcoming kingdom. Their request is the ultimate example of human self-centeredness in contrast to Jesus' humility and self-sacrifice.

It is not surprising that James and John make their move for supremacy at this point. After all, the two brothers, along with Peter, made up the privileged inner circle at the Transfiguration (Matt. 17:1-13). Furthermore, hadn't Jesus plainly rebuked Peter at Caesarea Philippi (Matt. 16:23)? And hadn't he received an implied reprimand in Matthew 19:30 in Jesus' response to his question of what he would get for following Him?

Now is their chance! So they come with their mother, who states their request. And she probably has excellent reasons to expect Jesus to grant it. Comparing Matthew 27:56 with Mark 15:40, we discover that her name is Salome, and John 19:25 provides evidence that she was the sister of Jesus' mother. That would make James and John full cousins of Jesus, and helps to explain why on the cross He committed His mother to the care of John (verses 26, 27). While we can't prove such identifications beyond a shadow of doubt, they are quite probable. They certainly help us understand "Aunt" Salome's aggressive request if it is a family matter.

The power play, however, puts the other 10 disciples in an uproar (Matt. 20:24). Unfortunately, their reaction is not because the 10 somehow grasped the error of the Zebedees' request, but because they also wanted the top spot.

There must be a lesson for me somewhere in this story.

Real Firstness

Jesus called them to Himself and said, "You know that the rulers of the Gentiles lord it over them, and those who are great exercise authority over them. Yet it shall not be so among you; but whoever desires to become great among you, let him be your servant. And whoever desires to be first among you, let him be your slave—just as the Son of Man did not come to be served, but to serve, and to give His life a ransom for many." Matt. 20:25-28, NKJV.

Correct ideas of Messiahship go hand in hand with right ideas on what it means to be a follower of the Messiah. And the disciples were having trouble with both.

Sin breeds sin. The wrongheaded ambition of James and John had stimulated intense jealousy in the rest of the disciples. The little band had reached a crisis point right at the edge, so to speak, of Jerusalem with its cross. They were torn apart by tensions that might permanently separate them and frustrate Jesus' purpose in calling them in the first place.

We don't know if Jesus felt tempted to give up on them, call them blockheads, and walk away. But certainly He must have sighed as He once again began to instruct the twelve on the basic principles of His kingdom.

This time His focus is on true greatness and what it really means to be first. His upside-down principles are just the opposite of those of the larger world. Unlike the world, where the greatest are rulers, in the kingdom of heaven the "great" (referring back to the Zebedees' request in Matthew 20:20, 21) are servants, and the "first" (referring back to the vineyard parable of verses 1-16) will be slaves. Jesus concludes by telling them that He Himself has not come to be served but to serve and to give His life.

He could not have outlined the concept of servant leadership more clearly. How unfortunate that down through history church leaders and Christians in general have not been any more drawn to that concept than were the disciples. The reason is simple: the servant leadership model goes against human nature. Its successful implementation demands both conversion and transformation.

Jesus has spent a lot of time on the twin themes of His cross and ours. Yet it is just as difficult to internalize the principle today as it was 20 centuries ago.

Lord, take my ears and help me hear. Take my life and live out Your principles in it today and tomorrow and every day. Amen.

The Beginning of the End

Jesus said, "Take away the stone." Martha, the sister of the dead man, said to him,
"Lord, by this time there will be an odor, for he has been dead four days."
. . . He cried with a loud voice, "Lazarus, come out." The dead man came out, his
hands and feet bound with bandages, and his face wrapped with a cloth. Jesus said
to them, "Unbind him, and let him go." John 11:39-44, RSV.

Here we find one of the most dramatic moments in the life of Jesus and His greatest miracle. The two other individuals whom the Gospels report that He had raised to life were only recently deceased. But here was one who had been dead for four days, and that was problematic in the warm climate of Palestine in which decomposition sets in rapidly.

There is something else important about this story. When Jesus had raised Jairus' daughter in Mark 5, He ordered almost everyone out of the room. And after the event He told them not to tell anyone. But now He operates before a large crowd, putting His reputation on the line as He shouts to Lazarus to come out.

And he did! It must have been a heart-stopping moment as they witnessed the bandaged figure staggering out from the tomb.

As He performed this miracle, Jesus undoubtedly had thoughts of His own approaching death and resurrection. The raising of Lazarus foreshadowed His own experience. But with differences. Lazarus was raised back to earthly existence, but Jesus to a heavenly ministry. While Lazarus would die again, Jesus would live forevermore.

The very publicness of the resurrection of Lazarus would lead to the final events of Jesus' earthly life. His disciples had warned Him not to go back to Judea because the Jewish leaders were looking for an excuse to kill Him (John 11:8). And now He had provided them with one. "From that day on they took counsel how to put him to death" (verse 53, RSV). Interestingly, they also put Lazarus on their hit list because many of the Jews were "believing in Jesus" as a result of the man's resurrection (John 12:10, 11, RSV).

This greatest of miracles had taken place in Bethany, just a few miles from Jerusalem. Soon Jesus would make His final entrance into the great city as the crowds surged into it for the Passover feast. And following that entry would come the climactic events of His life.

The Lazarus miracle indicates the life-giving power of Jesus. It is that power that forms the basis of the good news that He came from heaven to share with us.

A Public Messianic Statement

The disciples . . . brought the donkey. . . . Most of the crowd spread their cloaks on the road, and others cut branches from the trees and spread them on the road. And the crowds that went before him and that followed him were shouting, "Hosanna to the Son of David! Blessed is he who comes in the name of the Lord! Hosanna in the highest!" And when he entered Jerusalem, the whole city was stirred up, saying, "Who is this?" And the crowds said, "This is the prophet Jesus, from Nazareth of Galilee."
Matt. 21:6-11, ESV.

The time for privacy is over. In His triumphal entry into Jerusalem Jesus is making a public statement that He is the Messiah.

The surging crowd recognizes the moment by giving Him the red-carpet treatment as they spread branches and garments on the road for Him to ride over while shouting "Hosanna to the Son of David!" a title with unmistakable Messianic significance. "Hosanna" translates as "save, we pray thee." The people were ready for the salvational role of Jesus. But it would be much different from what they expected on this glorious day.

And where did the crowds come from? And why were they so enthusiastic? For one thing, it was the Passover season that celebrated God's deliverance of the nation from Egyptian bondage. Thus the roads teemed with people from all over the Jewish world heading for Jerusalem.

A second thing to note is that Lazarus had just been raised not far from the city. That outstanding miracle had caused widespread excitement.

But perhaps most important is the *manner* in which Jesus chose to enter the city. His deliberate choice fanned to white-hot flame the excitement and tension already in the air. The Gospels tell us that He entered town astride the colt of a donkey. That is interesting for a man who has just walked all the way from Galilee. Certainly He had no physical need to ride the last two miles. Furthermore, Jesus has always walked. This is the only time we find the adult Jesus riding in any of the Gospels. What He is doing is obviously deliberate.

It is guided by the prophecy of Zechariah 9:9, which says that Jerusalem's "king comes to you, righteous and victorious, lowly and riding on a donkey, on a colt, the foal of a donkey" (NIV). Jesus is making a definite Messianic statement. The crowds do not miss the point. And neither do the Jewish leaders, but to them it is a challenge rather than something to be joyful about.

Public Statement
Becomes Public Challenge

And Jesus went into the temple of God, and cast out all them that sold and bought in the temple, and overthrew the tables of the moneychangers, and the seats of them that sold doves, and said unto them, It is written, My house shall be called the house of prayer; but ye have made it a den of thieves. Matt. 21:12, 13.

With the cleansing of the Temple Jesus takes the battle into the very heart of the enemy camp. His demonstration in the Temple is no burst of enthusiasm or righteous anger stirred up by the momentary excitement of the triumphal entry. A reading of Matthew could give that impression, but Mark tells us that it was the "next day" after the entry when the cleansing took place (Mark 11:12, NIV). That is a significant bit of knowledge, since it definitely indicates that it was not some spur-of-the-moment challenge to the Jewish authorities. To the contrary, the fact that a night passes between the entry and the cleansing shows that we are dealing with a premeditated challenge whose purpose is to forcefully call the attention of the Jews to Jesus' mission. Thus in the cleansing we find Him making His Messianic claim and exerting His Messianic authority at the very heart of Judaism.

The challenge is now impossible for either the leaders or the common people to ignore. The common people flock to Jesus in the Temple and shout Messianic praises to the "Son of David" as He heals the blind and lame outcasts (Matt. 21:14, 15). The chief priests and the scribes react to all the celebration with indignation (verse 15). The enthusiasm of the crowds was bad enough out in the city, but now it has entered their own special territory and casts their lucrative Temple trade in an extremely insidious light.

Thus it is that in the Temple episode we find a turning point in the description of Jesus' enemies. Heretofore the gospel story has scarcely mentioned the high priests. But from now on out they will play a central role.

In the cleansing of the Temple Jesus has challenged and judged the formal religious power structure. The high priests will make common cause with the scribes and Pharisees to get rid of Him with a determination not present before. In cleansing the Temple He has truly proved Himself to be a dangerous enemy.

Father, help us as we meditate on the events leading up to the cross to see the importance and significance of Jesus' every step as He works out our salvation.

The Other Side of Gentle Jesus

In the morning, as he was returning to the city, he was hungry. And seeing a fig tree by the wayside he went to it, and found nothing on it but leaves only. And he said to it, "May no fruit ever come from you again!" And the fig tree withered at once. Matt. 21:18, 19, RSV.

At first glance it seems strange to find the story of the fig tree right after the cleansing of the Temple. But the placement is no accident. That becomes especially clear in Mark's Gospel, which splits the fig tree story into two parts (Mark 11:12-14 and 20-24) with the cleansing sandwiched in between them (verses 15-19).

Victor of Antioch (fifth century) clearly saw that connection in the oldest existing commentary on Mark. According to Victor, the withering of the fig tree was an acted parable in which Jesus "used the fig tree to set forth the judgment that was about to fall on Jerusalem."

In its context, the withered fig tree points to the Temple and its failure in preparing the Jewish people for the redemptive activity of the coming Messiah. Despite all that God had attempted to do through the Temple for His people, it had not borne fruit. And just as a tree that does not perform its proper function in bearing fruit gets cut down, so the Temple will meet its end.

By extension, the parable of the fruitless fig tree has much to say to all religionists and all religious institutions characterized by promise without fulfillment, by profession without practice. Whether it be the Jewish nation, the Jewish leaders, or ordinary Christians, Jesus is adamant throughout the Gospels that outward profession is not enough. "You will know them by their fruits" (Matt. 7:20, RSV). "Every tree that does not bear good fruit is cut down and thrown into the fire" (verse 19, RSV).

It has become fashionable for Christians to focus on the gentleness and kindness of Jesus and the Father to the exclusion of the "wrath of the Lamb" (Rev. 6:16). The plain fact is that the God of love calls His children to wake up before it is too late. Eventually the God of love will terminate the reign of sin and create a new heaven and earth.

And just as Jesus judged the barren fig tree, so He will someday judge the world. In fact, no one in the entire Bible had more to say about judgment than Jesus.

Today is a good one to examine my own "fruitiness." Let's be honest! Am I all show or is there depth and daily results of the gospel in my life?

Authorities in Conflict

*Jesus entered the temple courts, and, while he was teaching, the chief priests and the
elders of the people came to him. "By what authority are you doing these things?"
they asked. "And who gave you this authority?" Jesus replied, "I will also ask you one
question. If you answer me, I will tell you by what authority I am doing these things.
John's baptism—where did it come from? Was it from heaven, or of human origin?"*
Matt. 21:23-25, NIV.

J esus had challenged the authority of the Jewish leaders in His cleansing of
the Temple. Now they confront Him.

We need to note what they did not question. For one thing, they didn't
dispute the facts that He had authority or that He had been doing authoritative
things. He had certainly demonstrated that in the Temple cleansing. A second
thing that the delegation from the Sanhedrin did not contest was the righteousness of Jesus in cleansing the Temple. They knew that they had allowed
things in the Temple courts that were wrong.

On the other hand, they couldn't ignore what Jesus had done. After all, He
had acted as if He were Lord of the Temple and had a right to do what He did.
In that, He was usurping their prerogatives. Thus they had reasons to confront
Him. No one could deny them the right to question Him on the source of
His authority in His Temple-cleansing actions. After all, Jesus had no official
standing. Thus their challenge. But it had a hook in it. As William Barclay
points out, "They hoped to put Jesus into a dilemma. If He said He was acting
under His own authority they might well arrest Him as a megalomaniac before
He did any further damage." Yet "if He said He was acting on the authority of
God they might well arrest Him on an obvious charge of blasphemy."

Jesus was quite aware of the trap. His response would put them into a dilemma that was even worse. His counter question regarding the authority of
John the Baptist was a stroke of genius. They couldn't answer that the Baptist's
authority was from God because he had pointed to Jesus as the Lamb of God.
Yet they couldn't say that his authority came from men because the people held
that John was a prophet.

The stark alternatives left them with "we don't know" as the only possible
answer. Jesus retorted that their refusal to answer His question gave Him the
right to ignore theirs (see Matt. 21:27, NIV).

As Christians, we can learn much from the way that Jesus handled controversy. We need to keep both eyes open to His inspired strategy as He continues
to journey to the cross.

Confrontational Parable Number 1

What do you think? A man had two sons, and he came to the first and said, "Son, go, work today in my vineyard." He answered and said, "I will not," but afterward he regretted it and went. Then he came to the second and said likewise. And he answered and said, "I go, sir," but he did not go. Which of the two did the will of his father?
Matt. 21:28-31, NKJV.

W e have reached the final days of Jesus' life. And the Gospels indicate that He is on a collision course with the Jewish leadership. First came the triumphal entry, then the cleansing of the Temple, and finally the argument over His authority. Those events, which feature His Messianic role, reveal the growing rift between the Jewish leaders and the masses of the people, with the leaders rejecting Jesus and the latter group repeatedly demonstrating enthusiasm for Him.

Next we find Jesus teaching and dialoguing in the Temple courts. In the process, He presents several confrontational parables, all aimed at the Jewish leaders.

The initial parable is that of a father (God) and two sons. The first (who represents the tax collectors, prostitutes, and other outcasts) verbally refuses to labor in the father's vineyard but repents and works anyway. The second son (who represents the Jewish leaders) verbally agrees to obey but doesn't put his words into practice.

Jesus, using an excellent teaching technique, involves His audience in arriving at the parable's lesson. The answer is obvious. All through Matthew's Gospel it is not those who say "Lord, Lord" who enter the kingdom, but those who obey (see Matt. 7:21).

For Jesus, righteousness is not passive acceptance but active obedience. Faith is belief that acts. That is not salvation by works but rather the fact that love to God and other people flows naturally from the heart of a person who has met Jesus.

Thus His words stand against the so-called gospel of emotional revivalism that looks for mere verbal acceptance rather than a transformed life. Likewise, this parable puts the lid on the falsehood that suggests that believing certain doctrinal truths is the way of salvation. And again, the parable strikes at the heart of those forms of Christian assurance that tend to equate salvation with accepting Jesus at the point of justification. Jesus' teaching on assurance of salvation is based on both accepting Him and living the Christlike life.

And with that conclusion we have our marching orders for today and every day.

Confrontational Parable Number 2

"Hear another parable. There was a householder who planted a vineyard . . . and let it out to tenants, and went into another country. When the season of fruit drew near, he sent his servants to the tenants, to get his fruit; and the tenants took his servants and beat one, killed another, and stoned another. . . . Afterward he sent his son to them. . . . But . . . the tenants . . . killed him. When therefore the owner of the vineyard comes, what will he do to those tenants?" Matt. 21:33-40, RSV.

The second confrontational parable takes the sequence a giant step forward. Whereas the parable of the two sons pictured the resistance of the Jewish leaders in a passive mode, this one is active—so much so that it points both to rejecting the prophets and to killing the son. It would be almost impossible for any Jewish hearer to miss the allusion to God's much-loved Israel in the description of the vineyard. Isaiah 5:1-7 describes that vineyard in quite similar terms to what Jesus employs. But in Isaiah the fault lies with the vines, whereas here it is with the tenants. In both cases, the result of failure is divine judgment.

We can learn several lessons from the parable of the tenants. The first is that God is long-suffering. He does not send just one time, but keeps on sending. He does not give up easily on His children. A second lesson is just as obvious—the perversity of the tenants. If the major theme of the gospel story is God's love, a counterbalancing theme is humanity's rejection of that love. The tragedy of both the parable and history is that so often it has been God's own chosen people who have spurned His overtures.

The third lesson is the centrality and finality of sending the Son. Yet the tenants kill even Him. The parable pictures that act as ultimately bringing judgment on them.

A fourth lesson is that even though God's judgment may be long in coming, it is nonetheless certain and irreversible. The judgment of the particular tenants in Matthew 21 will come with the destruction of Jerusalem.

The parable's fifth lesson is the transfer of God's kingdom from the nation of Israel to a new people. "I tell you," Jesus says in His most explicit statement on the topic, "that the kingdom of God will be taken away from you and given to a people who will produce its fruit" (Matt. 21:43, NIV). That new people is the Christian church, which has inherited a continuation of the Jewish covenant promises and responsibilities.

May God help His new people not to exhibit the same perversity as the old.

Confrontational Parable Number 3

*Jesus spoke to them again in parables, saying, "The kingdom of heaven may be
compared to a king who gave a wedding feast for his son. And he sent out his slaves
to call those who had been invited to the wedding feast, and they were unwilling to
come. . . . Then he said to his slaves, 'The wedding is ready, but those who were invited were not worthy. Go therefore to the main highways, and as many as you find
there, invite to the wedding feast.' Those slaves went out into the streets and gathered
together all they found, both evil and good; and the wedding hall was filled with dinner guests. But when the king came in to look over the dinner guests, he saw a man
there who was not dressed in wedding clothes, and he said to him, 'Friend,
how did you come in here without wedding clothes?' And the man was speechless."*
Matt. 22:1-12, NASB.

The third confrontational parable is that of the wedding banquet. As in the first
two, it ends in judgment for those who reject the Father and the Son.

The parable divides naturally into two parts. The first deals with Jesus' historic
call to the Jews and ends with an explicit allusion to the destruction of Jerusalem in
verse 7. It replays many of the themes evident in the parable of the tenants.

But at verse 8 the parable makes a shift as it advances beyond the Jews to
those not initially invited to the banquet. Verses 8-10 foreshadow the gospel
invitation moving from its earlier preoccupation with the Jews to concern for
Gentiles in the larger world. Verse 9 begins with a close parallel to the great
gospel commission of Matthew 28:19, 20—"Go therefore . . ." The command to
preach to "both evil and good" reflects Christ's own preaching ministry. The
gospel is truly the "good news" that *everyone* is invited to the wedding.

But not all can stay. They must be in harmony with the king, who has commanded everyone to wear a wedding garment. Those without one are judged
unfit to remain at the feast.

A great deal of discussion has taken place as to the exact nature of the wedding garment. F. D. Bruner appears to be correct when he writes that "the wedding garment in the context of Matthew's Gospel is not passive, imputed (Pauline)
righteousness; it is active, moral (Matthean) righteousness (5:20 . . .); it is doing
God's will (7:21; 12:50 . . .); it is evidence of repentance by law-abiding discipleship
(3:7-10 . . .)." That interpretation is in line with Revelation 19:8, which tells us that
the fine linen of the redeemed "is the righteous deeds of the saints" (RSV).

Thus once again we find Jesus indicating that a genuine faith relationship
with Him includes not just believing but doing God's will. Faith is not mere
mental assent that Jesus is Lord. It includes living the Christ life.

Confrontation Is
a Two-way Street: Number 1

Then the Pharisees went and plotted how to entangle him in his words. And they
sent their disciples to him, along with the Herodians, saying, . . . "tell us . . . what you
think. Is it lawful to pay taxes to Caesar, or not?" But Jesus, aware of their malice,
said, "Why put me to the test, you hypocrites? Show me the coin for the tax." And
they brought him a denarius. And Jesus said to them, "Whose likeness and inscrip-
tion is this?" They said, "Caesar's." Then he said to them, "Therefore render to
Caesar the things that are Caesar's, and to God the things that are God's." When they
heard it, they marveled. Matt. 22:15-21, ESV.

Confrontation is a two-way street. When Jesus challenged the Jewish leaders in His parables, they were quick to counterattack. In the query about paying taxes they presented Him with a loaded question that contained a dilemma. If Jesus replies that it is unlawful to pay taxes to Caesar, they will promptly report Him to the Roman authorities, with arrest quickly following. On the other hand, if He approves the lawfulness of paying taxes to Caesar, He will lose influence in the eyes of the people. The Jews held that God alone was King and that to pay taxes to any earthly ruler was to admit the validity of that kingship and thus insult God. Whatever answer Jesus gives to His detractors will open Him to trouble.

Jesus' answer is both unique and wise. Asking to see one of their coins, He gets them to admit that it has Caesar's portrait on it. At that point He sets forth the maxim that both Caesar and God are to be paid their dues. That unexpected answer ends the attack. The Jewish leaders quickly see that Jesus has escaped from the trap they had so carefully laid for Him.

Perhaps the most remarkable thing about Jesus' answer is His point that Caesar's realm can be separated from God's. As a result, His followers hold dual citizenship in both the kingdom of God and in a particular nation.

Unfortunately, in a less-than-perfect world, a Christian's responsibility to those two realms comes into conflict from time to time. Matthew 22 does not tell us whether God's kingdom has priority over Caesar's or vice versa, or whether the two are equal. The early church had to work out that problem. While Paul and Peter argued that the rulers of earthly governments ought to be obeyed since they are God's agents (Rom. 13:1-7; 1 Peter 2:13, 14), the New Testament also makes it clear that when the dictates of an earthly ruler come into conflict with God's commands, the Christian "must obey God rather than human beings" (Acts 5:29, NIV).

Confrontation Is
a Two-way Street: Number 2

The same day Sadducees came to him, who say that there is no resurrection; and they asked him a question, saying, "Teacher, Moses said, 'If a man dies, having no children, his brother must marry the widow, and raise up children for his brother.' Now there were seven brothers among us; the first married, and died, and having no children left his wife to his brother. So too the second and third, down to the seventh. After them all, the woman died. In the resurrection, therefore, to which of the seven will she be wife? For they all had her." But Jesus answered them, "You are wrong, because you know neither the scriptures nor the power of God." Matt. 22:23-29, RSV.

The second question in the Jewish counterattack against Jesus comes from the Sadducees—the traditional enemies of the Pharisees. They had not only lined themselves up with the Roman rulers, but they rejected all Scripture except the Pentateuch (the five books of Moses). According to Josephus, the Sadducees held that "souls die with the bodies" (*Antiquities* 18.1. 4). Thus they denied the possibility of immortality and the resurrection from the dead.

Their acceptance of only the Pentateuch undergirds their question to Jesus in Matthew 22:25-28 about the woman who, according to levirate marriage custom (Deut. 25:5, 6), had seven husbands but no children. Their question sought not only to make light of the very idea of a resurrection, but, at a deeper level, to embarrass Jesus in public.

But once again, Jesus turns the argument against His detractors on two points. First, He suggested that their question is flawed because it is founded on error. Not knowing Scripture, He claims, they also fail to understand God and His power. Like so many modern people, they apparently thought of the future life as a slightly altered version of earthly life as we know it. Not so, says Jesus. God's new kingdom will be along different lines. He didn't tell the Sadducees what heaven would be like because their minds couldn't have grasped it if He had. But He did declare that life in the hereafter cannot be compared to the present one.

In the second part of His answer Jesus quotes from Exodus 3:6, demonstrating that the Sadducees were even ignorant of the part of Scripture that they accepted. God, Jesus noted, is the Deity not of the dead, but of the living, pointing forward to the resurrection of the patriarchs (Matt. 22:32).

Here is a challenge for modern Christians. Most of us probably view heaven in terms of earthly realities. What are the high points of that approach? What are its problems? In what ways does the Bible teaching on the topic transcend our usual ways of thinking about it?

Confrontation Is
a Two-way Street: Number 3

But when the Pharisees had heard that he had put the Sadducees to silence, they were gathered together. Then one of them, which was a lawyer, asked him a question, tempting him, and saying, Master, which is the great commandment in the law? Jesus said unto him, Thou shalt love the Lord thy God with all thy heart, and with all thy soul, and with all thy mind. Matt. 22:34-37.

This question, as with those of taxes to Caesar and the resurrection, was a major issue in the Jewish community of Jesus' day. Its legal scholars had concluded that Scripture contained 613 commandments, 365 prohibitions, and 248 positive injunctions. Among those 613 the rabbis differentiated between what they saw as the "heavy" and the "light" commandments. Jesus appears to have been alluding to that distinction when He said that "whoever then relaxes one of the *least* of these commandments and teaches men so, shall be called least in the kingdom of heaven" (Matt. 5:19, RSV).

In that context the question about the greatest commandment focuses on which was the most necessary to be observed. But some Jews disagreed even with the idea that some things were more basic than others. To them, just as with some Christians today, every command had equal weight. And so did every sin. You were either for God or against Him. Such believers across time have tended toward behavioral perfection in their daily lives.

But others of the Jews disagreed and debated endlessly as to which was the most basic of all laws. The scribe in Matthew 22 belonged to the latter group.

Which commandment would you select if a person hostile toward your religion should raise that question? Some Jews of old might have selected the fourth, with its injunction to keep the Sabbath holy as a sign of the specialness of God's covenant people. Others may have chosen one of the other commandments of the Decalogue.

But Jesus bypassed the Ten Commandments for one of the most familiar Bible texts in Jewish culture—Deuteronomy 6:4, 5: "Hear, O Israel: The Lord our God is one Lord; and you shall love the Lord your God with all your heart, and with all your soul, and with all your might" (RSV).

That verse was part of the Shema. It opened every Jewish service and formed a part of their morning prayer. In effect, Jesus defined the heart of religion as loving God with one's total being.

From that love should flow everything else in a believer's life.

Moving Beyond Confrontation

And the second is like unto it, Thou shalt love thy neighbour as thyself. On these two commandments hang all the law and the prophets. Matt. 22:39, 40.

Jesus' answer about loving God as the greatest command would have been satisfactory in answering the scribe's question. But He knew that some of us "religious types" do much better in what we think is loving God than we do in caring about other people.

As a result, He quoted a second great commandment from Leviticus 19:18, with its injunction to love one's neighbor. The underlying assumption is that it is impossible to truly love God without loving other people. Here we have one of the most important lessons in the entire body of Jesus' teaching. The apostle John put the matter succinctly when he wrote that whoever claims to love God, yet hates a brother or sister is a liar. For "whoever does not love their brother and sister, whom they have seen, cannot love God, whom they have not seen" (1 John 4:20, NIV). Again, "By this all men will know that you are my disciples, if you have love for one another" (John 13:35, RSV).

Jesus noted that love to God and love to one's neighbor is central to the Old Testament—"the law and the prophets" (Matt. 22:40). It would also become central to New Testament ethics. Thus Paul writes that "the whole law is fulfilled in one word, 'You shall love your neighbor as yourself'" (Gal. 5:14, RSV).

He repeats the same idea in Romans 13, in which he notes that "love is the fulfilling of the law" (verse 10, RSV). But in that chapter the apostle helps us see more clearly the relation of the command to love to the Ten Commandments. More specifically, he explicitly unites the commandments from the second table of the Decalogue to the second great commandment. Thus he ties such commandments as not killing, not stealing, and so on to the command to love other people (verses 9, 10). The same could be done for the first table and loving God. But Paul knew that the problem of most "religious" people was not in loving God but one another.

What a delightful place the church would be if more of its members took Jesus' answer to heart and put it into practice. Every congregation has "pious" members who act as if they can love God while being rude to other people. Beyond that, we continually encounter those who are extremely careful about how they keep the Sabbath and/or what they eat, but who are as difficult to live with as the devil himself.

Help me, Father, to get the point of true religion.

August 1

Christ's Unanswerable Question

While the Pharisees were gathered together, Jesus asked them a question, saying, "What do you think of the Christ? Whose son is he?" They said to him, "The son of David." He said to them, "How is it then that David, inspired by the Spirit, calls him Lord, saying, 'The Lord said to my Lord, Sit at my right hand, till I put thy enemies under thy feet'? If David thus calls him Lord, how is he his son?" And no one was able to answer him a word, nor from that day did any one dare to ask him any more questions. Matt. 22:41-46, RSV.

Here we have an argument that most modern Christians do not fully understand. But that was not so for the Jews of Jesus' day. We need to spend some time examining the issues He raised in this passage—issues central to the rest of the New Testament.

The first thing we should note is that Jesus' question regarding His identity is the same one He had brought up privately with the disciples on the road to Caesarea Philippi, when He asked them "Whom do men say that I am?" (Mark 8:27). Peter's answer was that Jesus is the Christ. And from that time forward Jesus began to explain to His disciples what it meant to be the Christ.

In Matthew 22 He moves from unfolding the significance of the Christ from the disciples to the Pharisees. But with them Jesus probes into "the Christ" and His relationship to David. To understand the passage it is important to remember that the Jews did not use Christ as a name but rather as a position. Thus Jesus framed His question in terms of "*the* Christ."

A second term that we need to understand is "son of David." Of all the titles for the Christ the most common was son of David. The Jews looked forward to a Messiah of the warrior-king type modeled by David. In that context, after the Pharisees publicly identified the Christ as the son of David, Jesus asked His most important and perceptive question: "How is it then that David, inspired by the Spirit, calls him Lord . . . ?"

Here Jesus had the Pharisees on the spot. His use of Psalm 110, which all agreed was Messianic, threw them into confusion, since in that passage David calls the Messiah his "Lord," the very word used in the Greek version of the Old Testament to translate Yahweh or God. The Pharisees recognized at this point that the Christ would not merely be David's son, but his divine Lord.

And with that, they realized that Jesus had bested them in their knowledge of the Bible. As a result, they feared to ask Him any more questions.

A Side Lesson in Messiahship

The Lord says to my lord:
"Sit at my right hand, till I
make your enemies your footstool." Psalm 110:1, RSV.

Yesterday we began to examine Jesus' use of Psalm 110. He had pointed out to the Pharisees that the coming Messiah/Christ would not only be a human being but would also be God. Thus "son of David," while being a true description of the Messiah, was an inadequate one. The Messiah would not only be David's Son but also his divine Lord.

Jesus accomplished at least three things in His exchange with the Pharisees. First, He publicly demonstrated their inadequacy as interpreters of Scripture. Second, He made an immense claim for Himself. The fault with the Pharisees was not that they had thought too highly of Messiah, but not highly enough. He would be divine—so divine that the great David hails Him as Lord (Yahweh). And in making that staggering claim for the Messiah, Jesus was advancing it for Himself, just as He had already done earlier in the week by riding in lowly triumph into Jerusalem and by claiming authority over the Temple.

A third implication arising from Jesus' use of Psalm 110 is that if the Messiah is not merely David's son, then David as a model for the Messiah is incomplete. Human kingship of the warrior variety was no longer an adequate understanding. As a result, we find Jesus accepting the titles of the Messiah and the son of David, but rejecting the limitations of the Jewish definitions. Jesus never came as a warrior king, but as the Lamb of God who would take away the sin of the world (John 1:29). And He was not merely seeking to deliver the Jews from the Romans, but to save His people everywhere from their sins (Matt. 1:21).

Jesus' use of Psalm 110:1 in Matthew 22 also reveals some things about His understanding of His mission: (1) that He would be victorious and sit at God's right hand, and (2) that He eventually would triumph over His enemies, who would become as a footstool.

Such confidence is crucial for believers as we face the onslaught of the world against our faith. It is little wonder that Psalm 110 became the most quoted Old Testament passage in the New, being alluded to or quoted 33 times. The book of Hebrews repeatedly uses the text to drive home the point that Christians can live in absolute confidence because they serve a risen Jesus who sits "at the right hand of the Majesty on high" (Heb. 1:3, RSV).

We can be thankful that Jesus is not merely David's son, but his victorious Lord.

Final Wake-up Call

Then Jesus said to the crowds and to his disciples, "The scribes and the Pharisees sit on Moses' seat, so practice and observe whatever they tell you—but not what they do. For they preach, but do not practice. They tie up heavy burdens, hard to bear, and lay them upon people's shoulders, but they themselves are not willing to move them with their finger. They do all these deeds to be seen by others." Matt. 23:1-5, ESV.

The verbal climax of Jesus' struggle with the scribes and Pharisees takes place in Matthew 23. Up to this point, He has done all He can to wake them up, but to no avail. Now the time for soft words and roundabout tactics is over. In His love, Jesus now makes a frontal assault. His time is running out, and they still have not heard Him.

Matthew 23 falls into three sections that run along a unified theme. Verses 1 to 12, given in the third person, present five characteristics for which Jesus rebukes the scribes and Pharisees. But before presenting them, Jesus highlights the importance of the office of the scribes and Pharisees. They "sit on Moses' seat" (verse 2). That is, they have the high privilege and responsibility of teaching God's Word to His people. It is in the light of that sacred and weighty role that we must view their shortcomings. Their faults are all the more serious because of their position.

Before looking at the negative characteristics described in this chapter, we need to recognize that not all Pharisees were as bad as those portrayed here. The Pharisees themselves had some of the same condemnations for their less-responsible fellows as did Jesus.

Another thing we should keep in mind is that Christian leaders and lay-people often emulate the traits of the Pharisees. While the Pharisees formed a historic party in Judaism, their spirit is rooted in human nature. Thus we Christians need to read the criticism of Matthew 23 with ourselves in mind.

Whenever we fail to practice what we preach (verse 3), are unwilling to carry out in our own lives what we prescribe for others (verse 4), love the show-off value of our religious accomplishments (verse 5), revel in honorific titles and in being shown respect (verses 6-10), and fail to realize that our ministry is a call to sacrificial service rather than an exalted status (verses 11, 12), we are acting as the worst of the Pharisees rather than followers of Jesus.

Help me, Lord, to come to grips with my own shortcomings in the light of Your life and Word.

Wrong Ways to "Play Church"

Woe to you, scribes and Pharisees, hypocrites! for you traverse sea and land to make
a single proselyte, and when he becomes a proselyte, you make him twice as much a
child of hell as yourselves. . . . Woe to you, scribes and Pharisees, hypocrites! for you
tithe mint and dill and cummin, and have neglected the weightier matters of the
law, justice and mercy and faith; these you ought to have done, without neglecting
the others. You blind guides, straining out a gnat and swallowing a camel!
Matt. 23:15-24, RSV.

The second section of Matthew 23, running from verses 13 through 32, Jesus presents in the second person. He enumerates the condemnations in this section in the form of seven "woes." In addition the segment calls the scribes and Pharisees "hypocrites" (play actors) six times and "blind" five times. At this point the confrontation of Jesus with the Jewish leaders has reached fever pitch. Even though He uttered His words in love, it is impossible to avoid their pointedness.

Here, as we noted earlier, before we get too critical of the ancient Jews, we need to realize that their faults tend to be a common characteristic of those who like to "play church," whether they be laity or clergy. The seven woes teach us that a great deal of difference exists between playing church and living the religion of Jesus.

The first woe deals with the failure of entering the kingdom while at the same time blocking others from entering (verse 13). Jesus, of course, had in mind the actions and words of the Pharisees that kept their followers from developing a faith relationship with Him. But the modern church still has its quota of such activity. The restricting can result from discouraging others through playing the role of the hypocrite, by perverting the teaching of Scripture, or by living a loveless life. Unfortunately, it doesn't take much skill or dedication to be a stumbling block to others.

The second woe focuses on those self-sacrificing types who do all they can to convert people to their legalistic ways. The upshot is that such converts wind up more miserable than before they encountered the missionaries' perverted view of religion (verse 15).

The final woe (verses 29-32) hits directly at the "monument keeping" of much organized religion. The greatest monument to true religion is not some celebration of the major religious events and personages of the past, but the spirit of the prophets living in our own lives in the present.

Sobering indeed are the ways good, sincere, religious people can go wrong. The seven woes are a call to self-examination and rededication for each of us.

August 5

The "Tough Love" of Jesus

You serpents, you viper's brood, how do you think you are going to avoid being condemned to the rubbish-heap? . . . Oh, Jerusalem, Jerusalem! You murder the prophets and stone the messengers that are sent to you. How often have I longed to gather your children round me like a bird gathering her brood together under her wing—and you would never have it. Now all you have left is your house. I tell you that you will never see me again till the day when you cry, "Blessed is he who comes in the name of the Lord!" Matt. 23:33-39, Phillips.

Some church members are just plain tough in their condemnation of others. Their concern is with purity, right conduct, correct music, and sanctified diet. They have no problem speaking their minds. And the result is that young people quit attending, new members get discouraged, and anybody with any spiritual sense begins to pray for the souls of such "righteous ones" and for the continued existence of true religion in the congregation.

Here we need to realize the difference between being hard and tough for the kingdom of God and exhibiting tough love in the spirit of Christ.

One of the unfortunate aspects of having only the written word is that it leaves us without the facial expressions and voice tonality. I can say the same thing in a spirit of love or one of meanness and harshness. It may be the same words, but the sense that comes across is totally different. We learn from Matthew 23 that Jesus ranks among those who are not afraid to confront error. But we also glimpse the spirit in which He did so.

When we are tempted to play the role of "spiritual storm troopers" we need to ponder the verses that highlight the spirit in which Jesus set forth the rebukes of Matthew 23. "O Jerusalem, Jerusalem, . . . ! How often would I have gathered your children together as a hen gathers her brood under her wings" (verse 37, RSV). It was in love and caringness that Jesus made His final appeal to the Jewish leaders to leave their false religiosity behind and turn to "the weightier matters of the law"—"justice and mercy" (verse 23, RSV). And it was with a broken heart that He realized that the majority of them would not change (verse 37).

With that rejection comes the foreshadowing of two events. One was the destruction of the Temple and Jerusalem with it (verse 38). And the second was His own return in the clouds of heaven (verse 39).

Lord, we have been sobered by the strong words of Jesus in the face of false ideas about religion. But we have been given hope by the spirit of love in which He spoke them. Help us to have both genuine religion and a proper spirit.

Introducing the Second Advent

Then Jesus went out and departed from the temple, and His disciples came up to show Him the buildings of the temple. And Jesus said to them, "Do you not see all these things? Assuredly, I say to you, not one stone shall be left here upon another, that shall not be thrown down."

Now as He sat on the Mount of Olives, the disciples came to Him privately, saying, "Tell us, when will these things be? And what will be the sign of Your coming, and of the end of the age?" Matt. 24:1-3, NKJV.

Matthew 24:1 has Jesus leaving the Temple for the last time. The disciples, having heard Him pronouncing it "forsaken and desolate" (Matt. 23:38, RSV), seemingly point out that the Temple looks just fine to them.

And a fine-looking building it was. Josephus, the first-century Jewish historian, writes that the outward face of the Temple "was covered all over with plates of gold of great weight, and, at the first rising of the sun, reflected back a very fiery splendour, and made those who forced themselves to look upon it to turn their eyes away, just as they would have done at the sun's own rays." At a distance, he continues, the Temple appeared "like a mountain covered with snow; for, as to those parts of it that were not gilt, they were exceeding white" (*Wars* 5. 5. 6).

The Temple was not only majestic; it was also massive. Josephus, in one place, indicates that some of the stones were 25 cubits (a cubit is 18-20 inches) long, 8 in height, and about 12 in breadth (*Antiquities* 15. 11. 3). In another place he tells us that other stones were up to 45 cubits (67-75 feet) in length (*Wars* 5. 5. 6). With those facts in mind, it is no wonder that the disciples experience shock when Jesus tells them that the massive Temple, one of the architectural wonders of the ancient world, would be totally destroyed, without one stone being left upon another.

To His followers such an event signaled the end of the world. The Temple was the focus of their earthly existence. And they couldn't even imagine a world without the great Jerusalem Temple. The disciples, seeking clarification, later ask Jesus three questions: (1) When will the Temple be destroyed? (2) What will be the sign of His return? (3) What will be the sign of the end of the age?

Jesus does not seek to correct their false understanding on the sequence of those events. In fact, His answer mixes the two events and their signs to such an extent that it is well-nigh impossible to disentangle them.

With Matthew 24 and its teachings on the second coming of Jesus we have come to a crucial aspect of the gospel story. We need to keep our eyes and ears open as we journey through Matthew 24 and 25.

August 7

A Side Lesson on
the Second Advent

As He was sitting on the Mount of Olives, the disciples came to Him privately, say-
ing, "Tell us, when will these things happen, and what will be the sign of Your com-
ing, and of the end of the age?" Matt. 24:3, NASB.

We noted yesterday that the disciples were confused about the relationship of the destruction of the Temple and the Second Advent. If I were
Jesus I would have put them straight on the topic and told them that they were
both coming but that 2,000 years would lapse between the two events.

But Jesus didn't follow my logic. His answer mixes the two events and their
signs in a manner that Christians have been hard put to disentangle.

One wonders at the logic of His strategy when He could have made things
clear. The only thing we can say for certain is that He deliberately mingled the
two events in His explanation.

But why? The chapter supplies us with the reasons. Foremost among them
is that Jesus is not so much seeking to tell us *when* the end will come as to alert
His hearers that they *must live in a state of continual expectancy* as they look for
the end. That aim becomes clear as Matthew 24 nears its end and enters into
the watch-and-be-ready counsels (verses 36, 42, 44, 50). The great parables of
chapter 25, which form the conclusion to the sermon, begin in chapter 24 and
continue to drive home the lessons of faithful waiting and responsible working
as Christ's followers anticipate the end of the age.

A second reason for His less-than-precise teaching strategy is that it forces
readers to continually rethink His teachings regarding the Second Advent as
they seek to penetrate His meaning. That approach is similar in some ways
to His use of parables. In Matthew 13:10-15 He intimated that He taught in
parables rather than in straightforward language because such teaching would
compel those who were truly interested to wrestle with the ultimate meaning
of what He said and thus make it their own.

As a result, the very ambiguity of some of His statements has driven readers to struggle with the significance and meaning of the topic. The result has
been an ongoing awareness and interest in the subject of the Second Coming.
Such a technique has aided people in identifying with the major point of His
sermon—to watch and be ready, because they truly know not the hour of the
Master's returning.

The Function of Signs

Take heed that no one leads you astray. For many will come in my name, saying,
"I am the Christ," and they will lead many astray. And you will hear of wars and
rumors of wars; see that you are not alarmed; for this must take place, but the end
is not yet. For nation will rise against nation, and kingdom against kingdom, and
there will be famines and earthquakes in various places: all this is but the beginning
of the birth-pangs. Matt. 24:5-8, RSV.

We would all like to have an indisputable sign that the Lord will be here in three years, three months, or even three days. Such an indication would stimulate us to get out of our chairs and begin earnest preparations for the event.

Significantly, that is exactly the kind of sign that Jesus never gave. And for good reasons.

In the Gospels we find the Jewish leadership repeatedly asking Jesus for various signs. But it is not until late in His ministry that the disciples do the same. They are especially interested in ones related to their confused conflation of the destruction of Jerusalem and the Second Advent. As a result, Jesus gives them a long list of markers beginning in Matthew 24:5. That list includes the emergence of false christs, wars and rumors of wars, nation rising against nation, famines, and earthquakes.

Unfortunately, those signs don't give us much specific information about the end of the age. After all, there have always been false messiahs, earthquakes, famines, and wars. What are we to make of such events, especially in light of the often overlooked statements in verses 6 and 8? Verse 6 tells us that such signs should not alarm us. They belong to the course of nature, "but the end is not yet" (RSV). In other words, they are indications that the end is coming, but they are not the real signs of *the* end. Verse 8 reinforces that thought with its teaching that "all these [signs] are the *beginning* of birth pains" (NIV).

It appears that such things are similar to the sign of the rainbow that God gave to Noah as a token of remembrance. Every time God's people saw the rainbow they remembered His covenant promise. So it is with wars, famines, and earthquakes. Each one is a reminder of earth's sickness and evidence that the faithful, covenant-keeping God has not yet finished the plan of salvation. Each of those signs is a promise that Christ will come again to complete the saving of "his people from their sins" (Matt. 1:21). Every falling star, every betrayal of trust, every tsunami and earthquake tell us that while Jesus' work is not yet finished, He will come again to rescue His people.

More on Signs

And this gospel of the kingdom will be preached in all the world as a witness to all the nations, and then the end will come. . . . As the lightning comes from the east and flashes to the west, so also will the coming of the Son of Man be. . . . Then the sign of the Son of Man will appear in heaven, and then all the tribes of the earth will mourn, and they will see the Son of Man coming on the clouds of heaven with power and great glory. Matt. 24:14-30, NKJV.

A careful reading of the text indicates that at least three signs in Matthew 24 are much more precise in their connection to the Second Coming than the recurring earthquakes and wars of verses 5-8. The first appears in verse 14 with its preaching of the gospel to all the world. That must have sounded like an impossible challenge to the few Galileans who first heard it. But the Christian church rapidly spread throughout the Roman Empire and beyond. And since the birth of modern missions two centuries ago, Christianity has become the most outreach-oriented of all faiths. It has permeated the far corners of the earth. Yet the missionary task is still not complete. R. H. Mounce appears to be correct when he states that "only when the church has completed its worldwide mission of evangelism will the Parousia [Second Coming] no longer be delayed."

The second concrete sign of the end occurs in verse 27, which pictures the coming of Christ as lightning visible to the entire earth. That sign, however, is not one proclaiming that the end is near. To the contrary, it indicates that it is in the process of taking place.

We find the only event actually called a sign in Matthew 24 in verses 30 and 31—"the sign of the Son of Man" appearing in the sky. Once again, it is not something pointing to the nearness of Jesus' coming, because it will take place as He comes in the clouds "with power and great glory," accompanied by "his angels" and "a great sound of a trumpet," the resurrection of the dead, and the ascension of living believers (see also 1 Thess. 4:16, 17; 1 Cor. 15:51-54).

Thus the pattern of Matthew 24 appears to be that the *real* signs are not those of nearness but ones of Christ's actual arrival. The less precise signs encourage believers to keep watching until that day.

The hope of the ages is the return of Jesus in the clouds of heaven. It is that event that makes it possible for Christians from all times and places to experience full salvation. No wonder Paul calls it our "blessed hope" (Titus 2:13).

The Sign of Jerusalem: Number 1

So when you see the desolating sacrilege spoken of by the prophet Daniel, standing in the holy place (let the reader understand), then let those who are in Judea flee to the mountains. . . . For then there will be great tribulation, such as has not been from the beginning of the world until now, no, and never will be. And if those days had not been shortened, no human being would be saved. Matt. 24:15-22, RSV.

W e should note that Matthew 24 has one other sign containing a great deal of precision—that of the destruction of Jerusalem and the Temple, a foreshadowing of the judgment and destruction of the entire world at the Second Advent.

Jesus predicted that the destruction of the Temple would be complete— "not one stone here will be left on another" (verse 2, NIV). Josephus, the Jewish historian who lived through the event, describes the almost unimaginable hardships during the final six-month siege. Not only does he claim that more than a million Jews died, but that the Romans took nearly 100,000 more captive. The famine was so bad that a mother is reported to have slain, roasted, and eaten her child (*Wars* 6. 3. 4). The Roman general Titus eventually ordered the entire city, including the Temple complex, razed to the ground, thus bringing to fulfillment Christ's prediction of verse 2.

But Christian believers, however, did not suffer the same fate as those Jews who had rejected Jesus as the Messiah. Christians had the counsel of Christ that we now find in Matthew 24. Verses 15 to 22 appear to be specifically directed toward the fall of Jerusalem and give directions as to when believers were to make their escape.

The Christians in Jerusalem were not only alerted to the coming crisis of the destruction of Jerusalem by the general sign of wars and rumors of wars, but they had specific counsel that when they saw "standing in the holy place 'the abomination that causes desolation,' spoken of through the prophet Daniel [9:27]" (verse 15, NIV), then those in Judea were to flee to the mountains (verse 16). Luke's rendering of this passage makes the meaning clearer: "When you see Jerusalem being surrounded by armies, you will know that its desolation is near. Then let those who are in Judea flee to the mountains, let those in the city get out, and let those in the country not enter the city. For this is the time of punishment in fulfillment of all that has been written" (Luke 21:20-22, NIV).

Tomorrow we will examine how accepting Jesus at His word saved the believers in Jerusalem.

The Sign of Jerusalem: Number 2

But when you see Jerusalem surrounded by armies, then know that its desolation has come near. Then let those who are in Judea flee to the mountains, and let those who are inside the city depart, and let not those who are out in the country enter it; for these are days of vengeance, to fulfil all that is written . . . Jerusalem will be trodden down by the Gentiles." Luke 21:20-24, RSV.

Yesterday we began to explore the prophetic warnings of Jesus that allowed His followers to escape the destruction of the city. The course of events themselves enabled the Christians to heed His warning.

In August of A.D. 66 Cestius (Rome's legate in Syria) attacked Jerusalem and then withdrew for some unknown reason, even though victory was within his grasp. Then in A.D. 67 and A.D. 68 Vespasian subdued Galilee and Judea, but delayed the siege of Jerusalem because of Emperor Nero's death. Not until the spring and summer of A.D. 70 did Jerusalem come under siege and be destroyed by Vespasian's son Titus. Sometime in the interval between the trouble of A.D. 66 and the destruction of A.D. 70, Eusebius (A.D. 263-339) tells us, "The members of the Jerusalem church, by means of an oracle given by revelation to acceptable persons there, were ordered to leave the City before the war began [in earnest] and settle in a town in Peraea called Pella. To Pella those who believed in Christ migrated from Jerusalem" (*Ecclesiastical History* 3. 5. 3).

Thus the Christians, following the warning of Christ in Matthew 24, Luke 21, and the unnamed prophet noted by Eusebius, fled the city and avoided its fate. Both that destruction and the salvation of Christians from catastrophe were signs of great significance concerning the second coming of Jesus and the end of the world. In the context of Matthew 24 they function as guarantees of the final annihilation of a sinful world and the ultimate salvation of those who believe in Jesus.

Ellen White summarizes it nicely when she writes that "the Saviour's prophecy concerning the visitation of judgments upon Jerusalem is to have another fulfillment, of which that terrible desolation was but a faint shadow. In the fate of the chosen city we may behold the doom of a world that has rejected God's mercy and trampled upon His law. . . . But in that day, as in the time of Jerusalem's destruction, God's people will be delivered" (*The Great Controversy*, pp. 36, 37).

Praise God for His providence.

Fig Lessons

Now learn the parable from the fig tree: when its branch has already become tender and puts forth its leaves, you know that summer is near; so, you too, when you see all these things, recognize that He is near, right at the door. . . . But of that day and hour no one knows, not even the angels of heaven, nor the Son, but the Father alone. For the coming of the Son of Man will be just like the days of Noah. . . . They did not understand until the flood came and took them all away. Matt. 24:32-39, NASB.

In Matthew 24:32-36 Jesus gives us two great truths about human knowledge of the Second Advent. The first is the lesson of the fig tree—one of the minority of trees in first-century Palestine that lost its leaves for winter. Just as the appearance of new leaves on the fig tree indicates that summer is approaching, so sensitive Christians can tell when Christ's appearing is near (verse 33). On the other hand, they can never know its exact time (verse 36).

Jesus goes on to give the illustration of Noah. Just as people "were eating and drinking, marrying and giving in marriage, up to the day Noah entered the ark," so will it be with the coming of the Son of man (verse 38, NIV).

Most explanations of that text imply that the sign of Noah will be great wickedness in the world, but that is not the only possible interpretation. The great wickedness understanding harks back to Genesis 6:5, which states that in Noah's time "the Lord saw that the wickedness of man was great in the earth, and that every imagination of the thoughts of his heart was only evil continually" (RSV). Note, however, that Genesis 6:5 is from God's perspective.

Matthew 24:37-39 can also be read from the human point of view. From that vantage, the text simply says that life near the end of time will continue as usual in the eyes of most people. After all, eating and drinking and marrying are normal activities. It is only the excesses of Noah's time and those implied just before the Second Advent that make them irregular. But most people, including many of those in the churches, will undoubtedly focus on the fact that life appears to be going on as usual until "the great surprise." They see nothing out of the ordinary.

That interpretation ties in nicely with those verses that compare the Second Advent to the coming of a thief (e.g., 1 Thess. 5:2). It also harmonizes with Matthew 24:40 and 41, which indicate the suddenness of the separation of the saved and the lost.

Lord, give me eyes to see fig trees and the events of earth from Your perspective.

August 13

A Side Lesson on
the Second Coming

They will see the Son of man coming in clouds with great power and glory. And then he will send out the angels, and gather his elect from the four winds, from the ends of the earth to the ends of heaven. Mark 13:26, 27, RSV.

The powers and warnings by Jesus in Matthew 24:1-41 are many and precious. Michael Green sums up the lessons of the passage in a helpful manner. First, he notes, the return of Christ will be personal as well as certain.

Second, history is going somewhere. It is not meaningless or random. Nor is it an endless cycle. "There will be a real end just as there was a real beginning. And at the end we shall find none other than Jesus Christ."

Third, the return of Christ points to the triumph of good over evil, the victory of God's purpose over human and cosmic rebellion.

Fourth, the return spells restoration. "There will be a new creation, a new heaven and earth, in which only goodness dwells" (see 2 Peter 3:11-13; Rev. 21:1-5).

Fifth, the return of Jesus points to judgment and separation. Some will be taken and some left (Matt. 24:40, 41). It will be a time when the secret thoughts of the heart and the innermost character become known to all.

Sixth, the return of Christ will be decisive. Signaling the end of the age, it ushers in the fullness of the kingdom. The time for repentance and change will be forever past.

Seventh, the return will be as sudden and unexpected as a flash of lightning in the sky (verse 27). "It will come out of the blue upon a heedless world."

Last, the return of Jesus will occur at a time known only to God the Father (verse 36). Preachers don't know the time, nor did the disciples. Even Jesus in His incarnate state did not know. God in His wisdom recognizes when it will be best to end earthly history. In the meantime, Christians are to be faithful in the face of hardships (verse 13) and watchful as they await the return of their Savior (verse 42).

It is to the topics of watchfulness and preparedness that Jesus turns to in the second half of His great sermon on His second coming. He will address the question of how His followers ought to live in light of His certain return.

And with that shift in emphasis we must "listen up" as our Lord provides us with priceless knowledge that we desperately need as we travel through endtimes.

Parable Number 1:
Watch for Christ's Return

Watch therefore: for ye know not what hour your Lord doth come. But know this, that
if the goodman of the house had known in what watch the thief would come,
he would have watched, and would not have suffered his house to be broken up.
Therefore be ye also ready: for in such an hour as ye think not the Son of man cometh.
Matt. 24:42-44.

The point of Matthew 24:37-41 is the absolute certainty and suddenness of the Second Advent. Neither God's people nor the wicked can predict the exact time of the event. Both are to some extent surprised as to its exact timing, but true believers have at least had their level of awareness raised by Jesus' counsel regarding signs.

Verse 42 brings us to a major transition in the Second Advent sermon of Matthew 24 and 25. Here we begin to find the practical outcome of the teaching in the first 41 verses of Matthew 24. If no one knows the time of the Advent except the Father (verse 36), then it behooves Christians to "watch," because they have no precise knowledge concerning what hour their Lord will return.

Then in verse 43 Jesus gives the first of five short parables showing people how to live in the light of His returning. In this one they are to be as alert as a householder who expects his house to be broken into. This short parable calls for a constant state of watchfulness and readiness for the Lord's return. After all, "the Son of Man will come at an hour when you do not expect him" (verse 44, NIV). Down through history, the time when Christ is least expected to return is always today.

William Barclay relates the fable of three apprentice devils who were coming to earth to complete their training. Each presented his plan to Satan for the ruination of humanity. The first proposed to tell people that there was no God. Satan replied that that would not delude many, since most have a gut feeling to the contrary. The second said he would proclaim that there was no hell. Satan rejected this tactic also, since most people have a sense that sin will receive its just deserts. "The third said, 'I will tell men that there is no hurry.' 'Go,' said Satan, 'and you will ruin men by the thousand.'"

The most dangerous delusion is that time will go on indefinitely. *Tomorrow* can be a dangerous word. It is against this attitude that Christ warns us in the first of His five parables on watchfulness and readiness.

Father, it seems as if time will go on forever. Help me ever to remember that
Your sure Word says that that is not so. Help me to keep the vividness of that
promise in my heart and mind.

August 15

Parable Number 2: Waiting Faithfully for Christ's Return

Who then is the faithful and wise servant, whom his master has set over his household, to give them their food at the proper time? Blessed is that servant whom his master when he comes will find so doing. Truly, I say to you, he will set him over all his possessions. But if that wicked servant says to himself, "My master is delayed," and begins to beat his fellow servants, and eats and drinks with the drunken, the master of that servant will come on a day when he does not expect him and at an hour he does not know, and will punish him, and put him with the hypocrites; there men will weep and gnash their teeth. Matt. 24:45-51, RSV.

The second parable continues the theme of urgency and watchfulness raised by the first, but with several added nuances. It sets forth the idea that Christians have duties and ethical responsibilities as they wait and watch. They are not to be idle. And in this story the householder's return gets delayed for reasons that the servants know nothing about.

Unfortunately, delay can lead to bad behavior. Since the servants are on their own in an uncertain situation, one of them allows baser passions to rise to the surface. That servant begins to be unkind to others and to live a loose life. After all, there seems plenty of time before the Master shows up.

But Jesus reiterates the lesson of the first parable: "the master of that servant will come on a day when he does not expect him and at an hour he does not know." Then Jesus adds a new aspect—one that will surface again in the conclusions of parables four and five (Matt. 25:30, 46). Unfaithful servants will lose their heavenly reward and will receive, instead, the same reward as the unfaithful Jews (Matt. 8:12), wicked people in general (Matt. 13:41, 42, 50), and the scribes and the Pharisees (Matt. 23:13, 15, 23, 25, 27, 29). The succeeding parables drive home the concept of faithfulness and watchfulness in a more complete way than the first one.

Hymnist Frank E. Belden captured the message of the first two parables in "We Know Not the Hour." Since we "know not the hour of the Master's appearing, . . . let us watch and be ready" for "He will come, hallelujah! hallelujah! He will come in the clouds of His Father's bright glory—But we know not the hour."

Good advice for people who all too easily forget that their Lord will return in spite of an extended delay that can lead to careless living.

And we are all those kinds of people.

Parable Number 3:
Prepare Now for Christ's Return

Then the kingdom of heaven shall be likened to ten virgins who took their lamps and went out to meet the bridegroom. Now five of them were wise, and five were foolish. Those who were foolish took their lamps and took no oil with them. . . . And at midnight a cry was heard: "Behold, the bridegroom is coming; go out to meet him!" . . . And while they [the foolish] went to buy [oil], the bridegroom came, and those who were ready went in with him to the wedding; and the door was shut. Matt. 25:1-10, NKJV.

The third parable on preparedness for the Second Advent (Matt. 25:1-13) continues the theme of waiting in watchful expectation, but once again the complexity of the message increases. This time the scene is a Palestinian wedding with Jesus as the Bridegroom.

Beyond the coming of the Bridegroom, the focus of the parable is on the 10 virgins and their lamps. In fact, the primary emphasis is really on the division between the virgins, with five being wise and five foolish. The difference between them has to do with the preparation they have made for the coming of the Bridegroom. All have lamps, but only half of them have sufficient oil.

Note that all 10 are outwardly Christians, for all of them are awaiting the Bridegroom. Also recognize that all 10 fall asleep.

A major point in the parable that we can all identify with is that the Bridegroom is "a *long time* in coming" (verse 5, NIV). That is why they are sleeping. Earthly necessities go on, even while Christ's followers anticipate His return. No one can exist in a constant state of high-pitched alert. And His delay tempts them to forget His return while they focus on the activities of this world. All sleep.

The difference between the wise and the foolish is not sleep but rather preparation for the return. Some have left preparation for the last minute, when it is too late. They pay deeply for their neglect. The door is shut (verse 10), their probation has closed (cf. Rev. 22:10, 11), and they miss the great "wedding supper of the Lamb" (Rev. 19:9, NIV) that takes place at the Second Advent (Matt. 25:11, 12).

Verse 13 gives the moral of the story: "Keep watch, because you do not know the day or the hour" (NIV). That theme, of course, undergirded the first two parables. But this one adds the facts of a long delay and that no individual can rely on another person's preparedness. In the judgment of God each one of us stands as an individual.

Parable Number 4: Working While Waiting and Watching

For it will be like a man going on a journey, who called his servants and entrusted to them his property. To one he gave five talents, to another two, to another one, to each according to his ability. Then he went away. He who had received the five talents went at once and traded with them, and he made five talents more. So also he who had the two talents made two talents more. But he who had received the one talent went and dug in the ground and hid his master's money. Now after a long time the master of those servants came and settled accounts with them.

Matt. 25:14-19, ESV.

The parable of the talents, in common with the three preceding parables, continues to emphasize being ready for the Master's return. But it begins to answer a question previously not addressed: what is readiness?

The story line is quite simple. A man (Christ) goes away and gives each of his servants talents (large amounts of money). The first two put their talents to work and increase their master's investment, while the third merely buries his in the ground for safekeeping.

But the master desires more than security from his investment. He expects the servants to use the talents to make a profit. That becomes evident when "after a long time" he returns for an accounting to determine the faithfulness of his servants in his absence. In the judgment scene that follows, he rewards the two servants who have been faithful, but he punishes the one who has done nothing (Matt. 25:24-30).

The lesson is clear. Readiness for the return of Christ does not mean passively waiting for the event. Rather, readiness is responsible activity that produces results that the Master can see and approve of.

We can also learn from this parable that God does not expect the same results from everybody. Christians have varying levels of ability. But it is not the amount of a person's ability that He evaluates in the judgment, but whether he or she has employed the full range of abilities that God has given them.

Another lesson from the parable is that the Lord rewards faithful people with even greater responsibility rather than with a pension. Greatness based on service (see Matt. 20:26-28) will continue in the age to come. It is an eternal principle of the kingdom of heaven. The book *Education* captures the concept nicely when it notes that true education "prepares the student for the joy of service in this world and for the higher joy of wider service in the world to come" (p. 13).

Parable Number 5: The Essential Work of the Waiting Ones

When the Son of man comes in his glory, and all the angels with him, then he will sit on his glorious throne. Before him will be gathered all the nations, and he will separate them one from another as a shepherd separates the sheep from the goats, and he will place the sheep at his right hand, but the goats at the left. Then the King will say to those at his right hand, "Come, O blessed of my Father, inherit the kingdom prepared for you from the foundation of the world. Matt. 25:31-34, RSV.

Whenever I preach on the parable of the sheep and the goats (Matt. 25:31-46) I always give people a homework assignment; namely, to count the question marks.

Jesus plainly teaches that the final judgment will be full of surprises. Many of the churchly types will find out they are goats, in spite of outward appearances, while many others will be surprised to discover that they are blessed as sheep.

The parable of the sheep and the goats brings the judgment theme that began in Matthew 23 to a climax. It also completes Jesus' developing teaching on readiness. Whereas the first three parables in the sequence of five placed the emphasis on watching (Matt. 24:42-25:13), and the fourth stressed working while watching (Matt. 25:14-30), this one (verses 31-46) is explicit as to the essential nature of that activity.

The story of the sheep and the goats is a vivid word picture of the final separation that will take place when Jesus comes in the clouds of heaven. It is a portrayal that allows for no middle ground or any second chances. One is either a sheep (a standard Old Testament symbol of God's people) *or* a goat. One is either assigned to the right (the symbol of favor) *or* the left (the symbol of disfavor). Nor is the decision of the judgment open to appeal. The scene is one of finality. Those individuals failing to utilize the waiting and watching time appropriately before the Second Advent eventually find themselves lost from the kingdom (verse 46).

As noted above, a crucial element in the parable is that of surprise. Both the sheep and the goats are startled at the king's verdict in their particular cases. Both groups question the decision (verses 37-39, 44).

The reason for the surprise, as Jesus makes clear, stems from a false understanding of religion, one held by most people.

We will return to that topic tomorrow. In the meantime, we need to begin to examine our own hearts and minds and lives as we contemplate our own idea of what it means to be religious and Christian.

Parable Number 5: Avoid Surprises

Come, you blessed of My Father, inherit the kingdom prepared for you from the foundation of the world: for I was hungry and you gave Me food; I was thirsty and you gave Me drink; I was a stranger and you took Me in; I was naked and you clothed Me; I was sick and You visited Me; I was in prison and you came to Me. Then the righteous will answer Him, saying, "Lord, when did we see You hungry and feed You, or thirsty and give You drink? When did we see You . . . in prison, and come to You?" And the King will answer and say to them, "Assuredly, I say to you, inasmuch as you did it to one of the least of these My brethren, you did it to Me."
Matt. 25:34-40, NKJV.

Did you see the question marks? We find even more as the parable moves toward its conclusion. One of its basic teachings is that the judgment is full of surprises.

The reason for them stems from the false understanding of true religion held by most people. The average person sees the heart of religion as believing in right doctrines or in practicing certain ritual and/or lifestyle duties. But that is not God's position. In one of the great Old Testament texts on the topic, God says through Micah that what He requires of His children is not outward behavior or ritual obedience but "to act justly and to love mercy and to walk humbly with your God" (Micah 6: 8, NIV). And in the first 24 chapters of Matthew Jesus has already quoted that verse three times (Matt. 9:13; 12:7; 23:23), each time in the context of verses dealing with a false understanding of genuine religion. The rest of the New Testament picks up on that same theme. Thus James can write: "Religion that God our Father accepts as pure and faultless is this: to look after orphans and widows in their distress and to keep oneself from being polluted by the world" (James 1:27, NIV). And Paul can state that "he whoever loves others has fulfilled the law" (Rom. 13:8-10, NIV; see also Gal. 5:14).

Nor has the first Gospel been silent on the topic of true religion and its rewards. Jesus put it most plainly when He claimed that "if anyone gives even a cup of cold water to one of these little ones who is my disciple, truly I tell you, that person will certainly not lose their reward" (Matt. 10:42, NIV). Again, Jesus noted that one can sum up the two great commandments as love to God and neighbor; He defined perfection in terms of being merciful to one's enemies (Matt. 5:43-48; Luke 6:36); and He specifically told the behaviorally oriented rich young ruler that if he would be perfect, he should sell his possessions and give to the poor and then his reward would be treasure in heaven (Matt. 19:21).

It is time for those who see doctrine and lifestyle or even prayer and Bible reading to be the heart of true religion to listen up. Those things are important, but there is something even more vital.

Parable Number 5:
The Core of True Religion

Then He will also say to those on the left hand, "Depart from Me, you cursed, into the everlasting fire prepared for the devil and his angels: for I was hungry and you gave Me no food; I was thirsty and you gave Me no drink; I was . . . naked and you did not clothe Me. . . ."
Then they also will answer Him, saying, "Lord, when did we see You hungry or thirsty or a stranger or naked or sick or in prison, and did not minister to You?"
Then He will answer them, saying, "Assuredly, I say to you, inasmuch as you did not do it to one of the least of these, you did not do it to Me." Matt. 25:41-45, NKJV.

In the overall context of the parable of the sheep and the goats, it is the Pharisees and their kind who are lost because they did not understand true religion. They had an outward form in doctrine, lifestyle, and religious ritual, but it hadn't entered their heart and made them more loving. Doctrine, lifestyle, and ritual are not ends in themselves, but rather a means to experiencing a transformed heart that leads to a life of loving and caring. Without the end product, those things that so-called religious, churchly people regard as important have no value. And those who focus on the wrong "religious" activities will be lost according to Jesus.

Ellen White sums up the teaching of Jesus nicely. Commenting on the parable of the sheep and the goats, she writes that Jesus "pictured to His disciples the scene of the great judgment day. And He represented its decision as turning upon one point. When the nations are gathered before Him, there will be but two classes, and their eternal destiny will be determined by what they have done or have neglected to do for Him in the person of the poor and the suffering" (*The Desire of Ages*, p. 637).

That is not salvation by works, but rather a heart response to the love of God—an internalization of that love that passes on to others His gifts to us. An important lesson of the parable is that the activities that really count are simple and uncalculating.

It is the unconscious internalization of God's love and its expression in daily life that is the one essential qualification for the kingdom of heaven. Such people have begun to live the principle of servanthood and greatness that has come up again and again in Jesus' teaching. They are safe to save for eternity, because they have internalized the principle of love, *the* principle of the kingdom. As a result, they have developed through grace that "righteousness [which] surpasses that of the Pharisees and the teachers of the law." Thus they are prepared to "enter the kingdom of heaven" (Matt. 5:20, NIV).

Father, help me to be one of those people.

Part 6

Turn Your Eyes Upon Jesus as the Crucified Lamb of God

The Final Trip to Jerusalem

When Jesus had finished all these sayings, he said to his disciples, "You know that after two days the Passover is coming, and the Son of man will be delivered up to be crucified."
Then the chief priests and the elders of the people gathered in the palace of the high priest, who was called Caiaphas, and took counsel together in order to arrest Jesus by stealth and kill him. But they said, "Not during the feast, lest there be a tumult among the people." Matt. 26:1-5, RSV.

The gospel story now shifts rapidly. Ever since Peter's confession that Jesus was the Christ events have been moving toward the cross as Jesus sought to help the disciples understand what it meant for Him to be the Christ. In that task He has largely failed. But He has provided them with much instruction that will enable them to put it all together when they recall His words after the Resurrection.

In the meantime, we need to recognize that Jesus' death is not an epilogue or an appendix to His life. To the contrary, it is His death that makes His life meaningful. After all, Jesus came to earth so that He could "give His life as a ransom for many" (Matt. 20:28, NIV). His blood was to be "poured out for many for the forgiveness of sins" (Matt. 26:28, NIV), and it was through His death and resurrection that He would "save his people from their sins" (Matt. 1:21).

Jesus' death is the focal point of the Gospels. Thus Martin Kähler's definition of the four Gospels as "passion narratives with extended introductions" puts the emphasis in the right place.

As Jesus makes His final journey to Jerusalem His general teaching and healing ministry has ended. We find few words from His mouth except those to His disciples, especially at the Last Supper and His prayer in Gethsemane. Rather, we watch the drama as the Jews, with the aid of their Roman adversaries, put their Messiah on the cross.

Jesus is not facing the cross as a pawn of events beyond His control. He knows what is going to happen and He could have refused to take this one-way trip to Jerusalem. But the Bible pictures Him to be in command of what happened. "I lay down my life, that I may take it again," He tells His disciples. "No one takes it from me, but I lay it down of my own accord" (John 10:17, 18, RSV).

But even though Jesus is in charge and has knowledge of what is transpiring, that does not mean that other forces are not maneuvering to bring about their own desired end. "Official" Jerusalem has rejected Him and is working toward His death.

Judas "Helps" Jesus

Then one of the twelve, who was called Judas Iscariot, went to the chief priests and said, "What will you give me if I deliver him to you?" And they paid him thirty pieces of silver. And from that moment he sought an opportunity to betray him.
Matt. 26:14-16, RSV.

The Jewish leaders were ready to move against Jesus, but they faced several problems. First, they dare not risk open action because the masses are favorable to Him (Matt. 26:5). Yet they are under the pressure of time. After all, if they delay their move until after the Passover, Jesus will presumably leave the city and thus elude their grasp.

Aid for their cause comes from a most unexpected source—one almost unbelievable: the defection of one of Jesus' 12 disciples. Judas Iscariot agrees to work as an inside man for 30 pieces of silver, the price of a slave (Zech. 11:12). He volunteers to arrange an opportune time for the Jewish leaders to arrest Jesus.

The Gospels all report Judas' betrayal, but none of them provides a reason for the action. In that absence, Bible students have suggested several possible reasons. One is that Judas became disillusioned with Jesus when he discovered He was a man of peace rather than a military Messiah who would overthrow the Romans.

But the only motive mentioned in the New Testament is money. It is no accident that Matthew places the story of the woman who anointed Jesus' feet between the story of the frustrated plotting of the Jewish leaders and the story of Judas' volunteering to betray Jesus.

The fourth Gospel helps us here. It tells us that Judas was especially upset because of the cost of the perfume (almost a year's wages) and that he was stealing from the disciples' communal money bag, which he carried (John 12:4-6).

But selfishness alone does not provide us with a sufficient interpretation for Judas' actions, especially since he still expected an earthly Messianic kingdom in which he would be a prominent leader. It seems that the best explanation is that through betrayal Judas sought to force the slow-moving Jesus into exerting His power and setting up His kingdom. Of all the possible constructions behind Judas' betrayal, this one best suits all the facts. And it also explains why Judas committed suicide when his plans went wrong.

Thought question: Am I ever guilty of pushing things a bit to get God moving in the direction I think He should go?

The Mary Choice

When Jesus was at Bethany in the house of Simon the leper, a woman came up to
him with an alabaster flask of very expensive ointment, and she poured it on his
head, as he sat at table. But when the disciples saw it, they were indignant, saying,
"Why this waste?" . . . But Jesus . . . said to them, "Why do you trouble the woman?
For she has done a beautiful thing to me. . . . In pouring this ointment on my body
she has done it to prepare me for burial." Matt. 26:6-12, RSV.

This story doesn't belong here in Jesus' very last entrance into Jerusalem. It is out of place. Matthew appears to have deliberately placed the account of the anointing between the plots of the Jewish leaders and Judas' offer to betray Jesus, even though he had to take the event out of its chronological setting to do so. John 12 situates the anointing six days before the Passover and puts the triumphal entry the "next day."

Yet Matthew does not include the story in the first Gospel merely to help explain Judas' actions. To the contrary, Mary's anointing has a message of its own. It is one of immense devotion that symbolizes her gratitude to Jesus. In sharp contrast to the Jewish leaders' and Judas' responses to Jesus in the story's immediate context, Mary's demonstrates her love for the One who has done so much for her personally and who has brought her brother Lazarus back to life.

Beyond that, the anointing is rich in symbolism. After all, the very meaning of Messiah or Christ is the "anointed one." Just as kings and priests received anointing in the Old Testament, so Mary anointed Jesus.

Perhaps the most surprising part of the anointing story is Jesus' explanation that Mary's deed is to prepare Him for burial. That statement indicates, once again, that Jesus is in control of the situation. After all, customarily, bodies did not get anointed for burial until after they were dead. Anointing was traditionally performed on corpses, not on living people, except in the case of criminals. Thus Jesus' interpretation of Mary's act seems to assume (correctly) that His death will be that of a criminal whose body will be buried without proper ceremony.

The stories of Judas and Mary bring us face-to-face with a crucial question. Where do we stand? Are we with the extravagant Mary, who selflessly gave her all to Jesus, or are we with the selfish Judas, who saw Jesus as a tool to serve his own needs? That is not an easy question to answer honestly, because a Judas lurks within the skin of each of us. Fortunately, a Mary also resides there. I make the choice as to which personality will dominate my own life.

The Final Passover

On the first day of Unleavened Bread the disciples came to Jesus, saying, "Where will you have us prepare for you to eat the passover?" He said, "Go into the city to a certain one, and say to him, 'The Teacher says, My time is at hand; I will keep the passover at your house with my disciples.'" And the disciples did as Jesus had directed them, and they prepared the passover. Matt. 26:17-19, RSV.

Jesus has been moving toward the cross ever since He first told His disciples about His coming death. Events since His triumphal entry into Jerusalem have begun to accelerate. The Jewish leaders have decided that the time has come to put Him to death. And Judas has volunteered his services to aid them in their designs.

The Passover is at hand. But Jesus and His disciples will eat it on Thursday, the evening before the regular Passover meal. In Jesus' case this is a necessity because He knows that He will be dead by Friday evening. The Passover lambs will be slain in the Temple on Friday afternoon, the very time that He will also die. That timing is significant, since, as Paul puts it, Jesus is "a Passover lamb sacrificed for us" (1 Cor. 5:7, Phillips).

The fact that Jesus died at the Passover was no accident. It was in God's plan from the beginning. The Passover finds its roots at the time of the Exodus from Egypt. God instituted it to commemorate the night of the Israelites' escape, when all the firstborn of the Egyptians perished. Each Jewish family was to slay a lamb and sprinkle the blood on the doorpost as a sign that their house should be passed over when sudden death invaded the homes of the Egyptians. The sprinkled blood would preserve the inhabitants of the house. And so it was that the blood of the Passover lamb spared God's people (Ex. 12). The New Testament views the Passover as symbolic of the work of Jesus.

J. C. Ryle notes that "*the intentional connection between the time of the Jewish passover and the time of Christ's death*" is of great significance. "We cannot doubt for a moment that it was not by chance, but by God's providential appointment, that our Lord was crucified in the Passover week. . . . It was meant to draw attention of the Jewish nation to Him as the true Lamb of God. It was meant to bring to their minds the true object and purpose of His death." And it was meant to be a sign of the "redemption and deliverance from the bondage of sin, which was to be brought in by our Lord Jesus Christ."

That fateful Passover is the pivot point of redemptive history.

Tension in the Room

Jesus, knowing that the Father had given all things into His hands, and that He had come forth from God and was going back to God, got up from supper, and laid aside His garments; and taking a towel, He girded Himself. Then He poured water into the basin and began to wash the disciples' feet and to wipe them with the towel with which He was girded. John 13:3-5, NASB.

Tension filled the room.

The disciples, Luke tells us, had been arguing about which of them was the greatest as they journeyed toward their Passover meal (Luke 22:24). Thus by the time they entered the room they were already agitated. More than a bit of pushing and jostling occurred as they seated themselves. Judas and John managed to score a victory over the equally aggressive Peter, with Judas gaining the place to Jesus' left and John to His right. They all wanted the most important positions.

The tension didn't dissipate after they took their seats. After all, there was something missing. It wasn't the water pitcher or the basin. They were in place. But there was no servant to wash their feet. On the dirt paths and roads of the day, a traveler's feet would be dusty upon arrival in the dry season and muddy during the wet. Animal waste fouled every street and path. As a result, on festal occasions a servant washed the participants' feet.

But there was no servant. As the disciples looked around the table, each determined that he would not assume that humiliating role. You could feel the tension in the air as they made no move to serve one another. Jesus, well aware of the dynamics, merely waited and watched to see what they would do.

In that explosive context He finally arose, girded on the towel, poured the water into the basin, and began to wash each disciple's feet.

What a demonstration! Here He was, "knowing that the Father had given all things into His hands" and that He would soon be sitting at His right hand in heaven, yet playing the part of the servant.

Jesus, sorrowful at the attitude of His followers, demonstrates the lesson that they need most. His whole life had been one of unselfish service. And now He had one last opportunity to demonstrate that principle in a way they would never forget.

Lord, there is tension in my heart also. I struggle between the principles of Jesus and those of the disciples. Help me.

Peter Gets a Lesson

He came to Simon Peter. He said to Him, "Lord, do You wash my feet?" Jesus an-
swered and said to him, "What I do you do not realize now, but you will understand
hereafter." Peter said to Him, "Never shall You wash my feet!" Jesus answered him,
"If I do not wash you, you have no part with Me." Simon Peter said to Him, "Lord,
then wash not only my feet, but also my hands and my head." Jesus said to him, "He
who has bathed needs only to wash his feet, but is completely clean; and you are
clean, but not all of you." John 13:6-10, NASB.

Peter was uncomfortable enough having been shut out of the two most prestigious table positions. And now he watched in horror as the foot-washing
Jesus served one disciple after another. But the crisis hit Peter as Jesus approached his own feet. Flustered and not knowing what to say or do, he blurted
out that he would never allow Jesus to wash his feet. But, to put it mildly, Jesus
asserted that what He was doing was essential, that if Peter would not allow
Him to serve him, then he could have no place as His follower. At that point the
ever-verbal disciple, not knowing what else to say, declared that Jesus should
wash not only his feet but all of him.

Jesus responded that Peter didn't need a complete bath, but only a cleansing
of his dirty feet. Here Christ probably alluded to the custom of bathing before
attending a feast. When guests arrived they needed only their feet cleansed.

We fail to see the importance and full significance of Christ's words if we
view them only in terms of physical bathing. They also contain a level of spiritual
meaning. Verse 10 reflects, by analogy, two kinds of spiritual cleansing. The first
is represented by baptism at the beginning of a Christian's life. At that point a
convert is forgiven of all sin and justified in the eyes of God. Having been sub-
merged in the watery grave of baptism, the new Christian is clean all over.

But as new believers move through life in their daily business, they make
sinful contact with the world and its contaminants. Worse yet, they make mistakes and commit sins. Such individuals have not apostatized or left Christ.
Thus they have no need of another full baptism. However, so to speak, they
have messed up their spiritual feet in their journey and need a partial cleansing
from time to time.

We should regard the foot-washing service in part as a mini-baptism. It
is a time in which individuals are cleansed and rededicate their lives to Jesus
as the Lord of their lives. They renew their vows of servanthood to the world
around them and to fellow church members.

A Neglected Blessing

So after he had washed their feet, and had taken his garments, and was set down again, he said unto them, Know ye what I have done to you? Ye call me Master and Lord: and ye say well; for so I am. If I then, your Lord and Master, have washed your feet; ye also ought to wash one another's feet. For I have given you an example, that you should do as I have done to you. Verily, verily, I say unto you, The servant is not greater than his lord; neither he that is sent greater than he that sent him. If ye know these things, happy are ye if ye do them. John 13:12-17.

One of the more curious aspects of the history of the church is that most religious bodies and Christians have placed a huge emphasis on that aspect of the Last Supper that deals with the bread and the wine but have almost totally neglected foot washing. Yet Christ commands both.

There are probably good reasons for that. After all, the death of Christ and His shed blood are central to what Christianity is all about. As a result, the broken bread representing Christ's body and the wine symbolizing His shed blood deserve an important place in Christianity.

But there is something else of importance in Jesus' teaching and example. That is the need for His followers to be spiritually ready to partake of the Communion symbols. Just as Jesus' first disciples needed to humble up and examine their hearts before eating the Communion meal, so likewise modern disciples must prepare their hearts and minds for the experience.

However, most of us moderns don't like the idea of washing someone else's feet any more than Peter did. I still remember the first time I attended a church that practiced foot washing. My whole mind and being rebelled against it. Yet I have discovered it to be a real blessing. I have found it to be not only an occasion of service to another person, but also an opportunity to confess my wrongs and shortcomings to both God and other people.

We all as humans have pride and we all have offended others in our families and in the church. The foot-washing experience is a time to humble up and to follow the example of our Lord. It is a time of spiritual renewal, a time to find others whom we have wronged, a time to make peace with them and our Lord. In short, it is a season of spiritual renewal, symbolized by a mini-baptism. Most important, it prepares us to sit at the Lord's table both in heart and mind as a healed community of sinners who have messed up our feet in the journey of life.

Tension Turns to Shock

When it was evening, he reclined with the twelve. And as they were eating, he said,
"Truly, I say to you, one of you will betray me." And they were very sorrowful and
began to say to him one after another, "Is it I, Lord?" He answered, "He who has
dipped his hand in the dish with me will betray me." . . . Judas, who would betray him,
answered, "Is it I, Rabbi?" He said to him, "You have said so." Matt. 26:20-25, ESV.

If Jesus had startled His followers by taking the towel and washing their feet, His announcement that one of them would betray Him was shock on steroids.

Prior to that Thursday evening He had indicated that He would die. But never has He tied one of the disciples to that event. For the first time He now states that a member of His own inner circle will play the part of betrayer. The effect on the twelve is traumatic. Matthew 26:22 tells us that they were "exceeding sorrowful" (KJV), "in great distress" (NEB), or "deeply grieved" (NASB). No matter how one translates the Greek, it reflects violent emotion and shock.

The revelation shakes up the disciples even to the point of self-doubt. Each in turn inquires, "Is it I, Lord?" And each expects a negative reply, as indicated by the New International Version's rendering: "Surely you don't mean me, Lord?" (verse 22).

It is of interest to note that Judas must have covered his tracks quite carefully. After all, no one asks, "Is it Judas?" Yet Judas knows. Caught off guard, he does not immediately join with the other disciples in inquiring if it is him. But he soon comes to his senses, realizing that if he fails to participate in the query it will identify him as the culprit. Thus he also says, "Is it I, Rabbi?" Note that Judas does not refer to Jesus as "Lord," as do the other disciples, but rather as "Rabbi"—a term of address appropriate for any Jewish teacher and one not used at all by the other disciples in the first Gospel.

Jesus does not respond to the questions of the other disciples, but He indicates to Judas His awareness that He will indeed be the betrayer. At that point Judas realizes that he has been found out. He also knows that he will have to act quickly if he is to successfully carry out his plan. It is about this time, John tells us, that "Satan entered into" Judas. Jesus told him that what he had to do should be done "quickly," and Judas "went immediately out" to put his plan into action (John 13:27-30).

We find a lesson even in this sad story. The church has never been pure. It has never existed with all of its members born-again Christians. We need to keep courage when even leaders fall by the way or turn against the faith.

The Beginning of the "Farewell Discourses"

When he [Judas] had gone out, Jesus said, "Now is the Son of man glorified, and in him God is glorified; if God is glorified in him, God will also glorify him in himself, and glorify him at once. Little children, yet a little while I am with you. You will seek me; and as I said to the Jews so now I say to you, 'Where I am going you cannot come.'" John 13:31-33, RSV.

The departure of Judas tells Jesus that His end rapidly approaches, that the tsunami of events will soon overtake Him. With the betrayer gone we find a turning point in the gospel story. Jesus is now free to say things that He hadn't been able to when Judas was there. He could not only teach more freely, but He must do so. He had been with His disciples for nearly three years, and they hadn't learned enough. They were not prepared for His departure. And Jesus has just a couple short hours left to teach them.

Here is where the "farewell discourses" begin. From John 13:31 through the end of chapter 16 Jesus will explain to them the fact that He is going away but that they can't follow Him yet. In those chapters He provides what He believed was the most precious and important instruction that He could leave with His followers as He was facing death. These men, though not ready, would soon be forced into assuming the leadership role that He Himself had provided up to then. The great prayer of John 17 follows the farewell discourses. All of this material appears only in the fourth Gospel. How thankful we should be that God saw fit to inspire John's Gospel as the last of the four to be added to the New Testament's presentation of the life and teachings of Jesus the Christ.

One thing to note about the instruction in the farewell discourses is that Jesus begins to talk about Himself in new ways. An example of that phenomenon is His statement in John 13:31 that He will soon be glorified. Previously His focus had been on the glory of God. But with Judas on the fast track to betrayal and with Jesus' death, resurrection, and ascension to heaven to sit on the right hand of the Father now looming, the time to openly speak of His own glorification has arrived. Verses 31 and 32 use the word "glory" five times as Jesus frankly tells His disciples that His hour has come in which He must leave them.

His final words, recorded in John 13:31 through the end of chapter 17, must have provided food for thought as the bereft disciples pondered their new mission without an earthly Jesus to lead them. With that reality we are in the same place as them. So listen carefully as Jesus provides essential material for each of us followers.

August 30

The Essence of Christianity
According to Jesus

A new commandment I give unto you, That ye love one another; as I have loved you, that ye also love one another. By this shall all men know that ye are my disciples, if ye have love one to another. John 13:34, 35.

It is one of those sermons that I will never forget. I had been preaching on one of my favorite topics and concluded with one of my favorite verses: "By this shall all men know you are My disciples, because you keep the Sabbath. By this shall all men know that you are My disciples, because you pay tithe. By this shall all men know that you are My disciples, because you eat the right things."

After the closing song a new convert ran up to me and excitedly wanted to know where that passage was. He apparently wanted the perfect Adventist proof text so that he could run home and use it on his parents and friends.

I noted to my somewhat disappointed friend that he hadn't listened to me very carefully. Whereas some people would love to find my enthusiastic paraphrase of Jesus' words in the Bible, what He actually said is "By this all men will know that you are my disciples, if you have love for one another" (John 13:35, RSV).

With those words Jesus has provided us with His personal definition of the essence of what it means to be a Christian. The tragedy is that countless church members miss that text. They are zealous about the doctrine of the Sabbath or the state of the dead, the true nature of Christ in His humanity, and the fine points of diet, but they fail in the one essential thing.

Please note that I labeled such people "church members" rather than "Christians." The frightful thing is that we can be members of the church without being Christians. We can have all the right doctrines and be "faultless" in our health reform and other practices and still be lost. In fact, some of those who are most excited about doctrine and lifestyle issues are "meaner than the devil" in their relationships to other people.

Christianity is not exchanging a false set of beliefs for true ones. Nor is it substituting abusive practices for healthier ones, even if the rationale for such changes is found in the Bible.

The proof of Christianity is a person's love and care for others. Christian doctrine and lifestyle issues find meaning within the context of that love. But outside of it even those with the best doctrine and most faultless lifestyle do not fit within Jesus' definition of what it means to be a Christian.

New Meaning for an Old Symbol

Now as they were eating, Jesus took bread, and blessed, and broke it, and gave it to the disciples and said, "Take, eat; this is my body." And he took a cup, and when he had given thanks he gave it to them, saying, "Drink of it, all of you; for this is my blood of the covenant, which is poured out for many for the forgiveness of sins. I tell you I shall not drink again of this fruit of the vine until that day when I drink it new with you in my Father's kingdom." Matt. 26:26-29, RSV.

Here we find Jesus supplying a new meaning for an old symbol. The old significance of the Passover meal centered on God's deliverance of His people from Egyptian bondage (Ex. 12:1-30). The new one has to do with their deliverance from sin through the sacrifice of Christ on the cross. Thus the new meal symbolizes an even greater rescue than the old.

As Jesus breaks the bread and passes it to His disciples, He says, "Take, eat; this is my body." He could have added "which will be broken for you" without doing violence to His intent. He next picks up the cup, indicating that it is His "blood of the covenant" that will be poured out for the forgiveness of our sins. Just as blood ratified the Old Testament covenant between God and His people, so will it now the new covenant prophesied in Jeremiah 31:31-34.

Jesus tells His disciples in words that they could hardly fail to understand that He would die in our place, as our substitute. Here is the foundation of the gospel. He bore the condemnation that was ours so that those who accept Him can participate in the life eternal that is His. He will die in our place. His blood will be poured out for the "forgiveness of [our] sins." For that we can praise God. From that substitutionary sacrifice all other blessings flow.

But there is something else of importance about Jesus' words on the Lord's Supper. Once again He demonstrates, even though He is facing death, that He is in control of events. He knows that He will rise to victory and that in the future He will celebrate with His followers when they drink of the fruit of the vine together in His eternal kingdom.

Christians of all persuasions, although differing in the exact symbolic meaning of the elements of the Last Supper, have made it a major event in their worship experience. Paul best captured the meaning of the service when he penned, "Whenever you eat this bread and drink this cup, you proclaim the Lord's death until he comes" (1 Cor. 11:26, NIV).

The new symbolism points in two directions. Backward to Christ's saving death and forward to His coming again to establish the fullness of His kingdom.

As we celebrate that Supper let us meditate on both the frightful reality that it symbolizes and the great promise it holds out to us.

Good News for Messed-up Disciples

And when they had sung a hymn, they went out to the Mount of Olives. Then Jesus said to them, "You will all fall away because of me this night. For it is written, 'I will strike the shepherd, and the sheep of the flock will be scattered.' But after I am raised up, I will go before you to Galilee." Peter answered him, "Though they fall away because of you, I will never fall away." Jesus said to him, "Truly, I tell you, this very night, before the rooster crows, you will deny me three times." Peter said to him, "Even if I must die with you, I will not deny you!" And all the disciples said the same. Matt. 26:30-35, ESV.

If Jesus' prediction that one of the twelve would betray Him shook the disciples, His new announcement that all of them would desert Him that very evening should have knocked them flat and woke them up at the same time.

But that is not what happened. They either didn't understand what Jesus was telling them in plain words or they chose not to believe Him.

Here we have a problem that we modern disciples can (or *should*) identify with. Whether we are willing to admit it or not, each of us tends to pick and choose those aspects of the Lord's teachings that we want to believe and emphasize. And the real problem is that we often ignore or skip over those areas of His counsel that we need to hear the most.

Be that as it may, today's passage presents several important truths. First, Jesus indicates once again that He is not stumbling toward the cross blindly. He knows what He is doing. And He even knows that He will rise again to meet His followers in Galilee.

A second truth in the passage is that Jesus' support group are stumbling in a massive way and have no knowledge of either what He is doing or how they will react. They are excellent examples of false self-confidence and total misunderstanding. Still visualizing Messiahship in terms of a conquering King rather than a suffering Servant, they have yet to grasp the very purpose of Jesus' sufferings. Such a misconception will disorient them in the time of crisis.

A third thing to note is the absolute grace of Jesus. In spite of their cockiness, failures, and betrayals, He will meet them in Galilee. There is grace supreme.

And in that grace you and I need to revel, because we also are messed-up disciples. Here is a promise worth remembering: Jesus doesn't reject us when we fail Him. He did not abandon His first disciples, but continued to work with them. So it is with us. No wonder the Bible calls the message of Jesus the "good news."

Good Reason for Untroubled Hearts

Let not your heart be troubled: ye believe in God, believe also in me. In my Father's house are many mansions: if it were not so, I would have told you. I go to prepare a place for you. And if I go and prepare a place for you, I will come again, and receive you unto myself; that where I am, there ye may be also. John 14:1-3.

Tough times are coming. But don't worry.

It is in the context of those two short statements that we need to understand today's Scripture reading and all of the counsel in Jesus' farewell discourses (John 13:31-16:33).

The events soon to overtake Jesus will flatten the faith and self-confidence of the disciples. But what comes out of the experience will be a more informed faith that is the genuine thing rather than the shadow of it that they possess on their final evening with Jesus.

The words of John 14:1-3 have comforted Christians for 2,000 years. And they will continue to do so until the end of time, because all of us face the death of loved ones, financial reversals, broken marriages, disease, aging, and the other realities of a disoriented world reeling under the effects of sin.

It is not only at funerals that we need to hear the precious promises of our passage for today. We require them every day.

"Let not your heart be troubled." Why? Because we have a Lord who died for us, got the victory over death, is ministering in heaven at this very moment on our behalf, and is coming again to take us home with Him. When we are walking with Jesus we can have peace no matter how bad it is around us.

"In my Father's house are many mansions." Unlike the exclusiveness and scarcity we face on earth, Jesus' future kingdom has room for all who desire to be there.

"I go to prepare a place for *you*." Mark the "you" as personal as you read this promise. (He is preparing a place for me! In that I can rejoice.)

And "I will come again," so that "where I am" you can be also. I don't know exactly what heaven will be like. But I do know that its central feature will be being with Jesus. One of the greatest things about heaven is that we will always be with Him. Nothing can ever separate us from Him—forever, and ever, and ever.

You see, my friend, you and I have no reason for troubled hearts.

September 3

Say Goodbye
to the Postmodern Jesus

Thomas said to him, "Lord, we do not know where you are going; how can we know the way?" Jesus said to him, "I am the way, and the truth, and the life; no one comes to the Father, but by me." John 14:5, 6, RSV.

Thomas may have had his faults, but at least he was honest. Again and again Jesus had told His followers what would soon take place. He had just finished explaining that He was going to the Father to prepare a place for them. And earlier He had noted that He had come from heaven and would be returning. Yet somehow they had not yet understood.

If they were confused as to His destination, they were doubly puzzled about the way to it. They still did not expect the path of the cross, even though Jesus had openly told them about His crucifixion several times. Here Jesus was at the end of His life and still the disciples were bewildered. They had been so blinded by their own view of truth that they could not understand His plain words. Fortunately one of their number was willing to open his mouth and express his doubts. He was too honest to wander in the dark without seeking clarification.

I say "fortunately," because in response to Thomas' question, Jesus provided the world with one of His greatest and most profound statements: "I am the way, and the truth, and the life; no one comes to the Father, but by me." Later a wiser Peter will say much the same thing in Acts 4:12, in which he asserts that "there is salvation in no one else, for there is no other name under heaven given among men by which we must be saved" (RSV).

In effect, Jesus is saying to Thomas, "Since I am *the* truth, *the* life, and *the* way, follow Me and you will be OK. I am the only way to life eternal." The statement is plain enough, but, interestingly, it is violently rejected by many even in the church today who view it as arrogant, exclusive, and "unchristian." For them Jesus is just another man, like Muhammad or Buddha. The theory is that all religions lead to the same place. Such are the fruits of the eighteenth-century Enlightenment having come to full fruition in postmodernism.

But even a cursory study indicates the uniqueness of Jesus and the fact that all religions are not heading to the same place or even in the same direction. Postmodernism has confused "bigheartedness" with the issue of truth.

When Jesus says He is the only way, He means it. And if we take His hand and follow His words and walk His life we will arrive at His heavenly destination.

Loving Jesus

If ye love me, keep my commandments. John 14:15.

With the idea set forth in this verse we have arrived at a theme that the apostle John will drive home again and again: namely, if we truly love God, we will keep His commandments, and if we truly love Jesus, we will obey His commandments.

One thing to note is that the commandments of God and Jesus are not different. After all, another great theme in the fourth Gospel is that Jesus and the Father are one. While They are distinct persons in the Godhead, They belong to the same united Trinity and share the same principles—so much so that Jesus could teach that if you have seen Him, you have seen the Father (John 14:9). In Scripture the commandments of God and those of Jesus are exactly the same. And at the foundation of all of them is one principle. Jesus identifies it concisely in John 15:12, in which He says: "This is my commandment, that you love one another as I have loved you" (RSV). And in verse 17 He again says, "This I command you, to love one another" (RSV).

Earlier in His ministry Jesus had asserted that the greatest commandment of the law was to love God with all our hearts and minds, and that inextricably connected to that injunction is the need to love our neighbors as our own selves (Matt. 22:36-40). Thus we can sum up the commandments of both God and Jesus in one great principle: love. Out of it flow all of the more specific laws, including the Ten Commandments. But it is the caring, outreaching principle of love that must be the motivating force undergirding true obedience. Jesus demonstrated that love in not only coming to earth, but in His daily life as He related to others.

Of all the New Testament writers, John is the most persistent in his call for Christ's followers to keep the commandments. In the first letter he writes that "we may be sure that we know him, if we keep his commandments. He who says 'I know him' but disobeys his commandments is a liar, and the truth is not in him" (1 John 2:3, 4, RSV). And in the book of Revelation John makes it clear that God will have a commandment-keeping people at the end of time (Rev. 12:17; 14:12).

Like the disciples of old, we need to take Jesus at His word. Obedience in the spirit of love was absolutely central to Him.

Help me, Father, not only to obey Your word, but to do so in the spirit of love.

September 5

Jesus' Greatest Gift to Us

And I will pray the Father, and he will give you another Counselor, to be with you for ever, even the Spirit of truth, whom the world cannot receive, because it neither sees him nor knows him; you know him, for he dwells with you, and will be in you.
John 14:16, 17, RSV.

With this passage we have arrived at another great theme of the fourth Gospel. More than in any book in the Bible, it is in John's Gospel that we find the most explicit and detailed understanding of the work of the Holy Spirit. Jesus will return to the topic repeatedly in chapters 15 and 16 as He seeks to prepare His discplies for leading His church after His death. The emphasis on the Spirit will climax on the day of Pentecost when the disciples are more fully empowered to carry out their task of taking the message of Jesus to the ends of the earth.

The gift of the Holy Spirit is absolutely central to the Christian life. Not only are true Christians born of the Spirit (John 1:12; 3:3, 5), but every act of their lives is guided by what Ellen White calls the "divine" "third person of the Godhead" (*Evangelism*, p. 617). "This promised blessing," we read in *The Desire of Ages* "brings all other blessings in its train" (p. 672). As Jesus prepared His disciples for His soon departure, it is no accident that He repeatedly taught them about the gift of the Spirit. It was their greatest need. And it remains the greatest need of those followers of the Lamb who live in the twenty-first century.

In John 14:16 Jesus does not give the promise of the Holy Spirit in isolation. In the previous verse He had told His followers that if they really loved Him they would keep His commandments. Given the perverseness of human nature, that is no easy task. In fact, fallen humans cannot obey them in the spirit of love without divine aid. Thus it is that the next words of Jesus are the promise of "another Counselor." "Counselor" is not a very meaningful translation of *paraklētos*, which literally means "one called to the side of." The most helpful rendering in English is "Helper" (NASB). The *paraklētos* is someone brought in to help when a person needs guidance and strength and direction. Jesus has performed those functions for His followers up until now. But His departure is at hand. So He promises them "another Helper."

Here we need to pause for a moment to think seriously about our own needs. It is all too easy for us to assume that we are self-sufficient—that we can make a success of our Christian experience through our own will and strength. But with such a perspective we are just as deceived as the disciples. *Our greatest need is the divine paraklētos.*

Hope in the Face
of Discouragement

I will not leave you desolate; I will come to you. Yet a little while, and the world will see me no more, but you will see me; because I live, you will live also. In that day you will know that I am in my Father, and you in me, and I in you. John 14:18-20, RSV.

By this time even the dullest of the disciples knew that something terrible was about to happen to Jesus, and, by extension, to them. After all, their well-being was totally tied to Jesus. They had given up all for Him. And now all He could talk about were foreboding topics that led nowhere but to death on a cross. That was hardly their view of Messiahship. And it was certainly not their understanding of the "benefit" for giving up all for this charismatic teacher. At no time since they began to follow Him had things looked so dim and hopeless.

It is in that context that Jesus said that He would not leave them desolate. "Desolate" is an interesting word. It translates the Greek *orphanos*, from which we get the word "orphan." Thus the New King James Version is quite correct with its translation that "I will not leave you orphans." With that thought Jesus is right back to John 14:1 with its "Let not your heart be troubled." "I am coming back for you," He asserted in verses 2 and 3. But that coming back would be at His second advent at the end of time.

John 14:18, however, presents a much more immediate coming. In a little while the world (those who cared nothing for Him or His message) would see Him no longer because of His death and burial. But "you," He tells the disciples, "will see me." And they did after His resurrection. As a result, they would not be orphaned at two levels. First, He would see them again after three days in the grave. And second, through the gift of the "Helper" or "Comforter" He would be with them as they faced the world without His physical presence.

But His promise is better than merely not being left desolate. "Because I live," He promised His followers, "you will also." One of the highest points of the gospel of Jesus is that He will share His victory over death with each of His followers.

These snapshots of discipleship are important for me in my own Christian walk. There are days when I feel desolate, hopeless, and forsaken. That's the bad news. But the good news is that I am not the orphan I feel like. I have a heavenly Father, a risen Lord, a powerful Helper, and the guarantee of life everlasting. I may be tempted today to let discouragement get the best of me. But what I need is to turn my eyes again to the realities I have in Jesus.

More on the Helper

These things I have spoken to you while abiding with you. But the Helper, the Holy Spirit, whom the Father will send in My name, He will teach you all things, and bring to your remembrance all that I said to you. Peace I leave with you; My peace I give to you; not as the world gives do I give to you. Do not let your heart be troubled, nor let it be fearful. You heard that I said to you, "I go away, and I will come to you." . . . Now I have told you before it happens, so that when it happens, you may believe. John 14:25-29, NASB.

More and more emphasis falls on the gift of the Holy Spirit as the farewell discourses proceed toward Gethsemane and the cross. In our Scripture reading for today Jesus tells us several more things about the One He will send to stand by every disciple's side after He has ascended to the Father.

The first thing Jesus explains about the Helper is that He will teach us all things. It is the Spirit who leads God's followers deeper and deeper into spiritual truth. That is why it is important to pray and invite His presence as we open our Bible for serious study. The same divine Person who inspired the prophets to write the Bible will unlock its meaning ever more fully to those dedicated to its study.

A second thing Jesus reveals about His gift of the Helper in John 14:25-29 is that He will remind us of what Jesus has said. That means several things. One is that in matters of faith the Spirit constantly brings into our consciousness the words and acts of Christ and His apostles. It is those teachings that form the basis of hope and the context in which followers of Jesus evaluate all their conclusions about the meaning and goals of life.

A third aspect of the Helper's guidance is that He keeps us on the right track in our conduct as we navigate the corridors of life. When we face difficult moral choices, it is the Helper who flashes the teachings of Christ through our minds to inform us of the best way to go.

We can thank God for all of those benefits of the Helper in our lives. But perhaps the most personal and precious is the gift of peace, which infuses our lives when we trust in God because of the accomplished victory of Jesus. Biblical peace is more than the absence of conflict. It is also that sense of well-being that God implants in our hearts and minds through the Spirit.

It is that sense of boundless peace that Jesus was seeking to leave with His followers in John 14. And it is what He desires to infuse in my life. But more than that, He desires me to be His Spirit-inspired agent of peace in my family and workplace today.

The "True" Vine

I am the true vine, and My Father is the vinedresser. Every branch in Me that does not bear fruit He takes away; and every branch that bears fruit He prunes, that it may bear more fruit. You are already clean because of the word which I have spoken to you. Abide in Me, and I in you. As the branch cannot bear fruit of itself, unless it abides in the vine, neither can you, unless you abide in Me. John 15:1-4, NKJV.

Most readers of the New Testament miss the full force of this passage. But that was not the case with the disciples. Being Jewish they saw the magnitude and meaning of Jesus' claim to be *the* vine.

Again and again the Old Testament pictures Israel as the vine and God's vineyard. "The vineyard of the Lord of hosts," claims Isaiah, "is the house of Israel, and the men of Judah his pleasant plant" (Isa. 5:7). And Jeremiah quotes God as saying to Israel, "I had planted you a noble vine" (Jer. 2:21, NKJV). "Thou hast brought a vine out of Egypt," says the psalmist (Ps. 80:8). As a result, the vine had become a symbol of Israel, so much so that they reproduced it on their coins when they were a free people. Thus to be a part of the vine meant to be an Israelite or Jew.

But the Old Testament teaching regarding the vine didn't end with the identity of Israel as God's vine. The downside of the symbolism is the fact that Scripture consistently associates with Israel the idea of degeneration. The point of Isaiah is that the vineyard had run wild. For Jeremiah the nation had turned from the "noble vine" that God had planted into a "degenerate plant of a strange vine" (Jer. 2:21). And for Hosea "Israel is an empty vine" (Hosea 10:1).

Those word pictures provide the background for Jesus' shocking claim that "I am *the* true vine." The implication of that claim, of course, was that being born a Jew did not automatically make a person a part of God's vineyard. To the contrary, Jesus is telling His Jewish hearers (and us) that to be a part of the true people of God we must be connected intimately to Him.

That thought will lead Jesus into a discussion in John 15:6-10 of what it means to abide in Him as branches tied closely to the true vine.

Before we examine those verses we need to meditate again on the way to eternal life. That path is not being born Baptist, Lutheran, Catholic, or even Adventist. At its core it is being connected to Jesus as our Savior, Lord, and Friend. Being a part of the Vine means that our lives and goals are totally in line with His.

September 9

The True Branches

I am the vine, you are the branches. He who abides in Me, and I in him, bears much fruit; for without Me you can do nothing. If anyone does not abide in Me, he is cast out as a branch and is withered; and they gather them and throw them into the fire, and they are burned. If you abide in Me, and My words abide in you, you will ask what you desire, and it shall be done for you. By this My Father is glorified, that you bear much fruit; so you will be My disciples. John 15:5-8, NKJV.

There are only two kinds of branches (that is, only two varieties of church members)—the fruitful and the barren. Those who are barren are cut off from the true vine. And those who remain get pruned by the hardships of life as God shapes them into ever more fruitful disciples.

Of course, none of us like to get pruned. But God uses the challenges of life to refine us as Christians. As Paul puts it in Romans, "we rejoice in our sufferings, knowing that suffering produces endurance, and endurance produces character, and character produces hope, and hope does not disappoint us, because God's love has been poured into our hearts through the Holy Spirit which has been given to us" (Rom. 5:3-5, RSV).

There is nothing that happens to us that God does not use to prune, cleanse, and shape us for His purposes and glory. In that we can be thankful, even though the process might be uncomfortable.

Pruning is what happens when the caring gardener prepares His vines to produce even more fruit. Some aspects of our lives get sheared off so that God might direct our energy to increase our productivity in bearing more and better fruit.

But what is the fruit? It comes in two varieties. One is the making of further disciples. God uses Christians to witness to His love and win others to the ways of Jesus.

A second form of fruit bearing is the development of Christian character. "The fruit of the Spirit," Paul tells us, "is love, joy, peace, patience, kindness, goodness, faithfulness, gentleness, self-control" (Gal. 5:22, 23, RSV).

Both types of fruit are intertwined in a person's life. After all, it is the beauty of a Christian's character that leads others to Jesus. And both types of fruit result from the work of the Holy Spirit. We can do nothing apart from Jesus and the Spirit. But with Them we naturally produce the sweet clusters of the vine.

Help me today, my Father, to stay connected to Jesus that I might be ever more fruitful.

More on True Fruit Bearing

If you keep my commandments, you will abide in my love, just as I have kept my Father's commandments and abide in his love. These things I have spoken to you, that my joy may be in you, and that your joy may be full. This is my commandment, that you love one another as I have loved you. Greater love has no man than this, that a man lay down his life for his friends. You are my friends if you do what I command you. . . . This I command you, to love one another. John 15:10-17, RSV.

Certain topics Jesus just couldn't seem to stay away from in His all-important final words to His disciples as they progress toward Gethsemane and the cross. Two of those words are "commandments" and "love." Jesus makes it absolutely clear that if we are abiding in Him we will obey His commandments. And He is equally adamant that anyone who abides in Him will be loving to others.

In reality those two results are really one. As we noted earlier, all of the commandments are based on the principle of love. One of the tragedies of the Pharisees is that they too often separated the two. And some church members do the same. They are obedient to all of God's commands, including the Ten Commandments, but they are all too often mean toward others both inside and outside of the church. But being connected to Jesus is more than outward obedience. It is a loving relationship with Him that spills over daily in love to those around us, even to our enemies and those who misuse us (Matt. 5:44).

Being connected to Jesus means living a life of self-sacrificing love, even to the extent, if necessary, of devoting our lives to the welfare of another. Jesus, of course, was originally speaking of the need of His warring disciples to get their act together by stopping their jostling for supremacy and letting love for one another fill their hearts and actions.

But His words are for me also. And I need them. My natural tendency is to love myself and use others toward that end. But Jesus calls for a reversal of that pattern. If I am truly abiding in Him, I will devote my life to being a blessing to others.

People have developed many descriptions of what it means to be a true Christian. But Jesus provides the best and most authoritative. We must have His love flowing out of our hearts that we might have true joy and be called His "friend" in the truest sense of the word.

September 11

The Negative Side
of Following Jesus

If the world hates you, know that it hated me before it hated you. If you were of the world, the world would love you as its own; but because you are not of the world, but I chose you out of the world, therefore the world hates you. Remember the word that I said to you: "A servant is not greater than his master." If they persecuted me, they will also persecute you. If they kept my word, they will also keep yours. But all these things they will do to you on account of my name, because they do not know him who sent me. John 15:18-21, ESV.

To hear some people talk you would think that Christianity is like a peaceful walk through a rose garden on a spring morning. If you love Jesus everything will go right. In fact, some assert, if you are having trouble it is because you are not living right, or that your heart has a shortage of faith and love. And some TV preachers even declare that if you are connected to Jesus, you will be blessed with overflowing wealth. Just plug into Him and the jackpot will open. Then there are the positive-thinker types who claim that the power of positive thinking will bring unimaginable blessings.

Jesus did not belong to that category. He knew that He was heading toward a cross. And that He would die not because He lacked faith, but rather because He had it. His trouble resulted not from the fact that He was out of harmony with God's will, but rather because He was actually following it.

Jesus knew one other thing: that His disciples would tread the same path. Nearly all of the original twelve would meet a violent death because of their faith. John would be an exception. But just because he was not martyred does not mean he would escape persecution. Tradition tells us that he was dipped in a tank of boiling oil for his faithfulness to the gospel.

And before the outward violence arrived, the disciples would face discrimination, be ignored by those they were trying to reach with the gospel message, and be labeled as troublers of the people.

Just as the disciples learned from Christ's experience, so we can learn from them. In the ceaseless spiritual warfare of a world lost in sin, those who stand for the principles of Christ must of necessity abandon its self-centered, self-glorifying principles. And that will continue to create a tension with nonbelievers that leads to rejection and at times to persecution.

The good news is that when we stand for Jesus, He will stand for us. We never face the trials of life alone.

The Work of the Spirit

When the Helper comes, whom I will send to you from the Father, that is the Spirit of truth who proceeds from the Father, He will testify about Me. John 15:26, NASB

It is to your advantage that I go away; for if I do not go away, the Helper will not come to you; but if I go, I will send Him to you. And He, when He comes, will convict the world concerning sin and righteousness and judgment. John 16:7, 8, NASB.

As they move toward the cross on their last evening with Jesus, the disciples are bewildered and grief-stricken. He keeps telling them that He will soon depart from them to a place that they could not go. But after they lost Him, what were they to do?

It is in that context that Jesus again tells them that He will send the Holy Spirit to be with them and guide them in their lives and ministry. They probably didn't understand the greatness of the gift of the Spirit on that discouraging evening. But after Pentecost they would.

In today's passage Jesus tells us four things about the work of the Holy Spirit. The first is that He will testify about Jesus. Here we have a most interesting fact. Of the three members of the divine Godhead we know least about the Spirit. Why? Because while Jesus came to demonstrate the nature and character of God and while the Spirit has inspired the whole New Testament to help us know Jesus, no one has filled in our knowledge of the Holy Spirit, the third member of the Trinity. As a result, some are tempted to think of Him as less important or less divine than the Father and the Son. But that is not the teaching of Scripture.

The good news is that on His last evening with His disciples Jesus provides us with a glimpse of the work of the Spirit in our lives. Not only does the Spirit testify of Jesus and help us understand His life and teaching, but He also convicts us of sin. That function is absolutely central to the plan of salvation, since without a clear sense of our sins and shortcomings we will feel no need of a Savior. Paul is quite clear that in the process of revealing to us our sin the Spirit uses God's law as the ideal model of the character traits and actions that He desires His followers to exhibit in their life (see Rom. 7:7).

On the opposite side of the convicting-of-sin coin is the Spirit's function of leading us to Jesus for forgiveness and a pattern for life. And closely related to those two functions is the Spirit's conviction of judgment for those who reject Jesus.

Today we need to thank Jesus again for the gift of the Helper. Without the Spirit a walk with Jesus would be impossible. The Holy Spirit is the dynamic force in our salvation.

September 13

Another Essential Work of the Spirit

I have many more things to say to you, but you cannot bear them now. But when He, the Spirit of truth, comes, He will guide you into all the truth; for He will not speak of His own initiative, but whatever He hears, He will speak; and He will disclose to you what is to come. He will glorify Me, for He will take of Mine and will disclose it to you. All things that the Father has are Mine; therefore I said that He takes of Mine and will disclose it to you. John 16:12-15, NASB.

Our mind is limited. We can absorb only so much. And when it overflows our abilities we end up bewildered and confused. That is the way it was with the disciples—they had reached the saturation point. But conditions change. And with new challenges and new situations comes the need for additional knowledge to both meet that new environment and to successfully navigate through it.

So it was with the disciples. As a result, Jesus told them that He had many things to tell them that they could not bear at that time. Some of them He would explain to them during the 40 days He spent with them between His resurrection and ascension. The Resurrection had changed everything for them. It had transformed their perspective on both Messiahship and discipleship. And Jesus used those days of instruction to advance them from being disciples to being apostles.

But the life of the church and the history of the world is a shifting canvas. As a result, Jesus sends the Spirit to continue to guide the church into all truth. The most significant step in that leading would be the inspiration of the books of the New Testament that put in permanent form not only the life and teachings of Jesus but the struggles and Spirit-inspired insights and experiences of the early church.

The prophecies of Revelation are a quite specific example of what Jesus had yet to tell His followers but knew they were not ready to hear during His earthly life. It is the Revelation from and about Jesus (mediated through the Holy Spirit). Repeatedly John declares to his readers, "Let him hear what the Spirit saith unto the churches" (Rev. 2:7).

The Spirit's guidance on how to apply and understand the Christ event didn't stop with the death of the last apostle. Paul tells us that the Spirit's inspired leading into all truth through the prophetic gift will last until the church reaches full maturity (Eph. 4:8-13). Thus the Spirit's role will last as long as we are on earth.

The most important thing we can do right now is to rededicate our hearts, minds, ears, and eyes to a clear hearing of the Word of Jesus through the Holy Spirit.

Jesus' Final Words to the Disciples

Jesus knew that they wanted to ask him; so he said to them, "Is this what you are asking yourselves, what I meant by saying, 'A little while, and you will not see me, and again a little while, and you will see me'? Truly, truly, I say to you, you will weep and lament, but the world will rejoice; you will be sorrowful, but your sorrow will turn to joy. . . .

"The hour is coming, indeed it has come, when you will be scattered, every man to his home, and will leave me alone; yet I am not alone, for the Father is with me. I have said this to you, that in me you may have peace. In the world you have tribulation; but be of good cheer, I have overcome the world." John 16:19-33, RSV.

His hour has come. He has time now only for a few short words of comfort and hope. Then Jesus will move beyond His farewell instructions that began in John 13 and offer His great prayer for them and the church in chapter 17. And finally comes the hike with the disciples across the Kidron Valley and up the slope to Gethsemane and His meeting with a band of Roman soldiers.

The time for final farewells has arrived. "A little while, and you will see me no more," Jesus tells His disciples. Then He adds that "again," after "a little while," they *would* see Him (John 16:16, RSV). As we might expect, that statement perplexed them, along with the one about His going to the Father (verse 17). The point to note is that His resurrection would turn their sorrow to joy (verse 20). That joy would so fill their hearts and minds that their lives would never be the same again.

But they can't perceive that yet. At the present all Jesus can do is make promises regarding the future. In the interim they must live by faith.

Yet faith is a fragile thing, even among those who knew Jesus the best. As a result, their confidence would soon shatter as He is arrested and they flee from the scene and desert their Lord. But He knows them. Not giving up on them, He will gather them again and send them to the ends of the earth to do great things in His name. Meanwhile, they can be of good cheer because they believe in One who has overcome the world and will share His victory with them.

These events have something in them for me. My faith is also fragile. And I also at times flee from Christ when the going gets too tough. But He doesn't forsake me even when I abandon Him. I also can be of good cheer because I have a Lord who understands and cares for me as an individual, even when I fail Him.

Christ's Great Prayer, Part 1

Father, the hour has come. Glorify your Son, that your Son may glorify you. For you granted him authority over all people that he might give eternal life to all those you have given him. Now this is eternal life: that they may know you, the only true God, and Jesus Christ, whom you have sent. I have brought you glory on earth by finishing the work you gave me to do. And now, Father, glorify me in your presence with the glory I had with you before the world began. John 17:1-5, NIV.

Jesus was a man of prayer. We all know that. But one of the peculiarities of Scripture is that we have very few of His personal prayers. Here in John 17 we have by far His longest prayer recorded in the Bible. John 17 is indeed the true "Lord's Prayer." It falls into three parts: (1) prayer for Himself in verses 1-5, (2) prayer for His disciples in verses 6-19, and (3) prayer for all believers in verses 20-26.

In the prayer itself we find Jesus peering through the events of the cross yet to come and into the future when He will resume His seat at the right hand on the heavenly throne.

His time or hour has come. The "hour" toward which Jesus had set the entire course of His life and ministry had finally arrived. The ultimate act of that hour of glory would be His death on the cross to redeem humanity from the curse of sin and to demonstrate to all the universe that the God of love is willing to sacrifice all for the eternal health of all creation in a planet gone wrong. The path to glory for Jesus would be through His death on the cross. But beyond the cross would be the glory of His resurrection, ascension to heaven, and installation on the throne of God represented in Revelation 4.

Included in His glory would be the human fruit of His labor—those who have eternal life through His completion of His Father's work on earth. And with eternal life we come to a highlighted concept in the fourth Gospel, which tells us again and again that eternal life has already begun for those who have accepted Jesus (John 3:36; 5:24). But in His prayer Jesus fills out the picture of eternal life a bit further when He identifies it with knowing Him and the Father.

In this great prayer we sense the victory that pulsates through Jesus' soul and into His words. He knows that the task is about finished and He can soon go home.

His accomplishment was not merely for Himself and God, but for you and me. As we study the prayer of John 17 we need to participate in its spirit.

Christ's Great Prayer, Part 2

I am not praying for the world but for those whom thou hast given me, for they are thine; . . . and I am glorified in them. . . . Holy Father, keep them in thy name, which thou hast given me, that they may be one, even as we are one. . . . I do not pray that thou shouldest take them out of the world, but that thou shouldest keep them from the evil one. They are not of the world, even as I am not of the world. Sanctify them in the truth; thy word is truth. As thou didst send me into the world, so I have sent them into the world. And for their sake I consecrate myself, that they also may be consecrated in truth. John 17:9-19, RSV.

In its second part the great climactic prayer of Jesus' ministry shifts from Himself to the disciples. He knows that their needs will be many after He departs to the Father.

The first thing to note is that He does not pray that God should take them out of the world. To the contrary, He knows that the world will be the place of their ministry. Therefore His prayer is not that they will find escape but rather victory. He never espoused the form of Christianity that buries itself in a monastery, but one that reaches out to help a lost and degenerate world. It is in the rough-and-tumble of life that His followers must live and work. While it is true that they require periods of prayer and meditation, those times are not ends in themselves but a means to the end. Christianity is never an abandonment of the world, but rather a desire to win the world. Christ prays for us as disciples because, even though we are in the world, we are not of the world.

A second thing to observe is that Jesus prayed for the unity of His disciples. They certainly needed it, having spent a great deal of time bickering over which of them was the greatest. And like other humans across time they had their petty jealousies and divisive ways. But Jesus' prayer for unity was not merely for them, but for us also. No church or congregation can be fully effective when its members are pulling in different directions.

A third aspect of the prayer is that God would protect His followers from the evil one. Jesus, unlike so many in our day, had a very clear understanding that there exists a powerful personality in the world seeking to derail each of us from our spiritual walk.

Last, Jesus prayed that they might be consecrated and equipped for their mission into the world.

That is a meaningful climax to His prayer for them. But it will have no effect unless we as disciples consecrate and set apart and dedicate our lives to Him. It is only when we consciously choose to place ourselves in His hands that Christ's prayer for us may be answered.

September 17

Christ's Great Prayer, Part 3

I do not pray for them alone, but also for those who will believe in Me through their word; that they all may be one, as You, Father, are in Me, and I in You; that they also may be one in Us, that the world may believe that You sent Me. . . . Father, I desire that they also whom You gave Me may be with Me where I am. . . .
O righteous Father! The world has not known You, but I have known You; and these have known that You sent Me. And I have declared to them Your name, and will declare it, that the love with which You loved Me may be in them, and I in them.
John 17:20-26, NKJV.

Jesus' prayer has moved from His personal concerns to the ends of the earth. First, He prayed for Himself as He faced the cross. Second, He prayed for His 12 disciples and for God's power to preserve them. Now in the third section He prays for all disciples in all corners of the earth until the end of time.

The final part of the prayer tells us certain things about Jesus. For one, it demonstrates His complete faith and absolute certainty. Here He is with a few stumbling, warring disciples and the cross facing Him, and yet He is praying for those who would believe on His name through their ministry. He didn't view the church as it was, but as it would be in the future. Jesus saw the future through eyes of faith established in confidence in the Father.

A second thing that this division of the prayer shows us about Jesus is that He had confidence in people. Through the eyes of faith He saw a movement growing out of the actions of a small group of individuals who were, to say the least, messed up. That confidence extends beyond those first followers to those who will have lived through all history and even to those of us at the end of time.

And as in the second part of the prayer, this third one has a focus on unity that we as His people might move beyond our self-centered differences to a love and oneness illustrated best by the divine Trinity. As Jesus and the Father and the Spirit are one in aim and purpose, so is Their church to be on earth. Why is that unity so important? "So that the world may know that thou hast sent me" (verse 23, RSV). Nothing is so disruptive of the church's witness to the world as disunity among those who claim to be following the same Lord. That thought brings us back to John 13:35 and its inspired insight that all will know we are Christians by our love for one another.

Father, enable me to have the mind of Jesus, the eyes of faith that see hope in even apparently hopeless situations and people. And enable me to move beyond myself to that Trinitarian love that is the basis of Your kingdom.

Moving Toward Gethsemane

Then Jesus came with them to a place called Gethsemane, and said to the disciples, "Sit here while I go and pray over there." And He took with Him Peter and the two sons of Zebedee, and He began to be sorrowful and deeply distressed. Then He said to them, "My soul is exceedingly sorrowful, even to death. Stay here and watch with Me."
Matt. 26:36-38, NKJV.

His hour has come! He has completed instructing the disciples. They may not have absorbed it yet, but the promised Holy Spirit would bring His words to their minds repeatedly after the Resurrection. Jesus had also prayed for them as a group one last time. And now the moment has arrived when He must leave them if He is to accomplish the mission He came to earth to carry out.

After the intercessory prayer recorded in John 17, the opening verses of chapter 18 tell us that after "Jesus had spoken these words, he went forth with his disciples across the Kidron valley, where there was a garden, which he and his disciples entered" (John 18:1, RSV).

Gethsemane is on the Mount of Olives. It is hardly a mountain in the strict sense of the word, but is more like a ridge running parallel to the Kidron Valley several hundred feet below. On the other side of the Kidron was the Temple, which was in full view from the height. Even today it provides the most impressive and least disturbed site of what Jesus actually did and saw in the area of the Holy City. A visitor stands among extremely old olive trees and gazes across the valley to the remains of the Temple wall.

It was from the Mount of Olives that Jesus began His triumphal entry into Jerusalem. On it He gave His great sermon on the Second Coming. And now He is returning to it as He moves toward His hour of destiny.

But others were also acquainted with His love for Gethsemane. "Now Judas," John tells us, "also knew the place; for Jesus often met there with his disciples" (John 18:2, RSV).

Jesus recognized that His hour of temptation had arrived and that He needed nothing so much as prayer as He encountered the greatest challenge of His life.

Although He would not back off of the road to the cross, He really didn't want to take it. Jesus, in His humanity, was caught in the tension. All He could do was pray.

In that conflict He faced a situation we also share to a much lesser extent. There are times in our lives when the only way forward is through serious prayer. In such crisis times we can advance only with God at our side.

The Struggle of Struggles

And going a little farther he fell on his face and prayed, "My Father, if it be possible,
let this cup pass from me; nevertheless, not as I will, but as thou wilt.". . .
Again, for the second time, he went away and prayed, "My Father, if this cannot pass
unless I drink it, thy will be done." . . . He went away and prayed for the third time,
saying the same words. Matt. 26:39-44, RSV.

Jesus has reached the crisis point of His life as the weakness of His humanity grapples with the will of God.

It is all too easy to view Him as some kind of superman who rode through life from one effortless victory to another. Not so! Like the rest of us, He struggled. But His battles were as much greater than ours as the magnitude of His mission exceeds the purpose of our lives. Daunted by the little temptations and challenges that come our way, we all too often cave in even before too much pressure is placed upon us. But if Jesus backed off, it would negate the entire reason for the Incarnation.

He faced only two options: to go forward to His once-for-all sacrifice on Calvary or to give up and let all of humanity reap its own destruction.

And the devil knew the stakes in the game. Up to then he had had his way on earth. But if Christ went through with His mission Satan knew that it would seal his own fate. The destiny of the world hung in the balances of what would take place in the next few hours.

It is in that tension that Christ entered Gethsemane. His thrice-repeated prayer shows Him struggling as never before as the major choice of His life loomed before Him.

Like other humans, He had no desire to experience the humiliating death of the cross. But that wasn't the real issue. The core problem was that on the cross He would die for the sins of all humanity. He would become sin for us (2 Cor. 5:21), taking upon Himself our curse (Gal. 3:13). That was the problem.

The Desire of Ages indicates that "He felt that by sin He was being separated from His Father. The gulf was so broad, so black, so deep, that His spirit shuddered before it. This agony He must not exert His divine power to escape. As man He must suffer the consequences of man's sin. As man He must endure the wrath of God against transgression" (p. 686).

It is with that weight upon Him that He struggled in agony, finally declaring that He would do God's will rather than His own.

Sleeping Through the Crisis

And he came to the disciples and found them sleeping; and he said to Peter, "So, could you not watch with me one hour? Watch and pray that you may not enter into temptation; the spirit indeed is willing, but the flesh is weak." . . . Again he came and found them sleeping, for their eyes were heavy. . . . Then he came to the disciples and said to them, "Are you still sleeping and taking your rest? Behold, the hour is at hand, and the Son of man is betrayed into the hands of sinners. Rise, let us be going; see, my betrayer is at hand." Matt. 26:40-46, RSV.

A nd what were the disciples doing as Jesus struggled in agony? Sleeping! They had been His closest followers for three years and yet they didn't seem to have the slightest conception of what was happening or what their Lord was going through.

Yet Jesus had selected Peter and the Zebedee brothers to accompany Him that fateful evening because He needed them desperately. Like other humans, Jesus desired human companionship and support in times of stress. But all they did during His struggle was to sleep. Jesus was truly alone.

But just a short time before, those very disciples had protested that they would die for Him. Now all they could do is sleep.

They had let their Lord down at the time when He needed them most. Yet He understood. The stress and excitement of the past few days had drained their strength and resistance. They truly were tired. And at that point we find the graciousness of Jesus. Even in the crisis of His life He realized that in their hearts they were sincere, even if they all too easily surrendered to their bodily demands and temptations.

Jesus forgave them. But what a blessing they missed! They needed the strength that could have come to them through prayer. Yet all they could do was sleep.

But that sleeping did not stop the wheels of history. They had missed their last opportunity to support their Lord in His earthly existence. The praying Jesus would move on to the cross. And the prayerless, sleeping disciples would rush into the future unprepared. All would soon abandon Him and Peter would deny Him. All had slept through their hour of opportunity.

Sleeping disciples are still with us today. Our spirits may be willing, yet all too often our flesh is weak. But now in this time of peace is the opportunity to become strong for the crisis that lies before us. Today is the day to wake up!

The Twisted Kiss

And while He was still speaking, behold, Judas, one of the twelve, with a great multitude with swords and clubs, came from the chief priests and elders of the people. Now His betrayer had given them a sign, saying, "Whomever I kiss, He is the One; seize Him." Immediately he went up to Jesus and said, "Greetings, Rabbi!" and kissed Him. Matt. 26:47-49, NKJV.

Why the kiss? Did the Jewish leaders and the Temple police really need to have Jesus pointed out to them?

It would be incredible if the Temple police and the others in the crowd couldn't identify the man who only days before had cleansed the Temple and driven out the money changers. And how could they not know by sight a person who had taught daily in the Temple courts?

The last thing they needed was an identification of Jesus. They were all too well aware of who He was and what He looked like.

What they required was not identification, but a convenient and safe place, given the crowds in Jerusalem for Passover and Jesus' popularity, to arrest Him. And that is what Judas had already provided them with.

Then why the kiss? The text itself may hint at the reason through the Greek words rendered into English as "kiss." In verse 48, Judas employs *phileō*, the normal word for kiss, as a sign that he will use to identify Jesus. But when it comes to the actual kiss in verse 49 the Greek is *kataphileō*, which, notes William Barclay, "is the word for a lover's kiss, and which means to kiss repeatedly, passionately, fervently."

Why the change of words? Because the sign of the kiss was not primarily for identity. If that had been the only reason, the kiss would have merely been an indication of hypocrisy.

But there appears to be something deeper in the twisted heart of Judas. His kiss was like that of a disciple who truly loved his master. Apparently Judas expected the occasion to stimulate Jesus to demonstrate His Messianic power and authority.

But it didn't work out that way. And the disillusioned Judas vanishes from the story until his suicide. He apparently can't even be located as a witness against Jesus during His trial. Judas had tried to force Jesus to use his approach. But all he ended up with was utter disillusionment.

How important that each of us seek to carry out God's work His way rather than our own. No matter how dedicated we are, if we are on our own path to success it is the wrong road.

Judas Didn't Stand Alone

And, behold, one of them which were with Jesus stretched out his hand, and drew his sword, and struck a servant of the high priest's, and smote off his ear. Then said Jesus unto him, Put up again thy sword into his place: for all they that take the sword shall perish with the sword. Matt. 26:51, 52.

Apparently Judas wasn't the only disciple seeking to get Jesus to provide a show of force.

John's Gospel fills in much of the information left out in Matthew's two short verses. After Judas' kiss, Jesus identified Himself as the one they had come to arrest. At that point the crowd "drew back and fell to the ground" (John 18:6, NKJV), apparently a sign of supernatural power given to wake them up to what they were doing.

But it didn't seem to wake anybody up except the disciples, who misinterpreted it. They "had thought that their Master would not suffer Himself to be taken. For the same power that had caused the mob to fall as dead men could keep them helpless, until Jesus and His companions could escape. They were disappointed and indignant as they saw the cords brought forward to bind the hands of Him whom they loved" (*The Desire of Ages*, p. 696).

At that point Peter came to life and decided to help out. Drawing his sword, he missed the head of the servant of the high priest but did manage to lop off one of his ears.

But it was all to no avail. Luke tells us that Jesus touched Malchus' ear and healed him (Luke 22:51). That turned out to be an eternal blessing to him. He had experienced the power of Jesus and had apparently accepted Him as His Savior by the time John wrote the gospel story. That is the reason he knew the servant's name. But all Peter got out of the experience was a mild rebuke from Jesus: "Put your sword into its sheath; shall I not drink the cup which the Father has given me?" (John 18:11, RSV).

So much for a flash of power that would initiate the Messianic kingdom, or at least an escape from the arresting officials. Judas and Peter had each failed in their quite different attempts. Jesus knew God's will and had accepted it. That kind of dedication was still future for Peter and his colleagues.

Help me, Father, not only to accept Your will but to give myself over to it. I have a Peter-person deep in my skin, and I would like right now to substitute it for a Jesus-person.

Jesus: Peaceful in Crisis

"Put your sword back into its place. . . . Do you think that I cannot appeal to my Father, and he will at once send me more than twelve legions of angels? But how then should the scriptures be fulfilled, that it must be so?" At that hour Jesus said to the crowds, "Have you come out as against a robber, with swords and clubs to capture me? Day after day I sat in the temple teaching, and you did not seize me. But all this has taken place, that the scriptures of the prophets might be fulfilled." Then all the disciples forsook him and fled. Matt. 26:52-56, RSV.

As the scene in the garden comes to a close the Jewish leaders finally have the troublesome Jesus in their hands.

But before exploring the trials of Jesus, we need to take one more look at the Gethsemane scene. We have already discussed the kissing Judas and Peter of the bloody sword. But there are others.

First, we see the Jews delegated to arrest Jesus. One would think that they would have woken up at the events that had taken place. After all, a supernatural force had knocked them to the ground. And then there is the case of the ear. It is easy to slice ears off, but quite a different thing to put them back on. They had witnessed a first-class miracle. Having always asked for a sign, now they had two of them. But they were not pleased. Acting like the blind, they completed the arrest. Only Malchus, the man of the ear, had apparently begun to think about the meaning of the events of that night.

Second, there were the disciples. Events had shattered their world. They had apparently believed that Jesus would summon legions of angels to rescue Him and set up His kingdom. Now, terrified and completely disorganized, all they can think of is saving their skins; and now they desert their Lord in His hour of need.

And then there is Jesus, who is calmly in control of the situation. How can that be when just a short time before He was in fierce agony in His Gethsemane prayers? The answer is that He had finally come to a full surrender. He had struggled mightily with His will in the face of the Father's and had chosen God's. And with that surrender came a peace that allowed Him to become "like a lamb that is led to the slaughter" (Isa. 53:7, RSV) so that Scripture might be fulfilled.

Surrender to God's will was the key in Jesus' life. It is only through surrender that we can obtain the peace that Christ had as He passed through life's crises.

The Trial of Jesus, Phase 1

*Then those who had seized Jesus led him to Caiaphas the high priest, where the
scribes and the elders had gathered. . . . The chief priests and the whole Council
were seeking false testimony against Jesus that they might put him to death, but they
found none, though many false witnesses came forward. At last two came forward
and said, "This man said, 'I am able to destroy the temple of God, and to rebuild
it in three days.'" And the high priest stood up and said, "Have you no answer to
make?" . . . But Jesus remained silent. And the high priest said to him, "I adjure you
by the living God, tell us if you are the Christ, the Son of God." Jesus said to him,
"You have said so. But I tell you, from now on you will see the Son of Man seated at
the right hand of power and coming on the clouds of heaven." Then the high priest
tore his robes and said, "He has uttered blasphemy." Matt. 26:57-65, ESV.*

The Jewish leaders have Jesus in their hands at last. Now they have a new
problem—what to do with Him. The issue is not their goal, but rather
how to get there.

The Sanhedrin's task is complex because although they are seeking the
death penalty, they have no authority to mete it out. The Romans, while using
local administration in conquered provinces whenever possible, kept the ultimate penalty in their own hands.

Thus the Jewish leaders face a crucial problem. They want to have Jesus
put to death for His Messianic claims, but the Romans did not accept blasphemy as a capital offense. As a result, the leaders of the Sanhedrin have a twofold
task before them. First, they must develop among their own members the need
to have Jesus executed for blasphemy—a matter of Jewish law. Second, they
must devise an appropriate strategy to induce the Roman governor to issue the
death penalty on the basis of Roman law.

After some less-than-successful maneuvering, the leadership finally fas-
tens a charge on Jesus, but it is not enough. At that point Caiaphas plainly asks
Jesus if He is the Christ.

The question was forthright. And so would be the answer. Jesus not only replies
in the affirmative, but goes on to say that in the future the members of the Sanhedrin
would see Him sitting at God's right hand and coming in the clouds of heaven.

That answer is all that Caiaphas needs. Blasphemy is punishable in the Old
Testament by stoning. The high priest has reached goal one. Now the task is to
transpose the Jewish accusation into a breach of Roman law serious enough to
require the death penalty.

*Help us, Father, as we watch the kingdoms of this world face off with Your
kingdom, to see Your hand at work in the complexities of life.*

September 25

The Trial of Peter, Phase 1

Peter followed him at a distance, as far as the courtyard of the high priest, and going inside he sat with the guards to see the end. . . . And a maid came up to him, and said, "You also were with Jesus the Galilean." But he denied it before them all, saying, "I do not know what you mean." And when he went out to the porch, another maid saw him, and she said to the bystanders, "This man was with Jesus of Nazareth." And again he denied it with an oath, "I do not know the man." Matt. 26:58-72, RSV.

Two trials were taking place that evening, one of Jesus and a second of His chief apostle.

Their responses under pressure would be very different, with Jesus standing firm and Peter caving in. But neither was the work of a moment. They reflect two paths that converged at the house of Caiaphas. We see them becoming evident in Gethsemane, where one Man prayed while the other slept, where one Man surrendered Himself totally to death on the cross while the other failed to face the events that would soon inundate both of them. In short, the differences in the two trials were not the decision of a moment, but reflect the differing habits of Jesus and Peter up to that time.

Perhaps the most remarkable thing about the incident is that Peter is there at all. Usually we fault him for his cowardice, but the fact that he followed Jesus, even if at a distance, says something about the man who had earlier in the evening pulled his sword in the face of a mob accompanied by a cohort of fully armed soldiers. Scripture tells us that all the disciples fled after Jesus' arrest. But at least two of them—Peter and John—had had second thoughts and had gone to Caiaphas' home. That took courage.

So far so good for Peter. Then that pesky servant girl shows up, claiming that he was a follower of Jesus. And how did she make that deduction? It wasn't all that difficult. John tells us that he and Peter both followed the procession to the high priest's house, but that John had been allowed into the courtyard because he was known to the high priest, while Peter remained outside the gate. So John went to the maid who kept the door and asked her to let Peter in. And, according to John, it was that very maid who first put the question to Peter (John 18:15-17).

The "fearless Peter" had come to his hour of trial. And he will fail miserably, not because of a momentary weakness, but as a result of habitual confidence in himself.

We can learn from Peter that our daily actions and attitudes are building characters that we must face in our own hour of trial.

The Trial of Peter, Phase 2

And a little later those who stood by came up and said to Peter, "Surely you also are one of them, for your speech betrays you." Then he began to curse and swear, saying, "I do not know the Man!" Immediately a rooster crowed. And Peter remembered the word of Jesus who had said to him, "Before the rooster crows, you will deny Me three times." So he went out and wept bitterly. Matt. 26:73-75, NKJV.

Peter's hour has come. And he fails, not only once but three times, with each episode becoming more damning.

Then, if possible, it worsens when a relative of Malchus of the healed ear identifies Peter because of his Galilean accent (John 18:26, 10; Mark 14:70). With this third accusation Peter totally unravels and begins "to curse and swear" that he doesn't "know the Man" (Mark 14:71, NKJV).

Peter had gone about as far as he could go in denial. There are at least three possibilities regarding the nature of his cursing and swearing. The first is that he used profanity. That would have been bad enough, but the meaning is probably deeper than that.

A second interpretation is that he swore by God's name that he didn't know Jesus, thereby couching his denial in the form of an oath that called God to witness as to its truthfulness.

The third possibility is even more damning than the first two. R. T. France suggests that Peter may even have uttered a curse upon Jesus to make it clear that he could not be a follower.

Whatever the nature of the swearing and cursing, it was a significant betrayal of Jesus by His chief disciple. At that point, at least three things happened. First, the cock crowed.

Second, as the cock crowed Jesus "turned and looked at Peter" (Luke 22:61, RSV). And what a searching gaze that must have been. Far from an "I told you so" kind of expression, Ellen White tells us that it was one of "deep pity and sorrow, but there was no anger there" (*The Desire of Ages*, p. 713). At that point Jesus' prophecy of his denial flashed upon Peter's mind.

Christ's look was more than he could bear. "He went out and wept bitterly." At that very point Peter's faith took a giant step forward. And Jesus knew the meaning of those repentant tears.

All of us can learn from Peter's experience. His core problem was not fear, but overconfidence. After all, no coward would have followed Jesus to that fateful courtyard. A second lesson is that while none of us are above reproach, none of us are yet beyond God's grace.

The Trial of Judas

When Judas, who had betrayed Him, saw that He had been condemned, he felt remorse and returned the thirty pieces of silver to the chief priests and elders, saying, "I have sinned by betraying innocent blood." But they said, "What is that to us? See to that yourself!" And he threw the pieces of silver into the temple sanctuary and departed; and he went away and hanged himself. Matt. 27:3-5, NASB.

The most unique thing about Judas' trial is that he passed judgment on himself. It is impossible for us to understand all that had gone through his twisted thinking prior to this time, but one thing is at last clear to him. He now understood the horror of what he had done. When he tried to return the money, the priests merely mocked him. Such are the friends of sin. They had used him for their purposes and then scorned him in his hour of need.

At that point Judas "threw the pieces of silver into the temple sanctuary." There are two important words in that sentence whose full meanings most translations, which state that he "threw down the money in the temple," fail to reflect.

The first is the word for Temple. It is not the general word for Temple (*hieron*), but the one for the actual Temple sanctuary. To get to it Judas had to pass through the Court of the Gentiles, the Court of the Women, and the Court of Israel. Beyond that he could not enter. He had come to the barrier that shut him out of the Court of the Priests. As a result, he had to yell his conversation with the priests.

That brings us to the second word of significance, usually translated as "threw down." The word also means "threw," "hurled," and "flung," a rendering demanded here by the Temple geography. He "hurled" the money at the mocking priests and went out to hang himself.

Such was the end of a man whose maneuverings had gone wrong. He had meant to force the reticent Jesus into displaying His power as the Messiah/King, but all he had accomplished was driving Christ to the cross. Judas' life was shattered.

Two lessons stand out from this experience. A first is that we often come to hate those things that we have gained from sin. The object of sinning in some cases becomes disgusting and revolting. So it was with Judas and with Amnon's conquest of his sister Tamar (2 Sam. 13:1-19).

A second lesson is that we cannot turn back the clock. All of us have times that we wish we could live over so that we could do things differently. But such is an impossibility. We and others must deal with the results of our actions. With that hard fact in mind, we need to be careful how we live each day.

The Trial of Jesus, Phase 2

When morning came, all the chief priests and the elders of the people took counsel against Jesus to put him to death; and they bound him and led him away and delivered him to Pilate. . . . The governor asked him, "Are you the King of the Jews?" Jesus said, "You have said so." But when he was accused by the chief priests and elders, he made no answer. Then Pilate said to him, "Do you not hear how many things they testify against you?" But he gave him no answer, not even to a single charge; so that the governor wondered greatly. Matt. 27:1-14, RSV.

The religious leaders had no time to waste. Roman legal proceedings began early so that by midmorning the ruling class could embark on pursuits of leisure. The Jews had decided for the death penalty, but a charge of blasphemy would hardly be sufficient to bring such a penalty from a Roman governor. He would see the whole problem as an internal Jewish squabble and throw the case out of court.

But the good news for the Jews is that blasphemy had a political interpretation. After all, wasn't the Messiah to be a warrior-king like David?

Matthew and Mark don't tell us the fancy footwork of the religious leaders in framing their official charge. But Luke does: "Then the whole company of them arose, and brought him before Pilate. And they began to accuse him, saying, 'We found this man perverting our nation, and forbidding us to give tribute to Caesar, and saying that he himself is Christ a king'" (Luke 23:1, 2, RSV).

The last thing Pilate (governor of Palestine from A.D. 26-36) needed was another run-in with the Jewish leaders, especially during the inflammatory Passover season when the minds of the people were already thinking of Exodus, liberation, and the overthrow of oppressors.

Pilate immediately sized up both the religious leaders and Jesus, easily concluding that He was no political threat. But he had to interrogate Him anyway. Jesus' reply to Pilate's question of kingship was guarded for good reason: "You have said so." Jesus didn't deny or admit it, partly because the charge was both true and false. It was true in that He was a King and had demonstrated that fact a few days before by riding into Jerusalem in princely fashion to the Hosannas of the crowd. But He wasn't a king in the political sense.

Jesus mounts no defense that could have won His freedom. Having surrendered to the Father's will in Gethsemane, He is now living out that decision.

Pilate, meanwhile, is left wondering what is taking place. Fortunately, he sees a way out of the predicament.

The Trial of Pilate, Phase 1

Now at the feast the governor was accustomed to release for the people any one prisoner whom they wanted. At that time they were holding a notorious prisoner, called Barabbas. . . . The governor said to them, "Which of the two do you want me to release for you?" And they said, "Barabbas." Pilate said to them, "Then what shall I do with Jesus who is called Christ?" They all said, "Crucify Him!" And he said, "Why, what evil has He done?" But they kept on shouting all the more, saying "Crucify Him!" Matt. 27:15-23, NASB.

Pilate had seen from the first that Jesus was innocent of being the kind of revolutionary that the Jewish leaders had accused Him of, and that they themselves were a crafty lot who obviously had cooked up the charges.

Even essentially evil men such as Pilate are not all bad. Even he had a spark of decency. That is evidenced by the fact that he didn't want to crucify an innocent man just to please the leaders. On the other hand, given his past, he needed to pacify the Jewish population in some way. Fortunately, he saw a way through the problem. He could appeal to his custom at Passover of releasing one prisoner to the population.

Quite aware that Jesus was extremely popular with the people, Pilate set the situation up in such a manner that the choice would be obvious and clearcut. Crowds had a few days earlier thronged Him as He made His triumphal entry into Jerusalem, throwing their cloaks before the feet of His donkey as they made the air ring with their songs of praises.

The other option Pilate offered them was the disgusting Barabbas, an insurrectionist "who had committed murder" (Mark 15:7, NIV). But in that he had underestimated the Jewish leaders. After all, a person repellent to Pilate could have a special appeal to a Jewish populace desiring freedom from Rome. Such a crowd could be led to clamor for Barabbas without too much difficulty. Then again, the mob may not have consisted of those who thought highly of Jesus, but one assembled for the occasion by the Jewish leaders.

So the crowd faces a choice. And what a choice it is. After all, Barabbas is an Aramaic name, *Bar-'Abba*, which means "son of the father." Thus the crowd had to decide which son of the father it wanted.

Its choice isn't altogether different from the ones you and I make every day. The question for me today is "What son do I desire?"

The Trial of Pilate, Phase 2

When Pilate saw that he was accomplishing nothing, but rather that a riot was starting, he took water and washed his hands in front of the crowd, saying, "I am innocent of this Man's blood; see to that yourselves." And all the people said, "His blood shall be on us and on our children!" Then he released Barabbas for them; but after having Jesus scourged, he handed Him over to be crucified. Matt. 27:24-26, NASB.

The Jewish leaders have Pilate on the spot, forcing his hand toward crucifixion even though he realizes Jesus is innocent. The turning point comes when some of the Jews cry out, "If you release this man, you are not Caesar's friend; every one who makes himself a king sets himself against Caesar" (John 19:12, RSV). The last thing the Roman governor could afford was to be accused before the emperor Tiberius of harboring a man who claimed to be king. With that threat the Jewish leaders hit Pilate at his weakest point. After all, one cannot expect the emperor to be merciful to an official who condones treason in the face of many witnesses.

With their accusations the Jewish leaders had bridged the gap between Jewish law and Roman law. They had transposed blasphemy in claiming Messiahship into revolutionary treason. Pilate now has a pretext for issuing the order for the death penalty, which he does, even though he sees through the thinly veiled Jewish plot.

John tells us that "he brought Jesus out and sat down on the judgment seat at a place called The Pavement. . . . He said to the Jews, 'Behold your King!'" They responded with further cries of crucifixion. And the outmaneuvered governor handed Him over to his soldiers to be crucified (verses 13-16, RSV).

At the same time Pilate sought to signify that he was not guilty by the symbolic act of washing his hands of the matter before the crowd. He had been warned by a sense of justice working on his conscience and through his wife's dream, but Pilate couldn't withstand the accusations of the Jewish leaders and the mob. So he issues the crucifixion order and washes his hands.

Pilate forgot only one thing: that responsibility is one thing we can never escape. Neither Pilate nor I can make a wrong choice and wash our hands of all responsibility. Accountability for my choices is something that is mine forever.

Father in heaven, help me to have the courage of my convictions and to make honest choices as I journey through life.

October 1

Degradation of the King

[Pilate], having scourged Jesus, delivered him to be crucified. Then the soldiers of the governor took Jesus into the praetorium, and they gathered the whole battalion before him. And they stripped him and put a scarlet robe upon him, and plaiting a crown of thorns they put it on his head, and put a reed in his right hand. And kneeling before him they mocked him, saying, "Hail, King of the Jews!" And they spat upon him, and took the reed and struck him on the head. And when they had mocked him, they stripped him of the robe, and put his own clothes on him, and led him away to crucify him. Matt. 27:26-31, RSV.

Scourging doesn't mean much to me. That's because I have never experienced one myself, or even seen one. Such cruelty is outlawed today.

But a Roman flogging was a brutal ordeal. The whip had long leather straps with sharpened pieces of metal and bone studded here and there. Such an instrument could tear a person's flesh down to the bone. Some victims never survived, while it drove others insane. But in Jesus' case it was merely a preliminary.

While I have never been scourged, I have been spit upon. I remember at age 18 standing in line one morning when a big gooey wad of saliva and mucus hit my head. I looked up to see a juvenile delinquent of about my age grinning down at me from an open platform several stories above me. There was no way I could get at him, but if I could have it would have been a violent scene. Few things in my life have been more disgusting and degrading.

Yet my experience isn't even the tip of an iceberg compared to what Jesus underwent at the hands of a coarse, rough, ignorant band of soldiers as they mocked and abused Him while awaiting the completion of preparations for the crucifixion.

Interestingly enough, the soldiers were the least to be blamed of those instrumental in the death of Jesus. They recently had accompanied Pilate to Jerusalem. As a result, they had no idea of who Jesus was. Unlike the Jews and Pilate, they acted in ignorance. To them He was merely a deluded Galilean. Having no hatred toward Him, they were merely doing what rough and ignorant people do in a sick world that earmarks some for mocking. But they did it. And Jesus suffered the disgrace and degradation of it all.

But He not only did it; He underwent it for me. Astounding! A member of the Godhead came and suffered unbearable shame for me!

What am I willing to do for Him?

A Painful Meeting

As they came out, they found a man of Cyrene, Simon by name. Him they compelled to bear His cross. Matt. 27:32, NKJV.

It all happened so quickly. Simon, a Jew from North Africa, is pushing through the crowd surging into Jerusalem for the Passover. At that same time a cohort of Roman soldiers is escorting a condemned man out of the city. Covered with blood from the usual precrucifixion flogging and staggering under the weight of the crossbeam of a cross, the man falls to the ground. Seeing the hopelessness of Jesus' situation, the soldiers grab Simon and press him into service.

It was the most important day of his life, but Simon had no way of realizing it at the time. All he knew was the splintery feel of the cross, the pushing of the soldiers as they tried to speed him through the thronging crowd, and the stares of those nearby as they mistakenly assumed that he was the condemned man. It was a shameful, unpleasant experience. But it changed his life.

But why Simon? How come the soldiers had selected him from the crowd? The Bible doesn't tell us. It may have been his strong build. Or it may be he just happened to be the nearest man when Jesus stumbled and fell. But there may have been a more attractive reason. Perhaps Simon's face and body language had shown signs of sympathy for Jesus and made him stand out from the indifferent crowd.

We don't know the "why" of Simon's selection, but we do know the "what" that came out of his short time with Jesus. In Mark's telling of the story he earmarks "Alexander and Rufus" as Simon's sons, indicating that they were known to the first readers of the second Gospel in Rome, its primary audience (Mark 15:21). In Romans 16:13 we find another tantalizing piece of information. "Greet Rufus," Paul wrote, "eminent in the Lord, also his mother and mine" (RSV).

We have no way of knowing if there is a relationship between Mark 15:21 and Romans 16:13, but we can be assured that Simon, on that fateful day on the road to Jerusalem, met Jesus as his Savior and, in turn, passed on that knowledge to his sons.

What a painful way to encounter Jesus. But what a reward. Jesus still meets men and women in painful situations—many upon beds of sickness, others in the shadow of bereavement. To all He offers a cross to carry and the honor of serving Him.

A "Crucified" Savior?

And when they were come to the place, which is called Calvary,
there they crucified him. Luke 23:33.

Crucifixion!
The very thought of it was enough to bring a case of chills to the hardiest inhabitants of the Roman world. A cruel form of capital punishment, crucifixion combined public shame with slow physical torture. Death on a cross, Martin Hengel writes, was not "just any kind of death. It was an utterly offensive affair, 'obscene'" in the fullest sense of the word. "Crucifixion was a punishment in which the caprice and sadism of the executioners was given full rein."

The public shame began with dragging the crossbeam of a cross through the streets to a place of public execution. In an era that lacked TV programs and movies to satiate the downward side of human desire for violence, crucifixion was often the "best show" in town for the bored and curious. The victims were stripped of all clothing and affixed to the cross in a manner that prohibited them from caring for their bodily needs or covering their nakedness from the taunts and indignities of spectators. When the execution party reached the place of crucifixion, soldiers fixed the crossbar to the upright beam. Next they stretched the prisoner out on it and drove the nails through soft flesh and hard bone. Finally, they raised the cross and dropped it with a flesh-tearing thud into the hole prepared for it.

The victim, being immobile, could not escape the burning Palestinian sun or fend off cold or insects. Since crucifixion affected no vital organs, death from fatigue, cramped muscles, hunger, and thirst came slowly, often after many days.

The Romans reserved crucifixion for the punishment of slaves and foreigners who were considered criminals and often used it as a public demonstration of the folly of rebelling against the empire.

Jews regarded anyone executed by crucifixion as rejected by the people of Israel, cursed by the law of God, and excluded from God's covenant with the Jewish people. To top it off, the Jews expected their Messiah to be a mighty conquering king, not a suffering criminal. No wonder Paul could refer to Christ's cross as "a stumbling block to Jews and foolishness to Gentiles" (1 Cor. 1:23, NIV).

Jesus was the only person in history to volunteer for that form of death. He came from heaven for it. At the cross the crucified God met my sins.

The Weight of Sin

Christ redeemed us from the curse of the law, having become a curse for us—for it is written, "Cursed be every one who hangs on a tree." Gal. 3:13, RSV.

C ursed be every one who does not abide by all things written in the book of the law, and do them" (Gal. 3:10, RSV, citing Deut. 27:26). One function of the law was to set forth God's ideal. A second of its purposes was to identify sin: "through the law comes knowledge of sin" (Rom. 3:20, RSV). The bad news is that "the wages of sin is death" (Rom. 6:23). And because "all have sinned and fall short of the glory of God" (Rom. 3:23), every human being since Adam has been under the curse of the law.

That's the bad news. The good news (literally "gospel") is that Jesus on the cross absorbed the curse for all of us and each of us.

It was not the physical punishment of the cross or the public indignation that made Jesus dread it so much, but the mental anguish accompanying His bearing of the sins of the world. *The Desire of Ages* helps us peer into that anguish: "The guilt of every descendant of Adam was pressing upon His heart. The wrath of God against sin, the terrible manifestation of His displeasure because of iniquity, filled the soul of His Son with consternation. All His life Christ had been publishing to a fallen world the good news of the Father's mercy and pardoning love. Salvation for the chief of sinners was His theme. But now with the terrible weight of guilt He bears, He cannot see the Father's reconciling face. The withdrawal of the divine countenance from the Saviour in this hour of supreme anguish pierced His heart with a sorrow that can never be fully understood by man. So great was this agony that His physical pain was hardly felt.

"Satan with his fierce temptations wrung the heart of Jesus. The Saviour could not see through the portals of the tomb. Hope did not present to Him His coming forth from the grave a conqueror, or tell Him of the Father's acceptance of the sacrifice. He feared that sin was so offensive to God that Their separation was to be eternal. Christ felt the anguish which the sinner will feel when mercy shall no longer plead for the guilty race. It was the sense of sin, bringing the Father's wrath upon Him as man's substitute, that made the cup He drank so bitter, and broke the heart of the Son of God" (*The Desire of Ages*, p. 753).

We have but the faintest of ideas of what the cross involved for Jesus. The tragedy of earth's history is that it means nothing to most people.

The Exchange of Calvary

He made Him who knew no sin to be sin for us, that we might become the righteousness of God in Him. 2 Cor. 5:21, NKJV.

Martin Luther, the great Reformer, captures the verse's intent. Writing to a monk in distress about his sins, Luther admonished: "Learn Christ and him crucified. Learn to pray to him and, despairing of yourself, say: 'Thou, Lord Jesus, art my righteousness, but I am thy sin. Thou hast taken upon thyself what is mine and hast given to me what is thine. Thou hast taken upon thyself what thou wast not and hast given to me what I was not.'" To Luther that was history's "great exchange."

But on that dreary day at Calvary the disciples of the crucified One didn't see it that way. "For the disciples who had followed Jesus to Jerusalem," penned Jürgen Moltmann, "his shameful death was not the consummation of his obedience to God nor a demonstration of martyrdom for his truth, but the rejection of his claim. It did not confirm their hopes in him, but . . . destroyed them." A crucified Messiah had never even entered the realm of their imaginations, in spite of the fact that Jesus had plainly told them several times the exact form of death that awaited Him.

We humans can be real blockheads when the ways of God cross our own visions of the good life and our goals. But since He always knows what He is talking about, perhaps it is time for us to open both eyes as we read His Word to us.

The Crucifixion may have been the darkest day in the disciples' lives, but it would not remain that way. His followers would soon see it as the high point of hope. Paul, for one, never ceased driving home the fact that the cross is the anchor point of redemption. It was the death of Jesus on the cross that made it possible for us to have His eternal life and His righteousness.

The apostle in part defined "the gospel" in terms of the brutal fact that "Christ died for our sins in accordance with the scriptures" (1 Cor. 15:1, 3, RSV). And the book of Hebrews asserts that Jesus died "once for all" and that "by a single offering" He made available the plan of salvation in all its fullness (Heb. 10:10, 14, RSV). It is Christ's spilled blood that forms the foundation for God's offer of saving grace to all who have faith in Jesus (see Rom. 3:23-25).

Father in heaven, I thank You for Jesus and fully accept Your "great exchange."

Enough Ignorance to Go Around

And when they had crucified Him, they divided up His garments among themselves by casting lots. And sitting down, they began to keep watch over Him there. And above His head they put up the charge against Him which read, "THIS IS JESUS THE KING OF THE JEWS." Matt. 27:35-37, NASB.

Meanings of the cross depend on the vantage point from which we view it. For the soldiers it was merely one more day of work. Another crucified cluster of Jewish scum. So what? And they passed some of the time gambling as they awaited the death of Jesus and the two robbers. They had not the foggiest idea of what they had done or its significance. Probably they would have laughed if told that they had just crucified the incarnate God, the active agent in the creation of heaven and earth. To them He was merely one more troublesome Jew.

Then there was that sign: "THIS IS JESUS THE KING OF THE JEWS." Here was a bit of payback from Pilate to the Jewish leaders who had bested him in his desire to free Jesus. He hadn't cared for Jesus as a person, but he was tired of the craftiness of the leading members of the Sanhedrin who were constantly causing him difficulties.

As a result, Pilate could send Jesus to a nasty death without remorse. But at the same time he took the opportunity to take a whack at the Jews with his sign.

And it did upset the leaders, especially since it was written in Hebrew, Latin, and Greek and thus could be read by many. That, John tells us, meant another trip for the Jewish leaders to Pilate requesting that he change the wording to "This man said, I am the king of the Jews." The Roman governor's answer was a smug one: "What I have written I have written" (see John 19:19-22, RSV).

Revenge is sweet. But beyond revenge Pilate's sign functioned as a billboard, announcing, in effect, that any person who posed as a king of the Jews could expect similar treatment. And that fact cut the Jews to the quick and flattened their pride.

But above all of the sparing, the most interesting aspect of the sign is that it was true. Jesus was in fact the Messiah/King of the Jews.

Pilate had the truth but didn't know it. The Jewish leaders had their Messiah but didn't recognize Him. The busy soldiers had participated in the central event of history but were not aware of it. It is no wonder that Jesus cried out, "Father, forgive them; for they know not what they do" (Luke 23:34, RSV). There is a wideness in God's mercy.

A Glimpse of Kingdom Faith

Two others also, who were criminals, were led away to be put to death with him.
. . . One of the criminals who were hanged railed at him, saying, "Are you not the
Christ? Save yourself and us!" But the other rebuked him, saying, "Do you not fear
God, since you are under the same sentence of condemnation? And we indeed justly;
for we are receiving the due reward of our deeds; but this man has done nothing
wrong." And he said, "Jesus, remember me when you come into your kingdom."
Luke 23:32-42, RSV.

A strange place for a conversation. Three naked, bleeding men, gasping for breath as they pushed up with their feet to let air into lungs constricted by the way they were affixed to their crosses. A more unlikely place for significant conversation is difficult to imagine. But there they are—two genuine criminals and the innocent Jesus.

Taking up the mocking flavor of the crowd, Matthew tells us, both robbers "reviled him in the same way" (Matt. 27:44, RSV). But that didn't go on forever. One of them sees something in Jesus that the careless crowd had missed.

But not the other thief, who sarcastically calls out, "Since you are the big-shot Christ, why don't you do something about it? Why don't you save yourself, and us while you are at it?"

At that point the other thief takes another look at Jesus and remembers what he had heard of His acts of healing and mercy. At that very point faith takes hold and hope ignites.

Mocking was not in short supply at the cross. But now comes a cry of conviction by a person who had seen beyond the exterior to the core of who Jesus was. "In Jesus, bruised, mocked, and hanging upon the cross, he sees the Lamb of God, that taketh away the sin of the world. Hope is mingled with anguish in his voice as the helpless, dying soul casts himself upon a dying Saviour. 'Lord, remember me,' he cries, 'when Thou comest into Thy kingdom'" (*The Desire of Ages*, p. 750).

Desperation and hope. Hopelessness and faith. Sinfulness and new possibilities. All of those thoughts and emotions surge through his mind as the Holy Spirit brings conviction to his heart and the power to speak for Christ.

Those same emotions need to flood our souls as we behold Jesus hanging on the cross. It is only when we finally give up on ourselves and see the hopelessness of our situation that we are willing to abandon our ways to the kingdom and cast ourselves upon His boundless mercy for the only way into His kingdom.

A Promise Extraordinary

And Jesus said to him, "Assuredly, I say to you, today
you will be with Me in Paradise." Luke 23:43, NKJV.

Here we have a controversial verse, especially since many teach that it offers proof positive that believers go to heaven the very moment they die. But before we get to that idea we need to examine what the verse says about Jesus and the thief.

When one looks at Jesus when He made this pledge, one wonders how He could in good conscience promise anybody anything. After all, He is in the process of dying the death of a condemned criminal. He is fastened to a cross with nails, is covered with blood and flies, and will soon end up in a hole in the ground. And then there were the taunting people surrounding the cross shouting out that if He was "the Christ of God, his Chosen One" He should prove it by saving Himself (Luke 23:35, 37, RSV).

We know now that by not saving Himself it became possible to save others, since it is through His death in our place that we have hope. But that wasn't evident as He hung upon the cross. He looked hopeless indeed.

Yet it is from His cross of death that He makes the remarkable promise to the thief that he will be with Him in Paradise or heaven. That promise indicates that He could at this point in His ordeal see beyond the tomb. By faith He realized that death was not the end for Him and that His life and death would make it possible for Him to save others.

Just as remarkable as the faith of Jesus is that of the thief, who even asks for such a promise as they both suffer on their crosses. Here is a man who believed in spite of *all* outward appearances.

We find another lesson here. Namely, that it is never too late to come to Jesus. As long as life remains there is hope.

Now, we need to ask, what exactly did Jesus promise? Most read the verse as if the thief would be with Jesus in heaven that very day. But, since there are no commas in a Greek sentence, it can also be translated as "I say to you today, you will be with Me in Paradise," meaning that Jesus was making the promise that very day.

Which is the correct placement of that controversial comma? Let's let Jesus answer. For one thing, He didn't go to heaven that day. Three days later He informed Mary that "I am not yet ascended to my Father" (John 20:17). And in other places He plainly told His disciples that He would reward His followers at His second coming, when He would return in triumph "in the glory of his Father with his angels" (Matt. 16:27).

October 9

The Paradox of a Crucified Messiah

Those who passed by derided him, wagging their heads and saying "You who would destroy the temple and build it in three days, save yourself! If you are the Son of God, come down from the cross." So also the chief priests, with the scribes and elders, mocked him, saying, "He saved others; he cannot save himself. He is the King of Israel; let him come down from the cross, and we will believe in him. He trusts in God; let God deliver him now, if he desires him; for he said, 'I am the Son of God.'" And the robbers who were crucified with him also reviled him in the same way.
Matt. 27:39-44, RSV.

How would you have responded to such people whom you were dying to save? If it were me I would have gotten off my cross and given them exactly what they deserved. I would show them in no uncertain terms who I was. They would be sorry that they had ever mocked me. I could, of course, destroy the whole mess of them by a limited atomic display. But then a slow fire would be more to my liking. Soon I would have them all begging and bowing.

We can be thankful that Jesus wasn't like me. But the interesting fact of the situation is that Jesus is the only crucified individual in history who could have gotten off His cross. He could have used His divine power to escape it. But the One "who knew no sin" chose to stay on it and die in our place, to become sin . . . , so that in him we might become the righteousness of God" (2 Cor. 5:21, RSV). "I lay down my life," we read in John's Gospel. "No one takes it from me, but I lay it down of my own accord. I have power to lay it down, and I have power to take it again" (John 10:17, 18, RSV). Jesus had a choice. And He decided to do God's will rather than His own. He chooses to remain on the cross.

The truth of the matter is that the Jewish leaders were quite correct when they shouted out "He saved others; he cannot save himself." The facts of the case are that if Jesus was save anyone, He could not leave the cross. For Jesus it was a physical possibility, but not a moral or spiritual one. To flee the cross would be to reject His role as the Lamb of God who was to die for the sins of the world (John 1:29).

Such is the paradox of paradoxes—a crucified Messiah, a dying Savior.

Today we can thank God that Jesus hung on the cross to the bitter end. It is because of that sacrifice on Calvary that we can share Paradise with Him for eternity.

A Side Lesson on
Staying on the Cross

Aha! You who destroy the temple and build it in three days, save Yourself and come down from the cross! Mark 15:29, 30, NKJV.

Jesus had two great core TEMPTATIONS in His life: (1) not to go to His cross, and (2) once there to get off of it.

He battled the first of those TEMPTATIONS throughout His life. The great climactic points of that struggle were at His wilderness temptations, in which Satan offered Him all of the world if He would just bow to him; after the feeding of the 5,000, when the crowd and the disciples wanted to crown Him King on the spot; at Caesarea Philippi, when Peter played the role of Satan by telling Jesus that He didn't need to go to the cross; and in Gethsemane, at which time Christ prayed desperately to be released from going to the cross, but finally surrendered to God's will. Each of those episodes was a TEMPTATION to avoid the cross, to achieve the crown without the Crucifixion.

The second aspect of His great TEMPTATION didn't take place until He was already on the cross. At that point TEMPTATION shifted to getting off the cross and using His dormant divine powers to give His hecklers exactly what they deserved.

TEMPTATION in our lives follows the same course as it did in Christ's. Too many of us seem to think that it is the urge to perform some evil act. Wrong! Those may be temptations, but they are not the essence of TEMPTATION.

As was the case for Jesus, the first avenue of my personal TEMPTATION is not to go to my cross. That is, the devil tempts me to live my own life, be my own person, and exert my own will rather than surrendering my life to God and living a life of service that represents the character of God and does His will. Avoiding the cross is the first great TEMPTATION for every person. But, as with Jesus, the only way to life eternal is to die to self, to be raised to a new way of life, and to live that life for Him.

That last point brings us to the second major area of our personal TEMPTA-TION—to get off of our cross. Once we have finally decided to get on our cross and live God's will, the devil then constantly hounds us to step off our crosses and give people who have irritated us or wronged us exactly what they deserve.

Father in heaven, help me today not only to go to the cross but, through Your power, to stay on it.

October 11

More About Staying on the Cross

The high priests, along with the religion scholars and leaders, were right there mix-
ing it up with the rest of them, having a great time poking fun at him: . . . "King of
Israel is he? Then let him get down from that cross. We'll all become believers then!"
Matt. 27:41, 42, Message.

For the past two days we have been meditating upon the great TEMPTA-
TION that leads to all the lesser temptations of life. In essence that TEMP-
TATION is to become the god of our lives, to do our own will. That is where
Adam and Eve went wrong. The eating of the fruit was only the result of a mi-
nor temptation after they had already fallen for Satan's great TEMPTATION.

Christ, as we noted earlier, experienced that TEMPTATION in two formats: not
going to the cross, and not staying on it. Today we will examine more fully how the
second aspect of TEMPTATION plays out in our daily life when we are tempted to
get off our cross, break our relationship with God, and do our own thing.

I have known for years that I cannot sincerely pray and commit a deliberate
act of sin at the same moment. I have experimented. Temptation becomes sin at
the point that I become conscious of the temptation. At that very moment I can
choose to do one of two things. I can reject the temptation through God's power,
or I can decide to dwell on the temptation and cherish it a bit. In other words, I
can ask God into my life to help me overcome, or I can tell Him to leave me alone
for a while so that I can enjoy my private sin. I comfort myself that I will pray
about it later. Too often, we are like Augustine, who, in suffering with the central
temptation of his life, prayed, "Make me chaste, Lord, but not quite yet."

The alternative is to come to God, saying, "Lord, I recognize this temptation for what it is, and I am going to pray right now." I have personally discovered that when I sincerely and perseveringly pray for victory, I lose the desire
for the sinful action. I believe that phenomenon is the power of God helping
me overcome both the specific temptation and the TEMPTATION to get off
my cross and live my life according to my own will.

But sometimes, to be honest, I don't want the power and the victory. Instead, I want the sin. At that point, I fall for TEMPTATION in the same way
that Eve did in Genesis 3. I have taken active charge of my own life and side-
lined God. To consistently choose TEMPTATION leads to a life of falling for
temptations as I separate myself from God.

Caring Until His End

Standing by the cross of Jesus were his mother, and his mother's sister, Mary the wife of Clopas, and Mary Magdalene. When Jesus saw his mother, and the disciple whom he loved standing near, he said to his mother, "Woman, behold your son!" Then he said to the disciple, "Behold, your mother!" And from that hour the disciple took her to his own home. John 19:25-27, RSV.

Jesus was not alone as He moved toward death. John mentions four women and himself, the only disciple specifically mentioned by the Gospels as a witness to the death of Jesus. Some of Jesus' followers may have opted to avoid the scene because it was always dangerous to be too closely identified with a condemned criminal.

But at least the four women had the courage to be with Him until the end. They were an interesting group. We know nothing of Mary the wife of Clopas, but the other three all feature in the gospel story.

The central woman, of course, was Jesus' mother. She had greeted His birth with such joy of promise to come. But early on the prophecy of Simeon in the Temple that His life would be a sword to pierce her own soul had disturbed her (Luke 2:35). And if she had been troubled at times during His ministry, what must her feelings and heart be like now. Still not understanding the nature of His mission, she suffered at the foot of the cross in silent agony. But her mother's love would not allow her even to think of staying away. This was her son.

Then there was Jesus' mother's sister. While John's Gospel does not identify her, a comparison of the parallel passages in Mark 15:40 and Matthew 27:56 makes it evident that she is Salome, the mother of James and John, the sons of Zebedee. She had earlier received a firm rebuke for trying to get her sons the top spots in Jesus' kingdom, but she had accepted it with a positive attitude. Now she is here at the crucifixion of her nephew.

Last, there is Mary Magdalene, from whom Jesus had cast out seven devils (Mark 16:9; Luke 8:2). She was eternally grateful for what He had done in her life.

But Jesus isn't quite finished with these women. Even on the cross in His own agony He could not forget His mother. With Joseph in his grave and His brothers not yet Christians, as the oldest son born to Mary, Jesus commits her to the care of His cousin John.

That action speaks volumes to those of us who still have parents. Our care for them must be central in our list of priorities.

October 13

Darkness in Two Flavors

Now from the sixth hour there was darkness over all the land until the ninth hour. And about the ninth hour Jesus cried with a loud voice, "Eli, Eli, lama sabachthani?" that is, "My God, my God, why hast thou forsaken me?" Matt. 27:45, 46, RSV.

Time passes slowly on the cross. Mark tells us that the Romans nailed Jesus to it at the third hour of the day or about 9:00 in the morning. He died at the ninth hour or about 3:00 in the afternoon. Six short hours to those enjoying life, but six hours that seemed like eternity to one hanging on a cross. If you have difficulty imagining what it was like, try picturing simultaneous surgery for six hours on several sensitive parts of your body without pain killer. But even then, you could never capture the pain of crucifixion. It made even strong men cry for death. Anything to get rid of the ceaseless pain.

For Jesus death came swiftly. Only six hours. Many hung on their crosses for days before entering the mercy of death. Halfway through those six hours, the Bible tells us, "there was darkness over the land until the ninth hour."

It was not an eclipse. The Gospel writers make no suggestion as to what caused the darkness. They simply record the fact that for three long hours it enveloped Jerusalem.

That three Gospels record the darkness indicates that it made a deep impression upon those who experienced it. One can only imagine the silence that must have fallen over the jeering crowd. Darkness at the height of day was enough to fill those experiencing it with a nameless terror. Something was happening as Jesus hung upon the cross, but they didn't know what.

But the darkness was not only in nature. It filled the soul of Christ. For at the ninth hour He cried, "My God, my God, why hast thou forsaken me?" (Mark 15:34, RSV).

The darkness overwhelming Jesus is even more amazing than that covering the land. His life had not been easy. In fact, He had had to face hatred and rejection on every side throughout His ministry. Yet He was a man of joy and positive expression.

The source of that joy was the deep conviction that He was never alone. "I and My Father are one." "I am in the Father and the Father in Me." "I am not alone, the Father is with Me." No matter what His outward circumstances, Jesus knew that the Father's smile rested on Him.

But now? Darkness!

Jesus' Dark Night of the Soul

At three o'clock Jesus groaned out of the depths, crying loudly, "Eloi, Eloi, lama sa-
bachthani?" which means, "My God, my God, why have you abandoned me?"
Mark 15:34, Message.

As we noted yesterday, throughout His life Jesus had always felt the presence of His Father, no matter how difficult things got. But now, on the
cross, it changed. Internal darkness reflected the external. Overwhelmed with
it, He felt Himself to be separated from the Father.

Without a word He had borne the pain of the nails, the mocking of the
people, and the jeers of the priests. But when He loses sight of God's approving
smile He breaks out into a heartbroken cry, "My God, my God, why have you
abandoned me?" Jesus had reached the midnight hour of His soul.

We will never fully understand what He was going through. But the fact
that that heartbroken cry of desolation came from a Jesus who had always felt
His Father's presence makes it utterly significant. The cry itself is a part of the
mystery of the cross.

The words themselves quote the first verse of Psalm 22, a psalm that parallels the events of the last ordeal of Jesus in many particulars. From the lips of
the psalmist the words form little more than a complaint of a lonely and deserted man. But from the lips of Jesus the same utterance demonstrates a depth
of meaning that the psalmist knew nothing about.

Why the cry from the cross? Certainly not from the fear of death. Once
you are on a cross, death is a friend.

There is something deeper here. And it is related to Christ's mission to
earth. On the cross, Jesus, the pure and upright God incarnate, was bearing the
sins of the world. As Isaiah 53 puts it, "he bore the sin of many," "the Lord has
laid on him the iniquity of us all" (verses 12, 6, RSV).

One of the bitter effects of sin is that it separates sinners from God. Adam and
Eve felt that separation. And so did Jesus, who became sin for us (2 Cor. 5:21).

But we need to be careful here. J. D. Jones points out that "it was not that
God had withdrawn His face or was angry with the Son Who was doing His
will. It was that these crowding sins of ours hid the vision of God's face." He had
lost the sense of the Father's presence. Although God had not deserted Him,
from the perspective of bearing sin on the cross He felt forsaken.

The good news is that, as in so many cases, feelings are not reality.

My Dark Night of the Soul

My God, my God, why have you forsaken me?
Why are you so far from saving me, from the words of my groaning?
O my God, I cry by day, but you do not answer, and by night, but I find no rest.
Psalm 22:1, 2, ESV.

In Psalm 22 we find David's cry of anguish in the midst of his suffering. Where is his God when he needs Him? Why is there no answer to his prayer? Has God truly forsaken him?

A study of the psalm itself points beyond David to the experience of Christ. And Jesus, aware of the depth of meaning in the psalm, may have memorized the words.

Feeling forsaken by God at times of stress is an experience all of us have from time to time. While as Christians we have our bright and sunny days, we also have periods of darkness when everything seems to go wrong and everyone is against us. "Where is your God now?" our mind screams out.

Just as Jesus had His own dark night of the soul, so did David, and so do I. At such times my prayers seem to go nowhere. Answers to them appear to be nonexistent.

At such times we need to take comfort from Jesus' dark night. The fact of the case is that God may be near to us even when we have lost sight of Him. Jesus on the cross may have felt forsaken, but, apart from His feelings, He was only "apparently forsaken of God" (*The Desire of Ages*, p. 756). God hadn't departed from Him. And the same Father stands by us in our hour of crises—in spite of our feelings.

Even in the depth of darkness, apparently forsaken, Jesus could address the Father as "*My* God," His personal Father. Even when Jesus could not see or feel the presence of God, He still clung to Him. Here is faith and trust in the midst of what seemed overwhelming gloom. To Jesus He was "*my* God" in spite of His feelings and of outward appearances. Here was the climax of Jesus' faith that "*my* God" would not let Him down.

In the end that faith in the unseen presence of the Father would allow Him to exit the cross with words of triumph as He shouted "It is finished" and committed His spirit to His Father. "*My* God" had been there all along even though Jesus did not feel His presence.

His experience has something important for me. Just as I have my midnights of the soul during which I feel abandoned by God, so I can keep the eyes of faith focused on "*my* God." Despite appearances and feelings, God has not forsaken us in times of trouble.

Peaceful Victory

And Jesus, crying out with a loud voice, said, "Father, into Your hands I commit My spirit." Having said this, He breathed His last. Luke 23:46, NASB.

The dark night of His soul has ended. Jesus has passed through the crisis of His life and knows that His Father has not forsaken Him.

The anguish is over. Trust and peace are in Christ's tone as He cries out with a "loud voice," "Father, into Your hands I commit My spirit."

Remarkable words for a Man who a few minutes before had felt utterly forsaken. They are words of faith. Jesus knew who His Father was. And He knew where He was going.

Jesus did not die as other humans. We die because we have no choice. Disease or injury takes us whether we like it or not. But even in death Jesus was different. He died as a volunteer. Of Himself He said, "I lay down my life, that I might take it again. No man taketh it from me, but I lay it down of myself. I have power to lay it down, and I have power to take it again" (John 10:17, 18). Jesus knew who He was. He realized the identity of His Father. And He recognized where He was going as He made His final commitment to God and breathed His last.

His experience has something to teach each of His followers. His death may have been unique in that it was voluntary, but every one of His followers has the privilege of meeting death with the calmness and sense of victory that He exhibited.

As with Him, I need have no fear of what some have called "the king of terrors." The work of Jesus has vanquished Satan. The devil can trouble our body for a season, but he cannot separate us from the love of God and the victory of Jesus.

The dying Stephen knew that as he cried out "Lord Jesus, receive my spirit" (Acts 7:59). The same great truth was in the mind of Paul when the time of his death was at hand: "I know whom I have believed, and am persuaded that he is able to keep that which I have committed unto him against that day" (2 Tim. 1:12).

Happy and blessed are those who stand with Jesus in life. The same shall eventually stand with Him again in the world to come.

We also can trust. Like Jesus, we know in whom we have believed. And we also can commit our spirit to Him as we face the end of our earthly journey.

October 17

Salvation Accomplished!

He said, "It is finished!" And bowing His head, He gave up His spirit.
John 19:30, NKJV.

In that verse we have the most important word in all the Bible. The words rendered in English as "It is finished!" are a single word in Greek—*tetelestai.*

The other three Gospels tell us that Jesus ended His earthly life with a "loud cry" or "loud voice," but do not indicate what Jesus said. Only John provides us with the words themselves. According to the fourth Gospel, Jesus' last words before His death were "It is finished!" "It's all done!" "It's complete!" (John 19:30).

All was finished, and Jesus knew it. But what was it that He had finished? His mission to earth. He had come to earth as God incarnate to demonstrate the love of God, live a perfect life, die for all who would believe in Him, and in the process defeat the devil and seal his doom. In short, through His death Jesus had accomplished salvation. Jesus had completed the work He came to do. Now He could go home to the Father.

As a result, "It is finished!" was not a moan or a sigh of one who had barely made it to the finish line. To the contrary, it was a shout of victory. "It is the cry," William Barclay writes, "of the man who has completed his task; it is the cry of the man who has won through the struggle; it is the cry of the man who has come out of the dark into the glory of the light, and who has grasped the crown. . . . Jesus died a victor and a conqueror with a shout of triumph on His lips."

And that victory contains the meaning of the cross. Jesus, who had lived a sinless life, had now become the spotless sacrificial Lamb of God who in dying took away the world's sins (John 1:29).

Christ has died. But the victory has been won. He has defeated Satan and set the course of history until at the end of time when the saved will again hear the words "It is done" (Rev. 21:6) at the setting up of a new heaven and a new earth as the new Jerusalem descends from heaven to earth (Rev. 21:1, 2).

Christ had completed His atoning work, but the reward of His followers will not be given in its fullness until He returns from heaven after preparing a place for them (John 14:1-3).

Meanwhile, as we wait we can rejoice in Jesus' accomplishments on the cross.

An Earthly Symbol
of Heavenly Things

And, behold, the veil of the temple was rent in twain from the top to the bottom.
Matt. 27:51.

At the very moment that Jesus cried "It is finished" and died on His cross, the curtain in the Temple ripped in two. Here we find one of the great symbols of the meaning of His death.

That curtain separated the two apartments of the Temple. Only the officiating priests could enter the first apartment, designated the holy place. But the second was even more sacred. Into that Most Holy Place only the high priest could enter, and he but once a year on the Day of Atonement, the day of Israel's year-end judgment.

The Gospel writers carefully point out that the curtain was torn "from top to bottom." Given the fact that the curtain was approximately 60 feet in height, the directional description of its ripping signifies a supernatural act, since a human tearing would have been from bottom to top.

The rending of that massive curtain signified several things. First, that the old system of ceremonies and sacrifices that pointed forward (Col. 2:17) to Jesus' sacrifice on the cross was now a thing of the past. Because the real sacrifice has taken place in which the Lamb of God had died for the sins of the world (John 1:29), the ceremonial system has served its purpose. The ripping of the curtain signifies that even the Most Holy Place of the earthly Temple is no longer sacred. The scene of action will now shift to heaven, where Jesus will minister in the "true" Temple (Heb. 8:1, 2) as High Priest for those who believe in Him.

A second major significance of the tearing of the curtain is that believers now have direct access to the Father through the sacrifice of Jesus and through His post-resurrection ministry in heaven. As Scripture puts it, we now "have confidence to enter the sanctuary ["holies" in Greek] by the blood of Jesus, by the new and living way which he opened for us through the curtain." Because of that access we can "draw near" to God "with a true heart in full assurance of faith" (Heb. 10:19-22, RSV).

The destruction of the curtain further symbolized the fulfillment of Jesus' saying that the Jerusalem Temple would be "forsaken" by God and left "desolate" (Matt. 23:38, RSV). The beginning of the desecration of the Temple took place with the tearing of the curtain. That event foreshadowed its complete destruction in A.D. 70.

Thank You, Lord, for not only providing Jesus as our Savior but for also opening up fuller access to Yourself through that event.

A Special Resurrection

And the earth quaked, and the rocks were split, and the graves were opened; and many bodies of the saints who had fallen asleep were raised; and coming out of the graves after His resurrection, they went into the holy city and appeared to many.
Matt. 27:51-53, NKJV.

At the same time as Christ's last victory cry and death several other events took place. Yesterday we examined the tearing of the Temple curtain. Another simultaneous happening was a massive earthquake that shook the entire area and apparently split open the earth in major fissures in several places. Whereas the rending of the curtain was not visible to all, everybody experienced the fearful earthquake.

A third supernatural incident at the death of Jesus was a special resurrection of some who had died. The only Gospel writer to mention it is Matthew. And in his account the sequence of events is not entirely clear. What he seems to be telling us is that the earth-shattering earthquake not only "split" rocks but also opened up many tombs. From the text above it is not clear if the individuals in those tombs arose at the time of His death or at His own resurrection. The latter seems to be the meaning of the passage. If that is so, the picture is of some of God's faithful ones arising out of their opened tombs on Resurrection morning and going into the city to bear witness to the power of Christ to resurrect.

The Bible does not tell us who these raised individuals were, and most commentators don't speculate on their identity. Ellen White makes the plausible suggestion that "they were those who had been co-laborers with God, and who at the cost of their lives had borne testimony to the truth" (*The Desire of Ages*, p. 786). Paul alludes to the fact that when the risen Jesus Himself later ascended to heaven He took the raised ones with Him (see Eph. 4:8).

We should not confuse this special resurrection with the general resurrection that occurs at the Second Advent. A limited number of faithful arose with Christ, but the bulk of God's people will sleep in their graves until His appearing at the end of time (1 Thess. 4:13-18; 1 Cor. 15:51-53).

What we do find in the event reported by Matthew is a clear teaching on the power of Christ to resurrect His followers. Because He lives, we shall also.

Firstfruits of the Cross

When the centurion and those who were with him, keeping watch over Jesus, saw the earthquake and what took place, they were filled with awe and said, "Truly this was the Son of God!" Matt. 27:54, ESV.

"Filled with awe." That is undoubtedly an understatement. One can only picture that Roman captain and his soldiers trembling at the supernatural darkness and the powerful earthquake and the victory-shouting death of this strange Captive whom they had been guarding.

We need to look a little more carefully at this centurion. He was undoubtedly a hardened man. Only such a person could stand up to the difficult duty of keeping down the boisterous population of Palestine. The Jews had no use for the Romans and made their contempt open through both minor and major acts of sabotage. The Romans reacted in kind. Violence had met violence on a consistent basis. The very centurion at the foot of Christ's cross had almost certainly participated in many crucifixions and witnessed people die the most agonizing of deaths. It was all part of his job.

But he sensed something different about this man, this death. As a result, we find an individual, who only a few minutes before may have been participating in cruel jesting, now confessing at the moment of Jesus' death that "Truly this was the Son of God." Even to this Gentile soldier and some of his men it was clear that there was something in the death of Jesus, together with the accompanying phenomena, that showed that He was not just another human being.

In the centurion's confession we find the beginning of the fulfillment of a prophecy that Jesus had made earlier: "I, if I be lifted up from the earth, will draw all men unto me" (John 12:32). Jesus had foretold the magnetic power of the cross. Now we find in the centurion the firstfruits of Christ's cross.

We should not overlook his declaration that Jesus was the Son of God. That was God's declaration at His baptism. It was Peter's breakthrough insight on the nature of Messiahship on the road to Caesarea Philippi. And now we find that truth in the mouth of a Gentile. With that the earthly story of the One who was to be "God with us" has come full circle.

Christ our Savior has the power to save because of who He is. And His cross is still drawing men and women to His divine person.

And Then There Were the Women

Many women were there looking on from a distance, who had followed Jesus from Galilee while ministering to Him. Among them was Mary Magdelene, and Mary the mother of James and Joseph, and the mother of the sons of Zebedee.
Matt. 27:55, 56, NASB.

Women!
Are they all that important? One would have to wonder by the record of a historic Christianity dominated overwhelmingly by males. But the Gospel writers seem to be of a different opinion. To them the women and their witness and ministry to Jesus were crucial to the story.

Matthew completes his presentation of the Crucifixion by telling us that there were "many women" there as witnesses. All four Gospels tell us that women remained at the cross until the end.

But where were the men? After Peter's repeated denial of Jesus, the only disciple Scripture mentions is John "the disciple whom he loved" (John 19:26, RSV). And John appears only in the fourth Gospel. Where are the men? Hiding most likely. After Jesus' arrest in Gethsemane they fled as fast as their legs could carry them. They had no desire at the time, apparently, to be too close to a condemned criminal.

Against that background of male failure, the courage and devotion of the women shines forth all the more brilliantly.

Matthew tells us not only that there were "many women," but that they were watching from "a distance." We don't know why they didn't come closer. It may have been that it was not safe to get too close to an execution when Jesus' enemies were in control. Perhaps it may be that it wasn't proper for women to attend a crucifixion. Or it could have been that they wanted to put some distance between themselves and the mockers.

What we do know is that they were close enough to hear when Jesus assigned His mother to John's care. But the most important thing we learn about those women is they were there at all.

In the absence of the male disciples, they provided support and a show of loyalty to the suffering Jesus when He needed it most. But this was not some new development. Matthew indicates that they had followed Him all the way from Galilee, ministering all the while to His needs. All along they had supplied the penniless Jesus what He had required for bodily survival. They had assumed the role of servant that Jesus' male followers had shunned.

May God continue to bless the ministry of the women among us.

Autopsy:
Death From a Broken Heart

Since it was the day of Preparation, in order to prevent the bodies from remaining on the cross on the sabbath (for that sabbath was a high day), the Jews asked Pilate that their legs might be broken, and that they might be taken away. So the soldiers came and broke the legs of the first, and of the other who had been crucified with him; but when they came to Jesus and saw that he was already dead, they did not break his legs. But one of the soldiers pierced his side with a spear, and at once there came out blood and water. . . . For these things took place that the scripture might be fulfilled, "Not a bone of him shall be broken." And again another scripture says, "They shall look on him whom they have pierced." John 19:31-37, RSV.

One male disciple did have the courage to stay with Jesus at the cross. It was the same disciple who had the "guts" to enter the courtyard of the high priest on the evening of Jesus' first trial. No wonder that John had a reputation as the disciple whom Jesus loved. He had the courage to stick with Him even though the authorities knew him to be one of Jesus' inner circle.

With those facts in mind, it is not surprising that John has something to report in his Gospel that the other three were apparently unaware of. He certifies the truth of what he has to say by pointing out that he was an eyewitness.

The first of the events he reports is the breaking of the legs of the criminals. Whereas the Romans would let a person hang suffering on a cross for days and then throw the body out for scavengers to eat, Jewish custom was much more merciful. The book of Deuteronomy stipulated that "if a man has committed a crime punishable by death and he is put to death, and you hang him on a tree, his body shall not remain all night upon the tree, but you shall bury him the same day" (Deut. 21:22, 23, RSV).

Thus it was not an accident that the Jewish leaders requested that the crucified men be removed from their crosses. But in this case it was even more important, since the next day was to be a high Sabbath when both the weekly Sabbath and the Passover day coincided.

The grim method of dispatching criminals still alive was to smash their limbs with a mallet until they died, but Jesus was already dead.

To make sure of His death a soldier speared Him in the chest. The result was a stream of blood and water. Now, dead people don't normally bleed. But it has been suggested that in cases of a ruptured heart the blood in the heart mixes with the fluid in the pericardium, which surrounds the heart. If that was the case, the spear's thrust hit that sack of fluid, indicating that Jesus had not died from His physical injuries but from a broken heart as He bore the sins of the world.

The Power of the Cross

After these things, Joseph of Arimathea, who was a disciple of Jesus, though a secret one because of his fear of the Jews, asked Pilate to let him take away the body of Jesus. Pilate gave him permission; so he came and removed his body. Nicodemus, who had at first come to Jesus by night, also came, bringing a mixture of myrrh and aloes, weighing about a hundred pounds. John 19:38, 39, NRSV.

With Joseph of Arimathea we have a new player in the gospel story. While he may have been a secret disciple up to the time of the cross, now he risks everything. He had no idea how the unstable Pilate would respond to his request to hand over the body of a man put to death for treason. On the other hand, he knew exactly how the Jewish leaders would react. For example, he could be certain that he would lose his standing in the Jewish community and his membership in the powerful Sanhedrin. Had he been a poor man he may have come out in the open sooner. But he had much to lose. After all, the Jewish leaders had agreed that those who became followers of Jesus should be put out of the synagogue—excommunicated (John 9:22).

And Joseph wasn't the only secret disciple to step forward at this hour of need. Nicodemus, whom we first met approaching Jesus at night (John 3:1-5) and later as he hesitantly speaks on behalf of Jesus (John 7:50-52), now comes boldly to the front. It was to Nicodemus that Jesus had first begun to develop the theme of His being lifted up in the same way that Moses had raised the serpent in the wilderness so that everyone who believes in Him might have eternal life (John 3:14-16). Jesus later added to that teaching when He noted that "when I am lifted up from the earth, [I] will draw all men to myself" (John 12:32, RSV).

And now that prophecy is being fulfilled. All of the disciples of Jesus except John might have been hiding in fear of being identified as followers of Jesus, but the drawing power of the cross has brought these two rich members of the Sanhedrin into the open.

Joseph and Nicodemus may have feared any association with Jesus while He was alive, but already the power of the cross was working to make cowards into heroes and waverers into individuals willing to make their faith known publicly. The cross had transformed them. The death of Jesus had done for them what His life had never accomplished. Their hearts broken in love, they were willing to risk everything for the One who had died for them.

They had discovered that no person can long remain a secret disciple. Eventually the secrecy will kill the discipleship or the discipleship will kill the secrecy.

Inspired Dedication

Pilate was surprised to hear that he was already dead. Summoning the centurion, he asked him if Jesus had already died. When he learned from the centurion that it was so, he gave the body to Joseph. So Joseph bought some linen cloth, took down the body, wrapped it in linen, and placed it in a tomb cut out of rock. Then he rolled a stone against the entrance of the tomb. Mary Magdalene and Mary the mother of Joseph saw where it was laid. Mark 15:44-47, NIV.

Whatever was to be done with the body of Jesus had to take place quickly. He had died at three on Friday afternoon and the Sabbath was rapidly approaching.

It frequently happened that criminals hung for days on their crosses before dying. Thus it surprised Pilate that Jesus had gone so quickly. And now there was the body. In most cases that would not have been an issue. Many of the crucified were never buried. Their bodies merely got taken down from their cross and left on the ground where wild dogs and vultures dealt with them. Others found burial in one of the cemeteries reserved for criminals and other undesirable individuals.

In that context, Pilate must have been shocked when approached by the wealthy and quite orthodox Joseph of Arimathea. To the Roman official it seemed merely one more perplexing situation in what undoubtedly was the most unusual crucifixion of his governship. We don't know what was going on in his mind, but we do know that he gave Joseph the body after he had ascertained that Jesus was truly dead.

According to John's Gospel, Joseph owned an unused tomb. Only a wealthy person could have owned such a burial chamber. Hewn out of solid rock, they often had several ledges on which to place the bodies. The tombs themselves were generally tall enough to stand in, but the doorway was probably not more than four feet high. A track was cut in stone on the outside, and when the body had been placed, a large circular stone was rolled along the track to close the entrance.

Jesus not only had a rich man's tomb, but also a preparation fit for a king. John tells us that Nicodemus brought about 100 pounds of spices, a gift that overshadowed the earlier anointing of Mary by 100 times. And the spices in that precrucifixion had been worth 100 days' wages (John 12:3-5). Truly it can be said that Jesus fulfilled the prophecy of Isaiah 53:9 that "they made his grave with the wicked and with a rich man in his death, although he had done no violence, and there was no deceit in his mouth" (RSV).

Help me, Father, to be as inspired to dedication by the death of Jesus as were Joseph and Nicodemus. May it continue to transform my life as it did theirs.

October 25

A Sabbath Lesson

And the women who had come with Him from Galilee followed after, and they observed the tomb and how His body was laid. Then they returned and prepared spices and fragrant oils. And they rested on the Sabbath according to the commandment. Luke 23:55, 56, NKJV.

M ore than the other Gospel writers, Luke goes out of his way to tell us that the disciples of Jesus rested on the Sabbath after the Crucifixion "according to the commandment." Here we find a theme that runs throughout the two long books contributed to the Bible by its only Gentile author.

One might have expected such comments from a person such as Matthew, who was writing for a Jewish audience. But Matthew didn't have to emphasize the Sabbath to a community of believers overly rigid on the topic. What his audience needed was a lesson on how to keep the day (see Matt. 12:1-12).

But Luke had a different problem. He needed to emphasize the Sabbath to a population of Christians made up of a large proportion of people without a strong Sabbath background. As a result, he highlights the fact that Jesus' followers faithfully observed the first Sabbath of the Christian Era. And, in the process, Luke makes it explicitly clear which day he was talking about. He makes prominent the fact that Jesus was crucified on Friday (Luke 23:54), rested on the Saturday Sabbath (verse 56), and resurrected on Sunday, the first day of the week (Luke 24:1-6).

It is not an isolated case of Luke's interest in the one commandment that begins with the word "remember" (Ex. 20:8). He had earlier stressed the fact that Jesus Himself had the "custom" of keeping the Sabbath (Luke 4:16). That, of course, one would expect, since Jesus was Jewish. But the statement about the disciples resting on the Sabbath makes it clear that Christ had given no instruction to the contrary during His earthly life.

Luke's purposefulness in highlighting the seventh-day Sabbath continues in the book of Acts, in which he consistently presents the apostles as worshipping on the Sabbath rather than Sunday (see, e.g., Acts 13:14, 42, 44; 17:2; 18:4), even when there are not enough Jews to form a congregation (Acts 16:13).

Luke the Gentile was inspired to present Sabbathkeeping in a way that the Jewish authors of the New Testament never did. For him it was truly a day to be underlined and remembered by the largely non-Jewish church to which he was writing. He knows nothing of another worship day, except the one given "according to the commandment."

Human Maneuvers
and Divine Providence

The next day, that is, after the Preparation, the chief priests and the Pharisees gathered before Pilate and said, "Sir, we remember how that imposter said, while he was still alive, 'After three days I will rise.' Therefore order the tomb to be made secure until the third day, lest his disciples go and steal him away and tell the people, 'He has risen from the dead,' and the last fraud will be worse than the first." Pilate said to them, "You have a guard of soldiers. Go, make it as secure as you can." So they went and made the tomb secure by sealing the stone and setting a guard. Matt. 27:62-66, ESV.

Here we find a passage full of surprises. The first is the fact that it is the Jewish leaders who remember that Jesus had promised to resurrect after His death. The disciples had completely overlooked that prediction even though Jesus had repeatedly told them that He would die and be resurrected (see Matt. 16:21; 17:23; 20:19; 12:40).

What they forgot, and apparently never even really heard, the Jewish leaders would remember, even though they did not believe it would take place. Rather, they feared that the disciples would steal the body and *claim* a resurrection. In that case, their lie concerning Jesus' resurrection would be worse than His lie that He was the Messiah.

The passage's second great surprise is that the Jewish leaders were so worried about that possibility and the crisis that would flow out of it that they take the unprecedented step of breaking their own extremely rigid Sabbath laws by visiting Pilate (an unclean Gentile) on their holy day to request a guard for Jesus' tomb. That breach of their usual practice indicates the depth of their fear of the dead man's disciples perpetrating a hoax. The Jewish establishment was willing to do anything to put an end to the Jesus problem.

Pilate's mind must have reeled as these events unfolded. But, presumably tired of the whole business, the governor readily agrees to cooperate with the troublesome leaders, since if he doesn't, and the body is gone on the third day, there will be no end to the problem. He thus grants the Jewish leaders a guard to seal the tomb and watch over it.

But in taking such precautions, Leon Morris points out, the Jewish leaders "did more than they knew. They ensured that there could be no nonsense about disciples stealing the body when in due course Jesus did rise from the dead. The precautions of his enemies would underline the truth of his resurrection."

Strange indeed are the wonders of God's providence. God can use anyone or anything to bring about His purposes on the stage of earth's history.

Part 7

Turn Your Eyes Upon Jesus as the Resurrected Lord

Turning Point

Now after the Sabbath, as it began to dawn toward the first day of the week, Mary Magdalene and the other Mary came to look at the grave. And behold, a severe earthquake had occurred, for an angel of the Lord descended from heaven and came and rolled away the stone and sat upon it. And his appearance was like lightning, and his clothing as white as snow. The guards shook for fear of him and became like dead men. Matt. 28:1-4, NASB.

We have been turning our eyes upon Jesus for 10 months. First we viewed Him as Eternal God, and then sequentially as Incarnate Christ, Ministering Servant, and Crucified Lamb. We have now come to another climactic event as we behold Jesus as our Resurrected Lord.

The world has never been the same since that early Sunday morning when the earth shook, the angel descended, and the tomb opened. It would impact the disciples on a magnitude far exceeding anything else in their relationship with Jesus. The Resurrection would propel them out of discipleship and into apostleship; out of being followers and into being aggressive leaders; out of fear and into victorious courage.

Yet nowhere in the history of Christianity do we find that event of events described. None of the New Testament writers attempt to portray the actual Resurrection. They merely treat it as a fact. The Gospels do, however, present the effects of Christ's resurrection along three lines: the empty tomb, the guards' fear, and Jesus' meeting with some of His followers.

Matthew opens up his account of the Resurrection story with Mary Magdalene and "the other Mary" coming to look at Jesus' grave. That "other Mary" is Mary the mother of James and Joses (Mark 16:1; 15:47). Here we find another interesting aspect of the gospel story. While Jesus' male disciples were hiding and hunkered down in fear, these women were out in the open and visiting His tomb.

How fitting it is that these two Marys should be the first to receive news of the risen Lord. After all, they had stayed with Him as He hung upon the cross, they had followed to see where He was laid in the tomb, and now they are rewarded for their love and faithfulness.

Here is a point worth remembering. It is not always the "greatest" or the most visible in the church who are most blessed in their journey with the Lord. But it is those who are most caring and most dedicated who have the privilege of the closest walk with Him and the fullest of His blessings.

October 28

A Moment to Remember

The angel said to the women, "Do not be afraid; for I know that you are looking for Jesus who has been crucified. He is not here, for He has risen, just as He said. Come, see the place where He was lying." Matt. 28:5, 6, NASB.

Some things you don't just forget. I remember precisely that I was washing my car on that sunny California autumn day when I heard the shattering news that President John F. Kennedy had been assassinated.

And I will never forget the moment that I first became aware of the September 11 disaster. Standing speechless in a phone booth at the Amsterdam airport, I suddenly realized why my ride had not picked me up. The world was reeling in shock and in the crisis of the moment I had been forgotten. The world had changed and my predicament was a side casualty.

We don't forget such events. Instead, we remember them as if they were yesterday. And we often share our story with others as we grapple with their meaning.

It was like that with the two Marys. They were shook up, to say the least, over what had happened the day before. The last thing they had expected was to see their precious Lord Jesus die on a cross. If my guess is right, they had spent a sleepless night, tossing and turning, crying their hearts out, and repeatedly asking, Why? But the only answer they received was silence, except for the similar tossings of others in the room. Disheartening misery and darkness was all they felt and saw. The light of their life had gone out.

Not being able to sleep, they rose early the next morning just to visit the tomb. They were going as mourners. Expecting nothing else, they just needed some peace and quiet.

But peace and quiet is the last thing they got. With an earthquake, stunned guards, and the presence of a brilliant angel they once again found their senses overpowered. Things were still changing as they faced new realities.

The God who had been silent on Crucifixion Friday was having the last word. With the words "He has risen" He had begun to answer their questions. Hope budded anew in their still uncomprehending hearts.

That is a moment that the two Marys never forgot. It is one that they told to their children and grandchildren. Through the gospel stories they are still telling it today. "He is risen" is the apex of the entire story of the incarnate Jesus. And "He is risen" are the words that still give us courage to move forward two millennia later.

HEARING Versus Hearing

But on the first day of the week, at early dawn, they went to the tomb, taking the spices which they had prepared. And they found the stone rolled away from the tomb, but when they went in they did not find the body. While they were perplexed about this, behold, two men stood by them in dazzling apparel; and as they were frightened and bowed their faces to the ground, the men said to them, "Why do you seek the living among the dead? Remember how he told you, while he was still in Galilee, that the Son of man must be delivered into the hand of sinful men, and be crucified, and on the third day rise." And they remembered his words. Luke 24:1-8, RSV.

They had a job to do and they knew it. Jesus had died late on Friday afternoon and there had been no time to prepare His body properly for burial before the Sabbath arrived. The body had merely been wound in linen and placed on a shelf, after which someone rolled the stone in front of the door and the Roman soldiers sealed it, with the Jewish leaders standing by to see that it was done correctly.

But the burial job had not been completed. The linen from the body would have to be unwound and rewound as they placed the spices into the folds of the winding sheet.

With that task in mind, some of the women arrived carrying the spices, presumably the ones purchased by Nicodemus. The last thing they expected was an empty tomb. Obviously they had not gone to the tomb while saying to themselves, "Well we have some spices just in case He is still dead, but we really think He is alive again." To the contrary. The women knew the basic fact of life that dead people remained that way.

But the empty tomb shifted their thinking, their immediate task, and their lives.

Yet they shouldn't have been surprised. After all, Jesus had repeatedly told them that on the third day He would rise.

Here we find a problem that we all suffer from. All too often we hear words but not meaning. Why? Because our minds are set. We know what we or our "group" believes. And those beliefs provide the framework in which we "hear" and interpret new ideas. Conclusions that don't fit into our mental frameworks we generally misunderstand if not reject.

You and I suffer from the same hearing problem as the disciples.

Open our ears, O Lord, that we might truly hear and be prepared for those events yet to come in the working out of Your great plan.

October 30

Resurrection Grace

[The angel] said to them, "Do not be alarmed. You seek Jesus of Nazareth, who was crucified. He is risen! He is not here. See the place where they laid Him. But go, tell His disciples—and Peter—that He is going before you into Galilee; there you will see Him, as He said to you." So they went out quickly and fled from the tomb, for they trembled and were amazed. And they said nothing to anyone, for they were afraid.
Mark 16:6-8, NKJV.

The resurrection of Jesus is the hinge of history. It is the transforming event in the lives of the disciples. How important it was that they hear the good news that "He is risen!"

Thus the command of the angel to tell the disciples. The most interesting aspect of that injunction is the addition of "and Peter."

Here is immediate grace in its most startling form. After all, the last we heard of the disciples in Mark was that they "all forsook him and fled" (Mark 14:50, RSV). And of Peter that he had cursed and swore that he didn't know Jesus, after which "he broke down and wept" (verses 71, 72, RSV).

Peter must have gone through utter despair in the three days since he had betrayed Jesus. It is significant that Mark is the only Gospel writer to record Jesus' special invitation to the fallen Peter. Peter himself had collaborated with Mark in the writing of his Gospel. All the other Gospel writers may have neglected the words "and Peter," but Peter never could. Those two words both shattered his despair and renewed his hope. The Jesus who had earlier urged him to forgive 70 times seven was doing that very thing for His fallen disciple.

Here is grace. Jesus didn't give Peter what he deserved. To the contrary, He offered him what he didn't deserve—forgiveness and restoration to apostleship. As James Edwards points out, "if the word of grace from the resurrected Lord includes a traitor like Peter, readers of the Gospel may rest assured that it includes those of their community who have also failed." And that goes for clergy also. We must never forget who Peter was and what he did. Yet Jesus forgave him.

That is truly "Amazing Grace," grace that stretches the imagination of even the most generous Christians. Could we do what Jesus did? Or, more pertinently, would we want Jesus to do the same for us were we in Peter's position?

"Amazing Grace" has long been my favorite song. If I had my way it would be sung after every sermon that I preach, every lecture that I give, every prayer that I offer, and every day that I live. We need to realize that "and Peter" means "and George," "and Mary," "and each of us."

Failure of the First Christian Sermon

It was Mary Magdalene, and Joanna, and Mary the mother of James, and other women that were with them, which told these things unto the apostles. And their words seemed to them as idle tales, and they believed them not. Luke 24:10, 11.

I n yesterday's reading an angel commanded the women to tell the disciples about the Resurrection, but they "fled from the tomb, for they trembled and were amazed. And they said nothing to anyone, for they were afraid" (Mark 16:8, NKJV).

It is not difficult to see why. After all, to arrive at a tomb looking for a dead body but finding a living angel would unnerve the strongest of us. What is not so easy to understand is their fear and their silence. After all, they had received a message of hope and joy along with a specific commission to pass it on to the disciples.

Up to this point the Gospels portray the women as consistently being brave and doing well. But now they fail. Their fear and disobedience demonstrate an apparent inability to truly believe the good news. They are speechless in the face of the command to speak.

Here we find a paradox. Throughout much of the gospel story Jesus has commanded individuals to remain silent about the truth of who He is, while they shout it out anyway. But now we have a specific directive to tell what they have seen and yet the women remain silent.

But not for long. It apparently took a while before the truthfulness and importance of what they had seen and heard worked through their astounded minds. Luke records that they eventually do tell the apostles.

Yet they did not believe the women. And perhaps that is why the women hadn't passed on the message in the first place. In Jewish society women did not count as witnesses. But God didn't see it that way. He chose women to be the first witnesses of the Resurrection. And beyond that, He, through an angel, commanded them to preach the first fully Christian sermon—"He is risen!" Yet the men, good Christians that they were, could not take it from the mouth of a woman.

That fact tells us two things. One is the stubbornness of some men. And the other is about God's willingness to use all people to spread the good news of salvation accomplished.

Too many of us are locked up in little boxes of our own making. Like the disciples, we miss blessings when we reject ideas that don't line up with our preconceptions. And, also like the disciples, we refuse even the gospel from people who don't fit "our" model of God's messengers.

November 1

Two Versions: One Story

But Peter got up and ran to the tomb; stooping and looking in, he saw the linen
cloths by themselves; then he went home, amazed at what had happened.
Luke 24:12, NRSV.

The most interesting thing about today's verse is that it does not appear in many modern translations of the Bible. Thus one can read the Revised Standard Version, the Revised English Bible, and others with the text moving immediately from verse 11 to verse 13, with verse 12 in a footnote stating that not all Greek manuscripts contain that passage. On the other hand, such versions as the New King James, the New American Standard Bible, and the New International Version contain the passage.

Here we have a problem that we should be aware of. Different Greek manuscripts vary at times, but the good news is that nearly all of the variations in the text are found in other parts of the Bible and thus very little is lost in the presentation. Beyond that, no major teaching of the Bible is at risk.

The interesting thing about Luke 24:12 is that John's Gospel takes up the same story. But John tells us that it was both he and Peter who, even though they had some doubts, ran to the tomb to see if the women's report might just be correct after all.

In John's account, "they both ran, but the other disciple [John] outran Peter and reached the tomb first; and stooping to look in, he saw the linen cloths lying there, but he did not go in" (John 20:4, 5, RSV). You see here that two of the "greatest" disciples still have some competitive spirit. But it is a transformed spirit. John goes on to give Peter his just credit: "Then Simon Peter came, following him [John], and went into the tomb. . . . Then the other disciple, who reached the tomb first, also went in, and he saw and believed; for as yet they did not know the scripture, that he must rise from the dead. Then the disciples went back to their homes" (verses 6-10, RSV).

We note several interesting things about John's and Mark's (Peter's) accounts of this event. One is that each of them presented it from his own perspective. The other is the truly wonderful fact that the four Gospels supplement each other, with each providing details left out by the others.

Inspiration never destroys the personalities of those who wrote the books of the Bible. Rather, the various personalities working under the guidance of the Holy Spirit give us differing insight into how God relates to and uses diverse individuals.

The Problem of the Missing Body

Some of the guard came into the city and reported to the chief priests all the things that had happened. When they had assembled with the elders and consulted together, they gave a large sum of money to the soldiers, saying, "Tell them, 'His disciples came at night and stole Him away while we slept.' And if this comes to the governor's ears, we will appease him and make you secure." So they took the money and did as they were instructed; and this saying is commonly reported among the Jews until this day. Matt. 28:11-15, NKJV.

If the Resurrection was proving to be rather incomprehensible to Jesus' followers, the missing body had become a major problem for both the Roman soldiers and the Jewish leaders. The first thing the soldiers do is to send a delegation into Jerusalem to report to the Jewish leaders what had happened. The paradox is that the very men who had predicted deceit by Jesus' followers (Matt. 27:63, 64) now turn to it themselves in order to cover up the Resurrection. Even more astounding is that they instruct the guards to tell the very story of the "missing" body that they had ordered the Romans to prevent. The Jewish leaders are desperate.

The soldiers are also in a jam. Their basic problem is that they do not have the corpse they had been sent to guard. But to say that they fell asleep is not much of a solution. After all, sleeping on guard was punishable by severe penalties. But the alternative of reporting the missing body would lead to the same result. Of course, they could tell the truth. But what Roman officer would believe such an improbable story?

All things considered, it seems best to the soldiers to accept the solution of the Jewish authorities and thus avoid certain punishment. The bribe of a "large sum of money" and the promise of the leaders to "appease" Pilate (who would soon be leaving the city) if the report reaches his ears quickly sweetened their move in that direction.

Matthew tells us that the soldiers agree to the deception. And, he notes, "This saying is commonly reported among the Jews until this day." In actual fact, the story continued to have circulation long after the death of the apostle. Justin Martyr (c. A.D. 100-165) tells us that in the middle of the second century the Jews were still repeating it.

Of course, the Jewish leaders didn't really have too many options. After all, they either had to stick by the lie, produce the body, or believe in the resurrection of Jesus. The last alternative was unacceptable. Thus, since they didn't have the body, they were stuck with the lie.

Trying to avoid the truth has led men and women down through time to strange mental and moral contortions. Unfortunately for that approach, it is always the truth that sets us free.

November 3

The Blinding Power of Failed Hope

That very day two of them were going to a village named Emmaus, about seven miles from Jerusalem, and talking with each other about all these things that had happened. While they were talking and discussing together, Jesus himself drew near and went with them. But their eyes were kept from recognizing him. And he said to them, "What is this conversation which you are holding with each other as you walk?" And they stood still, looking sad. Then one of them, named Cleopas, answered him, "Are you the only visitor to Jerusalem who does not know the things that have happened there in these days?" And he said to them, "What things?" And they said to him, "Concerning Jesus of Nazareth, who was a prophet mighty in deed and word before God and all the people, and how our chief priests and rulers delivered him up to be condemned to death, and crucified him. But we had hoped that he was the one to redeem Israel." Luke 24:13-21, RSV.

Luke is perhaps the greatest storyteller in the New Testament. His portrayal of the prodigal son (Luke 15) and the praying Pharisee and tax collector (Luke 18:9-14) especially engages our minds and hearts. The story of the walk to Emmaus ranks with those other sketches.

Told only by Luke, this story is not significant just because of an artistry that draws in the reader. Its importance also centers on its message, which speaks to bewildered people down to the end of time.

In many ways the confusion of the two followers of Jesus catches us by surprise. After all, His followers always recognized Him during later appearances. But not in these earlier ones. Thus the problem is not that the resurrected Jesus is unrecognizable. Rather, Luke tells us that "their eyes were kept from recognizing him."

I don't know exactly what that means. But I do know that yesterday I had a similar experience. I failed to notice a visiting friend in our Sabbath school class because I was expecting to see someone else. My mind had so focused on one identity that I could not place a familiar face until after my mind could sort out the pieces. Once that happened, I wondered how I could ever have been so stupid.

Something like that happened on the road to Emmaus. The disciples had expected Jesus to be the political redeemer of Israel from Rome. But instead of delivering them, He had died at Roman hands. Stupefying confusion blinded their eyes. Subsequently, they couldn't even recognize Jesus when He was with them.

There is encouragement for us here. Sometimes in our walk through life we feel confused and lonely. In our lostness we wonder where Jesus is. But often the problem is not His absence, but our lack of vision, something that only later events in God's providence can make plain.

New Eyes for New Reading

"We had hoped that he was the one to redeem Israel. Yes, and besides all this, it is the third day since this happened. Moreover, some women of our company amazed us. They were at the tomb early in the morning and did not find his body; and they came back saying that they had even seen a vision of angels, who said that he was alive. Some of those who were with us went to the tomb, and found it just as the women had said; but him they did not see." And he said to them, "O foolish men, and slow of heart to believe all that the prophets have spoken! Was it not necessary that the Christ should suffer these things and enter into his glory?" And beginning with Moses and all the prophets, he interpreted to them in all the scriptures the things concerning himself. Luke 24:21-27, RSV.

That was a Bible study I would like to have attended. Here we find the Lord Himself explaining the meaning of the Old Testament in light of the events later recorded in the New. Underlying Jesus' presentation are the facts that we need the entire Bible if we are truly to understand His life and work and that we most fully understand the Old Testament when interpreted through the lens of the New. God has one redemptive message that runs throughout the Bible. It is foreshadowed in the Hebrew Bible but dealt with explicitly in the New Testament.

We don't know exactly what passages Jesus utilized in His Bible study regarding His followers' mistaken ideas about Him. But a prime candidate would be the meaning of the sacrificial lamb that stood at the center of Jewish worship.

It was one thing for John the Baptist to proclaim Jesus as the Lamb of God who would take away sin (John 1:29). But it must have been almost impossible for the Jews, including the disciples, to understand the meaning of that statement. They were not expecting a messiah who would die for their sins, but a conquering warrior. In the light of Calvary and the Resurrection, however, the Old Testament took on new meaning as the Lamb Himself explained things.

One passage Jesus undoubtedly treated is Isaiah 53, with its talk of God's Servant being rejected and despised, bearing our griefs, being "wounded for our transgressions," being "numbered with the transgressors," bearing the sins of many, dying with the wicked, and being buried in association with the rich.

Suddenly it all came together. The two men saw redemption and Messiahship and the Old Testament in new ways. Their eyes were opened and their hearts warmed. Jesus was no longer a false hope but their resurrected Lord. The Bible itself held the key to both their discouragement and to their victorious future. Now they saw Jesus the Lamb as the center of Scripture from beginning to end.

November 5

A Tale of Two Meals

So they drew near to the village to which they were going. He appeared to be going further, but they constrained him, saying, "Stay with us, for it is toward evening and the day is now far spent." So he went in to stay with them. When he was at table with them, he took the bread and blessed, and broke it, and gave it to them. And their eyes were opened and they recognized him; and he vanished out of their sight.
Luke 24:28-31, RSV.

Meals are important in the Bible. The feeding of the 4,000 and the 5,000 were memorable events, as was the Last Supper. But here we need to go back to the first meal described in Scripture: "So when the woman saw that the tree was good for food, and that it was a delight to the eyes, and that the tree was to be desired to make one wise, she took of its fruit and ate; and she also gave some to her husband, and he ate. Then the eyes of both were opened, and they knew that they were naked; and they sewed fig leaves together and made themselves aprons" to cover their nakedness (Gen. 3:6, 7, RSV).

I would like to suggest that we can sum up the Bible message as a tale of two eye-opening meals. The first was an earth-shaping event. With it came the entrance of sin, death, and the other miseries that have provided a centerfold for the history of a world that has jumped its track and has been in the process of self-destruction. That meal also led to a long list of human ways to solve the problems caused by sin, the first being a human-generated approach to salvation and redemption. Human beings can solve the problem, runs the subtheme. We can use fig leaves to cover our nakedness. If that doesn't fully do the trick, we can overthrow the powers of darkness through force. And with that came the vision of a very human Messiah.

The second meal put an end to all that human-centered speculation. This time, however, eyes opened more fully to the divine solution to the difficulties that had entered at the first meal.

When the eyes of those two disciples were opened, they truly saw the meaning of Christ's death and His all-important resurrection. They clearly recognized that the curse of sin had met its defeat, that death itself had suffered a fatal blow, that new possibilities were on the horizon.

Jesus was alive! Not like Jairus' daughter, or the son of the widow of Nain, or the resurrected Lazarus. They would have to face death again. But here is One who has gone through death and come out the other side as victor.

Their eyes were opened. Because of their resurrected Lord everything took on bright new meaning. And those new eyes are also for you and me.

The Warm Hearts of
the Redeemed Community

And their eyes were opened and they recognized him; and he vanished out of their sight. They said to each other, "Did not our hearts burn within us while he talked to us on the road, while he opened to us the scriptures?" And they rose that same hour and returned to Jerusalem; and they found the eleven gathered together and those who were with them, who said, "The Lord has risen indeed, and has appeared to Simon!" Then they told what had happened on the road, and how he was known to them in the breaking of the bread. Luke 24:31-35, RSV.

Their eyes had been opened! Suddenly everything had made sense! Now they knew why their hearts had felt a burning glow while they had journeyed for two hours as the "Stranger" had explained things to them.

Already when they had begun the seven-mile trudge to Emmaus it had been late, and by the time they had arrived the day was "far spent" (verse 29). And then there was a meal that consumed more time.

But they forget all that when their eyes are opened and they grasp the gospel story and the meaning of Christ's death and resurrection. Now all they can do, in spite of the lateness of the hour, is to return to Jerusalem and share the good news about Jesus.

But the return trip is hardly the mournful trudge of the earlier journey. Now their feet fairly fly as they race back to that upper room where the disciples had been hiding, mourning, and commiserating. Having found Jesus, they could hardly wait to share it with others. I can imagine that they easily made the seven-mile trip in an hour or less. And they aren't even tired. All that is gone, along with their discouragement. Their eyes had been opened! Now that they had discovered the truth, their only desire is to bring it to others.

That's what happens to everyone who truly discovers Jesus. It is excitement, witnessing, and sharing in community that has stood at the heart of Christianity for 2,000 years. Christianity is not a solitary experience—it is communal. It is rejoicing with others who have also had their eyes opened. And it is taking the message of a risen Savior to those who are still blind and need hope.

Our passage for today closes with a note about Peter. Jesus had gone out of His way to comfort this man who had fallen from the path. Scripture makes special mention of Jesus' opening of His fallen disciples' eyes also.

Here is love! Here is grace! Here is what the Christian faith is all about—Jesus coming to seek and to save that which is lost (Luke 19:10). Here is true redemption.

More Eye Surgery

While they were still talking about this, Jesus himself stood among them and said to them, "Peace be with you." They were startled and frightened, thinking they saw a ghost. He said to them, "Why are you troubled, and why do doubts rise in your minds? Look at my hands and my feet. It is I myself! Touch me and see; a ghost does not have flesh and bones, as you see I have." When he had said this, he showed them his hands and feet. And while they still did not believe it because of joy and amazement, he asked them, "Do you have anything here to eat?" They gave him a piece of broiled fish, and he took it and ate it in their presence. Luke 24:36-43, NIV.

Talk about confusion!

The words that catch my attention are "They still did not believe it because of joy and amazement"(verse 41). The Revised Standard Version translates the passage as "they still disbelieved for joy, and wondered," and Moffatt renders it as "they could not believe it, for sheer joy; they were lost in wonder."

Whatever it was that they were experiencing, one fact stands out above all others: what had happened in the past 24 hours had totally overwhelmed Jesus' disciples. Their entire worldview had turned upside down as they oscillated between total despair and unbelievable joy. Now they were just plainly confused, as well as being frightened.

Jesus' task is to open their eyes a bit further by clarifying their vision, something that He does in three steps. First, He had to straighten out the disciples' misconceptions. They had swallowed some of the contemporary mythology about ghosts. He didn't explicitly correct them about the superstition, but He did demonstrate beyond a shadow of the doubt that His resurrected body was genuine flesh and blood. Seeing His pierced hands and feet and touching them helped. But the ultimate proof was His eating a piece of fish.

The second thing Jesus did at that point, John tells us, is that "he breathed on them, and said to them, 'Receive the Holy Spirit'" (John 20:22, RSV). The gift of the Spirit would continually lead them into further truth and a correcting of their eyesight.

Last, Luke tells us that Jesus took the roomful of disciples through the same Bible study regarding the Old Testament's presentation of His mission that He had earlier given to the two on the road to Emmaus. Thus "He opened their understanding, that they might comprehend the Scriptures" (Luke 24:45, NKJV).

Father, even today the Resurrection event seems too good to be true. Guide us as You did the disciples of old into an ever clearer and firmer faith is our prayer. Amen.

Strength Through Differences

Now Thomas, called the Twin, one of the twelve, was not with them when Jesus came. The other disciples therefore said to him, "We have seen the Lord." So he said to them, "Unless I see in His hands the print of the nails, and put my finger into the print of the nails, and put my hand into His side, I will not believe." And after eight days His disciples were again inside, and Thomas with them. Jesus came, the doors being shut, and stood in the midst, and said, "Peace to you!" Then He said to Thomas, "Reach your finger here, and look at My hands; and reach your hand here, and put it into My side. Do not be unbelieving, but believing." John 20:24-27, NKJV.

What do we know about Thomas the disciple? Not much! Outside of John's Gospel the only mentions of him appear in the lists of the disciples. But John provides us with a handful of passages that give us a glimmer of this "man in the background."

We first meet him as an individual disciple in John 11:16. Jesus had decided to go to Bethany after He had heard about the death of Lazarus. Thomas' response is revealing: "Let us also go, that we may die with him" (RSV). That short quotation provides us with a small glimpse of the man. It lets us know that Thomas was both courageous and pessimistic. He didn't expect much good to come out of the journey, but he was willing to accompany Jesus on it anyway. Thus we see loyalty to Him as a third characteristic.

The only other place we find Thomas speaking before today's passage is in John 14:5. Jesus had just told the disciples that they should not let their hearts be troubled because He was going to prepare a place for them and would return. He closed His brief presentation of the Second Advent by saying "and you know the way where I am going." Thomas' response was, "Lord, we do not know where you are going; how can we know the way?" (verses 4, 5, RSV).

In effect, Thomas was implying that Jesus hadn't made things clear enough. He was a person willing to move forward, but he wanted sufficient information before doing so.

That is what we find in John 20. But there the picture deepens a bit. We find Thomas unwilling to believe in the word of others. What they were claiming seemed to be too good to be true. They might have gotten one another overly excited and created something out of a sheer longing for release from agony and pain. His pessimistic nature with its desire for full information again surfaced. But when he met the resurrected Jesus his faith also came to fullness.

Some of us are like the hesitant Thomas, while others are like the impetuous Peter. If we were all Peters the church might run before it had sufficient knowledge. But if we were all Thomases we might never get started. The church of Christ needs both types for proper balance.

Thomas Sees the Light

*Thomas answered and said to Him, "My Lord and my God!" Jesus said to him,
"Because you have seen Me, have you believed? Blessed are they who did not see,
and yet believed."
Therefore many other signs Jesus performed in the presence of the disciples,
which are not written in this book; but these have been written that you may believe
that Jesus is the Christ, the Son of God; and that believing you may have life in His
name. John 20:28-31, NASB.*

His doubts removed, all Thomas could say is "My Lord and my God!" The hesitant disciple had come to faith. And that faith would shape the rest of his life. While the book of Acts (which focuses on Peter's proclamation in Jerusalem in the early part and Paul's work for the Gentiles in the latter) does not feature his future activities, a strong tradition in the early church tells us that Thomas, the courageous disciple who needed to know for sure before he moved, became the pioneer missionary to Persia and India. Southern India has an indigenous group known for centuries as Thomas Christians. They claim that he suffered martyrdom on St. Thomas Mount near Madras.

While we cannot prove that tradition (at least to the exacting standards of Thomas himself), we do know beyond a shadow of a doubt what drove the man for the rest of his life—the conviction that Jesus is "my Lord and my God." That firm belief became the guiding force and anchor point in his life.

But more important yet, it is the foundation for all Christianity. With that declaration by Thomas the Gospel of John has come full circle. Thomas is the first person in John to address Jesus as "God." Yet that is the truth that begins the fourth Gospel: "In the beginning was the Word, and the Word was with God, and the Word was God. . . . And the Word became flesh and dwelt among us" (John 1:1-14, RSV).

After that introduction, John guides his readers in a journey of discovery as we ourselves come to the conclusion, through the experiences of Thomas and others, that Jesus of Nazareth is indeed the Messiah, the Son of God. John tells us in his statement of purpose that he selected the material for his Gospel so that we might come to the same conclusion as Thomas ("That you may believe that Jesus is the Christ, the Son of God") and thereby obtain life eternal (John 20:30, 31, RSV).

John sought to demonstrate that apostolic conviction as firmly and certainly as possible because he knew that we could never be first-person witnesses to the Resurrection, but would of necessity have to rely on inspired Scripture. Thus *"blessed are those who have not seen and yet believe"* (verse 29, RSV).

Gospel Foundations

Now I would remind you, brothers, of the gospel I preached to you, which you received, in which you stand, and by which you are saved, if you hold fast to the word I preached to you—unless you believed in vain. For I delivered to you as of first importance what I also received: that Christ died for our sins in accordance with the Scriptures, that he was buried, that he was raised on the third day.
1 Cor. 15:1-4, ESV.

In our journey of turning our eyes upon Jesus we have witnessed His incarnation, His sinless life, His sacrificial death, and His resurrection from the dead. We have come to the end of His earthly life, but not to the end of His influence and work.

The ongoing impact of Christ on the world is summed up in one word: "gospel," which literally means "good news."

The apostle Paul is the Bible writer who most fully defines the saving gospel. Today we need to let his thoughts on the topic soak into our minds. One of Paul's best definitions appears in 1 Corinthians 15:1-4. The twin facts that Jesus died for our sins and that He rose that we might have life are the very foundation of the saving gospel. His death alone didn't save. Dead Saviors can't help anyone. Thus Jesus' resurrection is absolutely crucial to the good news. It is in many ways its central feature.

But before exploring further the significance of the Resurrection, we need to take a look at other aspects of the gospel, remembering all the while that they also rest on the bedrock accomplishments of Christ's death and resurrection.

Paul expounds on the word "gospel" again in Romans 1:16, 17, in which he claims that he is "not ashamed of the gospel: it is the power of God for salvation to every one who has faith, to the Jew first and also to the Greek. For in [the gospel] the righteousness of God is revealed through faith for faith; as it is written, 'He who through faith is righteous shall live'" (RSV). It is from that passage that we get the phrase "righteousness by faith."

Another passage, even though it doesn't use the word "gospel," certainly highlights its content. "For by grace you have been saved through faith; and this is not your own doing, it is the gift of God—not because of works, lest any man should boast" (Eph. 2:8, 9, RSV).

We need to read those passages again and again and meditate upon their meaning for our lives, remembering all the while that the saving power of the gospel in our lives is founded upon the two great anchor points of Christ's life that we have spent so much time on this year—His death for "my sins" and His resurrection that "I" also might have life.

November 11

Resurrection Power

He appeared to Cephas, then to the twelve. Then he appeared to more than five hundred brethren at one time, most of whom are still alive, though some have fallen asleep. Then he appeared to James, then to all the apostles. Last of all, as to one untimely born, he appeared also to me. 1 Cor. 15:5-8, RSV.

Paul has a burden on the topic of the Resurrection. So much so that he devotes what is probably his most extensive discussion on any single topic to Christ's resurrection and its meaning for our lives. The 58 verses of 1 Corinthians 15 are his tour de force on the Resurrection.

But Paul was not alone in this opinion. All of the Gospels, the books of Acts and Revelation, and the rest of the New Testament highlight the fact that "He has risen!"

Why? Because without that central fact we have nothing to believe in but a man who was a "nice guy" and had some good things to say while He was alive, but is now dead and powerless. That might be an adequate foundation for a philosophic school, but not for Christianity, a faith anchored in the reality that Christ lives and is a force in every believer's life. Because He lives, we as His followers have hope in both the present and the future.

But the Greek world in which Christianity was born doubted bodily resurrection and even the value of the body itself. Thus we find the great pains the New Testament writers expended to demonstrate not only that Christ rose, but that He did so with a physical body that they could see and touch, a body that could even eat fish. He was not a phantom or a ghost or a disembodied spirit, but the risen Lord Jesus who appeared to hundreds of witnesses, some of them very skeptical.

Paul himself had been one of those skeptics. To the pre-Christian Paul the resurrection of Jesus had been merely one more superstition cooked up by the disciples. His response to the "myth" was to stomp it out in a wave of persecution. And he did so until he himself met the resurrected Christ on the road to Damascus.

After that the reality of the Resurrection became the central point of his life. Paul surrendered his life to the direction and power of his resurrected Lord. And Jesus used him mightily.

The same resurrected Lord wants to take each of our lives and fill them with hope and energy and purpose. The only question is whether we will let Him.

Lord, thank You for the possibility of resurrection power. I accept it this day for the direction and energizing of my life.

Keys to the Grave

Do not be afraid, I am the first and the last, the living one. I am he who was dead, and now you see me alive for timeless ages! I hold in my hand the keys of death and the grave. Rev. 1:17, 18, Phillips.

D o not be afraid." Those words are remarkably similar to Jesus' "Let not your heart be troubled" on the night before His crucifixion (John 14:1-3). In the earlier passage Jesus tied the reason not to fear to His second advent. He was going to prepare a place for them and would return so that they could be with Him. John 14:1-3 does not mention His resurrection, but it is obviously implied.

Here in Revelation 1:17 and 18 mention of the Second Coming is not in the verses. But we do find it in verse 7, in which John declares that Jesus will come in the clouds and that "every eye will see him" (RSV). He can return because He is "the living one" who "was dead" but is "now . . . alive."

That is good news, but in the last part of verse 18 it gets even better. "I hold in my hand," declares the living One, "the keys of death and the grave." In ancient palaces the one who held the keys was an important person. That individual could admit or shut out people from the king's presence. The keys were a symbol of authority.

It is in the light of that fact that we can evaluate Jesus' statement on having the keys of death and the grave. All kinds of people could put individuals to death. There is no secret to that. Just pull a trigger and you can send someone on a one-way trip to the cemetery.

But the reverse is not so easy. It is impossible to bring people back to life, no matter how much money or power you have.

That is where Jesus' victory over death comes in. His resurrection demonstrated for all time that He alone has the keys of death and the grave.

As a result, His resurrection is a guarantee of that of His followers. Thus Christians have no need to fear. We serve a risen Lord! Nothing can happen to us that He cannot reverse—even death itself.

He not only arose, but He is "alive for evermore" (verse 18, RSV). Jesus did not rise to die again, but is the "living one, . . . alive for timeless ages." And with His keys He offers that same eternal life to each of His followers.

The final word: Fear not; we serve a risen Lord who will come again to provide His followers with life throughout the ages of eternity.

November 13

The Key to Apostolic Power

Then Peter, filled with the Holy Spirit, said to them, "Rulers of the people and elders, if we are being examined today concerning a good deed done to a cripple, by what means has this man been healed, be it known to you, and to all the people of Israel, that by the name of Jesus Christ of Nazareth, whom you crucified, whom God raised from the dead, by him this man is standing before you well. This is the stone which was rejected by you builders, but which has become the head of the corner. And there is salvation in no one else, for there is no other name under heaven given among men by which we must be saved." Acts 4:8-12, RSV.

Is this the same Peter who a few weeks before was shaking with fear and hiding lest he be identified as a follower of Jesus? Is this the same person who cursed and swore that he didn't know Jesus and that he was not His disciple?

Yes and no. Yes because he had the same body and name. But no because the cowardly Peter had been transformed, so much so that he now fearlessly addresses the powerful Sanhedrin, the governing body of the Jews, the very same group that had sentenced Jesus to death.

Acts 4 continues on to say that the Jewish rulers "when they saw the boldness of Peter and John, and perceived that they were uneducated, common men, . . . wondered; and they recognized that they had been with Jesus" (verse 13, RSV).

Not knowing what to do with the troublesome apostles, the Jewish leaders "charged them not to speak or teach at all in the name of Jesus. But Peter and John answered them, 'Whether it is right in the sight of God to listen to you rather than to God, you must judge; for we cannot but speak of what we have seen and heard'" (verses 18-20, RSV).

Later, after the authorities imprisoned them for their faith, the transformed Peter and his colleagues, having been released miraculously, were found "standing in the temple and teaching the people" openly (Acts 5:17-25, RSV). When brought again before the Sanhedrin, "Peter and the apostles answered, 'We must obey God rather than men. The God of our fathers raised Jesus whom you killed by hanging on a tree. God exalted him at his right hand as Leader and Savior, to give repentance to Israel and forgiveness of sins. And we are witnesses to these things" (verses 29-32, RSV).

The preaching of Christ's resurrection provided the central certainty in the apostolic message. They no longer feared because they now served a risen Lord who had the keys of death and the grave. Not even powerful people could do anything to them. Having seen the risen One, they knew what they were talking about. And no one could shut them up.

Such is the transforming power of resurrection faith.

Centrality of the Key

Paul, a servant of Jesus Christ, called to be an apostle and set apart for the gospel
of God—the gospel he promised beforehand through his prophets in the Holy
Scriptures regarding his Son, who as to his earthly life was a descendant of David,
and who through the Spirit of holiness was appointed the Son of God in power by
his resurrection from the dead: Jesus Christ our Lord. Through him we received
grace and apostleship. Rom. 1:1-5, NIV.

The words we want to focus on are "through the Spirit of holiness [Jesus] was appointed the Son of God in power by his resurrection from the dead." *The Message* renders verses 3 and 4 helpfully: "His descent from David roots him in history; his unique identity as Son of God was shown by the Spirit when Jesus was raised from the dead, setting him apart as the Messiah, our Master."

If Jesus had come to earth and merely lived a good (even perfect) life and died a violent death, He would have been just one more noble and heroic person. But still dead like the rest of them.

The good news, Paul reminds us, is about not merely another good man who came to an unjust end. To the contrary, His resurrection demonstrates Him to be the powerful Son of God. The good news is that Jesus lives to continue His work for those who have accepted Him. Thus His resurrection also stands at the center of Paul's gospel message. "Before that" event, Anders Nygren points out, Jesus "was the Son of God in weakness and lowliness. Through the resurrection He became the Son of God in power."

Christ's resurrection, as I noted before, is the hinge of history. Without it Christianity would have never existed. It would have ended in a Palestinian grave, with a few frightened disciples trying to keep the memory of Jesus of Nazareth alive until they finally died or gave up in discouragement. William Barclay is right on target when he asserts that "one thing is certain—if Jesus had not risen from the dead we would never have heard of Him."

But Jesus did arise. And that single fact transformed and energized His followers. His was a victory over death. And in the long run it signals the end of death itself. The Resurrection is the great victory of God the Father and Jesus over Satan and the forces and power of death. It demonstrates that God is truly in control.

Without the Resurrection, Christianity would have nothing to offer the world but a few nice ideas. But with the Resurrection came power to the disciples and hope to a lost and suffering world.

Praise God that Jesus has risen!

November 15

Pitiable, Foolish, Keyless "Christianity"

If Christ is not risen, your faith is futile; you are still in your sins! Then also those who have fallen asleep in Christ have perished. If in this life only we have hope in Christ, we are of all men the most pitiable. 1 Cor. 15:17-19, NKJV.

B ut," Paul goes on to say, "now Christ is risen from the dead, and has become the firstfruits of those who have fallen asleep. For since by man came death, by Man also came the resurrection of the dead. For as in Adam all die, even so in Christ all shall be made alive. But each one in his own order: Christ the firstfruits, afterward those who are Christ's at His coming. Then comes the end, when He delivers the kingdom to God the Father" (1 Cor. 15:20-24, NKJV).

A resurrectionless Christianity is the height of folly, making Christians, as Paul put it, the most pitiable of all people. People who claim the name of Christ without His resurrection have kept the husk but have thrown away the fruit. They are living a powerless falsehood.

Yet that is exactly what some of the Corinthians had done. Paul's massive assault on the topic in 1 Corinthians 15 sought to put them straight by highlighting the truth of the Resurrection and the foolishness of rejecting it—a path that leads to meaningless "Christianity."

The interesting thing about the Corinthian crisis is that theologians and ministers reinvented it during the Enlightenment period, and it became a major plank in the belief system of the mainline Protestant denominations of the twentieth century.

Modern people were just too smart to believe in such foolishness. Dead people don't come to life. The disciples invented the idea to cover up their mistake. H. Richard Niebuhr summed up modernistic Christianity when he penned that "a God without wrath brought men without sin into a kingdom without judgment through the ministrations of a Christ without a cross." And, he could have added, "without a resurrection." The result was a form of religion focused on ethics and doing good.

The upshot was powerless churches that would eventually begin to shrink and die. They had thrown away the core of the biblical message. And with that one stroke, as I have said in my *Apocalyptic Vision and the Neutering of Adventism*, they managed to emasculate themselves.

Such will be the fate of any movement that turns its back on the pillar truths that made it strong. And for all of Christianity there is no more vital and important *fact* than the risen Christ.

Jesus Comes When We Need Him

After this Jesus revealed himself again to the disciples by the Sea of Tiberias; and he revealed himself in this way. Simon Peter, Thomas called the Twin, Nathanael of Cana in Galilee, the sons of Zebedee, and two others of his disciples were together. Simon Peter said to them, "I am going fishing." They said to him, "We will go with you." They went out and got into the boat; but that night they caught nothing. Just as day was breaking, Jesus stood on the beach, yet the disciples did not know that it was Jesus. . . . He said to them, "Cast the net on the right side of the boat, and you will find some [fish]." So they cast it, and now they were not able to haul it in, for the quantity of fish. That disciple whom Jesus loved said to Peter, "It is the Lord!" When Simon Peter heard that it was the Lord, he put on his clothes . . . and sprang into the sea. But the other disciples came in the boat, dragging the net full of fish. John 21:1-8, RSV.

Why had they gone fishing? I can't say for sure. But I do know that when I am discouraged I like to just get away from it all, to find some peace and quiet. One of my escapes is to read beside a fast-running stream. Another is to go fishing.

But these seven disciples may have had a deeper reason. The Crucifixion had destroyed their world. And while it is true that the resurrected Jesus had appeared to them twice already, they weren't altogether sure what to make out of life. They were still in a fog of confusion. And for Peter there was still that business of his denial that continued to trouble him day and night.

Without any sure guidance for the future, perhaps the best thing to do was to get on with life. The world they knew was fishing. Seemed strange, going back, but they had families to feed. Perhaps they should settle down and do something sensible for a change. Like earning money.

Good idea. But it didn't work. They fished all night with no results. But at dawn this "guy" shows up on the beach and starts asking them questions. They don't recognize Him at first. But as soon as He tells them where to get the fish and they get enough to feed the whole village with one cast of their net, they know exactly who He is.

The troubled Peter immediately jumps into the water and swims to shore, even though he knew full well that he was abandoning his share of the work of getting the boat and its catch back to his six friends.

Why? Because Peter was a tormented man who had sinned grievously and could hardly sleep at night. He needed healing but didn't know what to do about it. And then Jesus came.

But then He always comes. No matter what you and I have done, Jesus makes Himself available to us for our healing and restoration. That is a part of His resurrection ministry. The good news is that He comes to us when we need Him.

November 17

A Tale of Two Fires

So when they got out on the land, they saw a charcoal fire already laid and fish placed on it, and bread. . . . Jesus said to them, "Come and have breakfast." . . . So when they had finished breakfast, Jesus said to Simon Peter, "Simon, son of John, do you love Me more than these?" He said to Him, "Yes, Lord; You know that I love You." He said to him, "Tend My lambs." He said to him again a second time, "Simon, son of John, do you love Me?" He said to Him, "Yes, Lord; You know that I love You." He said to him, "Shepherd My sheep." He said to him the third time, "Simon, son of John, do you love Me?" Peter was grieved because He said to him the third time, "Do you love Me?" And he said to Him, "Lord, You know all things; You know that I love You." Jesus said to him, "Tend My sheep." John 21:9-17, NASB.

It all began and ended around two charcoal fires. Before that first fire Peter was the most exuberant of the disciples, telling Jesus that he would never let Him down, that he would follow Him no matter where the path led—even to prison or death. He claimed that he was willing to lay down his life for Christ.

And then came that charcoal fire, where the servants of the high priest and certain officers stood around warming themselves (John 18:18). Peter joined them. Fateful move. Beginning at that fire he would step by step deny Christ three times, eventually cursing and swearing that he did not know Him. During the days and nights of agony that followed, Peter could never forgive himself. Having sinned in an almost unimaginable way, he could never escape the genuine guilt of his betrayal. Life had lost its sparkle.

The second charcoal fire reminded Peter of the first one. The very smell brought back memories. Jesus knew what he had done. God knew. John knew. And Peter *knew*. Not even the Resurrection itself could dispel his feelings of guilt and the haunting memory. Only revisiting the scene in a healing context would ever help.

Around that second charcoal fire the number three is again significant. But this time it relates to three questions from Jesus and three agonizing responses from Peter. As the charcoal fire burns, the number three becomes a reminder of Peter's betrayal of the Lamb that takes away the sin of the world (John 1:29). And, to Peter's inexpressible relief, the Lamb takes his sin away. But Jesus doesn't just say "It's all right, forget about it." No, three times He recommissions His fallen disciple to work for Him.

There is something for each of us in this story. If we are awake at all to spiritual things, we will notice the smell of a charcoal fire in the air that we breathe. But there is also our Lord willing not only to forgive us but to restore us.

An End That Is a Beginning

Then the eleven disciples went away into Galilee, to the mountain which Jesus had appointed for them. When they saw Him, they worshiped Him; but some doubted. And Jesus came and spoke to them, saying, "All authority has been given to Me in heaven and on earth. Go therefore and make disciples of all nations, baptizing them in the name of the Father and of the Son and of the Holy Spirit, teaching them to observe all things that I have commanded you; and lo, I am with you always, even to the end of the age." Amen. Matt. 28:16-20, NKJV.

Matthew's concluding paragraph finds the resurrected Jesus meeting with His disciples and apparently some of the more than 500 who saw Him in His resurrected body before He ascended. That meeting began in worship and ended in service.

We should note several things about verses 16-20. First, those present worship Jesus, but some doubt. With the hesitating Thomas having finally accepted the resurrection of Jesus, the 11 disciples were definitely among those who worshipped Him. The doubters were evidently some of the more than 500 witnesses to the Resurrection who had not seen Him up to that time. But the fact that the disciples and others worshipped Jesus is important. For Jews to take that step meant that they had accepted His full divinity as an equal with the Father.

Second, Jesus received "all authority . . . in heaven and on earth." Authority has been a major issue throughout the gospel story, and world dominion was the issue in the third temptation when Satan offered Jesus "all the kingdoms of the world." But Jesus had chosen the way of the cross. And because of His victorious life, death, and resurrection, He has "all authority" for dominion in "all nations" for all time. Jesus is truly Lord.

Third, Jesus delegates His authority to His followers for the express purpose of enabling them to go into all the world to make disciples and baptize them in the "name" of the Trinity (name is in the singular, thereby indicating that the three Persons of the Godhead are united). Part of their commission is not only to teach the full message of Jesus, but also to observe His teachings. Obedience for Jesus was never an option. Christianity is not merely a change of belief, but a transformation in how people live. Fourth, Jesus will be with His church until the end of the age. He continues to be "God with us" (Matt. 1:23) as long as time shall last.

With what has been called the gospel commission we have come to the end of the story of Jesus in Matthew. But the ending is really a beginning. The teachings in this verse would eventually stimulate Jesus' followers to take His message to the ends of the earth. It is a mission in which we twenty-first-century disciples still participate. Christianity may begin in worship, but it always ends in service.

The Waiting Time

You are witnesses of these things. And behold, I send the promise of my Father upon you; but stay in the city, until you are clothed with power from on high.
Luke 24:48, 49, RSV.

To them he presented himself alive after his passion by many proofs, appearing to them during forty days, and speaking of the kingdom of God. And while staying with them he charged them not to depart from Jerusalem, but to wait for the promise of the Father, which, he said, "you heard from me, for John baptized with water, but before many days you shall be baptized with the Holy Spirit" Acts 1:3-5, RSV.

Luke ends his Gospel and begins his history of the early Christian church in Acts of the Apostles with the same thought. Namely, that Jesus charged His followers not to move forward in His Great Commission to them to take the gospel message to the world until they had received the power of the Holy Spirit to accomplish the task.

That was just the advice they needed at that time. Filled with the excitement of the Resurrection, the natural thing would be to rush out and tell others about the greatest truth in history.

But Jesus recognized that they were not ready for action yet. He realized that even though they had the truth of the gospel message, they still lacked the power to preach it successfully. "The Saviour knew that no argument, however logical, would melt hard hearts or break through the crust of worldliness and selfishness. He knew that His disciples must receive the heavenly endowment; that the gospel would be effective only as it was proclaimed by hearts made warm and lips made eloquent by a living knowledge of Him who is the way, the truth, and the life. The work committed to the disciples would require great efficiency; for the tide of evil ran deep and strong against them. A vigilant, determined leader was in command of the forces of darkness, and the followers of Christ could battle for the right only through the help that God, by His Spirit, would give them" (*The Acts of the Apostles*, p. 31).

One of the most difficult truths for genuine believers to grasp is that waiting is often more important than action. Too many of us are like Peter. We jump into action before we know exactly what we are doing—we charge ahead without the power to accomplish the task.

Waiting time must always precede exploits. Study, prayer, discussion, and sharing wisdom are important. The time for action will come after we have the Spirit's power and direction and wisdom to carry out our Lord's mission according to His will.

Jesus' Mission Plan, Part 1

But ye shall receive power, after that the Holy Ghost is come upon you: and ye shall be witnesses unto me both in Jerusalem, and in all Judaea, and in Samaria, and unto the uttermost part of the earth. Acts 1:8.

Jesus had a plan. A successful mission is not something that just happens. It needs thought, direction, and power. The first step in Jesus' massive plan was for His followers to be fully equipped for their daunting task. That would take not only knowledge, which He had supplied them with while He was on earth, but divine power.

The Greek word for "power" is *dynamis*, from which we derive our word "dynamite." I vividly remember a trip I took across the desert of southern California nearly 50 years ago. What caught my attention was a blinding flash on a mountain some miles in the distance. Next, I saw a huge cloud of dirt and debris. At that point the first sound waves shook my car, and I realized that I had witnessed a mighty explosion. The explosive agent in that case had undoubtedly been dynamite. Dynamite is a form of *dynamis* or power. Paul ties the gospel message to that same force when he writes that "the gospel . . . is the power of God that brings salvation to everyone who believes" (Rom. 1:16, NIV).

One reason that he is not ashamed of the gospel is that it is backed by God's power. And one thing the apostle makes crystal clear in the early chapters of Romans is that people are unable to save themselves from the hold of sin. No matter how hard they try, they can't free themselves from its ravages. That's where God's power comes in. He can do what we cannot.

That truth applies to both the saving of sinners and the spreading of the truth of the gospel. And it is the Holy Spirit who is God's agent in those tasks. The work of the Spirit undergirds all true Christian evangelism. Without the Spirit there is no *dynamis*.

That brings us to part 2 in Jesus' mission plan. He calls His Spirit-empowered followers to be His agents or witnesses. Here we find another important Greek word, *martys*, from which we get the English word "martyr." Originally the word stood for someone bearing witness in a court of law. But in the New Testament it came to mean one who witnessed or bore testimony to the truth of the gospel of Christ. Eventually it signified someone willing to die rather than give up Jesus and the preaching of His message.

God is still calling people to be His witnesses in power. Today He is summoning me and you personally. How shall we respond?

Jesus' Mission Plan, Part 2

But you are to be given power when the Holy Spirit has come to you. You will be witnesses to me, not only in Jerusalem, not only throughout Judea, not only in Sa-maria, but to the ends of the earth. Acts 1:8, Phillips.

When we think of world mission we too often have a mental image of going far away to some foreign land where the "heathen" have never heard about Jesus. Christ, Himself, set forward just the opposite program. His command is for us to start with the "heathen" in our own town.

For the earliest disciples that meant Jerusalem. Jesus had sown gospel seed in the Jewish metropolis for years. It was there that He "had been condemned and crucified. In Jerusalem were many who secretly believed Jesus of Nazareth to be the Messiah, and many who had been deceived by priests and rulers. To these the gospel must be proclaimed" (*The Acts of the Apostles*, p. 31).

What we find in the book of Acts is the filling out of the mission program or schedule set forth in Acts 1:8. Obeying Jesus' advice, His followers first preached the gospel in Jerusalem. And the fruit came fast because of the many waiting hearts who had already known about Jesus but had not yet decided to dedicate their lives to Him. The harvest was now ripe and about 3,000 Jewish believers would be baptized on the day of Pentecost (Acts 2:41), with more joining the church with each passing day (verse 47). Even "a great many of the priests" became "obedient to the faith" (Acts 6:7, RSV).

While the first post-Pentecostal step in Christian mission took place in Jerusalem (Acts 2-6), the martyrdom of Stephen (Acts 7) led to the believers being "scattered throughout the region of Judea and Samaria" (Acts 8:1, NKJV). And with that event the action of Christian mission broadened, like the rings in water caused by a falling stone. Acts 8 highlights the ministry of Philip in Samaria. Then Acts 10 features Peter reluctantly bringing the message of Christ to a Gentile. And with the conversion of Cornelius the non-Jew the way opened for the gospel to go to the rest of the world, a process that Acts sets forth in the work of the apostle Paul from Acts 13 to 28.

Paul's work, of course, is just one arm of the apostolic mission to take the gospel to the ends of the earth. As we noted earlier, Thomas carried it to Persia and probably India. Others proclaimed Christ in Africa and other places. The ever-widening circle of Christian outreach will continue until the "whole world" has heard the message of the risen Christ. "Then the end will come" (Matt. 24:14, RSV).

A Faith-building Event

*Now when He had spoken these things, while they watched, He was taken up, and
a cloud received Him out of their sight. And while they looked steadfastly toward
heaven as He went up, behold, two men stood by them in white apparel, who also
said, "Men of Galilee, why do you stand gazing up into heaven? This same Jesus,
who was taken up from you into heaven, will so come in like manner as you saw
Him go into heaven." Acts 1:9-11, NKJV.*

The next essential step in the ministry of Jesus for a lost world has arrived.
We have seen so far His incarnation, sinless life, death, and resurrection.
Now we witness His ascension. And here we can be thankful for Luke, the only
Bible writer who describes this event.

The first thing we should note about the Ascension is that it was public.
And that was important. The alternative would have been a quiet disappearance that left Jesus' bewildered followers puzzled as to where He had gone.
That would have resulted in a picture of Jesus appearing to His disciples less
and less often until they finally saw Him no more. Eventually they would have
wondered what they believed in.

But Jesus didn't do it that way. All the leading disciples and many others
saw Him rise from the earth and return to heaven—an event they would never
forget. They served a Lord who had not only risen from the grave but also from
the earth. The manner in which Jesus departed was faith building. It had to
bring to the minds of the disciples Jesus' words on the night before His crucifixion when He told His followers not to let their hearts be troubled because He
was returning to heaven to prepare a place for them and would come again for
them. The public manner of the Ascension was a visible, public demonstration
of the first half of that promise.

One of the more interesting aspects of today's passage is the question of the
angels: "Why do you stand gazing up into heaven?" The answer seems to be
obvious. If we saw someone from our church (or anyone else) floating toward
heaven, we would be left both gawking and speechless.

The public ascension of Jesus was absolutely essential for the disciples. Because of it they knew that they served a risen Lord who had gone to heaven to
minister in their behalf. They weren't altogether sure what that meant. But they
could have faith that they were not alone.

And we have that same faith.

*Thank You, Father, for the ascension of Jesus. As we meditate upon that
event may its meaning become ever more clear in our hearts and minds.*

November 23

Preparing for Action

Then he led them out as far as Bethany, and lifting up his hands he blessed them. While he blessed them, he parted from them, and was carried up into heaven. And they returned to Jerusalem with great joy, and were continually in the temple bless-ing God. Luke 24:50-53, RSV.

H ere is Luke's other account of the Ascension. Jesus had been with His fol-lowers for 40 days since the cross, offering them "many proofs, appearing to them . . . , and speaking of the kingdom of God" (Acts 1:3, RSV).

And now He was leaving as the disciples stood awestruck as He was caught up to heaven. But the angels assured them that He would return for them in just as public a way as they had seen Him go (verse 11).

Christ's ascension divided their lives into two parts. It signified an ending of their apprenticeship, in which they had been daily taught by the incarnate Jesus. And it also signaled a beginning, in which they would be left to guide and shepherd the church of their risen Lord.

Luke 24:53 tells us that after witnessing the Ascension they "returned to Jerusalem with great joy, and were continually in the temple blessing God" (RSV). That is probably an understatement. My guess is that the apostles and their friends must have fairly skipped all the way back to Jerusalem, shouting to each other as they recounted the events of the past few weeks. They had a great deal to rejoice over. Beyond the shadow of a doubt they knew that they had a friend in heaven. And they couldn't keep their mouths shut.

But they also had other things to attend to. The Ascension took place 40 days after Passover. And Pentecost would occur at day 50. In the interim Jesus had commanded them not to depart from Jerusalem, but to await the promised power of the Holy Spirit.

Acts records that they returned to Jerusalem and "went up to the upper room, where they were staying." Then Luke tells us, after listing the disciples, that "all these with one accord devoted themselves to prayer, together with the women and Mary the mother of Jesus, and with his brothers" (Acts 1:12-14, RSV).

Christianity is more than public rejoicing in the Temple. It is also praying to God in the privacy of our own upper room as we seek Him out for power to witness more effectively to other believers and to the world around us.

The truth of the matter is that in the long run we need quiet time with God if our public work for Him is to have authenticity and power.

Inaugural Event

Then I looked, and I heard around the throne and the living creatures and the elders the voice of many angels, numbering myriads of myriads and thousands of thousands, saying with a loud voice, "Worthy is the Lamb who was slain, to receive power and wealth and wisdom and might and honor and glory and blessing!" And I heard every creature in heaven and on earth and under the earth and in the sea, and all therein, saying, "To him who sits upon the throne and to the Lamb be bless- ing and honor and glory and might for ever and ever!" And the four living creatures said, "Amen!" and the elders fell down and worshiped. Rev. 5:11-14, RSV.

The scene now shifts. The Ascension not only means that the resurrected Christ departs from the earth, but also that He arrives in heaven. And He doesn't do so merely as a weary pilgrim but as a conquering King. Jesus has completed the work that He left His place in heaven to accomplish. Now He is inaugurated or, more accurately, reinaugurated as the one worthy to take an equal place with the Father on His throne.

Thus the scene shifts from the disciples rejoicing in the earthly Temple to the angelic hosts praising in the heavenly Temple. In that great Temple scene Revelation 4 and 5 present a sequence of praises as the Lamb rejoins the Father on inauguration day.

The praises focus on Jesus' worthiness as "the Lamb who was slain." At the cross heaven defeated Satan. That event assured the security of a universe in trouble. It is now history. The present for the heavenly throng is praise and adoration in the superlative.

And what is the worthy inaugural Lamb to receive? Power for one thing. The risen Christ, sitting on the throne of the universe, will be able to dispense power to His followers on earth. The first earthward expression of that power takes place on the day of Pentecost when the apostles receive the blessing of the Holy Spirit. Thus the inauguration had an earthly side. Once again we see a connection between events on earth and heavenly realities. With Jesus on the throne His followers on earth are assured of heavenly gifts.

Power, of course, is but one item in the list of gifts to the Lamb who was slain—wealth, wisdom, might, honor, glory, and blessing are also His. The in- augural scene closes with the entire universe joining in on the greatest praise session in the history of the universe.

As we seek to grasp the reality and wonder of these events, we need carefully to study and meditate upon the songs in Revelation 4 and 5. They will help us enter more fully into true worship as we apply these lessons to our daily devotional life.

November 25

A Tale of Two Inaugurals

When the day of Pentecost had come, they were all together in one place. And suddenly a sound came from heaven like the rush of a mighty wind, and it filled all the house where they were sitting. And there appeared to them as tongues of fire, distributed and resting on each one of them. And they were all filled with the Holy Spirit and began to speak in other tongues, as the Spirit gave them utterance. . . . When they heard this [Peter's message] they were cut to the heart, and said to Peter and the rest of the apostles, "Brethren, what shall we do?" And Peter said to them, "Repent, and be baptized every one of you in the name of Jesus Christ for the forgiveness of your sins. . . . There were added that day about three thousand souls. Acts 2:1-41, RSV.

The great event in the throne room of heaven at the inaugural of Christ had accompanying events on earth that signaled the beginning of a new age in which Christ's followers would eventually become a force on earth through the power of the Holy Spirit.

Ellen White illustrates the connection between the two inaugurals when she writes that "the Pentecostal outpouring was Heaven's communication that the Redeemer's inauguration was accomplished. According to His promise He had sent the Holy Spirit from heaven to His followers as a token that He had, as priest and king, received all authority in heaven and on earth, and was the Anointed One over His people" (*The Acts of the Apostles*, p. 39).

The Jewish holiday of Pentecost was the very best day of the year for such a demonstration. Pentecost means "fiftieth," and took place 50 days after Passover and the Feast of Unleavened Bread. The Hebrew calendar called it the Feast of Weeks (since it took place a week of weeks after the Passover and its related events) and the Feast of Firstfruits (since on that day the priests offered two loaves of grain in thankfulness for the beginning of the grain harvest).

By that time of year (early June) travel was safer and Jerusalem hosted the largest and most varied assortment of worshippers of any time of the year. People from all over the empire would be in the city.

It was a propitious time for Christ's inaugural in heaven and His initiation of a new era on earth. On the day of Pentecost, through the mighty Spirit-empowered preaching of Peter, type met antitype and the meaning of "firstfruits" took on new significance as the firstfruits of the Christian message came in through the power of the Spirit. That day about 3,000 individuals accepted the message of Jesus Christ as the crucified and resurrected Lord and Messiah.

But Pentecost was only the beginning of the new age in God's work. Christ's inaugural blessing will remain with His church until His return at the end of the age. With the bestowal of the Spirit heaven poured out its richest gift.

A Friend on the Throne

He [Jesus] is the radiance of His [God's] glory and the exact representation of His
nature, and upholds all things by the word of His power. When He [Jesus] had made
purification of sins, He sat down at the right hand of the Majesty on high.
Heb. 1:3, NASB.

So, we need to ask, where did Jesus go when He ascended?
Stephen answered that question in reporting the vision he received just before he became the first Christian martyr. In it he saw the risen Jesus in heaven
at the right hand of God (Acts 7:56).

But it is the book of Hebrews more than any other in the Bible that describes where Jesus went and what He has been doing for the past 2,000 years.
The opening verses tell us that after "He had made purification of sins, He sat
down at the right hand of" God. And Hebrews 1:8 highlights both Jesus' divinity and His place on the throne. "But of the Son," we read, "Thy throne, O God,
is for ever and ever, the righteous scepter is the scepter of thy kingdom" (RSV).

Today's passage has two important ideas, the first is that the divine Jesus
did indeed take His seat on the governing throne of the universe in the place of
honor at the right hand of the Father. In using that terminology the author of
Hebrews is alluding to Psalm 110:1: "The Lord said to my lord: 'Sit at my right
hand, till I make your enemies your footstool'" (RSV). That verse is the most
cited Old Testament verse in the New Testament, and it undergirds much of
the presentation in the entire book of Hebrews.

Of special interest in Hebrews 1:3 is that Jesus "sat down" at God's right
hand. Earthly priests stood while performing their functions because they
were continually offering sacrifices. But Jesus, who died "once for all" (Heb.
10:10, 14), had put an end to the need for any further sacrifice. His sacrificial
work had been accomplished and never needs to be repeated. Thus the words
"sat down" have an air of finality about them. Jesus "had made purification of
sins." It was a completed work. He could now "sit down."

The Gospels highlight the great substitutionary sacrifice of Christ, "the
Lamb of God, who takes away the sin of the world" (John 1:29, RSV). That part
of Christ's work is over. He now moves on to the priestly aspect of His work,
which is the focal point of the book of Hebrews. Another way of saying it is that
in the Gospels Jesus accomplished our salvation, while in His heavenly priesthood He will apply the benefits of what He has done to each of His followers.

November 27

Jesus' Work in Heaven

We have such a High Priest, who is seated at the right hand of the throne of the Majesty in the heavens, a Minister of the sanctuary and of the true tabernacle which the Lord erected, and not man. Heb. 8:1, 2, NKJV.

W e have a High Priest in heaven. With that statement we know what Jesus has been doing since the Ascension. He had finished the sacrificial aspect of His ministry and has moved to the priestly.

In describing His priestly ministry the book of Hebrews becomes quite specific. Jesus is not merely somewhere up in heaven, but is ministering in the "true tabernacle which the lord erected, and not man." Prior to these verses, Hebrews has indicated the existence of a heavenly sanctuary. But in today's passage the book begins to present the heavenly sanctuary as the seat of God's operations.

The idea of a heavenly sanctuary wasn't completely new to the Jewish mind. Several pre-Christian Jewish documents allude to it. Central to their understanding was Exodus 25:8, 9, in which God told Moses regarding the Israelites, "Let them make me a sanctuary, that I may dwell in their midst. According to all that I show you concerning the *pattern* of the tabernacle, and of all its furniture, so shall you make it" (RSV). Hebrews 8 utilizes Exodus 25 as the foundation for its presentation of the heavenly sanctuary, or the "true tabernacle," that provided the "pattern" for the wilderness sanctuary and its ministries, which were only a "copy and shadow" of heavenly realities (Heb. 8:5, NKJV). Later Jewish thought also connected God's throne to the heavenly Temple (see Isa. 6:1).

Thus the idea of a heavenly sanctuary that contains God's throne was nothing new to Jewish thinking. The concept that would have been novel to them was the fact that Jesus was now there serving as high priest in their behalf.

What the book of Hebrews is arguing is that Christ's ministry is the real thing, while the Levitical ministry was merely an illustration that pointed toward His future work. Just as all of the animal sacrifices foretell Jesus' once-for-all sacrifice as the Lamb of God and the real Passover (1 Cor. 5:7), in the same way the earthly sanctuary directed attention to the true sanctuary in heaven.

In short, priestly ministry has shifted from earth to heaven and to Jesus as the true High Priest. The rending of the curtain from top to bottom at the very time of His sacrifice on the cross signaled the transfer (Matt. 27:51). The Most Holy of the earthly Temple was no longer holy.

It is time to turn our eyes to heaven and what Jesus is now doing for us.

Coming Boldly Before God's Throne

Seeing then that we have a great High Priest who has passed through the heavens,
Jesus the Son of God, let us hold fast our confession. For we do not have a High
Priest who cannot sympathize with our weaknesses, but was in all points tempted as
we are, yet without sin. Let us therefore come boldly to the throne of grace, that we
may obtain mercy and find grace to help in time of need. Heb. 4:14-16, NKJV.

One of the most significant truths in the New Testament is that "we have a great High Priest" who passed through the atmospheric and starry heavens after His ascension to meet God.

He is the Son of God, and thus has access to the Father. But Jesus is much more than a divine Being "out there." At His incarnation He became "God with us" (Matt. 1:23). As a result, He can "sympathize with our weaknesses" because He "was in all points tempted as we are." Jesus understands us in ways that would not have been possible had He not partaken of our sufferings. Here is a unique Person—one who has access to both God and individual humans. In that position He serves as the link between sinful people and a holy God. Thus He is our High Priest—the bridge between two incompatible worlds.

We should not pass over lightly the humanness of Jesus highlighted in today's verses. In the Greek world into which Jesus was born, the idea of God was that of detachment from humanity. Philo (a Jewish theologian/philosopher contemporary with Jesus and the apostles) promoted that detachment in the person of the high priest when he wrote that such an individual needs "to show himself superior to pity, and pass the whole of his life exempt from all sorrow" (*The Special Laws* 1:115).

Jesus was plainly the opposite of the Greek ideal. He became flesh and blood and suffered from the same types of temptations that we do. As a result, He understands us. He is one of us—we are His brothers and sisters (Heb. 2:10). It is because of that experience that He can sympathize with us as we face trials, temptations, and even death—He has passed through all of those things.

Therefore, the book of Hebrews tells us, we can come "boldly to the throne of grace" to find both mercy and grace in our times of distress. Because we have such a High Priest the doors of the heavenly Temple are wide open to us. No matter how dark our sin, no matter how deep our hurt, no matter how profound our disillusionment, we are welcomed at the throne of God by a High Priest who truly understands us.

Today as we bow before the throne of the Almighty let us praise Him again that we can come "boldly" rather than with fear or doubt. Our High Priest is there, ever willing to help us.

November 29

Jesus: The Better Way

He entered once for all into the Holy Place ["Holies" in Greek], taking not the blood
of goats and calves but his own blood, thus securing an eternal redemption.
Heb. 9:12, RSV.

J esus didn't enter the throne room of heaven (called the "Holies" in Hebrews,
the name for the heavenly Temple) empty-handed. He entered as our High
Priest who had also been our sacrifice. On the cross He had died for my sins that
I might have His righteousness (2 Cor. 5:21). It is little wonder that the songwrit-
ers speak of "the cleansing blood." Hebrews 9:22 helps us see the importance
of that sacrifice when it notes that "without the shedding of blood there is no
forgiveness of sins" (RSV). Of course, as Hebrews argues, the repeated Jewish
sacrifices could never take away sin and its penalty. All they could do was point
to the "Lamb of God," who would remove the sin of the world. Hebrews 9:23, 24
highlights that truth when it tells us that "it was necessary for the copies of the
heavenly things to be purified with these rites [the repeated sacrifice of sheep
and goats], but the heavenly things themselves with better sacrifices [Christ's
atoning death] than these. For Christ has entered, not into a sanctuary ["holies"
in Greek] made with hands, a copy of the true one, but into heaven itself, now to
appear in the presence of God on our behalf" (RSV).

One of the key phrases in this section of the book of Hebrews is "once for
all." Christ "once for all . . . offered up himself" (Heb. 7:27, RSV). He appeared
"once for all at the end of the age to put away sin by the sacrifice of himself"
(Heb. 9:26, RSV). "We have all been sanctified through the offering of the body
of Jesus Christ once for all" (Heb. 10:10, RSV). And "he entered once for all
into the [Holies], taking not the blood of goats and calves but his own blood,
thus securing an eternal redemption" (Heb. 9:12, RSV).

Those verses bring us to another key word in the book of Hebrews—"better."
The whole book builds on that term. Thus Jesus is better than the angels (Heb.
1:4-2:18), better than Moses and Joshua (Heb. 3:1-4:13), and better than Aaron
(Heb. 4:14-6:20). He also has a better priesthood (Heb. 7:1-28), a better covenant
(Heb. 8:1-10:18), and faith in Him is a better way (Heb. 10:19-11:40).

For all of those reasons believers in Him can come boldly before the throne
with full assurance that they have a sympathetic High Priest in heaven who is
taking care of the sin problem in terms of its effects in the universe and in their
personal lives.

Thank You, Father, for the heavenly object lesson of the sanctuary that helps
us to understand the reality of what Jesus is now doing for us in heaven.

He Is Able!

The former priests were many in number, because they were prevented by death
from continuing in office; but he [Jesus] holds his priesthood permanently, because
he continues for ever. Consequently he is able for all time to save those who draw
near to God through him, since he always lives to make intercession for them.
Heb. 7:23-25, RSV.

He is able"! Possibly the most profound words in human history. Jesus is able to "save them to the uttermost that come unto God by him" (Heb. 7:25, KJV), because He not only offered a better sacrifice, but also has a better priesthood, one that will continue until sin is no more and atonement is complete.

"He is able." Those who trust in Jesus need not fear. His hand is not shortened that it cannot save (Isa. 50:2). Unlike the Levitical priests who died, the resurrected Jesus is always there for His people.

Beyond that, "He is able" to save fully and completely ("to the uttermost"). He can do what the Levitical priests could not. Because of that we as Christians have a "better hope" (Heb. 7:19).

At this point we need to ask what it means to be saved "to the uttermost" or "completely" (Heb. 7:25, NIV). We see one aspect reflected in the Revised Standard Version's translation: "He is able for all time to save those who draw near to God through him." That meaning is certainly in the context, but extent in time doesn't capture the full contextual implications. Hebrews 7:27 goes on to speak of human sin and the ineffectiveness of the Levitical sacrifices as opposed to the efficacious once-for-all sacrifice of Jesus that solved the sin problem once and for all. Thus Christ's saving "to the uttermost" implies that Jesus rescues us from all that we need redemption from—that His salvation is complete deliverance from the sin problem.

W. H. Griffith Thomas, combining that thought with the temporal one, writes that "looking back over the past, we have been saved from the condemnation and guilt of sin; looking round upon the present, we are being saved from the power, love, and defilement of sin; looking forward to the future, we shall be saved from the very presence of sin in the glorified state above."

In short, Jesus is able to "save to the uttermost" not only because He lives, but also because He intercedes for those who come to Him. He returned to heaven as a victorious conqueror who died and rose again and sits on God's throne as an equal.

For all of those reasons and more, "He is able"!

December 1

"We Have an Advocate"!

My little children, I am writing these things to you so that you may not sin. But if anyone does sin, we have an advocate with the Father, Jesus Christ the righteous. He is the propitiation for our sins, and not for ours only but also for the sins of the whole world.
1 John 2:1, 2, ESV.

We have an advocate." Here we find the same idea that we did in yesterday's passage when it said that Jesus "always lives to make intercession" for those who come to Him (Heb. 7:25, RSV). The two verses are really speaking to the same point—that our intercessor is our advocate.

But in 1 John we find an extension and filling out of the meaning of the intercessor of Hebrews 7:25. The context of 1 John 2:1, with its statement of Jesus being our advocate, is the problem of sin. The same verse tells us that it is God's will that we don't sin.

That is good and well. But John, like the rest of the Bible writers, knows that all people do commit acts of sin, in spite of their good intentions and God's ideal. That is why a few verses earlier he wrote that "if we say that we have no sin, we deceive ourselves, and the truth is not in us" (1 John 1:8). We find that same forthrightness in verse 10, in which the apostle declares that "if we say that we have not sinned, we make [God] a liar, and his word is not in us." Those two verses enclose verse 9, which plainly states that "if we confess our sins, he is faithful and just to forgive us our sins, and to cleanse us from all unrighteousness."

John is a realist. He doesn't beat around the bush regarding human sinfulness. Confession of the truth of our sins is the way to go rather than denial.

It is in that context that we find John's words about sinners having an advocate with the Father. That context also helps us understand the meaning of Jesus' advocacy or intercession. When under the convicting power of the Holy Spirit sinners come boldly before the throne of God in prayers of confession and repentance, Jesus the risen conqueror notes to God that they have accepted Him by faith. At that point both He and the more than willing Father forgive the repentant sinner on the basis of Christ's atoning sacrifice (or propitiation) made on the cross (1 John 2:2).

"We have an advocate"! "He is able"! We can come "boldly" before the throne. And we leave God's presence both forgiven and cleansed. Amen!

We Have an Intercessor!

If God is for us, who is against us? He who did not withhold his own Son but gave him up for all of us, will he not with him also give us everything else? Who will bring any charge against God's elect? It is God who justifies. Who is to condemn? It is Christ Jesus, who died, yes, who was raised, who is at the right hand of God, who indeed intercedes for us. Who will separate us from the love of Christ? Will hardship, or distress, or persecution, or famine, or nakedness, or peril, or sword? . . . No, in all these things we are more than conquerors through him who loved us. Rom. 8:31-37, NRSV.

As Christians, we never stand alone. We have a friend in heaven who ensures the eternal salvation of all who come to Him. Part of Christ's work in the heavenly sanctuary is to be an intercessor who guarantees the salvation of each of His followers. Leon Morris refers to today's passage as "the Christian's triumph song."

Nothing can separate us from the love of God because we have a Friend in heaven. Perhaps it is more accurate to say Friends, because God so loved us that He gave His Son. And it is God who justifies all who come to Him through Christ. Then who is left to condemn? Paul asks in Romans 8:34. His answer is emphatic. It is Christ Jesus. And that is good news.

Why? Because, the apostle says, Christ is on our side. Here we need to remember that while He was on earth He told us that "the Father judgeth no man, but hath committed all judgment unto the Son" (John 5:22). Thus even though "we must all appear before the judgment seat of Christ" to answer for our lives (2 Cor. 5:10), Christians (those who have a continuing faith relationship with God through Jesus) have absolutely nothing to fear. Again, why? Because He (1) died for them, (2) was raised from the dead, (3) is sitting at the right hand of God, and (4) is presently interceding for Christians as their heavenly High Priest.

Here is the best of good news. Christ gave His life for the sins of His followers. As a result, there is "now no condemnation for those who are in Christ Jesus" (Rom. 8:1, RSV). Having absorbed the penalty for those "in Him." He will not turn around and pronounce judgment against His followers for the very sins that He died for.

To the contrary, Jesus is currently "at the right hand of God" in the heavenly throne room, where He intercedes for us as our High Priest.

The biblical doctrine of the judgment is a reality. But if the judge is on our side, there is no way that we can come under condemnation. We are safe in Jesus. Nothing can separate us from the love of God except our own personal decision to reject the One who is currently interceding for us in the Temple above.

December 3

Jesus' Prayer-answering Ministry

I write these things to you who believe in the name of the Son of God so that you may know that you have eternal life. This is the confidence we have in approaching God: that if we ask anything according to his will, he hears us. And if we know that he hears us—whatever we ask—we know that we have what we asked of him.
1 John 5:13-15, NIV.

Jesus in His heavenly high priestly ministry not only functions as one who can save to the uttermost as our advocate and intercessor, but He also has a ministry of answering the prayers of His followers still on earth.

During His days of walking with the disciples He had repeatedly told them that their prayers would be answered. And now that He is in heaven John reveals a few more of the details of how prayer works. At the center, as we might expect, is Jesus Himself. Because of His earthly work for us we can come confidently before the Father in His name, knowing "that if we ask anything according to his will, he hears us. And if we know that he hears us," we have assurance that God the Father and God the Son will respond to our prayers through the activity of God the Holy Spirit and the angels who do His bidding. Such is Christ's heavenly ministry of answering prayer. We have a Friend in heaven who became one of us and knows our needs through firsthand experience and is more than willing to facilitate the answering of the prayers of His saints. The ministry of prayer is a central function in His priestly activity in our day.

As we think about the verses for today's reading we see that John has the interesting habit of stating the purpose of his writing near the end of the document rather than at the beginning. Thus toward the conclusion of the fourth Gospel he tells his readers that these things "are written that you may believe that Jesus is the Christ, the Son of God, and that in believing you may have life in his name" (John 20:31, RSV).

He does the same thing in quite similar words in 1 John 5:13, but with a major difference. He composed the Gospel so that the readers might come to a belief in Jesus and so have life. The letter, however, he penned to those who were already believers but had had their faith shaken by internal conflict in their congregations. They had become unsettled about their standing before God and needed to regain confidence.

Some of us are in that latter category. We have accepted Jesus but have been battered by our own shortcomings and perhaps hurt by members of the church who in their carelessness have rattled our faith. John wants us to know that in spite of all the challenges we face and all the roadblocks life has thrown in our path, we can have confidence that we have a Friend in heaven intent in answering all prayers asked according to God's will.

The Setting of the Final Judgment

As I looked, thrones were placed and one that was ancient of days took his seat; his
raiment was white as snow, and the hair of his head like pure wool; his throne was
fiery flames, its wheels were burning fire. A stream of fire issued and came forth
from before him; a thousand thousands served him, and ten thousand times ten
thousand stood before him; the court sat in judgment, and the books were opened.
Dan. 7:9, 10, RSV.

Another aspect of Christ's heavenly ministry is that of judgment. Just as the ancient Jewish year had a day of judgment connected to the ministry of the earthly sanctuary near its end in the annual Day of Atonement *(Yom Kippur)*, so the Bible tells us that the heavenly pattern will also. Daniel 7 presents us with the most graphic scene of that heavenly judgment, which represents the final act of Christ's high priestly ministry. In the flow of history that judgment takes place during the final phases of the little horn's reign (verse 8) and near the time when God gives the kingdom to the saints (verses 14, 26, 27). In other words, the book of Daniel pictures it as occurring right before Christ comes again. After the judgment is complete, Christ will, so to speak, lay aside His priestly robes and don those of a conquering king.

Before we get to Jesus' place in the judgment we need to take a closer look at Daniel's portrayal of the judgment scene itself. "Majestic" is the only way we can describe it. Even the size of the heavenly throne room, represented in the earthly model by the Most Holy Place, beggars our imaginations. Visualizing a room large enough to contain millions of angelic beings is beyond our comprehension. We can say the same for the dynamism and glory of the place. Here we need to be careful, though. The prophet puts before us a picture beyond our imagination and comprehension. As a result, we can grasp the general picture of what is happening but its details are beyond us. We have a snapshot rather than a detailed explanation of what is happening.

But even from that we learn several quite distinct facts. One is that of glory. The vision depicts Jesus and the Father in terms of light and fire as They sit upon the throne. Another image is that of action with thousands and millions of angels performing works of service both in relation to God and to the universe.

But the defining picture is that of the judgment being set, with all eyes focused on the process. The judgment is a public event based upon evidence (books). God wants all the universe to know that He has done the best thing possible in His handling of the sin problem on earth that led to the incarnation of the Son.

The words "thrones were placed" "and the books were opened" signal not only the judgment but the beginning of the end of earthly history.

December 5

Judgment Result Number 1:
Christ Is Vindicated

I kept looking in the night visions, and behold, with the clouds of heaven One like a Son of Man was coming, and He came up to the Ancient of Days and was presented before Him. And to Him was given dominion, glory and a kingdom, that all peoples, nations and men of every language might serve Him. His dominion is an everlasting dominion which will not pass away; and His kingdom is one which will not be destroyed. Dan. 7:13, 14, NASB.

This passage is pregnant with meaning. Taken in the context of the flow of Daniel 7, the verses do not speak about the Second Advent, but rather of Christ's coming to the judgment scene. The stage was set for it in verses 9 and 10, which pictured the public placement of thrones, the arrival of the Father, and the opening of the books containing the evidence that forms the basis of the final judgment. Now, Daniel describes Christ as "One like a Son of Man" joining the Father in the final work of judgment before They bring an end to earthly history.

The vision shows that the judgment ends in favor of Jesus, who at its conclusion receives everlasting dominion. That decree seals forever the fate of Satan and renders God's universe secure for the eternal ages to come. And Jesus' vindicating judgment involves His followers in the victory. Thus a judgment in favor of the work of Jesus on earth is also a verdict for the final and eternal justification of those who have chosen to accept the benefits of His incarnation, life, death, and resurrection.

One of the most interesting things about this judgment scene is that it pictures Jesus as "One like a Son of Man." It is the verse that led Him to choose that title as His favorite description of Himself during His earthly ministry. He chose it rather than Messiah or Christ because that designation had acquired too many ideas related to a conquering king. To avoid that, Jesus elected to identify Himself as "the Son of Man."

Interestingly, John the revelator picks up the title of the Son of Man again in Revelation 14:14-16 to depict Jesus coming in the clouds of heaven at the end of time to take His people home. As a result, we can see that the Jews were not altogether wrong when they visualized the Messiah as a conquering king. But they weren't completely correct, either. In reality, the ministry of Jesus as the Son of Man has two aspects—the first as suffering servant and the second as coming King. The final judgment utilizes the accomplishments of the first phase of His work as the justification for the second, in which He is given everlasting dominion.

Judgment Result Number 2: Christ's Followers Are Vindicated

I was watching; and the same horn was making war against the saints, and prevailing against them, until the Ancient of Days came, and a judgment was made in favor of the saints of the Most High. . . . The court shall be seated, and they shall take away his [the little horn's] dominion, to consume and destroy it forever. Then the kingdom and dominion, and the greatness of the kingdoms under the whole heaven, shall be given to the people, the saints of the Most High. His kingdom is an everlasting kingdom, and all dominions shall serve and obey Him. Dan. 7:21-27, NKJV.

I vividly remember my introduction to the topic of the pre-Advent judgment. One of my first visits to an Adventist church took place when I was an 18-year-old private in the army. I went because I wanted to be with my girlfriend, but what I observed astounded me. Up front stood an "old" woman (she was probably 40) who had an exceptionally long and bony finger that she utilized in pointing to each of us teenagers. Her message was that we had better lie awake at night and recall and confess each and every sin that we had ever committed, because if we missed one we would end up in the hot place. The judgment had begun, and who knew when our individual names might surface in it.

That is what I have come to see as the bad-news version of the judgment, a fear-laden approach that does not line up with Scripture. In the Bible the judgment is always for the saints. Unlike human judges, God is not neutral. He is actively on the side of those at whom the devil is pointing an accusatory finger. He so loved the world that He sent Jesus to die for us (John 3:16). But the Father went further than that; He has even given over the final authority of judgment to Jesus (John 5:22). That is the concluding aspect of His high priestly ministry in heaven. Jesus our Savior is also Jesus our Judge. And those who have accepted His redeeming work have nothing to fear in the final judgment. In fact, the Bible describes their judgment as gospel—good news.

Thus in Revelation 6:10 it is the saints who cry out "how long" before the beginning of the judgment that will set things right. Scripture pictures them as looking forward to God's judgment with joyful anticipation. And in Revelation 18:20 the judgment is for the saints and against Babylon.

Too many people have thought of the final judgment as a kind of medieval inquisition headed up by a vengeful God. Not so! Rather, God's purpose is to demonstrate that believers have accepted Jesus. The judgment does not seek to keep people out of the kingdom, but to vindicate as many as possible so that they can go home with Jesus when He comes again.

December 7

Judgment Completed

What is a man profited, if he shall gain the whole world, and lose his own soul? or what shall a man give in exchange for his soul? For the Son of man shall come in the glory of his Father with his angels; and then he shall reward every man according to his works. Matt. 16:26, 27.

When Christ completes His priestly work of judgment in the heavenly sanctuary, He returns to earth to reward those who have accepted His grace and let it change their lives. Of course, some will have opted for some other reward. But the very logic of the flow of events demands the type of pre-Advent judgment set forth in Daniel 7: first comes the judgment and then follows the Advent with its rewards.

That judgment, of course, is not for God's information. Rather, it is public because others need to be convinced that He is doing the right thing in saving some but not others. The open nature of the event is the reason the Bible talks about "books" that record people's lives. What they have done is crucial in the judgment.

Here we have a problem. After all, Paul makes it clear that we are not justified or counted righteous because of our works (Rom. 3:20), but saved fully and entirely by grace (Eph. 2:8-10). And that is absolutely true. But grace doesn't merely forgive and justify—it also transforms, empowers, and sanctifies.

To put it another way, if you have been justified by grace your whole life will change. You will not be able to continue in the same old self-centered way. Jesus makes a difference in how people behave and think. Saved people will live by a different set of principles, and those principles will determine what they "do" in life.

In other words, our actions indicate either salvation in the heart or a lack thereof. According to Jesus, both the heart and the life come up for review in the final judgment. Even Paul teaches that point when he writes that God "will render to every man according to his works" (Rom. 2:6, RSV). And as we have seen, Jesus was big on "doing" since the beginning of His ministry: "Not every one who says to me, 'Lord, Lord,' shall enter the kingdom of heaven, but he who does the will of my Father in heaven" (Matt. 7:21, RSV).

So the judgment is based on how those who claim to be Christians have lived their lives. And when the evidence is in and has been set forth for all to see in the pre-Advent judgment, then Jesus "shall come . . . with his angels" to "reward every man according to his works." What a glorious prospect for God's people. It is a day worth living for.

The Silent Close of Jesus' Work in Heaven

Let the evildoer still do evil, and the filthy still be filthy, and the righteous still do right, and the holy still be holy. Behold, I am coming soon, bringing my recompense, to repay every one for what he has done. I am the Alpha and the Omega, the first and the last, the beginning and the end. Rev. 22:11-13, RSV.

Contrary to popular opinion, time will not go on and on indefinitely into the future. There will come a point when God decides finally to put a stop to the misery, death, and disease that we call earthly history. That ending, the Bible describes as a public event. But preceding the Second Advent there will be an invisible one that takes place when the heavenly pre-Advent judgment has been completed and every person has made a decision either for or against Jesus.

Jesus Himself describes that sequence in Revelation 22:11, 12. Earthly probation will close, eternally sealing the fate of all. Then He returns to reward each person according to their life's decisions.

The Great Controversy describes the close of probation in the following way: "When the work of the investigative judgment closes, the destiny of all will have been decided for life or death. Probation is ended a short time before the appearing of the Lord in the clouds of heaven. Christ in the Revelation, looking forward to that time, declares: 'He that is unjust, let him be unjust still: and he which is filthy, let him be filthy still: and he that is righteous, let him be righteous still: and he that is holy, let him be holy still. And, behold, I come quickly'" (pp. 490, 491).

The interesting thing about the conclusion of human probation is that it has no visible sign that it has occurred. The Second Advent and the rapture of the saints, as we will soon see, are visible. But the close of probation takes place as men and women go about their daily business. "Men will be planting and building, eating and drinking, all unconscious that the final, irrvocable decision has been pronounced in the sanctuary above. Before the flood, after Noah entered the ark, God shut him in and shut the ungodly out; but for seven days the people, knowing not that their doom was fixed, continued their careless, pleasure-loving life and mocked the warnings of impending judgment. 'So,' says the Saviour, 'shall also the coming of the Son of man be.' Matthew 24:39. Silently, unnoticed as the midnight thief, will come the decisive hour which marks the fixing of every man's destiny" (*ibid.*, p. 491).

According to Jesus, now is the time to get right with God. Today we must let His grace fill our hearts and change our lives.

December 9

Troublesome Times

At that time shall arise Michael, the great prince who has charge of your people. And there shall be a time of trouble, such as never has been since there was a nation till that time; but at that time your people shall be delivered, every one whose name shall be found written in the book. Dan. 12:1, RSV.

Christ's work in the heavenly sanctuary has come to an end. As He completes it Daniel pictures Him as standing up as He prepares to return to earth for His people.

The pre-Advent judgment has ceased, probation has closed, and the great High Priest has stood. Yet something else happens at this momentous time. The earth descends into a "time of trouble" unequaled in earthly history. That difficult time undoubtedly is brought about when the "four angels standing at the four corners of the earth, holding back the four winds of the earth" (Rev. 7:1, RSV) finally let loose of their hold and allow the devil to operate more freely throughout the earth.

Now, the earth has always seen trouble. Jesus pointed that out when He told His disciples that "you will hear of wars and rumors of wars; see that you are not alarmed; for this must take place, but the end is not yet. For nation will rise against nation, and kingdom against kingdom, and there will be famines and earthquakes in various places: all this is but the beginning of the birth-pangs" (Matt. 24:6-8, RSV).

As noted earlier, earth has always experienced wars, earthquakes, and so on. But the Bible is clear that the beginning of birth pangs will be followed by their end as the earth enters a time of trouble such as never was, during which Satan's evil forces have freedom to do their will. At such a time, Jesus tells us, there will be "men fainting with fear and with foreboding of what is coming on the world" (Luke 21:26, RSV).

It will be a time of chaos. Not only will the economic and physical world be in upheaval, but there will inevitably arise trouble in the spiritual realm as people begin to blame one another for what is happening. And as in all such times in prior history religious strife will rage as the earthly forces of Satan turn upon believers in Jesus. Revelation 13 and other places in John's apocalypse depict some of that aggression.

It is during that crisis point in history, as God's people are seemingly being overwhelmed in what Daniel describes as the time of trouble, that Jesus returns to deliver them.

Father, help us today to stick close to You as we prepare for those things that will come upon the earth.

Part 8

Turn Your Eyes Upon Jesus as the Coming King

December 10

Christianity's Defining Word: Hope

For the grace of God that brings salvation has appeared to all men, teaching us that, denying ungodliness and worldly lusts, we should live soberly, righteously, and godly in the present age, looking for the blessed hope and glorious appearing of our great God and Savior Jesus Christ, who gave Himself for us, that He might redeem us.
Titus 2:11-14, NKJV.

It seems like just yesterday, but it was really more than 50 years ago. In my younger years I had a friend whom we referred to as D. G. I never did know what the initials stood for, but that is what we all called him. He was a regular sort of kid and a good friend to hang around.

Somehow we lost track of each other. Then when I was 16 or so I had occasion to stop by his house. What I saw shocked me. Beer cans littered the yard. More beer cans had been thrown carelessly throughout the house. There were beer cans everywhere! I had seen plenty of beer cans in my short life, but nothing like that.

As a result, I asked the natural question—What's going on here? Then I heard the shocking news. Sixteen-year-old D. G. had died of leukemia a few days before, and, not knowing what else to do, his parents had thrown an all-out beer party for him and his friends for his last weekend of life.

I was doubly dumbfounded. First, because of the untimely death of a boy who had been my friend. And, second, because hosting a beer party was the only thing that his apparently adult parents could come up with as a send-off.

At that time I had no problem with beer parties. But even my agnostic, hedonistic mind had a difficult time grasping the poverty of his death. It forced me to face some important questions. Was escape from reality through alcohol the best thing this family could think of in the face of death? Do not life and death deserve some dignity? Is there any meaning to life after all, or was I, as a wandering teenager, to continue to live my own life alternating between study and work and meaningless stupor? In short, is there any hope in life?

It would be three more years before I discovered the answer. And since that time what Paul calls the "blessed hope," the hope that surpasses all others, has guided my life.

In many ways the words "having hope" signify more than any others what it means to be a Christian. We may face crises and death in this life but we know that this life is not all there is. We have the "blessed hope" of a new life when Jesus returns in the clouds of heaven.

Half Saved

*He has appeared once for all at the end of the age to remove sin by the sacrifice
of himself. And just as it is appointed for mortals to die once, and after that the
judgment, so Christ, having been offered once to bear the sins of many, will appear
a second time, not to deal with sin, but to save those who are eagerly waiting for him.*
Heb. 9:26-28, NRSV.

Here is a passage that finds echoes in many places in the New Testament. The book of Hebrews tells us that Christ accomplished His sacrificial work when He died once for all on the cross. While that never needs to be repeated, by itself it leaves people only "half saved." He has yet to "appear a second time, not to deal [again] with sin, but to save those who are eagerly waiting for him."

Wait a minute! Aren't Christians already saved? Doesn't Ephesians 2:8 plainly teach through its use of the past tense that believers "have been saved" (NKJV) by grace through faith?

Those things are definitely true. So, we must ask, if Jesus has already redeemed Christians, how come Hebrews says that Jesus will return "to save those who are eagerly waiting for him"? How can they be saved but not yet saved? Before answering, we should realize that Paul takes up the topic in Romans 13, in which he appeals for Christians "to wake from sleep. For salvation is nearer to us now than when we first believed" (verse 11, RSV).

Part of the answer to the half-saved dilemma is that Romans speaks of salvation from three different perspectives. One of them, justification, is past for believers. Another, glorification, is future. And the third, sanctification, is a present reality. Thus Christian living takes place between two great events. The first being justification, when believers gave their hearts to Christ. The second is His return at the end of the age.

And with that phrase, "end of the age," we hit upon the two great events that encompass all the New Testament era. The first is the beginning of the kingdom of God, which Jesus asserted He had inaugurated when He began His earthly ministry (Matt. 4:17). The second is the consummation of the kingdom, when Christ comes again.

That thought takes us to Romans 8:23, in which the apostle states that Christians "have the first fruits of the Spirit," but that they "groan inwardly as [they] wait for adoption as sons" and "the redemption of [their] bodies" (RSV).

The plain fact is that as believers we are half saved and half redeemed. The fullness of that salvation hope will not come until Jesus returns at the end of the age and gives us new bodies to go with our new hearts and wills.

December 12

Our Doubts
Don't Change God's Plans

Scoffers will come in the last days with scoffing, following their own sinful desires. They will say, "Where is the promise of his coming? For ever since the fathers fell asleep, all things are continuing as they were from the beginning of creation." For they deliberately overlook this fact, that the heavens existed long ago, and the earth was formed out of water and through water by the word of God, and that by means of these the world that then existed was deluged with water and perished. But by the same word the heavens and earth that now exist are stored up for fire, being kept until the day of judgment and destruction of the ungodly. 2 Peter 3:3-7, ESV.

Doubting comes easy, especially when it involves the Second Advent. Day follows day and year follows year and the flow of history goes on and on. And with the lulling passing of time the return of Christ falls into the background of our thinking—transformed into a bit of New Testament mythology or perhaps a pious wish that we think about when we are ill or lose a loved one. But once the crisis is over, our thought patterns get back to "normal" as we plow all our resources into making our earthly future bright and happy.

I remember how vivid the promise of the Second Coming was when I first became a Christian at the age of 19. I was sure I would never reach the age of 30. In fact, I did my last two years of college in one so that I would have a chance to preach before the end.

That was more than 50 years ago. And time still continues relentlessly. Down through history that perception has led many people to scoff at the Bible's teaching on the Advent and to live according to "their own sinful desires," noting that things are as they always have been.

It is at that point that the aggressive Peter jumps into action, noting that the earth-centered philosophy of uniformitarianism overlooks two major facts. First, that there was a beginning when God created the earth. And second, that there had been a massive flood in the time of Noah that had destroyed the civilization of that day. Both of those facts, Peter claims, God brought about by His intervention in history. They were divine actions impossible to predict from the viewpoint of the evolutionary flow of time. And just as certain, he asserts, is the second coming of Jesus.

For Peter, following the teaching of his Lord, the Second Advent is a certain event. And all the doubting and scoffing and wild living by humans will not change that fact.

His words are a wake-up call to all of us. We need to be preparing our lives for more than just a comfortable retirement with our grandchildren. The *fact* of the Second Advent is just as certain as the reality of the earth on which we live and the air that we breathe.

Why Jesus Waits

But do not ignore this one fact, beloved, that with the Lord one day is as a thousand years, and a thousand years as one day. The Lord is not slow about his promise as some count slowness, but is forbearing toward you, not wishing that any should perish, but that all should reach repentance. But the day of the Lord will come like a thief, and then the heavens will pass away with a loud noise, and the elements will be dissolved with fire, and the earth and the works that are upon it will be burned up.
2 Peter 3:8-10, RSV.

Surely I am coming soon" (Rev. 22:20, RSV). The last words of Jesus in the Bible, we find them repeated three times in Revelation 22. When I get to heaven I want to ask Him what He meant. After all, it has been more than 2,000 years. And, no matter how patient you are, that is hardly soon.

Peter, a man not always known for his patience, may have been asking himself the same question. I don't know what he was thinking, but I do know that he has provided us with an inspired answer.

He handles the topic on two levels. The first is that God doesn't have the same level of impatience as humans. In fact, He doesn't even view time as we do. Our personal lives are bounded by birth and death. In between we may have 60 or 70 or even 100 years. But when death comes time is over for us. We are very conscious of time and its shortness. As I grow older I find myself taking a greater interest in obituaries. My consciousness of the time I have remaining becomes more acute with each passing decade.

But what if I existed from eternity in the past through eternity in the future? Time would take on new meanings. So it is with God. The time panic of humans does not cause Him to forget His ultimate purpose on earth.

And that purpose is Peter's second response to God's delay in returning. Namely, He allows time to go on because He desires to give as many people as possible a chance to repent and enter His kingdom. From that perspective, the delay itself is an act of mercy.

Yet the end will come, and when it does it will happen spectacularly with loud noises and fire and earth-shaking events.

But the Second Advent itself will arrive like a thief to a scoffing world lulled by its amusements. And here we have another possible meaning for Christ's final words in Scripture. The word used for "soon" also means "quickly." When the clock of heaven signals the end of time, Jesus will quickly come in the clouds and earth's affairs will wind up rapidly for both scoffers and believers.

December 14

"The Greatest Show on Earth"

As the lightning comes from the east and shines as far as the west, so will be the coming of the Son of man. . . . Then will appear the sign of the Son of man in heaven, and then all the tribes of the earth will mourn, and they will see the Son of man coming on the clouds of heaven with power and great glory; and he will send out his angels with a loud trumpet call, and they will gather his elect from the four winds, from one end of heaven to the other. Matt. 24:27-31, RSV.

One thing is certain about the second coming of Jesus—everybody will know when it takes place. Some things happen in secret, while others are public. Jesus Himself described His return as the most public event in history. The timing may be a secret, and the event will sneak up on the world like a thief in the night, but the experience itself will be spectacular. All eyes will see it, whether we want to or not. The Second Coming, when it takes place, is not an option for viewing. You can't switch channels or turn off the set. It is the historical event that will end history. As such, it will affect every person living on the earth at the time.

From our earthly perspective it may seem that time is stretching indefinitely from the past into the future, but that is merely an illusion. With the "sign" of Jesus' appearing in the clouds of heaven with a host of angels, it is all over. Time may seem to be dragging on, but when Jesus comes He will, as He claimed in His last words to the church in the Bible, do so "quickly" (Rev. 22:7, 12, 20).

We need to look again at the descriptions of that return that Jesus used in today's verses.

- It will be like lightning flashing across the heavens.
- It will take place with dynamic power.
- It will be an event of great glory.
- A multitude of angels will accompany Jesus.
- A loud trumpet call will rattle the heavens.
- And there will be a gathering of the elect from all across the face of the earth.

Some years ago I saw a movie called *The Greatest Show on Earth*. It featured the circus in its heyday—a time when everybody in town showed up for the circus parade as it headed toward the fairgrounds where the great tents were pitched.

"The Truly Greatest Show on Earth" is yet future. Nothing will be able to compare with it in terms of brightness and glory.

That is one show I want to see. But, I should add, from the right seat.

Dominion Reversal

Then the seventh angel sounded: And there were loud voices in heaven, saying, "The
kingdoms of this world have become the kingdoms of our Lord and of His Christ,
and He shall reign forever and ever!" And the twenty-four elders who sat before God
on their thrones fell on their faces and worshiped God, saying:
"We give You thanks, O Lord God Almighty,
The One who is and who was and who is to come,
Because You have taken Your great power and reigned.
The nations were angry, and Your wrath has come,
And the time of the dead, that they should be judged,
And that You should reward Your servants the prophets and the saints,
And those who fear Your name, small and great,
And should destroy those who destroy the earth." Rev. 11:15-18, NKJV.

When the seventh angel sounds, the chain of events pictured in Revelation's seven trumpets reaches its climax and earth's history rushes to an end.

That time will be one of power reversal. One of the key words in Bible prophecy is "dominion." That is particularly true of Daniel 7, which predicts a future time when the dominion of the devil and his agents will be "taken away" (verse 26, RSV) and given to Christ (verse 14). And "his dominion is an everlasting dominion, which shall not pass away" (verse 14, RSV).

The focal point of Bible prophecy in Daniel and Revelation is dominion. It centers on the question of who is in charge. Thus the great panoramic vision of Daniel 7 (and its parallels in both apocalyptic books) features a sequence of earthly rulers, including Babylon, Persia, Greece, Rome, and the power that would make great claims for itself, who seek to change God's law, and persecute God's people throughout much of Christian history (verse 25).

But those earthly rulers were really only a front for Satan, who sought to control world events from behind the scenes. It was the devil himself who claimed dominion over this world. Paul referred to that reality when he spoke of "the world rulers of this present darkness" (Eph. 6:12, RSV) and "the prince of the power of the air" (Eph. 2:2, RSV).

God has permitted the forces of darkness to run the earth, utilizing their own principles. And human history demonstrates the destructiveness of that rule. The final judgment is not merely about humans, but about God and His justice.

God allows history to play out until the principles of the two kingdoms are visible to the heavenly hosts. And then, with the approval of the angelic multitudes, Jesus resumes His rightful place as the true prince of our world.

December 16

"Fear" Is More Than Respect

When he opened the sixth seal, I looked, and behold, there was a great earthquake;
and the sun became black as sackcloth, the full moon became like blood, and the stars
of the sky fell to the earth as the fig tree sheds its winter fruit when shaken by a gale;
the sky vanished like a scroll that is rolled up, and every mountain and island was
removed from its place. Then the kings of the earth and the great men and the generals
and the rich and the strong, and every one, slave and free, hid in the caves and among
the rocks of the mountains, calling to the mountains and rocks, "Fall on us and hide us
from the face of him who is seated on the throne, and from the wrath of the Lamb; for
the great day of their wrath has come, and who can stand before it?"
Rev. 6:12-17, RSV.

As I noted a few days ago, I want to be seated in the right section when the world sees Jesus coming in the clouds of heaven. Not all will be filled with joy when that happens.

The biblical descriptions of the day itself beggar the imagination from both the perspective of glory and from that of disaster. In today's passage John seems to be struggling with how to depict earth's end. Nothing will remain untouched.

The description reminds me of that day when I stood at ground zero in Hiroshima, Japan—the very spot above which the first atomic bomb used in wrath detonated. The impression in my mind was one of awe and fright as the destructive forces of even that simple (in the light of modern capabilities) bomb impressed themselves upon my mind. Yet that explosion is as nothing compared to what will happen at the end of world history.

"Fear" is the only word that we can use to capture the reaction of those who have chosen to live by destructive principles opposed to God and His kingdom. All they want to do is to escape from the Lamb. But that is nothing new. They have rejected Him throughout their lives.

When many modern people read that one of the Bible's last warnings is to call men and women to "fear God and give him glory, for the hour of his judgment has come" (Rev. 14:7, RSV), they interpret fear merely as "respect." It is respect, but, as today's passage makes clear, it is much more than that.

When dominion gets reversed at the end of time many of those who created fear in others during their lives will suffer from fear themselves as they see their kingdoms and ways of life brought to an end.

This is not the Bible's most pleasant teaching. But it is an important one as we line up for seats in what will truly be "The Greatest Show on Earth."

The Wrath of the Lamb

And [they] said to the mountains and rocks, Fall on us, and hide us from the face of him that sitteth on the throne, and from the wrath of the Lamb: For the great day of his wrath is come; and who shall be able to stand? Rev. 6:16, 17.

Who has ever heard of a wrathful lamb? The two words don't even seem to go together. But then neither do the descriptions in Revelation of Jesus as both the Lamb of God and the Lion of the tribe of Judah. Perhaps we need to take a second look to see what John is reporting.

Most people see "wrath" as a nasty word. And many theologians have worked hard to remove all divine wrath from their teachings. But what is unpopular with them is quite popular with God. The number of Bible references to God's wrath exceeds 580. Writers have utilized barrels of ink to explain away God's wrath, but in the final analysis the Lamb of God and the Lion of the tribe of Judah will act to end the problem of sin.

But let's not go astray here. God's wrath is not an emotional anger comparable to human rage. To the contrary, it is a function of His love. God hates the sin that continues to destroy the lives and happiness of His created beings. He is weary of dead babies, cancer, and blindness; rape, murder, and theft; holocausts, Rwandas, and Iraqs.

In His timing God will respond to the souls under the altar whom John pictures as crying out, "O Sovereign Lord . . . how long" before You put an end to the mess we call world history (Rev. 6:10, NLT)? As W. L. Walker declares, "God's wrath only goes forth because God is love, and because sin is that which injures His children and is opposed to the purpose of His love." And Alan Richardson points out that "only a certain kind of degenerate Protestant theology has attempted to contrast the wrath of God with the mercy of Christ."

God, as the Bible portrays Him, cannot and will not forever stand idly by while His creation suffers. His reaction is judgment on that sin that is destroying His people. We should see that judgment as the real meaning of biblical wrath. God condemns sin in judgment and will eventually eradicate it completely. The first step takes place at Jesus' second advent. The second will occur at the end of the millennium according to Revelation 20:11-15.

The plain fact is that if we have only the Lamb of God who died for us, we have only half a gospel. The Lamb has been slaughtered, yet God's children continue to suffer. The climactic phase of the Lamb's work is His function as the Lion of the tribe of Judah at the end of time.

December 18

The Kingly Lamb

After this I heard what seemed to be the loud voice of a great multitude in heaven, crying, "Hallelujah! Salvation and glory and power belong to our God, for his judgments are true and just."... Then I saw heaven opened, and behold, a white horse! He who sat upon it is called Faithful and True, and in righteousness he judges and makes war. His eyes are like a flame of fire, and on his head are many diadems; and he has a name inscribed which no one knows but himself.... And the armies of heaven, arrayed in fine linen, white and pure, followed him on white horses.... On his robe and on his thigh he has a name inscribed, King of kings and Lord of lords.
Rev. 19:1-16, RSV.

How does an earthly writer describe a heavenly coming? How does one imprisoned on the Isle of Patmos write about glory and victory? Not very easily. John's language is symbolic throughout Revelation 19 as he seeks to portray the majestic return of the humble Lamb of God who has become the majestic "King of kings and Lord of lords" to rescue His people and destroy those who have wreaked havoc on the earth.

A lot has happened in the life of John. He first knew Jesus as a humble man who healed the sick and fed the multitudes—a man who submissively went to the cross. But now, some 60 years later, that same John receives a glimpse of the humble Galilean in all of His glory.

And here it is that we find the Messiah King that John, Peter, and the Jews in general expected at the First Advent. Deep in Jewish history, as we have seen many times during the year, was the Bible-based belief in a Christ who would come to rescue His people as a conquering David—a Man of war who would release His people from oppression and bondage.

That is what the disciples fully expected of Jesus back in His earthly journey. Their minds had collapsed His two comings into one, and they were totally bewildered when their Christ was led to the cross as a lamb.

But now it is clear to John. The Christ had to become the sacrificial Lamb before He could in righteousness and justice and love assume the role of the conquering King of all nations. At last the fullness of the kingdom has come.

The One who is called "Faithful and True" is returning to fulfill the promises He made on earth. The white horse symbolizes both purity and conquering royalty. And God's people both in heaven and on earth are filled with praise as their Lord at last puts an end to sin.

As the old song goes, "What a day of rejoicing that will be" when we see our personal Savior coming to take us home. I want to be ready to meet my Lord on that day. I look forward to it with all of my heart.

Earth's Greatest Supper

Then I heard what seemed to be the voice of a great multitude, like the sound of many waters and like the sound of mighty thunderpeals, crying, "Hallelujah! For the Lord our God the almighty reigns. Let us rejoice and exult and give him the glory, for the marriage of the Lamb has come, and his Bride has made herself ready; it was granted her to be clothed with fine linen, bright and pure"—for the fine linen is the righteous deeds of the saints. And the angel said to me, "Write this: Blessed are those who are invited to the marriage supper of the Lamb." And he said to me, "These are true words of God." Rev. 19:6-9, RSV.

Earth's palaces throughout history have seen a lot of famous suppers, which people anticipated with enthusiasm and expectation. But none will be greater than the marriage supper of the Lamb, at which time Jesus receives His kingdom, figuratively described in Revelation 21 as the "new Jerusalem . . . prepared as a bride adorned for her husband" (Rev. 21:2, RSV).

Here we have a banquet rooted deeply in biblical history. The prophet Isaiah spoke of it 700 years before Christ's incarnation: "On this mountain the Lord of hosts will make for all peoples a feast of fat things. . . . He will swallow up death for ever, and the Lord God will wipe away tears from all faces, and the reproach of his people he will take away from all the earth, for the Lord has spoken. It will be said on that day, 'Lo, this is our God; we have waited for him, that he might save us. This is the Lord; we have waited for him; let us be glad and rejoice in his salvation'" (Isa. 25:6-9, RSV).

And Jesus prophesied of that feast when He said that "many will come from east and west and sit at table with Abraham, Isaac, and Jacob in the kingdom of heaven" (Matt. 8:11, RSV). He alluded to it again at the Last Supper when He took the cup and said, "I shall not drink again of this fruit of the vine until that day when I drink it new with you in my Father's kingdom" (Matt. 26:29, RSV).

The great supper of the ages has arrived in Revelation 19. And, as in the parable of the 10 virgins, it portrays the waiting saints as guests invited to the wedding (Matt. 25:1-10). They are not only invited, but Revelation 19:8 has them properly clothed for the occasion. Saved by grace, that same grace has made a difference in their lives as they lived for God and His principles. Thus not only is their King represented as coming on a white horse, but their glistening robes are described as "bright and pure" linen consisting of "the righteous deeds of the saints" (RSV). God's saving, transforming, empowering grace has made a difference in their lives, and they are ready for earth's greatest supper—the climactic feast of the ages.

More on "Hope"

But I would not have you to be ignorant, brethren, concerning them which are asleep, that ye sorrow not, even as others which have no hope. 1 Thess. 4:13.

With today's verse we come to Paul's most extensive treatment of the Second Advent. And in terms of the details about the resurrection of the saints it is the most complete in the New Testament, with 1 Corinthians 15:51-55 coming in as a close second.

The apostle begins his discussion with a statement regarding "hope." We have already seen how Paul viewed the Second Advent as "the blessed hope" (Titus 2:13). But here in 1 Thessalonians he expands on that hope and makes some of its implications explicit.

The recently converted believers in Thessalonica needed such hope. The death of some of their number had caught them by surprise. Undoubtedly they had assumed that all believers would live until Christ returned.

But some hadn't made it, and the Thessalonica church members had had the sorrowful task of burying them. What would become of such individuals?

Here is a problem that troubles people in every generation. After all, none of us escapes death. So what is the meaning of death, or even of a life destined to end in such a useless manner? It is a question that has challenged philosophers and theologians and ordinary people across the ages. Paul's answer is the most satisfactory ever given.

He writes that he doesn't want them to be ignorant about those who were sleeping in death. The apostle didn't want the death of loved ones to shatter the faith of those he was writing to. He didn't want them to be people of "no hope."

"No hope" are the words that set the apostle up for the discussion of the resurrection of the saints, a topic he begins to undertake in 1 Thessalonians 4:14.

But before moving to his presentation we will examine Paul's understanding of Christianity as a religion of hope. In his letter to the Romans he refers to God as the "God of hope" (Rom. 15:13) and notes that as Christians we "rejoice in our hope of sharing the glory of God" (Rom. 5:2, RSV).

Hope in the Bible, I should point out, is not wishful thinking but a knowledge that something will happen. And confidence about what God will do in the future rests upon what He has done in the past. Therefore, Paul writes, "whatever was written in former days was written for our instruction, that by steadfastness and by the encouragement of the scriptures we might have hope" (Rom. 15:4, RSV).

Resurrection Hope

For since we believe that Jesus died and rose, even so God will take with Him those who have fallen asleep in Jesus. 1 Thess. 4:14, my translation.

The "for" at the head of verse 14 refers us back to verse 13, which noted that Christians are not like those who have no hope in the face of death. Why? "For," or because, "we believe that Jesus died and rose" and that "God will take with Him those who have fallen asleep in Jesus." Thus Paul builds the Christian case for hope in two propositions: (1) Jesus died and rose, and (2) because He rose, those who have accepted Him will rise also.

Jesus is coming again. That is the primary "blessed hope." But now he adds breadth and depth to that hope in his discussion of the promised resurrection. To the apostle these teachings stand at the heart of the gospel of Jesus Christ, the one who died and rose again that we might share his victory (1 Cor. 15:1-3, 22, 23).

The perceptive reader will have noted that I did not use one of the standard translations for today's reading but substituted my own translation. Let me explain the implications here.

Every published translation that I consulted renders the verse something like this: "For if we believe that Jesus died and rose again, even so God will *bring* with Him those who sleep in Jesus" (NKJV). The word we want to look at is "bring." I translated it as "take." The Greek word includes both of those meanings, and either is a permissible rendering. But the two translations have quite different meanings: either Jesus will *"bring"* with Him those who supposedly went to heaven at death, or Jesus will "take" to heaven those whom He resurrects at the Second Advent.

The reason that nearly all translators render *agō* as "bring" is that they truly believe that people go to heaven when they die. My translation, of course, holds that the dead are asleep in their graves until Jesus returns.

Here we have a problem. Is the correct translation merely my theology against theirs? The good news is that the context solves the problem. Verse 16 clearly teaches that all are asleep (dead) in their earthly graves until the wake-up call on resurrection day. Martin Luther, the fountainhead of the Reformation, explains that truth when he writes that "we are to sleep until he comes and knocks on the grave and says, 'Dr. Martin, get up.' Then I will rise in a moment and will be eternally happy with him."

Thank You, Father, for the extensiveness of the blessedness in "the blessed hope."

December 22

A Tale of Two Ascensions

For this we say to you by the word of the Lord, that we who are alive and remain until the coming of the Lord, will not precede those who have fallen asleep. For the Lord Himself will descend from heaven with a shout, with the voice of the archangel and with the trumpet of God, and the dead in Christ will rise first. Then we who are alive and remain will be caught up together with them in the clouds to meet the Lord in the air, and so shall we always be with the Lord. Therefore comfort one another with these words. 1 Thess. 4:15-18, NASB.

With verses 15-17 we come to one of the most insightful pictures of the return of Jesus recorded in the New Testament. As we read these verses we need to remember that Paul's purpose in writing is pastoral. Some of the believers have been disoriented by the death of others in the church, and he responds with words of comfort and assurance.

We have seen in verses 13 and 14 that the apostle did not want them ignorant on the topic, and that just as Jesus rose from the grave so would His followers. Now in verses 15-17 Paul states plainly what he had only hinted at in verse 13.

And his words of hope must have been extremely comforting to the distressed believers. For one thing, in verse 15 he lets them know that those who had died and were sleeping in their graves would have absolutely no disadvantage at the Second Advent. To the contrary, they would have the honor of firstness. The apostle notes that the living "will not precede those who have fallen asleep." He goes out of his way to emphasize his point by using an emphatic negative. The more accurate is "most certainly not" rather than merely "not." He wants them to have complete assurance on the point that is troubling them.

With verse 16 we can feel the excitement building up in Paul as he describes the Second Advent itself. Not only will the Lord return from heaven, as He had promised His earliest disciples (Acts 1:11; John 14:1-3), but He will do so with glory and fanfare as the trumpets blare and the archangel shouts as He calls the dead from their graves.

But for those living at the return of Jesus the best is yet to come. In verse 17 Paul adds that "we who are alive and remain will be caught up together with them [those who have been resurrected] in the clouds to meet the Lord in the air."

What a promise! Just as Jesus arose from the dead, so will those who believe in Him! And just as He ascended to heaven, so will all of those who have trusted in Him! They will be caught up in the clouds to meet Him in the air!

As Paul tells the story, the "blessed hope" just gets better and better.

The Not-So-Secret Rapture

For the Lord himself shall descend from heaven with a shout, with the voice of the
archangel, and with the trump[et] of God: and the dead in Christ shall rise first:
Then we which are alive and remain shall be caught up together with them in the
clouds, to meet the Lord in the air: and so shall we ever be with the Lord.
1 Thess. 4:16, 17.

In these verses we find the Bible's most vivid description of the rapture. Paul writes that "we who are alive, who are left, shall be caught up together with them [the resurrected dead] in the clouds to meet the Lord in the air" (1 Thess. 4:17, RSV).

The words to watch are "caught up." The Greek word behind the translation means "to seize," to "snatch away," and to "transport hastily." It has worked its way into English as "rapture" through the Latin *rapio*. So when Paul speaks of the end-time rapture he means the event in which God's people are "caught up," or raptured, at the Second Advent to meet Him who is coming in the clouds of heaven.

With verse 17 in mind, it is little wonder that Christians like to talk about the rapture. But what is inconceivable is that some have concluded that it would be secret.

Paul tells us just how secret it is. First, he ties the rapture to the Second Advent. That is, it will take place at the same time that Jesus returns. And how hidden is His coming? According to Jesus Himself, it would be as visible as the lightning that flashes across the heavens (Matt. 24:27). And the book of Revelation tells us that when He returns "every eye will see him" (Rev. 1:7, NKJV).

But Paul adds to that lack of secrecy when he tells us that "the Lord himself will descend from heaven with a cry of command, with the archangel's call, and with the sound of the trumpet of God" (1 Thess. 4:16, RSV). All the noise and calling and victorious trumpeting have the effect of awakening those asleep in their graves. The coming will be just as audible as it will be visible.

The rapture and the Second Advent are the opposite of secret. They will be accompanied by a massive shout, the voice of an archangel, the blaring of a trumpet (verse 16), a heavenly display that will be as visible as lightning illuminating the sky (Matt. 24:27), something so widespread that every eye will see it (Rev. 1:7), and around the entire world the opening of the graves and resurrection of the dead who had accepted Jesus as their Lord (1 Thess. 4:16; 1 Cor. 15:52).

It appears that the not-so-secret rapture will indeed be the greatest show on earth. I look forward with all my heart to that day!

December 24

Immortal Saints

Behold, I tell you a mystery: We shall not all sleep, but we shall all be changed—in a moment, in the twinkling of an eye, at the last trumpet. For the trumpet will sound, and the dead will be raised incorruptible, and we shall be changed. For this corruptible must put on incorruption, and this mortal must put on immortality. So when this corruptible has put on incorruption, and this mortal has put on immortality, then shall be brought to pass the saying that is written: "Death is swallowed up in victory."
1 Cor. 15:51-54, NKJV.

Nothing captures this scene more vividly than a passage from *The Great Controversy*: "Amid the reeling of the earth, the flash of lightning, and the roar of thunder, the voice of the Son of God calls forth the sleeping saints. He looks upon the graves of the righteous, then, raising His hands to heaven, He cries: 'Awake, awake, awake, ye that sleep in the dust, and arise!' Throughout the length and breadth of the earth the dead shall hear that voice, and they that hear shall live. And the whole earth shall ring with the tread of the exceeding great army of every nation, kindred, tongue, and people. From the prison house of death they come, clothed with immortal glory, crying: 'O death, where is thy sting? O grave, where is thy victory?' 1 Corinthians 15:55. And the living righteous and the risen saints unite their voices in a long, glad shout of victory. . . .

"All arise with the freshness and vigor of eternal youth. In the beginning, man was created in the likeness of God, not only in character, but in form and feature. Sin defaced and almost obliterated the divine image; but Christ came to restore that which had been lost. He will change our vile bodies and fashion them like unto His glorious body. The mortal, corruptible form, devoid of comeliness, once polluted with sin, becomes perfect, beautiful, and immortal. All blemishes and deformities are left in the grave. Restored to the tree of life in the long-lost Eden, the redeemed will 'grow up' (Malachi 4:2) to the full stature of the race in its primeval glory. The last lingering traces of the curse of sin will be removed, and Christ's faithful ones will appear in 'the beauty of the Lord our God,' in mind and soul and body reflecting the perfect image of their Lord. Oh, wonderful redemption! long talked of, long hoped for, contemplated with eager anticipation, but never fully understood" (pp. 644, 645).

Some may speak of immortal souls, but the Bible is clear that immortality is a gift bestowed at the Second Advent. Until that time the dead sleep in their graves. But when He comes again, He will complete His victory over death with the resurrection of those who have accepted Him and the transformation of their bodies and the granting of immortality. Such is the victory of the followers of Him who has the keys of death and the grave (Rev. 1:18).

Being Ready for Jesus to Come

The day of the Lord will come as a thief in the night, in the which the heavens shall pass away with a great noise, and the elements shall melt with fervent heat, the earth also and the works that are therein shall be burned up. Seeing then that all these things shall be dissolved, what manner of persons ought ye to be in all holy conversation [conduct] and godliness, looking for and hasting unto the coming of the day of God, wherein the heavens being on fire shall be dissolved, and the elements shall melt with fervent heat? Nevertheless we, according to his promise, look for new heavens and a new earth, wherein dwelleth righteousness. Wherefore, beloved, seeing that ye look for such things, be diligent that ye may be found of him in peace, without spot, and blameless. 2 Peter 3:10-14.

What kind of person should I be in the face of the unprecedented events coming upon the earth? Jesus tried to tell us the answer to that question when He ministered on earth for those three years. We find it in the Sermon on the Mount in His call for His followers to be humble, meek, merciful, pure in heart, peacemakers, and individuals who hunger and thirst after righteousness more than anything else in their lives (Matt. 5:3-9).

Another part of His answer appears in His response to the lawyer about the greatest commandment of all. I still need to hear His words more fully and apply them to my life: "You shall love the Lord your God with all your heart, and with all your soul, and with all your mind. This is the great and first commandment. And a second is like it, You shall love your neighbor as yourself. On these two commandments depend all the law and the prophets" (Matt. 22:37-40, RSV), including the Ten Commandments, which are extensions and applications of the two great commandments (Rom. 13:8-10; Gal. 5:14).

And yet another aspect of how to be ready occurs in the parable of the sheep and the goats, in which we discover that the last judgment centers upon our acts of mercy and justice to those who need help the most in this life. The caring, giving life of the servant is the life that Jesus modeled in His earthly existence. And it is those characteristics He will be looking for in those He takes to heaven with Him.

We are, to be sure, saved by His grace. But that same grace transforms His followers and step-by-step forms them into His likeness. What kind of people do we need to be like on "that day"? The short answer is that we need to be like Him.

Father in heaven, I look forward to the coming of Jesus. Help me, Father, to let You change me from the inside out so that I might be ready to stand on "that day."

Heaven: A Negative Perspective

Then I saw a new heaven and a new earth; for the first heaven and the first earth had passed away, and the sea was no more. And I saw the holy city, new Jerusalem, coming down out of heaven from God, prepared as a bride adorned for her husband; and I heard a loud voice from the throne saying, "Behold, the dwelling place of God is with men. He will dwell with them, and they shall be his people, and God himself will be with them; he will wipe away every tear from their eyes, and death shall be no more, neither shall there be mourning nor crying nor pain any more, for the former things have passed away." And he who sat upon the throne said, "Behold, I make all things new." Also he said, "Write this, for these words are trustworthy and true."
Rev. 21:1-5, RSV.

Jesus has returned (Rev. 19) and taken His people, who have been caught up in the air to meet Him, back to heaven with Him (1 Thess. 4:17; John 14:1-3). There they spent the 1,000-year period known as the millennium fellowshipping with God and one another and becoming absolutely convinced that God had done the very best thing in the face of the crisis caused by sin (Rev. 20:4-6). When all are satisfied, sin and sinners and Satan himself are put to rest in what John the revelator calls "the second death" (Rev. 20:7-15).

It is at that point in time that the new Jerusalem descends to a re-created earth (Rev. 21:1; 2 Peter 3:13). The book of Revelation describes that re-creation as the restoration of Edenic conditions. Sin is only a memory as God's saints who have been saved through the varied work of Jesus spend the eternal ages headquartered on Planet Earth.

One of the most interesting things about that heavenly place is that Jesus reveals it to John in the negative. There is a good reason for that. Part of it is that the human mind with its limited experience cannot grasp the glories of God's realm. It is beyond the scope of their thinking and thus impossible to describe.

But we earthlings do know what we have to face in this earth and what we would like to escape from.

As a result, we find the book of Revelation telling us that the heavenly realm will have no more tears, or any pain or death or mourning. It even tells us that there will be no more sea (Rev. 21:1)—representing in symbolic terms that the entire earth will be agriculturally fruitful—that there will be no more hunger.

I am glad for the negatives. I look forward to an existence not bounded by death and not interrupted by illness. But such negatives provide only the slightest glimmer of what awaits those who choose to live with Jesus throughout infinite time.

Heaven: A Positive Perspective

Then he showed me the river of the water of life, bright as crystal, flowing from the throne of God and of the Lamb through the middle of the street of the city; also, on either side of the river, the tree of life with its twelve kinds of fruit, yielding its fruit each month; and the leaves of the tree were for the healing of the nations. There shall no more be anything accursed, but the throne of God and of the Lamb shall be in it, and his servants shall worship him; they shall see his face, and his name shall be on their foreheads. And night shall be no more; they need no light of lamp or sun, for the Lord God will be their light, and they shall reign for ever and ever. Rev. 22:1-5, RSV.

Eden restored is the best way to describe the re-created earth on which the redeemed from all ages will spend eternity. And the best thing about it will be the presence of Jesus Himself. He may be in a spiritual sense the light of our life during our present earthly journey, but there His glory will literally be all the light we need. Now, I have to admit that I do not fully understand such things. But I look forward to learning about them in the heavenly school.

Isaiah presents a peek into heavenly conditions in a way that we can understand. His word pictures have been some of my favorites from the beginning of my Christian walk.

"The wolf shall dwell with the lamb,
   and the leopard shall lie down with the kid,
   and the calf and the lion and the fatling together,
   and a little child shall lead them.
The cow and the bear shall feed;
   their young shall lie down together; and the lion shall eat straw like the ox. . . .
They shall not hurt or destroy in all my holy mountain;
   for the earth shall be full of the knowledge of the Lord
   as the waters cover the sea" (Isa. 11:6-9, RSV).

Again we read: "Then the eyes of the blind shall be opened, and the ears of the deaf unstopped; then shall the lame man leap like a hart, and the tongue of the dumb sing for joy. For waters shall break forth in the wilderness, and streams in the desert" (Isa. 35:5, 6, RSV).

Here we have snapshots of the heavenly new earth of the saved. No wonder Isaiah tells us that "the ransomed of the Lord shall . . . come to Zion with singing; everlasting joy shall be upon their heads; [and] they shall obtain joy and gladness, and sorrow and sighing shall flee away" (verse 10, RSV). All I can add to those word pictures is a heartfelt Amen!

Part 9

Turn Your Eyes Upon Jesus as Your Personal Savior

Jesus the Eternal and Omnipotent

"I am the Alpha and the Omega," says the Lord God, who is and who was and who is to come, the Almighty. Rev. 1:8, RSV.

And He said to me, "It is done! I am the Alpha and the Omega, the Beginning and the End. I will give of the fountain of the water of life freely to him who thirsts. He who overcomes shall inherit all things, and I will be his God and he shall be My son." Rev. 21:6, 7, NKJV.

Behold, I am coming quickly, and My reward is with Me, to render to every man according to what he has done. I am the Alpha and the Omega, the first and the last, the beginning and the end." Rev. 22:12, 13, NASB.

One of the more interesting titles of Jesus is the fact that He is "the Alpha and the Omega." But is He? In the first use of the term in Revelation it seems to be referring to God the Father. But in the last Jesus uses it of Himself. We have something precious here in the full equality of Jesus and the Father. Both of them are the Alpha and the Omega. *Alpha* is the first letter in the Greek alphabet and *omega* the last.

The Jews had a similar saying. The first letter in the Hebrew alphabet is *aleph*, while the last is *taw*. The rabbis said that Adam transgressed the law, but Abraham kept the law from *aleph* to *taw*. Again, they declared that God had blessed Israel from *aleph* to *taw*. That expression, like "the alpha and the omega," indicates a completeness that lacks nothing. When used of Deity it means that God and Christ are complete—that They lack nothing.

That is the kind of infinite Jesus whom we serve. Like the Father, He is one "who is and who was and who is to come." He is "the first and the last, the beginning and the end."

Both of those expressions signify the absolute eternalness of Jesus. Thus He was before time began, He is now, and He will be through the ages without end. He is One in whom people trusted in the past. Now He is one in whom we can put our trust at this present moment. And there can be no event or time in the future in which He will let us down.

Another description used of God the Father and Jesus in the alpha and omega passages is that They are "the Almighty," a phrase used numerous times in the New Testament, almost all of them being in Revelation. Our lives may look weak. And even the church may appear insignificant compared with the forces of the world. But those things are not where we are to focus. "Almighty" describes God and Jesus as Those who control all things, who hold all in Their grasp.

We serve a Lord who is not short of power. He is still "God with us" (Matt. 1:23).

December 29

Where to End?

Jesus did many other things as well. If every one of them were written down, I suppose that even the whole world would not have room for the books that would be written. John 21:25, NIV.

We began this year's journey of turning our eyes upon Jesus with the question of "where to begin?" And that certainly is a problem. After all, if we had begun it with His birth in Bethlehem we would have missed most of the story.

We now face the same problem at the journey's conclusion. Where to end? is a question that must be asked. How do you bring to completion a life that resurrected from death, a life that has the keys of death and the grave and continues on eternally?

The answer, of course, is that there is no ending. The story of Jesus goes on and on. And like a mighty river, it picks up strength and added texture as it flows from eternity in the past to eternity in the future.

The apostle John helps us catch a glimpse of the problem of even chronicling the events and teachings of Jesus' earthly life, stating that if the whole story were told, "even the whole world would not have room for the books that would be written." John himself had opened up new realms in the life of Jesus that the other Gospel writers had neglected. Even a casual comparison of the fourth Gospel with the other three helps us see how much material he added to our store of knowledge. And yet that is only one little step toward what could be added to even our understanding of Jesus' earthly life. And even a full accounting of those 33 years would be hardly the tip of an iceberg compared with a detailed narrative of His eternal existence.

Such unwritten "gospels" will be part of our study for eternity. Meanwhile, in what the four evangelists have provided for us we have all we need to know for salvation.

How to end the story for now is the problem. Perhaps the best way is with the final paragraph in *The Great Controversy*, which reflects a completed atonement: "The great controversy is ended. Sin and sinners are no more. The entire universe is clean. One pulse of harmony and gladness beats through the vast creation. From Him who created all, flow life and light and gladness, throughout the realms of illimitable space. From the minutest atom to the greatest world, all things, animate and inanimate, in their unshadowed beauty and perfect joy, declare that God is love" (p. 678).

Not a bad ending for a story that has no end.

Jesus' Final Invitation

"I Jesus have sent my angel to you with this testimony for the churches. I am the root and the offspring of David, the bright morning star." The Spirit and the Bride say, "Come." And let him who hears say, "Come." And let him who is thirsty come, let him who desires take the water of life without price. Rev. 22:16, 17, RSV.

The book of Revelation is all about Jesus. It begins with Him as the Lord of the churches as He walks among the candlesticks. From there it moves on to His heavenly coronation as the Lamb of God and the Lion of the tribe of Judah in chapters 4 and 5. And after featuring Him in world history it concludes with a vision of His coming in the clouds of heaven as a glorious conquering King who spends eternity with the redeemed of all the ages.

Near the end of the book we find His last invitation to you and me. It is a simple "come," made more profound by repetition in the context of a hushed universe before whom He highlights the fact that He is "the root and the off-spring of David and the bright and morning star."

Near the beginning of Revelation we also find an invitation from Jesus. "Behold," He says, "I stand at the door and knock; if any one hears my voice and opens the door, I will come in to him and eat with him, and he with me. He who conquers, I will grant him to sit with me on my throne, as I myself conquered and sat down with my Father on his throne. He who has an ear, let him hear what the Spirit says to the churches" (Rev. 3:20-22, RSV).

In response to that invitation Ellen White writes that "Jesus is daily saying to you, 'Behold, I stand at the door, and knock. . . .' Jesus has given His precious life for you, that you may become a partaker of the divine nature, having escaped the corruption that is in the world through lust. Then give yourself to Him as a pledge of grateful love. Were it not for the love freely given us of Christ, we should now be in hopeless despair, in spiritual midnight. Thank God every day that He gave us Jesus" (*Sons and Daughters of God*, p. 238).

It all sounds so deceptively easy—"come," "open," "give." And it is simple.

You and I have choices. We can have a life without hope or we can keep our eyes fixed on Jesus, give our lives to Him, and walk with Him every day of our lives.

The choice is simple, but also individual. Don't just look at Jesus, my friend, but do something about it. Right now!

December 31

Keep Turning Your Eyes Upon Jesus

Behold the Lamb of God, which taketh away the sin of the world. John 1:29.

We have spent a year beholding the Lamb. Our theme song for the year has been "Turn Your Eyes Upon Jesus." There is no better place for our gaze. During our final time together let us sing through its chorus one more time:

"Turn your eyes upon Jesus,
Look full in His wonderful face;
And the things of earth will grow strangely dim
In the light of His glory and grace."

We have turned our eyes upon Jesus as the eternal God, the incarnate Christ, One who ministered on earth, the crucified Lamb, the resurrected Lord, the coming King, and our personal Savior. Also, we have looked upon Him in His weakness and His strength, in His humility and His glory, and as the Babe in Bethlehem and the infinite God of the universe.

We have looked. That is true. But we also need to keep on looking every day until He returns in the clouds of heaven. Then we need to keep on looking at Him throughout the ceaseless ages of eternity.

But with that looking comes the need to do something with this Lamb who died for each of us. In the end we each face the question that Pilate put to the Jews: "What shall I do with the man whom you call the King of the Jews?" (Mark 15:12, RSV).

I see you fidgeting over there. But let's face it; fidgeting doesn't solve the issue. What are you going to do with the salvation through Jesus that you have meditated upon for the past 365 days? What are you personally going to do with Jesus?

The answer of the Jews to Pilate was loud and clear: "Crucify Him! Crucify Him!" And Pilate did. That is still a live option for us. The other option is that we will let Him crucify us and resurrect us to a new way of life in Him.

God is waiting for our response. He realizes the depth of our need. But He also knows the depth and height and breadth of His grace provided through the Lamb of God who died to take away the sin of the world.

Not only do we need to keep on every day turning our eyes upon Jesus, we also must daily make Him the ruling Lord of our life.

Today, Father, we thank You for Your greatest gift. But more than that, we want to recommit our lives to walking with our resurrected Lord each of our days here on earth that we might continue to behold Him throughout the eternal ages. Amen!

Scripture Index